D0886617

Black Students on WHITE CAMPUSES:

The Impacts of Increased Black Enrollments

Black
Students on
WHITE
CAMPUSES:

The Impacts of Increased Black Enrollments

Marvin W. Peterson·Robert T. Blackburn·Zelda F. Gamson
Carlos H. Arce·Roselle W. Davenport·James R. Mingle

Survey Research Center • Institute for Social Research • The University of Michigan

ISR Code No. 3985

Library of Congress Catalog Card No. LC 78-60965
ISBN 0-87944-221-2 clothbound

Published by the Institute for Social Research,
The University of Michigan, Ann Arbor, MI 48106

Published 1978
Cover Design by University Publications,
The University of Michigan

Preface

The participation and support of many groups and individuals were necessary in the course of this study. We are indebted to the people in the participating institutions who were willing to receive an outside group on their campuses delving into a very sensitive issue and sometimes painful memories. We are especially grateful to the many individuals and groups who not only consented to be interviewed, but often went to great lengths to provide materials, make arrangements, and give other assistance. We also appreciate the assistance of the several graduate students who participated in the research and, too, we appreciate the forbearance of our colleagues in the Center for the Study of Higher Education who were burdened by a heavier load during our involvement in this study. A personal note of thanks is due Dorothy Walker, who kept us organized and proved a much valued source of support and optimism. Finally, we acknowledge the support from the National Institute of Mental Health which made the study possible.

Contents

Part I

Evolution of a Complex Social Issue:

The Basis for the Study

1

Introduction

Robert T. Blackburn

This book addresses the question of the responsiveness of colleges and universities to black students. It also has implications for the broader question of general institutional and organizational responsiveness to particular clienteles. In addition, we have attempted to trace the implications of how the influx of black students within educational institutions may affect other new client groups (e.g., other minorities, women, adult students) and the response of colleges and universities to external pressures. This is a crucial question for a fundamental understanding of the relations between institutions of higher learning and the larger society. To what extent and in what ways have colleges and universities responded to major social changes in American society? How have they been carried into and communicated within these institutions? With what effects?

We know that change in higher education in the past has occurred slowly and often fortuitously. A number of observers, writing about the post-World War II era, have remarked on the magisterial pace of curricular change and the homogeneity of whatever changes did occur (Jencks and Riesman 1968; Hodgkinson 1971; Martin 1969; Dressel and De Lisle 1969; Brick and McGrath 1969). The turbulence of the late 1960s, however, had its effects across the landscape of higher education, particularly in loosening degree requirements and in opening up a wide range of new subjects and options in the undergraduate curriculum (Pace 1974; Blackburn et al. 1976).

3

Academe as a whole has been more responsive to external forces than it has been willing to admit. This has been especially true with respect to the entry of new kinds of students, especially minorities in recent years. But even the dramatic and accelerated entry of blacks into higher education was not as unique or as sudden as it appeared. The long-run trend in higher education has been growth in absolute numbers as well as in the percentage of youths continuing their education beyond high school (at least until a few years ago). Some short-term reversals have occurred—in the early 1930s, for example, and during major wars—but more often than not, a fair number of first generation students populated campuses. The long-run trend has been to increase the diversity of students entering American colleges and universities.

For the most part, these new student groups entered gradually enough so that colleges and universities could accommodate them without strain—the goal for the new clients as well as for the institutions was assimilation. There were instances in the past, however, when new clients had profound impacts on the institutions which received them and major changes were made. Women are one example (Feldman 1974); veterans are another. And the large influx of the children of Jewish immigrants around 1920 brought a new group to American institutions, primarily in New York City (Steinberg 1974).

The rapid expansion of higher education in the 1960s is not unique either. In the decades following the Civil War, the number of institutions of higher learning almost tripled (from 500 to 1,400 between 1870 and 1920) and enrollments grew by 5,000 percent (from 20,000 to 1,100,000). With the emergence of the modern university during this period, school after school was added to the arts and science colleges in response to society's need for the preparation and certification of professionals (Veysey 1965). These earlier growth spurts played a part in beginning to introduce new clienteles to the campuses.

Large federal support of higher education, which many in the 1960s said compromised the autonomy of universities and made them agents of unpopular policy, is also not limited to the recent past. While federal participation in higher education has been irregular, it dates from before the Morrill Act of 1862. By 1930, the U. S. government was spending $23 million a year on higher education and designating the educational activities that were to receive aid (Brubacher and Rudy 1968). Health, Education and Welfare mandates and state boards of control also have their forerunners. For example, during the Great Depression, more than one state government acted to increase its institutional control under the guise of efficiency through external coordination.

Since well over half of those who are professors today were not in academic positions prior to 1960 (which means that their professional lives have spanned a period of comfortable budgets and general public endorsement of higher education), it is not surprising to hear so many express surprise at the external pressures now being directed at colleges and universities. But crises and change have been the norm, not the exception (Kerr 1975). A money shortage is not only not new today, it is perhaps the one threat to colleges and universities that has been continuous. The Depression reduced faculty salaries to such a level that professors were still earning less in 1942 than they were in 1931. Even when enrollment expansion was rapid (in the late 1940s or 1960s, for example) and overall growth was meteoric, dollar support always lagged at least a year behind (Henry 1975).

Nor are today's verbal assaults on colleges and universities a first in higher education. Going back but a generation or two (and it began long before then), God-fearing Americans worried about the loss of moral standards among the golden youth of the Roaring Twenties. The 1930s were filled with charges that faculty who were attracted to Russian socialism were seducing youth into communism.

In sum, much of what was unique to colleges and universities in the 1960s—and to the entry of black students in particular—is not because these institutions have been unresponsive to external social, political, and economic forces. Naturally, each period brings its novel events, but from a longer perspective the character of these events has not changed appreciably over time. There have been student demonstrations on campus, faculty debates on what should be taught and to whom, new student clienteles, and pressures from various private and governmental groups.

Before discussing the principal forces which came into prominence in the 1960s and which encompassed the rise in black enrollments, it is important to note that contests between the university and society have a single aim—control of the organization. Whether the issue has been academic freedom, war, foreign ideologies, or efficiency, those within the colleges and universities have fought to maximize their power to act independently and to retain the freedom to criticize those upon whose support they depend, while those outside of academe have moved to gain as much control over the institutions as they can muster. The contest is a continuing one—and a crucial one. As we shall see, what was new and of great significance in the 1960s was that the struggles were waged on the campus itself.

THE PROBLEM AND ITS SIGNIFICANCE

The absorption of black students into higher education has not been a simple matter, especially in those predominantly white institutions which have experienced a rapid increase in black enrollments the last few years. The sharpest delineation of the problem is likely to be drawn in four-year institutions where, in the past, faculty members and administrators could count on large segments of the student body with the requisite skills, motivations, and family backgrounds to adapt fairly easily to the academic program and collegiate environment.

It can no longer be assumed that these attributes are already held by all the minority students, of whom blacks make up the largest proportion, now entering higher education. Large numbers of black youths, with strong assent from their families, expect to continue in some form of post-secondary education; in some cases, young blacks hold this expectation to a greater degree than do other youths from comparable social classes (Antonovsky 1967; Bayer and Boruch 1969a; Centra 1970; Hunt and Hardt 1969; Kandel 1971; Knoell 1971; Veroff and Peele 1969; Watley 1971a). This is true despite major barriers to college entry and completion: black students come from poorer families, work more at outside jobs, and need more financial assistance (Bayer and Boruch 1969a; Centra 1970; Watley 1971; Willingham 1970); and their average academic aptitudes and performance, as measured by standardized tests, are considerably lower than the average for white students (Crossland 1971; Astin 1969; Bayer and Boruch 1969; Kendrick 1968).

Although black students do not differ much from white students in their reasons for attending college (Centra 1970), blacks show much greater dissatisfaction with the collegiate experience (Centra 1970; Hedegard and Brown 1969; Fenstemacher 1971). Perhaps related to black students' greater dissatisfaction is the difference between black and white perceptions of the "racial environment." Blacks are more likely to be aware of their minority status on white campuses and to see their colleges as places where friendships are determined by race and background. One researcher (Fenstemacher 1971), in a study of Black Opportunity Award students at The University of Michigan, concluded that blacks felt more antagonistic as a *result* of their college experiences. This may have been a passing phase. A more recent study (Boyd 1974) of black undergraduates in 40 predominantly white institutions concluded that black students are generally opposed to separatist philosophies and policies.

With all of these discontinuities between the typical black student and the typical white institution, most studies have documented the average or even better than average persistence of black students (Astin 1969; Bayer and Boruch 1969a,b; Clark and Plotkin 1963; Clift 1969; Harrison 1959; Hedegard and Brown 1969; Milton 1970; Rossman et al. 1975).

Black students, then, are attending white institutions of higher education in increasing numbers, bringing with them high expectations for success. Despite disparities between them and typical white students in academic preparation and financial security, and a subsequent disillusionment among large numbers of black students with the actual college experience, black students persist in college to a surprising degree.

Yet little is known about their impact on the institutions they have attended. Many writers who published studies of minority students at the height of black student activism in the late 1960s and early 1970s raised questions about the short- and long-term impact of the presence of black students in white colleges and universities. Bayer and Boruch wrote in 1969:

> What new needs and demands might be placed on academic institutions as a result of . . . special assistance and admissions programs are largely unknown. Pressures are being applied now to institute new curricula, special remedial programs, enhanced academic and personal counseling services, and other new or revised student services. However, the short- and long-term effects on the composition of the student body, the characteristics of an institution's programs, and an institution's productivity and output have been largely unconsidered (1969b, p. 371).

Two years later, Melnick (1971) concluded with the following statement in his review of research on programs for the disadvantaged in higher education:

> Little is known about how to implement or develop special teacher strategies for college-aged disadvantaged, nor is there obvious agreement whether, in fact, there should be such a focus. Programs have differed from school to school; with some the emphasis has been on easy admission, and a "sink or swim" attitude afterwards, with others there have been counseling efforts but no modifications of curricula, with still others there have been special classes, special requirements, special rates of amassing credits (p. 32).

The same year, Fred Crossland of the Ford Foundation (1971) offered the following speculation at the end of a lengthy review of blacks in higher education:

> Virtually all of the growth of minority enrollment will be in
> historically nonblack colleges . . . Institutions of higher learning will
> continue to change rapidly. Reforms initiated in the last five years
> are only beginning to gain momentum, and further changes in ad-
> ministration, pedagogy, curriculum, and institutional purpose seem
> inevitable. It is likely that the net result of these changes will be to
> make colleges and universities more flexible and more hospitable to
> minority students (pp. 106–107).

There have been no definitive answers to the questions inherent
in this issue and, despite speculations and hortatory accounts, there
has been no systematic investigation of the impact of blacks on colleges and universities *after* the period of student activism and heightened attention to minorities. Yet this is the crucial question for research. It is not enough to point to the myriad reforms initiated during the 1960s in the country and in higher education. Many of these
reforms have followed the "boom and bust" cycle of change characteristic of other turbulent periods in the United States—and many
Americans, including writers on higher education, display a peculiar
amnesia about recent history. Yet the real test of reform is whether it
continues past early spurts of enthusiasm and militancy into less
dramatic, more constricted circumstances.

The research reported in this book was undertaken at a time
(1974 and 1975) when the impact of black students on white colleges
and universities had had the opportunity to become routinized if it
was to occur at all. By 1974, the theatrics of student militancy had
become muted. A new generation of students—inheritors of "the
movement"—was taking over. The psychologies and realities of retrenchment were beginning to supplant expansion. And blacks no
longer provided hot topics and agendas for colleges and universities.

The time was ripe, then, to examine closely what had happened in
white colleges and universities after the height of the influx of black
students between 1968 and 1972. With the help of a grant from the
National Institute of Mental Health, our research group—including
both faculty and students from The University of Michigan's Center
for the Study of Higher Education—chose to study a small group of
institutions, each of which had sharply increased its admissions of
black students between 1968 and 1972, in order to investigate their
responses to black students. Working with the Institute for Social
Research, we selected colleges and universities in the Midwest, Pennsylvania, and New York as our sample for this research.

Less important to us—though not completely ignored—was the
issue of the response of black students to the institutions they at-

tended, the concern of most writing in this field. Rather, we wanted to assess the impact of black students on the administration and organization of colleges and universities; on faculty and curricula; on the allocation of resources; and on student culture.

ORGANIZATION OF THE BOOK

With these original questions in mind, we have organized this book around critical periods, theories, and institutional segments. At the outset, it is important to recognize that while many of our questions derive from theories of how organizations change—particularly in response to new human input—this book does not test hypotheses. It lies somewhere between description and theory. Our analytic strategy has been inductive. By paying close attention to the key events and actors surrounding the entry of black students to the 13 campuses, we have been able to identify several patterns of response. While the various patterns of response have grown from the particular histories and institutional characteristics we observed, they allow us to look beyond the particular and enable us to understand the dynamics of change in higher education more generally.

In Part I, "The Evolution of a Complex Social Issue," we examine the legal, social, and political movements related to civil rights and race relations since the 1930s (Chapter 2) and the implications of these movements for higher education (Chapter 3). The increased role of state and federal government in pressing for more minority enrollments, specific historical patterns of black enrollments, and early programs for blacks are also reviewed in Chapter 3. Chapter 4 turns to the chronology of the study and its evolutionary, two-stage design. The selection of the sample institutions and the issues involved in studying such a sensitive issue are then discussed.

Part II, "The Determinants and Dynamics of Change," follows the entry of black students into the 13 institutions and looks at their impact in a variety of areas. Chapter 5 presents short vignettes which highlight the major dynamics accompanying the entry of blacks into each of the 13 institutions. (The reader who wants a quick review of what happened on the 13 campuses should turn directly to Chapter 5.) In Chapter 6 we look at the environmental forces which supported or resisted the increased black enrollments, as well as the institutional factors predisposing them to change their enrollment patterns. Chapter 7 describes the events which led to dramatic shifts in black

enrollments and the initial responses to blacks. Chapter 8 examines
the patterns of conflicts that erupted between the new black students
and the institutions shortly after the increase in enrollments and
some of the dynamics of that period. The importance of symbolic
struggles and the roles of key personalities—critical to the understanding of the impact of black students—are then discussed.

Part III, "Institutional Impacts and Responses," examines responses in particular sectors. Chapter 9 describes the development
and comprehensiveness of academic and supportive services, the integration of these services into the institutions, and institutional commitment to them. Chapter 10 deals with the role of students, both
blacks and whites, in the early black enrollment increases. The student role in institutional conflicts, in the development of interracial
patterns, and in the growth of black student organizations are discussed; a typology of the student racial climate is also presented. In
Chapter 11 we examine the impact of blacks on administrative, faculty, and other governance patterns and the key roles played by black
and white administrators and faculty.

Part IV, "The 1975 Perspective: Integration, Segregation, or Pluralism," introduces the results of surveys of faculty and administrators
at 4 of the 13 institutions. In Chapter 12 we compare administrator
and faculty perceptions of the impact of increased black enrollments,
campus racial climate, and institutional goals and commitments.
Chapter 13 examines faculty and departmental responses to blacks,
looking particularly at the relationships among faculty characteristics, disciplines, and departmental contexts. We compare the
survey results for the 4 institutions in Chapter 14 and examine their
differences according to the strategies of response described in earlier
chapters.

In Part V, "Evolution or Revolution: The Process Reviewed," we
present a five-stage model of institutional experiences with increased
black enrollment (Chapter 15). The model identifies crucial impact
issues, and response strategies for each stage and, from these, projects
future institutionalization or rejection of responses to black students.
Chapter 16 reviews the nature of the problem and the response conditions represented by this study. A final discussion on the meaning of
and conditions for response draws on the evidence presented here to
define the meaning of institutional response to new clienteles.

2

Civil Rights and Race Relations

Zelda F. Gamson

It is difficult to identify a specific event or an exact year as the clear turning point in the admissions of substantial numbers of black students to white colleges and universities. The murder of Dr. Martin Luther King, Jr., in 1968 comes closest to playing this role. King's death led to active minority recruitment by white colleges and universities and to a range of academic and nonacademic programs, often in response to the pressure from black students; but his death also marked the end of an earlier era. We need to retreat a few years to gain a proper perspective of the events that began circa 1968.

PRE-1954:
EARLY LEGAL ATTACKS ON EDUCATIONAL SEGREGATION

The beginning of the era of increased civil rights activism is usually marked by the Supreme Court decision of May 1954 in the *Brown* v. *Topeka, Kansas, Board of Education* case, which finally ended legal segregation in public elementary and secondary schools. The *Brown* case, itself, can be viewed as both a beginning and an end. It opened a period of increased civil rights activism, and it ended legal sanction for segregation. The separate but equal doctrine, laid down in the *Plessy* v. *Ferguson* decision by the Supreme Court in 1896, had been

under attack for years prior to the *Brown* case in numerous court
cases focusing on graduate and professional education, many of them
organized and backed by the National Association for the Advance-
ment of Colored People (NAACP).

Until the thirties, such cases had been settled in accordance with
Plessy v. *Ferguson*. The shift occurred in a series of decisions which
extended over the Depression years and through World War II. In
1935, the *Donald Murray* case attacked segregation by the University
of Maryland Law School, to which Mr. Murray was eventually admitted. In 1938, the *Gaines* case attacked segregation at the University
of Missouri, and the Supreme Court ruled that the state of Missouri
either had to provide blacks with equal law school facilities or admit
them to the University of Missouri Law School. The *Bluford* case in
Missouri led to the establishment of the School of Journalism at Lin-
coln University. The results of the litigation in the 1930s were decidedly mixed: challenges against segregation at the University of North
Carolina and the University of Tennessee were lost, and a case
against the University of Kentucky resulted not in desegregation but
in the opening of a school of engineering at a black college, Kentucky
State. The University of Maryland became the only white institution
opened to blacks as a result of the litigation in this period. In order to
avoid integration, a number of southern states started poorly supported graduate and professional schools at black institutions.

Things began to shift in the 1940s. The University of West Virginia voluntarily admitted a black to graduate school in 1940, and
the University of Arkansas admitted its first black in 1948. The
Sweatt v. *Painter* case in 1948 resulted in a ruling by the U.S. Supreme Court that a black be admitted to the University of Texas Law
School because the law school at black Texas Southern University did
not afford equal facilities. In the *McLaurin* case, the Supreme Court
ruled that a black did not receive equal treatment at the University
of Oklahoma if he was required to sit at a separate table in the
university library and occupy a specific seat in a classroom or dining
room. Other significant cases which resulted in desegration rulings
were *McLaurin* v. *the University of Oklahoma, Sepuels* v. *the University of Oklahoma, McCready* v. *the University of Maryland,* and *Johnson* v. *the University of Kentucky*. Between 1948 and 1961, legal efforts finally opened white colleges and universities to blacks in all
southern states except Alabama, Mississippi, and South Carolina
(Bowles and DeCosta 1971).

Around the same time, a number of cases attacked segregation in
other regions of the country; these litigations followed the modest

economic gains of blacks during World War II, the large black migration northward during and after the war, and the increased pace of
desegregation in the armed services. In 1944, the Supreme Court
ruled against segregation in interstate transportation and, in 1947,
against the whites-only Democratic primary in the South. *Shelly* v.
Kraemer struck down restrictive covenants in housing in 1948. In
1947, President Truman's Committee on Civil Rights called for the
elimination of segregation and, in 1948, Truman asked Congress to
set up a permanent Fair Employment Practices Commission. A few
years earlier (1942), the Congress on Racial Equality (CORE) had
been founded as an outgrowth of the pacifist Fellowship of Reconcilia-
tion and began to develop techniques, later adopted by an enlarged
civil rights movement, of nonviolent resistance to segregation in restaurants, housing, amusement parks, and interstate transportation.

1954–1964: FROM CIVIL RIGHTS TO BLACK POWER

In 1951, the NAACP decided to challenge segregation directly in
elementary and secondary schools. In a series of four cases—*Brown* v.
Topeka, Kansas, Board of Education (1951), *Clarendon County, South
Carolina* (1951), *Wilmington, Delaware* (1951), and *Prince Edward,
Virginia* (1952)—segregation in public schools was eventually declared illegal. On May 7, 1954, the unanimous decision of the Supreme Court in the *Brown* decision spelled out the case against the
inherently discriminatory treatment of black children implied by the
separate but equal doctrine.
   The court's decision had a profound psychological impact on
blacks and southern whites at the time. In the South, whites reacted
immediately and bitterly to what they saw as coercion by the court
when attempts were made to implement the *Brown* decision in Little
Rock and sporadically throughout the South. Later, in the early
1960s, their anger increased when the federal government attempted
to enforce the law and protect blacks by sending in federal marshals
and calling out the National Guard in Alabama and Mississippi.
Southern resistance continued throughout this period.
   For blacks, on the other hand, the Supreme Court decision gave
legitimacy to a new kind of activism; at the same time, it drew attention to the gap between democratic ideals and the realities of life for
nearly every black in the United States. Later, the reaction to this
gap was to be radicalization and an increased sense of black national-

ism. In the late 1950s, however, the mood was one of hope and energy.[1] Long-standing organizations with a base in the black middle class, such as the NAACP and the Urban League, began to expand. CORE began to recruit a larger national membership. New civil rights organizations were to follow soon, most prominently the Southern Christian Leadership Conference (SCLC), in 1957, and the Student Non-Violent Coordinating Committee (SNCC), in 1960.

With active support from some northern whites, most notably college students and members of liberal churches such as the Quakers, and with the more passive support of others, civil rights activism focused initially on hastening desegregation "with all deliberate speed"—the phrase used by the Supreme Court in its implementation of school desegregation. Efforts broadened to other kinds of segregation and discrimination. In 1955, just one year after the Supreme Court decision, segregation on buses and other public facilities became a target when Rosa Parks, a middle-aged black seamstress, refused to give up her bus seat to a white man in Montgomery, Alabama. The ensuing Montgomery bus boycott catapulted to national prominence its leader, Rev. Martin Luther King, Jr. The Freedom Rides organized by CORE in 1961, with the participation of whites and blacks of all ages, continued the attack on segregation in interstate transportation. The Freedom Rides became a base for the recruitment of white college students and faculty who later became involved in the voter registration drives organized by SNCC.

Next to the Supreme Court decision of 1954, the Woolworth lunch counter sit-in of 1960 in Greensboro, North Carolina, became a turning point in the history of the civil rights movement. By all accounts a spontaneous event, the sit-in by a group of students from the all-black North Carolina Agricultural and Technical College in Greensboro began the attack on segregation in public eating facilities in the South, and it later spurred demonstrations over discrimination in all public facilities, housing, and employment. In the wake of the sit-in, CORE organized a nationwide boycott of Woolworth stores which drew whites' attention to the civil rights movement in large numbers for the first time.

The drama of the sit-in attracted the attention of the whole nation to the situation of blacks in the South and it laid the groundwork for a new phase of the civil rights movement. SNCC was founded soon after the Greensboro sit-in at a meeting called by Martin Luther King at Shaw College in Raleigh, North Carolina. The Greensboro sit-in rapidly mobilized large numbers of students in black colleges for the civil rights struggle—by 1965, close to 70 percent of the student body in some colleges.[2] A small number of white college students, politically inert during the 1950s, began to go "down south" to work with rural blacks through SNCC and other organizations. Some of these students later became active in the Students for a Democratic Society, founded in 1962, and in the activist movements in the universities during the mid- to late 1960s. The time was more than ripe for a major movement.

The civil rights struggle became "the movement" for many blacks and some whites during the following six years. The alliance between blacks and liberal northern whites, however fragile it turned out to be, was the crucial fact about the success of the civil rights movement in those early years. White guilt and outrage over blatant injustices against blacks, combined with the soberness and moral tone of nonviolent doctrine and practice, evoked great sympathy for the civil rights movement in the North. Whites provided the cadres and, in some cases, the leadership for civil rights organizations in the first years of the movement. They gave support through dollars and were important in setting a generally favorable climate of opinion in the North.[3] They responded to and, to some extent, were responsible for the attention to civil rights issues in the press and on television. Imprinted on the memory of those old enough to remember are the images of young black children being escorted into all-white southern schools, accompanied by the jeers and threats of white parents. The pictures tumble one over the other: Central High School in Little Rock, Arkansas in 1955; burning busses in 1961; the hate-filled, distorted faces on white housewives in New Orleans; fire hoses, dogs, and beatings in Montgomery, Birmingham, Selma, and other places; Sheriffs Bull Conner and Lawrence Rainey; James Meredith at Ole Miss in 1962; George Wallace at the University of Alabama in 1963.

Black nonviolence had its counterpoint in white violence. Sanctioned by southern authorities, white violence meant that the gains achieved by the civil rights activists were costly in the extreme. Ostracism, isolation, and fear were part of the daily experience of activists in the South. Arrests were commonplace. A series of murders of black and white civil rights workers—Liuzzo, Edwards, Cheney, Goodman, Schwerner, and Evers—which went unpunished increased the terror and anger of the civil rights activists and of the southern blacks they were trying to reach.

Meanwhile, the federal government responded as blacks set the agenda; the interplay during the civil rights years between the government and civil rights advocates was another important backdrop to the dramas which were being played out. The Department of Justice, under Attorney General Robert Kennedy, instituted voting rights suits early in the 1960s—more than 30 cases by 1962.[4] President Kennedy sent deputy marshals to Mississippi and federalized the National Guard when violence erupted in 1962 over the admission of James Meredith to the University of Mississippi. In 1963, when Governor George Wallace opposed the court-ordered admission of two black students to the University of Alabama, Kennedy issued a proclamation on the unlawful obstruction of justice and an executive order authorizing the use of armed forces in Alabama.

As civil rights became a central issue in American politics in the 1960s, blacks in other parts of the world were gaining attention. Black Africans were revolting against colonial empires throughout Africa, and European control in Africa began to weaken. The admission of Ghana to the United Nations in 1957 coincided with the attempted admission of a handful of black students to Central High School in Little Rock. The black African nations began to emerge as a force in the United Nations, as a source of pride and cultural resurgence to American blacks, and undoubtedly as a factor in the sensitivity of the federal government to racial issues in the United States.[5]

The Civil Rights Act of 1964, initiated by Kennedy and broadened by Johnson, allowed the Attorney General to start school desegregation suits and the federal government to withhold funds from segregated school districts. It forbade discrimination in voting or registration procedures and segregation in public hotels, restaurants, shops, libraries, services, transportation, or places of recreation. Strong protection for black voters came with the Civil Rights Act of 1965, which did away with literacy tests and allowed the use of federal registrars when state registrars were discriminatory. Title VI of the Civil Rights Act of 1964, which prohibits all forms of racial discrimination in programs receiving federal assistance and requires termination of this assistance to recipients who fail to comply, and Executive Order 11246 of 1965, which prohibits employment discrimination on the basis of race, color, religion, sex, or national origin by federal contractors and subcontractors, also applied to higher education.[6]

Throughout the early 1960s the southern civil rights movement had remained nonviolent, and Martin Luther King and other civil rights veterans continued to set the ideological and tactical tone of the movement—with somewhat grudging support from the younger, more impatient new activists. Perhaps the greatest triumph of the moderate integrationist leaders was the massive, emotional March on Washington in 1963 in support of the Civil Rights Act which passed in Congress the following year. But as southern white violence against civil rights workers continued and, as the movement began to attract an even younger and more diverse group who saw support from the federal government as slow in coming and meager when it did come, the activists in SNCC and CORE became increasingly militant. It was not long before the struggle began to turn inward and organizational troubles intensified. Blacks began to criticize whites for taking over leadership positions, for not really understanding the black situation, for harboring unconscious racial prejudice, for unwittingly supporting racism in American institutions.

Moderates and radicals of both races began to split. In 1966, James Meredith was shot while walking for freedom in Mississippi. CORE, NAACP, and SNCC took over his march. Sometime during the march the phrase "Black Power," which had been in circulation among civil rights activists prior to the march, was picked up by the press. But the feeling of "the movement" as an interracial effort was over. Whites were expelled or voluntarily departed from SNCC and CORE. Black Power as an ideology and a strategy, as a means of self-defense, as a path of self-consciousness and pride, began to be enunciated by young blacks who had been through the civil rights movement as well as by others who had not.[7]

To some extent, the tension between integrationist and separatist elements had always been present in the civil rights movement, but as long as gains were being made through the courts and through other legitimate means, the integrationists dominated. The direct action approach of Martin Luther King was an early sign that blacks could not rely on strictly legitimate means. When, in the eyes of civil rights workers, the nonviolence of direct action seemed to do little more than activate violence on the part of whites, the integrationist position began to lose its weight and power. Ironically, the Civil Rights Act of 1964 and 1965 came too late to heal the split between the moderates and the militants in the civil rights movement. A new stage in black-white relations had been reached and the setting shifted northward.

CIVIL RIGHTS MOVES NORTH

While the major action of the civil rights movement occurred in the South, important developments were occurring around the same time among northern blacks. The black middle class was consolidating gains it had made after World War II. Removed from them were developments among the black masses. With the large black migration to northern cities during and after the war, black ghettos became filled with people who were living in overcrowded, overpriced dwellings in poor repair, in neighborhoods which bred crime and dependence on welfare and where high rates of unemployment and family disruption were experienced. The northern ghettos provided fertile soil for the Black Muslims, who were growing in strength at about the same time the civil rights movement was flourishing in the South.

Urban riots began erupting regularly during the 1960s (though they were certainly not a new invention—American cities have had a history of racial and ethnic riots): in 1963, Birmingham, Savannah, Cambridge, Md., Chicago, and Philadelphia; in 1964, Jacksonville, Cleveland, St. Augustine, Philadelphia, Mississippi, New York, Rochester, and Jersey City; in 1965, Watts and Bogalusa, La.; in 1966, Watts, Chicago, Cleveland, and Baltimore; in 1967, Detroit, Nashville, Houston, Tampa, Atlanta, Newark, Plainfield, and New Brunswick. In 1968, there were riots in 36 states and hundreds of cities following the assassination of Martin Luther King. The urban riots represented a deep, and increasingly widespread, alienation among blacks in America. Surveys have documented the support for the urban riots among the general black population, particularly among urban youth, and among both the well-educated and the less educated. As Schuman and Hatchett (1974) note, "the riots *crystallized* the belief among many blacks that progress was too slight and their status in American society still basically frustrating. In one way, of course, the riots were simply a continuation of the black protest movements that had been gathering steam over the past decade . . . In another sense, the riots—and even more, the support they engendered in the black population—precipitated increased disillusionment with the more disciplined and optimistic earlier civil rights movement led by men like Martin Luther King."[8]

As civil rights activists moved north, they became more militant. Some had to leave the country, some disappeared entirely, and others were driven to more extreme acts by their own logic and by the logic of police harrassment. Revolution against capitalist oppression seemed the only answer for some. Rap Brown, a well-educated and articulate SNCC leader, moved in a brief two years from a belief in integration to separatism to revolution. In 1968 he was twice arrested on vague charges, and he endured a 43-day hunger strike while in jail. In an open letter from jail he wrote: "Our will to live must no longer supersede our will to fight, for our fighting will determine if our race shall live. To desire freedom is not enough. We must move from resistance to aggression, from revolt to revolution" (Ellison, 1974).[9]

In 1966, just as the civil rights movement was beginning to fall apart, the Black Panther Party was founded by young blacks in Oakland, California. Within the next few years, the Panthers were to provide a glittering array of articulate, angry spokespersons: George Mason Murray; Huey Newton; Bobby Seale; Eldridge Cleaver; George Jackson; Angela Davis. Initially biracial and coalitionist in its politics, the Panthers' sophisticated young leaders included ex-SNCC workers Stokely Carmichael, James Forman, and Rap Brown. Panther chapters spread quickly in cities across the country, but police harrassment, infiltration, conflicts with the various black nationalist groups that were springing up regularly during that time, and internal splits eventually decimated the organization. Its own overblown rhetoric did not help, and the Panthers found they could not count on the liberal support, white or black, that moderate civil rights organizations had attracted earlier. Official repression of the Panthers went unchecked in the late 1960s. By the spring of 1970, 38 Panthers were dead, at least 12 shot by police (Ellison, 1974). Panther Leader Bobby Seale was one of the defendants in the celebrated Chicago conspiracy trial after the 1968 Democratic Convention. Eldridge Cleaver later fled the country rather than serve a prison sentence.

The violence by whites which accompanied the efforts of the civil rights movement was undoubtedly a force in undermining it in the South. The violence against northern black activists was also costly. A series of trials and deaths thinned the ranks of the Panthers, although they continue today in a more subdued way in several cities. Indeed, the story of that decade is a story of violence, from Vietnam to the assassinations of John Kennedy, Malcolm X, Martin Luther King, and Robert Kennedy. By the time of the King assassination, integrationism had already lost its hegemony in black movements, and pessimism and alienation among large sectors of the black population had already set in.[10]

Notes

[1]See Howard Schuman and Shirley Hatchett (1974). These researchers note changes in black attitudes in the mid-60s which showed perceptions of increased contact with white people and optimism about change in the racial situation in the United States. By the late 60s and early 70s, however, disillusionment and pessimism about

the possibility for substantial change had increased. "System blame" rather than self-blame became more prevalent among blacks, particularly among youth. For a discussion of the complexity of these dynamics among college students at black colleges during the 1960s, see Patricia Gurin and Edgar G. Epps (1975).

[2]Gurin and Epps (1975) document the widespread support and activity of students in black colleges during this period. Three-quarters of their sample students in black colleges reported in 1970 that they had participated in some form of political activity during their college years. Harris and Gallup polls for 1967 and 1968 showed that only 20 percent of the nation's college students had participated in some form of politics in college.

[3]Survey researchers have noted a transformation in white racial attitudes, particularly among the young, which began in the 1940s when whites began to express relatively more liberal racial attitudes. This trend has continued over the past three decades. See, for example, Paul B. Sheatsley (1960); Mildred Swartz (1967); Andrew M. Greeley and Paul B. Sheatsley (1971); Angus Campbell (1971); Otis Dudley Duncan, Howard Schuman, and Beverly Duncan (1973).

[4]Civil rights had been a political issue in earlier administrations but gained national prominence in the 1960 contest between Nixon and Kennedy. Pressed by black organizations at the time, the Roosevelt, Truman, and Eisenhower administrations recognized the plight of blacks as a political issue. The southern bolting of the Democratic Party after the nomination of Harry Truman in 1948 was due to a large extent to Truman's support of the Fair Employment Practices Commission and other efforts to end segregation. In the 1960 campaign, John Kennedy came out as a stong advocate of civil rights and, in the heat of the campaign, showed his support by telephoning Mrs. Martin Luther King to express his sympathy when her husband was jailed in Atlanta. Also, Robert Kennedy helped to secure King's release.

[5]Skolnick, in a staff report to the National Commission on the Causes and Prevention of Violence in 1968, writes in a section reprinted in Yetman and Steele (1972):

> The rise of these new states, especially when coupled with the exigencies of Cold War diplomacy, has meant that since World War II American leaders have been well aware that the way blacks are treated at home has important ramifications for world affairs. A number of American black militants have looked to the UN specifically as an arena for bringing black grievances before the world. As Colonialism disintegrates, the previously unquestioned authority of the white world likewise disintegrates, and with it the capacity of a predominantly white society to maintain its privileges. Black militants are aware of this, and recognize the impact it may have. (p. 545)

[6]The revelant laws and regulations prohibiting discrimination in employment, salaries, fringe benefits, admissions, etc., include:
1. Executive Order 11246, as amended by 11375;
2. Title VII of the Civil Rights Act of 1964, as amended by the Equal Employment Opportunity Act of 1972;
3. Equal Pay Act of 1963, as amended by the Education Amendments of 1972 (Higher Education Act);
4. Title IX of the Education Amendments of 1972 (Higher Education Act);
5. Title VII (Section 799A) and title VIII (Section 845) of the Public Health Manpower Act and the Nurse Training Amendments Act of 1971.

The Director of the Higher Education Division of the Department of Health, Education and Welfare's Office for Civil Rights is responsible for enforcing most of these provisions. For a full description and analysis of legal mandates for affirmative action, see Jamie B. Catlin, John A. Seeley, and Margaret Talburtt, 1974.

[7]See Carmichael and Hamilton (1967) for the major statement of this position.

[8]Pages 124–125. For data on responses to the riots, see Campbell and Schuman (1968). See also Caplan and Paige (1968).

[9]Quoted by Ellison, 1974.

[10]For a report on a 1974 survey of black and white attitudes, see "Cross-Racial Contact Increases in Seventies: Attitude Gap Narrows for Blacks and Whites," *ISR Newsletter,* (Institute for Social Research, The University of Michigan), Autumn 1975.

3

Implications of the Social Context for Higher Education

Zelda F. Gamson and Carlos H. Arce

It is sometimes thought that the campus unrest of 1968, which expanded considerably after King's assassination, was the major cause of the increase in black enrollments in northern colleges and universities. On closer inspection, however, the unrest—and the assassination itself—appear to have merely sped up the trends that had already begun. A large wing of the black movement had moved north before 1968. King and the SCLC and other civil rights organizations had continued their work in the South, although the moderate organizations began to focus increasingly on integration in the North, where *de facto* rather than *de jure* segregation became the target of legal attacks. The struggle raged in the late 1960s between the moderate integrationists and the militant non-integrationists in the North. Desegregation and equality continued to be the bywords for some; liberation and autonomy for others. Community control over schools came to be seen as more desirable than integration among some black leaders such as those in CORE. The emphasis in the schools was on service to black needs through quality education that would incorporate black history and culture into the school curricula. The disorders which took place after King's death were sparked by riots in schools and colleges and were often led by a new group of self-aware young blacks who had grown up with the interesting amalgam of recent history we have just sketched: the measured, religious tones of Martin Luther King; the strident, messianic language of black nationalists and Black Muslims; the political awareness and glamour of the Black Panthers; and the street wisdom and volatility of the black urban underclass.

THE FEDERAL ROLE

The racial activism of the late 1950s and the 1960s was interspersed with growing governmental activity in protecting the civil rights of blacks. The activism frequently triggered governmental response and the combined impact of the two was felt in many sectors of American society, particularly in higher education.

By the time of King's assassination, the role of the federal government in promoting legal desegregation and in providing financial support for bringing minorities into colleges and universities was firmly established. Although enforcement of Title VI of the Civil Rights Act was sporadic, it did begin to bring in more black students. In 1969 and 1970, HEW and the Office of Civil Rights notified ten states that they must formulate desegregation plans for their colleges and universities.[1]

More dramatic has been the unprecedented role of the federal government in providing financial aid. A few private sources for financial aid to black students had been in existence for many years before the federal government entered the picture. The National Scholarship Service and Fund for Negro Students (NSSFNS), established in 1948, has had the longest history of giving financial aid to black high school students and helping them enroll in predominantly white institutions. The National Achievement Program, begun in 1964 with a $7 million grant from the Ford Foundation to the National Scholarship Service, was used principally for black students who sought to attend prestigious colleges of the North.

Prior to 1965, the federal government's involvement in financial aid programs was limited to National Defense Student Loans (NDSL)—now called National Direct Student Loans. Of no small impact, however, between 1958 and 1972–73 it provided nearly $2.2 billion to educational institutions to make direct loans to student borrowers at low interest and with liberal repayment provisions. The passage of the Higher Education Act in 1965, with provisions for a series of new financial aid programs, greatly accelerated the federal government's encouragement of equal access to higher education. Not since the G.I. Bill which followed World War II had legislation had such an influence on opening post-secondary education to new kinds of students.

The Higher Education Act of 1965 added three major new programs: College Work-Study (CWS), Educational Opportunity Grants (EOG) (replaced under the 1972 Higher Education Amendments by the Supplemental Education Opportunity Grant program), and the Guaranteed Student Loan Program (GSL). These programs began to receive substantial funding by 1968. Over $1 million in federal funds went into Opportunity Grants in fiscal year 1968; in 1974, this figure reached beyond $6 million. Over $2 billion went to institutions participating in the College Work-Study program from its inception to 1973–74, and nearly six million Guaranteed Student Loans had been made by the same year, bringing the annual volume of loans close to $1 billion.

Title VI of the Higher Education Act provided money for a variety of special programs aimed at the disadvantaged, including Talent Search and Upward Bound (over $220 million through fiscal year 1974). These programs were aimed at identifying needs and providing special help and remedial programs in high school and during the freshman year of college.

Beginning in the late 1960s, numerous states instituted their own scholarship and grant programs, which have grown considerably in size and dollar support within a short period of time. In 1969–70, 19 states were providing $199.9 million to nearly 471,000 students. Estimates for 1975–76 placed the number of states with scholarship and grant programs at 43, with total support close to half a billion dollars.

At the federal level, the 1972 Higher Education Amendments revised some of the programs of the 1965 act and added the Basic Educational Opportunity Grants (BEOG). Taking the philosophy and approach of the G.I. Bill, the new grants were based on the concept of entitlement. When fully funded, low income students could expect to receive the cost of their education per year or $1,400, whichever was less. Students could take the grants to the institutions of their choice (including a large number of proprietary institutions previously excluded from federal student aid programs).

The Civil Rights Act of 1964 mandated a census of all higher education institutions which identified students by race and ethnic identification. This monitoring device, which runs counter to earlier race-blind practices in colleges and universities admissions, had a profound effect on enrollment of blacks—despite early resistance from liberals and integrationists who viewed such enumeration as a possible violation of civil rights, and from conservatives who feared federal control and opposed the entry of minorities.

The first survey of minority enrollments was undertaken by James S. Coleman in 1965 as part of the Project on Equality of Educational Opportunity (Coleman et al. 1966). It was not until 1967 that a full compliance survey of enrollments was first introduced by the Office of Civil Rights; but the data from this survey were not analyzed, nor was a report disseminated. However, raw enrollment percentage figures were published in *The Chronicle of Higher Education* in April 1968 under the ominous title "Armed with Racial Survey, HEW Probes Campus Bias." Since 1968, the Office of Civil Rights has conducted biennial surveys requiring increasingly more detail.

BLACK ENROLLMENTS IN HIGHER EDUCATION

Historical Trends

The level of black participation in desegregated institutions is difficult to assess both because of its low magnitude and because of the general failure to maintain full data relating to it. Until fairly recently, there were two important features that distinguished and severely limited most "head counts" of blacks in colleges and make the retrospective measurement of enrollment patterns difficult. The first is that racial classifications were considered illegal or were at least discouraged in most statistical surveys by governmental agencies or educational associations. The second is that black enrollments in colleges were considered synonymous with enrollments in the historically black colleges. This perception went together with a general neglect of the enrollment of blacks in white colleges, which has always been grossly underrepresentative of the black population. It is nevertheless possible to generate annual estimates of total black college-level enrollments through Bureau of the Census school enrollment survey data which have been available since the end of World War II; these estimates can also be adjusted to show black enrollments in colleges which were not historically black.[2]

The historical portrait of black enrollments and their determinants is presented in Figure 3-1. The number and percentage of blacks attending college, including the white colleges, increased sharply immediately after World War II and more moderately after the Ko-

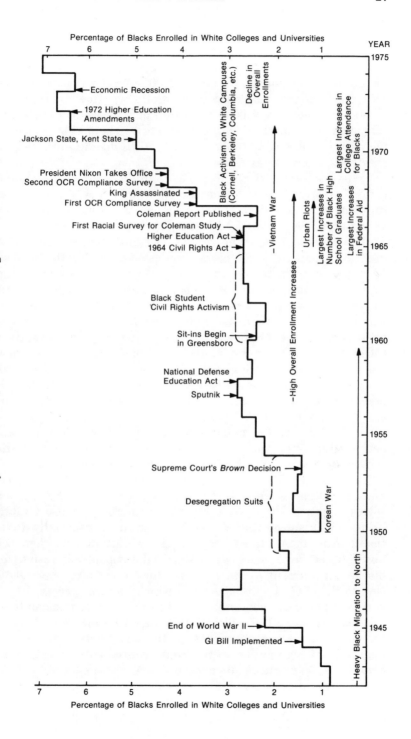

FIGURE 3-1

Historical Summary of Black Enrollments in White Colleges and Universities

rean War. Between the two wars, there were substantial declines in black enrollments to pre-1940 levels. After the Korean War and following the Supreme Court's antisegregation decisions, black enrollments increased rapidly and leveled off in 1956 at about 5 percent of total enrollments and 3 percent of enrollments in white colleges. This leveling off indicated that black enrollments were increasing at rates comparable to those of white students in the 1950s. Black enrollments remained at a stable level for a full decade until 1967, when they began to climb again.

When viewed historically, black enrollment in white higher educational institutions is a complex phenomenon. The sharp black enrollment increases since 1967 have been the result of the confluence of numerous forces which had their effect as major black demographic shifts were occurring. The most important demographic factor has been the expansion of the black population in the North and West due to migration from the South after World War II. As blacks migrated to western and north central urban centers, educational institutions in these areas became more accessible to them. Thus, beyond any deliberate plan to increase black enrollments, by 1967 conditions were ripe for greater black representation in predominantly white colleges and universities. These same conditions, however, also provided a "natural setting" for significant black enrollment growth prior to 1967, which was less noticeable because it took place during periods when white enrollments were increasing at least as quickly and sometimes even faster.

In a context of demographic change, other pressures came together to give impetus to the steady black enrollment growth through the 1960s and to the sharp and conspicuous increases in 1967 and following years. The two major sources of these pressures to increase black enrollments were the federal government and the blacks themselves (supported by nonblack sympathizers). They also combined to bring about substantial demographic change, especially in educational attainment. Increased educational attainment then brought about higher and more widespread educational aspirations among blacks. Attainment and aspirations fueled and often provided direction to the civil rights movement, which in turn increased the pressure on the federal government and institutions to respond to blacks.

Federal support of a direct and indirect nature caused significant increases in black enrollments. In the mid-1950s, judicial decisions ending legal segregation in the South caused noticeable increases in overall black enrollments nationally. A decade later, in the mid-1960s, legislative activity also provided an impetus for increases in black enrollment. At first, legal decisions and legislative acts were viewed in many sectors of higher education as distant and even irrelevant. Subsequent data collections from every institution could not be so perceived. The 1965 Office of Education Enrollment Survey, with its request for racial data for the Coleman study, and the first Office for Civil Rights "compliance" survey in 1967 underscored the seriousness of the government's intentions in promoting equal opportunity for blacks in higher education.

Judicial decisions, legislative acts, and federal bureaucratic activity account for only part of the federal impact. If these represented a stick wielded before higher education, there was also the carrot of federal financial support which expanded simultaneously with civil rights legislation. The various federal aid programs dramatically altered the amount and type of funding for student financial aid. These changes were closely linked to expansion of educational opportunity and, subsequently, to increased black enrollment in white colleges and universities.

The other major source of external pressure was the social-political activity of blacks themselves. This pressure was both direct and indirect. Indirectly, the civil rights movement pressured the federal government to act and thus to offer the carrot and stick to higher education. The gradual movement of black civil rights activity to higher education as a target during the 1960s climaxed in 1967–68. Extensive and diverse demands on particular institutions and on the overall enterprise called for commitments by the colleges and universities themselves to increase opportunities for blacks. For several years, black activism was a primary pressure on academe to continue earlier enrollment increases.

The two major turning points in this history of black enrollment were thus in 1954 and 1967. In both years, the increases followed close on the heels of considerable federal civil rights activity, judicial in 1954 and legislative in 1967. The increases of the 1944 to 1947 period, although temporary, also support an external explanation of black enrollment increase. Military participation and use of G. I. Bill benefits seem to have influenced these increases. The elimination of these outside inducements brought a quick end to the black enrollment increases until 1954.

Institutional and Regional Trends

Short of a major data collection effort, it is not possible to assess in any systematic fashion the distribution of black enrollments in particular institutions prior to 1968. However, OCR compliance reports permit such an analysis for 1968–1974, the period on which this study is focused. Figure 3-2 shows the mean percentages of black enrollments for the years 1968, 1970, 1972, and 1974 by region and for different institutional types.

Overall black enrollment has been and remains proportionately higher in the lower degree level institutions of higher education.

FIGURE 3-2

Black Enrollment by Type of Institution and by Region, 1968–1974

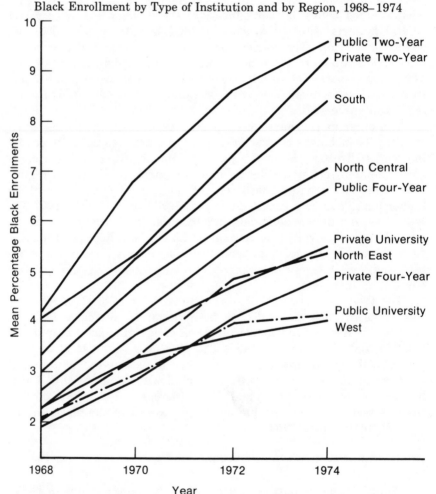

SOURCE: Aggregated data from Office for Civil Rights Reports.

However, there are variations by degree level and control, as shown in Figure 3-2. Among universities, private institutions have made greater increases and reached higher black enrollment levels than public ones. Among private institutions generally, the universities enroll larger proportions of black students than do the private liberal arts colleges. On the other hand, in the public institutions the relative enrollment is inversely related to degree level: the largest percentages are in the community colleges and the lowest are in the universities.

Black student enrollments vary substantially by region (Figure 3-2); they are highest in the South, decrease from the North Central region to the Northeast, and are lowest in the West. In general, this parallels the proportion of blacks in the regional population reported in the 1970 census: 19.7 percent in the South; 8.9 percent in the Northeast; 8.1 percent in the North Central area; and 4.9 percent in the West. While the rate of regional underenrollment (percentage of blacks in the population minus the percentage of blacks enrolled in college) was most severe in the South, the rate of increase of black college enrollments from 1968 to 1974 was directly related to the degree of underenrollment. The percentage of black college enrollments by 1974 was still increasing rapidly in the South, where underenrollment was the largest (over 10 percent). It has increased most gradually in the West, where regional underenrollment of blacks in higher education was quite small (around 1 percent).

WHITE INSTITUTIONS' RESPONSES TO BLACK STUDENTS

With these changes in enrollment patterns, black students began to be concentrated in large enough numbers on some campuses to organize politically. Astin et al. (1975) concluded that racial protests tended to "work."[3] While only 28 percent of all institutions in 1968–69 instituted ethnic studies courses, programs, or departments, 63 percent of those experiencing severe protest initiated such changes. This relationship between protest activity and institutional response held up under controls for student and institutional characteristics. In 1971, Astin and Bayer suggested a "critical mass" hypothesis to explain the incidence of black student protests. While the *proportion* of black students at predominantly white institutions was not related to protests over racial policies, the absolute *number* was. About tactics the author concluded that "institutions seemed somewhat more

BLACK STUDENTS ON WHITE CAMPUSES

willing to make concessions to black students when their tactics were extreme but not violent" (Astin et al., 1975, p. 151).

From the federal government, the foundations, and the institutions came a proliferation of ideas and funds to develop special programs. There were remedial programs such as Project Opportunity and a variety of Educational Opportunity Programs. There were preparatory programs such as the Transitional Year Program and Upward Bound. There were special admissions and financial aid programs; counseling, tutoring, and special classes; cultural programs and social activities.

Black Studies

A large number of black colleges and universities had been offering black-oriented courses in history and other fields since the 1920s. The first recognized black studies program at a predominantly white college or university was officially established at San Francisco State College in 1968 under the directorship of Nathan Hare. In the same year, a conference of prestigious scholars met at Yale to lay the groundwork for Afro-American studies. Black and ethnic studies caught on quickly across the country: a survey of 451 institutions of higher education in the fall of 1972 indicated that two-thirds offered at least one ethnic studies area (Dutton 1973). These ranged from a focus on a single ethnic group to a general ethnic studies focus, from degree to nondegree status, from interdepartmental programs to independent centers and freestanding departments. Shoenfeld (1972), in a 1969 survey of 132 institutions, found the establishment of some black studies program to be the most common student-initiated change during the late 1960s. Most surveys conducted in 1969 and 1970 indicated that slightly fewer than 50 percent of all institutions offered black studies courses (McKee 1971).

It appears that the total number of institutions offering such courses did not expand after this initial burst of activity. Dutton, in a 1973 ACE study which sampled 20 percent of the population, estimated that 49 percent of all institutions offered at least one course in black studies in the fall of 1972. Sixty-one percent of all institutions offered either black, Chicano, Asian-American, or multi-ethnic courses. Even though the total number of institutions offering such courses has remained stable, the number of institutions offering substantial programs (usually meaning major, minor, or "certificate") continued to rise. Dutton estimated that, as of the academic year 1972–73, 182 institutions offered majors in black studies and 96 offered minors.

Dutton found ethnic and black studies to be most common in universities and least common in two-year institutions. Dutton estimated that over 81 percent of all universities offered at least one course in black studies, while only 37 percent of two-year institutions did so. With 47 percent of midwestern institutions offering black studies courses, this regional group is quite close to the estimate for the country as a whole.

Unmeasured, yet probably more significant in determining the overall curriculum response, is the degree to which students not majoring in black studies take courses in the area. Dutton estimates black studies course enrollments at near 143,000 in the fall term of 1972. There is some indication, however, that interest in black and/or ethnic studies is waning among undergraduates; very few recently intended to pursue them as a major field of study.[5]

Less is known about the organizational patterns, staffing, and budgeting of black studies programs. Ford (1973) provides one of the most recent observations. He identifies three types of organizational arrangements: the *interdisciplinary approach,* with a director who obtains his staff through the regular departments and the device of joint appointments (75 percent of all programs); the *independent or semi-autonomous department* or institute which accounted for fewer than 25 percent of the programs; and finally a small number of *separate and fully autonomous* schools or colleges with the same privileges as other units of the university or larger state system (e.g., Malcolm X in Chicago and Third World College at the San Diego campus of the University of California).

A smaller study of ten university programs conducted in 1970 supports Ford's findings (Academy for Educational Development 1971). Of the ten schools, which included a number of prestigious research institutions and major black universities, seven had taken the interdisciplinary approach, two had semi-autonomous institutes and one had an independent departmental arrangement. The staffs were generally small, with teaching faculty coming almost exclusively from other departments. Budgets ranged from a low of $57,000 to a high of $150,000. Fair (1973) surveyed Illinois colleges and universities operating black studies programs and found that directors were generally black males between the ages of 22 and 40.

The literature on black studies programs reveals substantial consistency among institutions on the problems seen to be of critical importance—and wide disagreement over the prospects for the future. Shortages of money and staff, intra-university conflict concerning the availability of faculty, and problems surrounding the intellectual validity of black studies are the questions cited most often (Academy for Educational Development 1971; Ford 1973).

Remedial Programs

While the literature seems to reflect a declining interest in compensatory programs, survey research indicates continued growth. Gordon and Wilkerson (1966) estimated that 37 percent of all institutions had compensatory programs, and only about 50 schools conducted "substantial" programs. Egerton set the figure in 1968 at about 50 percent. A 1973 survey conducted by ACE estimated that 61 percent of all institutions were conducting remedial programs, with the highest percentage among public community colleges and the lowest among private colleges and universities.

We can divide compensatory education programs into three basic types: *pre-entrance programs,* such as Upward Bound and summer "orientations" run by individual institutions; *transitional programs* of a nonintegrated nature, often one year in length and usually found in the more prestigious colleges and universities (e.g., Brandeis and Yale); and *integrated approaches* which combine remedial work with the regular undergraduate curriculum.

By far the most common form of compensatory education, itself quite varied in technique and approach, is the integrated approach where remedial work is made available to regularly matriculated students. The literature also reflects a decline in "special" programs for the disadvantaged (both because of the expense and the opposition from minorities) and a shift toward a wide range of supportive services in the area of guidance and counseling. Reflecting the general milieu in higher education, there also appears to be a current emphasis on black adults—programs for black women, black veterans, etc. Jacoby (1972), in an article on Michigan State, discusses the existence of a nonrecognized "basic track" for students with low high school averages and board scores (a combination of rural whites and minorities). This may well be a practice followed by institutions seeking to avoid "special" labels.

Other Organizational Responses

In addition to spurring the development of black studies programs, remedial courses, and counseling services, the presence of blacks in colleges in increasing numbers has brought a variety of political, social, and cultural organizations formed by blacks themselves. These organizations appear to be pervasive, even in schools with relatively small black enrollments. Lyons (1973), in a 1969 survey of 140 institutions, found that 62 of the 68 responding institutions had black student organizations. Two-thirds of these groups perceived their primary function as political. Record (1974b) believes that as blacks become more professionally and occupationally oriented, specific limited-purpose organizations will replace the broader political organizations now in existence. Developments in medicine and law student bodies already mark this trend.

FACULTY AND ADMINISTRATIVE RESPONSE TO BLACK STUDENTS

From the beginning of the confrontation period, the response of faculty to black students has been especially problematic. The atmosphere in which the first confrontations took place was chaotic and confused. In reading reports of the period, one is struck by the level of confusion and fear which pervaded faculties and by the suddenness with which normally deliberate and slow-moving faculties were confronted with the necessity of making major curricular changes.[6]

Ironically, while one of the principal demands of this period centered on an academic issue—mainly the initiation of black studies—the involvement of the faculty was minimal. Negotiations usually took place between a small group of black students and executive officers of the institution. When faculty were involved, they often found their recommendations ignored or circumvented by a central administration responding to more direct pressure and confrontation tactics. Rosovsky (1969) notes that at Harvard when the issue of autonomy for the Afro-American Studies Program (which gave extraordinary power to its students) was presented to the faculty, the measure was passed in an atmosphere of fear and "liberal guilt."

While the tactics employed for implementing changes circumvented the usual academic modes, it was the rhetoric and apparent rejection of the tradition of integration which turned many faculty against the demands of black students for separate programs. Etzioni (1970), in an essay defending black studies as a "bridging" instrument, wrote:

It is hoped that the total rejection of the white world and the demand for total autonomy are only transitory stages, a step on the road from

being oppressed and suppressed to that of membership in the society
as a semi-autonomous community, proud of its own positive values
(p. 219).

It is difficult to determine how universal this particular senti-
ment was at the time. The literature of the day (and it continues)
certainly contains ample and vociferous opposition to black studies
and special programs of admission and support. Admission and support programs (remedial and social) seemed to engender far less hostility than the black studies issue. This may be partly the result of
the rhetoric accompanying early proposals which were often presented in words that indicated white scholarship—especially in the
social sciences and humanities.

Robert Blauner (1972), writing from a position to the left of the
majority of faculty and generalizing from his experience at Berkeley,
called the influx of black students into universities a severe test of
the liberalism of white faculty. Faculty, he claims, were "jolted from
complacency." The tranquility of their privileged positions had been
disturbed and they did not like it. There was a paradox, Blauner said,
between faculty conservatism at home and liberalism in the world.
While faculty tended to support civil liberties, opposed the war in
Vietnam, and supported liberal economic and social measures, they
nevertheless jealously guarded their "craft autonomy" and authority
over entrance into the discipline.[7] Scientific methodology itself,
Blauner noted, is a conservative, painstaking, step-by-step process.
Organizationally, the departmental structure tends to limit vision;
Blauner contrasted the more positive responses of administrators to
blacks with the generally negative responses of faculty. Blauner also
believes that the call for special admissions policies conflicted with
the central value of the liberal philosophy—that of universalism as
opposed to particularism.

Within the classroom, Blauner concluded, white faculty were
often intimidated by vocal new blacks who challenged what had previously been passively accepted. Faculty (at least at a place like Berkeley) found that they did not like teaching third world students. White
faculty applied a double standard in grading. "Many third world students became adept at hustling for grades, working on professors'
guilt, confusion, and general ignorance of the cultural patterns and
survival techniques of the racially oppressed (Blauner 275)."

Lipset and Ladd (1972), working with the Carnegie Survey of
Faculty conducted in 1969, devised a "Black Support Scale." The scale
consisted of three items: (1) relaxation of requirements for minority

faculty hiring, (2) lowering of admission standards for minorities, and (3) support of a program of black studies. As in other measures of liberal versus conservative values, faculty in the social sciences and, secondly, in the humanities were more supportive than those in the biological and physical sciences. Engineering and agriculture ranked lowest.

In one of few studies to date which attempted to assess the impact of open admissions on faculty—a survey conducted in 1971 a few months after the advent of open admissions at City University of New York (CUNY)—Rossman et al. (1975) asked faculty, students, and administrators for their reactions to open admissions. The author found a solid base of support—with the administration slightly more favorable than faculty. About nine out of ten faculty members agreed with general statements about open admissions being a good idea because it equalized opportunity. Few felt that separate colleges should be established. Further, over 80 percent of the faculty felt that the same performance standards should be employed in awarding degrees. Forty-one percent of the faculty in the four-year colleges felt that the academic reputation of the school would be hurt. Instructors and lecturers who had joined the faculty recently were less anxious about this matter than older, higher-ranking colleagues. In general, however, age, sex, race, credentials, rank, and length of employment were unrelated to attitudes on open admissions. Slightly over one-third of the faculty said that open admissions had had no effect on their teaching. Most of the others said they had changed either their teaching styles or course content. Twenty-five percent said they had lowered their grading standards as a result of open admissions (pp. 125–127).

Record (1974a) attempted to assess the impact of the introduction of black studies on sociologists with specialities in the area of race and ethnic relations. Comparing responses of over 200 sociologists in 70 different colleges and universities, he distinguished four types: *embracers, accommodaters, antagonists,* and *dropouts.* In general, he found that young sociologists, blacks, and, to a lesser degree, women were more favorably disposed toward black studies, while Jews were generally less receptive. Interestingly, the "embracers" (who accounted for 28 percent of his sample) consisted of a mixed group of both radical sociologists and conservatives "who welcomed black studies as a containment and decompression area," as well as traditional academicians who saw black studies as a "landing place for marginal or deficient black students combed out of sociology classes" (1974a, p. 366). The "dropouts" included a group of black and white sociologists who had had traumatic experiences during the confrontation period; this was a substantial group, about 20 percent of the total sample.

Less has been written on the response of administrators to black students. As we have noted, administrators have been more involved in negotiations with black students and have generally been viewed as more responsive. This involvement took its toll, however. Most of the administrators whom Astin et al. (1975) interviewed felt that unrest and student dissatisfaction had lessened their authority. They complained of increased demands on their time and of feeling "overworked and harassed" (p. 155). Lindahl (1973), in interviews conducted in the winter of 1970, found that "campus conflict" and "political interference" were often cited by exadministrators as reasons for leaving.

Black faculty, recruited in greater numbers to white campuses in the early seventies as a result of student pressure and federal requirements for affirmative action, have been the subject of recent research.[8] In their 1975 survey of faculty, Lipset and Ladd (*Chronicle of Higher Education,* September 22, 1975) found that the overall proportion of black faculty had remained at about the same level over the previous decade. The proportion of blacks was not greater among young faculty than among older age groups, and they were clustered at less prestigious institutions.

Estimates we have made from 1969 to 1973 ACE surveys indicate that black faculty comprised 2.9 percent of all college and university faculty in 1973, while the percentage was 2.2 in 1969. These percentages included more black women than black men in both years. The greatest increase in black faculty since 1969 occurred in two-year colleges, especially among black women. Four-year colleges and universities increased black faculty representation, both male and female, by 0.4 percent in the four-year period, although the largest proportion of blacks are in four-year colleges (5.4 percent). (Undoubtedly this figure represents the faculties in predominantly black colleges.) Less than 1 percent of the faculty in predominantly white universities are black.

A number of studies have examined role conflict among black faculty who, more often than not, have found themselves in positions calling for various responses to different constituents. Cox (1971) found that black administrators in community colleges had high perceptions of role conflict and appeared to have more duties than white administrators. Noting the high level of turnover among black studies directors and blacks in teacher-counselor roles, Rist (1970) concluded that such positions often create intolerable tensions which are best resolved by resignation. The level of power at which blacks find themselves is also a source of frustration. Moore and Wagstaff (1974) call this the "assistant to" phenomenon: blacks in administrative positions, while recruited as a result of affirmative action programs, held staff positions outside of the main lines of decision making. Kirkmon (1972) found that minority administrators in California community colleges perceived their roles as holding minimum responsibility. At the same time, they felt that they had a large degree of freedom to plan, make judgments, and express and discuss opinions. It may be that blacks are gaining autonomy and power in areas of minor importance.

Black faculty are often torn between loyalty to their discipline and the demands of black students for black studies programs (Record 1974a). Rafky (1973), in a national sampling of black faculty attitudes toward black studies and black students, found that a full 20 percent of black faculty outside of black studies had no contact with black students. However, he did find a high degree of support for these programs—but it was by no means unanimous. Richard Garcia (1974), in an essay on hiring practices, notes that faculty committees often assume that minority faculty members will take leadership roles in minority student affairs. This is not only an untenable position for a beginning faculty member, but, Garcia claims, often an unwanted one.

STUDENT RESPONSE

Three studies have been published in recent years which add significantly to our knowledge of black students in the context of predominantly white institutions. Willie and Sakuma (1972), in a variation of the "critical mass" hypothesis, concluded in their study of four New York state campuses that there must be a minimum number of black students on a campus in order to provide sufficient opportunities for satisfactory adjustment. On campuses where the number was fewer than 75, blacks "suffered the social consequences" of a limited range of personalities with whom to develop compatable relationships (p. 105). They also noted the lack of trust between blacks and whites as an important consequence of racial discrimination. Out of this problem a new role has emerged in higher education institutions, that of the black advisor.

> The black advisor performs a sort of holding operation, supporting
> the black students until the institution can demonstrate to them
> that it is trustworthy and reliable. Without a black advisor, the
> black students would despair. (p. 106)

Rossman et al. (1975) concluded that the results of the first year
of an open admissions policy at CUNY would support a decision to
implement open admissions throughout the university system. Most
students (both regular and open admission) expressed satisfaction
with the first year of college experience, and retention rates were
similar to national averages. Freshmen significantly raised reading
and math achievement scores during the year, with increases about
the same for open admissions and regular students. By the end of the
first year, open admission students had increased their scores to
about the level of regular students when they first entered college.

William Boyd II (1974), in a nationwide survey of black students
in 1972–73, found that black students want desegregation to continue
and that the most important changes for the future are continued
increases in the number of black faculty and students. Black students
were generally opposed to separatist philosophy and policies. Fifty-
nine percent indicated that race was not a dominant influence in
their choice of friends and activities, and only 15 percent expressed a
preference for all-black or minority housing. One out of two felt that
they had been discriminated against—with faculty members being
the primary source. Nevertheless, nearly two-thirds expressed satisfaction with their college experience. Students from private colleges
and universities were more likely to perceive their institutions as
responsive than students from the public sector. Location was also
revealed as an important situational factor. Forty-six percent of the
black students in nonmetropolitan colleges viewed location as a negative characteristic, compared to only 13 percent of the students in
metropolitan institutions.

THE FUTURE

The changes in higher education we have reviewed in this chapter occurred within a very short span of time—no more than three or
four years—and they were painful and difficult for both blacks and
whites. For blacks, there was tension between integration and separation, between personal mobility and loyalty to other blacks, between political and academic goals. For whites, guilt and varying

degrees of pressure often produced overreaction to black demands or incomprehension. Lower-class blacks and middle-class whites spoke to one another from vastly different cultural experiences and values (and middle-class blacks were often caught in the middle). There is no question that higher education has responded to these and many other forces for change.

The gains of the 1960s were won at great cost to those who struggled to achieve them. Many of the black students in white colleges and universities today are the beneficiaries. The impact on whites of the recent entry of large numbers of black students, however, is virtually unknown. This is the question we explored in our study of 13 colleges and universities.

Notes

[1]The directive quickly suffered from the virtual ending of executive branch enforcement of civil rights legislation by the Nixon administration. In the fall of 1970, however, the NAACP Legal Defense Fund took the federal government to court and asked that HEW enforce the law—that is, terminate funds to institutions engaged in racial discrimination. On November 16, 1972, U.S. District Judge John H. Pratt ruled that HEW had indeed failed to enforce Title VI. The U.S. Court of Appeals for the District of Columbia upheld his decision and the ten states were required to produce desegregation plans for their institutions to be submitted by June, 1974. These plans have been proceeding slowly.

[2]This discussion and the following statistical history are based on Arce (1976). This study reviews the quality of major primary sources of black enrollment data and concludes that census data on black enrollments are slightly inflated but generally provide a reliable measure of the proportion of blacks in predominantly white colleges and universities.

[3]Astin and his colleagues analyzed data from a number of national surveys of institutions and students conducted during the sixties and seventies. They note that in the 1969–70 "peak year," 80 percent of the four-year institutions and 67 percent of all institutions experienced student protest over some issue. While not as prevalent as protests over the environment or the war in Vietnam, protests over campus racial issues were significant in number. An estimated 16 percent of all institutions experienced a protest over these issues in 1959–70.

[4]The authors noted that private universities were most susceptible to protest and that size, selectivity, and curriculum diversity were also positively related to protest during the peak period.

[5]The Chronicle of Higher Education, September 15, 1975, reports that, of the 607,819 high school students who took the SAT in 1974–75, 165 said they intended to major in black studies and an additional 336 chose some other subfield of ethnic studies.

[6]See especially Rosovsky (1969), Hayashi (1972), and Gamson (1973) for accounts

of events at Harvard, Berkeley, and Michigan. For a discussion of the period and the issues it raised, see Nichols and Mills (1970) and Riesman and Stadtman (1973).

[7]To classify such a large and diverse group as college faculties in the United States as liberal or conservative is a dubious undertaking. The Carnegie/ACE surveys of 1968–1969 and 1972–1973 contradict the belief that faculties overall are liberal. In 1972–73, 44 percent of faculty members indicated that they considered themselves politically conservative (see Bayer 1974, p. 63). On the other hand, Ladd and Lipset, working from 1975 data, located the American academic on the left or liberal side of the political spectrum as compared to all other occupational groups; at the same time, they found sharp divisions within this group. While close to half support the conservative side of many major issues, the liberals are found among the most prominent and influential faculty, whose scholarly concerns most involve them with public policy. Thus the public image is one of an overwhelmingly liberal academia.

[8]For a study of black faculty, see Moore and Wagstaff (1974).

4

Chronology of the Study and First Steps

Robert T. Blackburn, Zelda F. Gamson,
and Marvin W. Peterson

The study we are about to describe arose as much from concern with a compelling human problem as it did from scientific curiosity. Because we were dealing with the results of unusual historical events, we did not expect to find theories which would help us generate specific hypotheses or techniques for analyzing the material we collected. We did start out with a very general framework for understanding the way universities and colleges were structured. We even had some expectations about how they would respond to pressures and opportunities to enroll black students. And we certainly had hunches about what we would find, questions to ask, leads to track down. The collective experience of our research team in academe and in civil rights and campus activism totaled to almost 100 years. These experiences did not suddenly disappear when we donned our "research suits"—they infused every aspect of our study from beginning to end. This chapter describes the assumptions we began with and how these assumptions affected crucial early decisions about defining a sample of colleges and universities, how and whom to interview, what information to collect, when to move on to our second stage, and what to do with what we had learned.

We began discussing the possibility of doing a study of institutional responses to black students in 1971, when it was becoming apparent that the entry of large numbers of minority students could have profound implications for higher education. After more than a year of discussion and planning, we submitted a proposal to the National Institute of Mental Health for a pilot study in a number of selected institutions. The proposal was eventually approved but the funds were impounded, along with those of many other projects, by the Nixon administration. It was not until the late spring of 1974 that we learned the funds would be released. This turn of events had the fortuitous effect of putting us in the field at a time when the issue of blacks on most campuses had cooled down. Indeed, in the short space of the two years between the submission of the proposal and its funding, the presence of blacks in predominantly white colleges and universities became more commonplace. This may have had positive effects on our study. By 1974–75, responses to blacks had become stabilized. The situation was clearer than it would have been two years earlier, when most of the campuses in our study were just starting to sort out what had happened to them in the throes of the black activism of the late 1960s and early 1970s. This was a definite advantage for us, since the "responses" we were interested in were developed enough to be examined.

THEORETICAL FOCUS AND VARIABLES

We started out with a general view of institutions of higher education as "open systems" which must deal with certain internal and external problems. Internally, colleges and universities must provide conditions so that the people who keep them going—faculty members, administrators, students—can more or less perform the institutionally defined tasks. Externally, they must deal with both threatening and supportive groups in such a way as to maximize both institutional integrity and responsiveness.

More than most organizations, a college or university is a human organization—its products, processes, and raw materials are primarily people-related. However anarchic and disorderly they may sometimes seem (Cohen and March 1974), colleges and universities are not just an undifferentiated conglomerate of people. They follow fairly regular patterns of behavior and define regular relationships among the people within them in such a way as to enable them to function as organized entities which accomplish certain purposes.

The activities and interactions of students, faculty, staff, and administrators constitute patterns of behavior that describe the university's varying processes—teaching, research, admissions, placement, decision making, communication, conflict resolution, etc. The processes themselves lead to certain outcomes such as producing degrees and research ("productive"); allocating resources and evaluating effectiveness ("managerial"); limiting the stress on or providing rewards to human beings ("maintenance"); maintaining external relations ("boundary"); and responding to new realities or planning ("adaptive").

These outcomes are produced by the operation of three fairly distinct subsystems: the formal organization, the social organization, and technology. The *formal organization* includes the formally approved set of positions, committees, and programs (the organization chart) and the goals, policies, rules, and regulations by which they are related. The *social organization* refers to the informal groups of people that emerge in any organization based on personal needs, motives, expectations, values, and interests. These groups often develop attitudes toward their work and/or patterns of behavior that may or may not be consistent with the requirements of the formal organization. Finally, the *technology* of an organization refers to the physical mechanisms and techniques used. In a university the kinds of teaching materials, the kind of budget format, or the mode of information handling are examples.

All three of these subsystems obviously are affected by the kinds of inputs the university receives. The inputs in turn influence the way people behave and the manner in which the processes contribute to outcomes. What is less obvious, but widely recognized by social and organizational theorists, is that changes in any of the subsystems are likely to affect the others.

In this study the major change is in the human input—the introduction of black students with new characteristics, abilities, expectations, and needs. We were interested in learning what happened to colleges and universities when this new clientele appeared in sharply increased numbers over a short period of time. How did the formal organizations respond? Were new departments, committees, and positions formed? Did goals change? How was the social organization affected? How did faculties respond to black students in their classes? Were new groupings found among the faculties? Among students? How did majority students feel about minority students, and vice versa? How did they actually interact—in the dorms, in class, in meetings, in informal situations? How was technology adapted to the

presence of a new student clientele? Were there new curricula or
courses? Did teaching practices change? Did new forms of information
gathering begin to appear?

Whether through changes in the formal, social, or technological
structures, how were the institutions' processes of accomplishing
their goals affected? Did typical patterns of decision making and communication undergo a shift in the period of increased black enrollment? What about the institutions' relations with their local communities? Were new resources attracted? Was money redistributed? Of
course, as we have seen in Chapter 3, not all colleges and universities
in the U.S. faced these questions; some chose not to enroll significantly increased numbers of minority students. Others, among them
the most prestigious private colleges in the country, have been able to
find minority students from the top ability and social class strata. But
many colleges and universities have had to wrestle more painfully
with the problem. What did they do?

When we started out, we assumed there were three possible responses for each of the educational institutions. One was to do nothing;
many schools developed no special programs or courses. Another was
to insulate the rest of the institution by developing programs which
were administratively, socially, politically, and culturally separate. A
third response was to develop new programs or to expand old programs
within the regular units, essentially integrating the problem of edu-
cating minority students into the overall teaching process.

It was difficult for us to know in advance whether particular
programs with the same name were separate or integrated. A remedial program, for example, may be organized as a new service function completely isolated from the academic function, as an arm of the
administration which is staffed by nonacademic counseling staff. Or
it could be a decentralized operation located and staffed within an
academic department. The implications of these different arrangements, both for students and for the institution, would be very different indeed.

It is also difficult to judge in advance whether a primarily separate program would have a greater or lesser institutional impact than
an integrated one. On the one hand, a separate program may have
low institutional impact because it is turned inward. At the same
time, separateness may give such a program new freedom and internal cohesion. An integrated program, on the other hand, is likely to
be high in its impact in the institution as a whole, but, because it
may have to adapt to existing conditions, it may be less adventurous
and cohesive than a separate program.

The chapters to follow will address some of these issues. At the outset, we began with certain expectations about what we would find. We expected, for example, that when there was a great disparity between white and black aptitudes, and when the reputation of the faculty was high, conflict would be high. We expected that most of the responsibility for administering and enacting the programs would be vested in a new group of specialists and that few faculty members would be involved in the program. We expected to find little impact on the student culture and to see the development of dual environments for blacks and whites.

Among faculty, we expected that those with the greatest commitment to traditional academic values would tend to retrench in response to black students and to become less involved in the affairs of the university. Those faculty members who saw the university as a social change agent and who took a "developmental" view of undergraduate education would be more likely to alter their teaching behavior and adjust their work priorities in accommodation to black students. In general, we thought overall faculty responses to black students would be ambivalent and erratic.

In the administrative area, we expected that institutions which had experienced great conflict would be more likely to have separate and highly autonomous programs for blacks. We expected that administrators, as they usually do, would pay greater attention to relationships with external groups and that they would create new offices within the central administration with special expertise related to blacks. We expected that there would be substantial modification of decision-making structures and greater formalization of policy with respect to blacks.

In the student area, we expected to find the greatest responsiveness to the entry of black students among white students who were actively involved in student groups, particularly political groups. We thought there would be efforts among these white students to form alliances with active black students; but as blacks entered institutions in increasing numbers and engaged in negotiations with administrators with some success, we expected to find some hostility between black and white student groups in the short run and indifference in the long run. The access to and responsiveness of administrators to black students, we expected, would stimulate an interest among organized black students in questions of governance and student participation in institutional decision making.

As we turn to the design and methodology section we shall see that many, but not all, of our questions were answerable. In later chapters, we will see that many of our formulations were too simplistic. In addition, the adaptations we had to make in conducting the study—necessitated both because of the sensitivity of the problem and because of complications in data collection—led us in directions we had not planned or anticipated.

DESIGN

The study was conducted in two stages. In the first stage, we visited 13 colleges and universities selected because they had experienced a substantial increase in black enrollments between 1968 and 1972. The second stage focused on 4 of the 13 institutions for an extensive survey of students, faculty, and administrators.

One restriction we encountered at the very beginning resulted from the resources available and the time allotted for completion of the study. We had only enough staff and funds to study a limited number of colleges and universities and, hence, could not control for all the variables we deemed important. Fiscal realities also confined our geographic coverage to the upper Midwest. While we went as far east and west as we could, we did not reach New England or west of Minnesota and Iowa. We do not believe unsampled areas had experiences that were dependent upon geography, although institutions in the South could well have been quite different from any we encountered and our study does not include their experiences.

A second kind of restriction stems from the research question itself. We studied only colleges and universities that had an "appreciable" black enrollment increase in a four-year time span. We do not know about colleges and universities which had smaller increases, none at all, or declines, nor do we know about those institutions which had substantial black enrollments by 1968.

Third, the sensitive nature of the issue itself and the absence of reliable information required that we be flexible in our design and procedures. What was done at each stage, the complexities encountered, and the dependency of the second stage on the first stage gave us, in essence, an evolutionary research design—Stage I results modified Stage II plans. In retrospect, we do not see how it could have been otherwise; at the outset, however, we held rather strong expectations about what we would find in the field that were ultimately not fully supported.

We were aware that type of control, institutional complexity, student selectivity, and type of institutional response would affect the impact of increased black enrollments on the institutions we would study. Public institutions are more responsive to pressure groups than are private institutions and have fewer options available to them. At the same time, institutions under private control usually have higher student tuitions. If a private college or university decides to recruit blacks in large numbers, the institution's financial burden is likely to be proportionately larger than it will be for colleges and universities in the public sector (although theirs is not small either).

Regarding institutional complexity, a four-year college can be expected to be more totally affected than would a university composed of a number of separate and highly autonomous colleges. The decisions made by a small, private liberal arts college would affect its entire faculty—while the school of engineering, for example, within a large university might remain relatively untouched by increased black enrollment.

Student selectivity was expected to have different kinds of effects. When an institution's SAT cutoff scores are very high, the pool of blacks meeting these standards is generally small. When new admissions practices are effected, remedial measures become a greater concern. In contrast, an open-admissions institution has a different set of problems since minority students are not the only ones who need special attention.

Finally, the pattern of institutional response to the presence of black students is related to other impacts. Greater staff isolation and less institutional influence and legitimacy would result for a separate black studies unit than for a series of black studies courses within a number of different departments.

Selection of the Institutions

We were interested in institutions where the possible impact would be greatest. Therefore, we selected institutions in which the black enrollment increase took place rapidly and reached a fairly high level. The percentage increase for blacks was important for us, for it would be this rather than an actual "head count" that would force the institution to respond in some way. At the same time, numbers were also important, for if there were only a handful of blacks, adding a few more could produce a large percentage increase even though the total number would still be small. At the other extreme, if the institution had had a significant number of blacks for some time it would be more likely to have made accommodations already and would be less likely to make new ones if the number of black students were to increase appreciably. Our solution to the instances of extremes was to eliminate those colleges and universities which in 1968 had fewer than 50 blacks or more than 3 percent. We then arbitrarily defined a "significant" increase as at least a doubling of the percentage of blacks from Fall 1968 to Fall 1972.[1]

American Council on Education data from Alexander Astin's studies and Office of Civil Rights reports were used to identify institutions meeting our enrollment criteria. There were 133 colleges and universities in the midwestern states, Pennsylvania, and New York that met our minimum size requirements; of these, 55 had at least doubled the percentage of black students between 1968 and 1972. On the basis of the best information we could obtain on type of control, selectivity, size, and type of program response, we invited 14 colleges and universities to participate in our study; 13 of these accepted. We initially told the participating institutions that they would remain anonymous in any reports we wrote but later thought better of this when it became clear that institutional identification would make our findings more comprehensible to readers. Ten of the 13 agreed to release their names. Two of the 3 institutions, all universities, that wished to remain anonymous were selected for the Stage II surveys; we have assigned them pseudonyms. Table 4-1 lists the 13 institutions by name or pseudonym, according to size, control, and selectivity.

An abstract of Stage I of our research, specifying the research questions and the demands to be made on the institution, was sent to the presidents of the selected institutions, along with a letter requesting their participation. This abstract is presented in Appendix A.

Stage I: Institutional Visits

The interview schedule for Stage I was designed to tap institutional responses in four areas: administrative, faculty, and academic or curricular responses and responses within the student culture. Four research questions cut across these areas: (1) What were the events and conditions leading to increased black enrollments and how were they reflected in each area? (2) What changes in program and structure had taken place in response to black students in each area? (3) How did changes affect existing structures, roles, and performance? (4) What was the impact on decision making, communication, allocation of resources, and other important processes or patterns in each area? The final interview schedule for Stage I of the study appears in Appendix B.

TABLE 4-1

Institutions in the Study by Control, Size, and Selectivity

Control and Size	Selectivity	
	Lower	Higher
Private		
Small*	Lewis University (Illinois)	Carleton College (Minnesota)
	Bradley University (Illinois)	Macalester College (Minnesota)
Large*	"Metropolitan University" (Midwestern State)	Northwestern University (Illinois)
Public		
Small†	University of Missouri–Kansas City (Missouri)	Clarion State‡ (Pennsylvania)
	California State College (Pennsylvania)	
Large†	Bowling Green State University (Ohio)	State University of New York–Brockport (New York)
	"University of the City" (Eastern State)	"State University" (Midwestern State)

*Size classifications were relative to other private institutions.
†Size classifications were relative to other public institutions.
‡Less selective by 1972.

Pretesting of earlier versions of the interview guide led to minor modifications. A pilot run at The University of Michigan was used as an interviewer training session in which subjects were interviewed by staff pairs, who took turns as interviewer and observer. Problems of interview length and the subjects' memories of the sequence of events were encountered and built into the final version of the interview guide. Reminders of the sequence of historical events (date of Martin Luther King's assassination, for example) were prepared for interviewees.

Each participating institution appointed a liaison person who sent available documents in advance, arranged interview schedules with individuals designated ahead of time (presidents, vice presidents, deans, and directors of admissions, minority affairs, and financial aid; representatives of student groups; key faculty members), and provided campus accommodations and assisted in arranging interviews with other individuals once our team arrived on campus.

We conducted the institutional visits in teams of three or four, which usually included one or two senior researchers and two graduate student research assistants. The teams included both blacks and whites, males and females. We opened each visit with a briefing with the institutional liaison person, who would give us a quick review of the history of the institution's relationship with blacks and introduced us to key figures to interview. We found that we could conduct most of our interviews in three days, even in the larger, complex universities in our sample.[2] These were extremely intense visits, during which we began to build up a collective picture of what had happened to increase black enrollment, of major events on the campuses, and of significant responses to blacks within the institution.

Interviews generally lasted about an hour. Since our questions focused primarily on "facts"—events, positions, finances, and programs—rather than attitudes, we spent a good portion of our time interviewing people who held formal responsibility for dealing with minority students and with the senior administrators. We spoke with faculty leaders and with department chairman but not very much with rank and file faculty. We were weak in the coverage of students and our only interviews with students were with the campus leaders. Furthermore, the time we spent with students was very small compared to the time we spent interviewing administrators and faculty. In sum, then, the institutional visits covered the formal life of the institution more thoroughly than the social structure; administrators more than faculty; administrators and faculty more than students. This strategy made sense, however, for the kinds of things we wanted to find out, which were often inaccessible or unknown to ordinary faculty members and students, and we knew we would give the students a chance to have their say in our attitudinal survey at four of the institutions.

Our interview teams met at the end of each day of interviewing to review notes, to reconcile differences in perception, and to delineate questions requiring further exploration. Several of these team sessions were tape-recorded; these recordings were an invaluable source for interpreting the data we brought back to Ann Arbor for the final writeup of the case studies.

All interviews were carefully written up or recorded as close to verbatim as possible on the interview guide. These, plus institutional records, statistics, and documents furnished the primary materials for a detailed case study of each institution. The first draft of the case study was written by the senior researcher in charge of each institutional visit, with major input from the other team members. These drafts were then sent back to the institutions for critique and review. Not all responded. Those who did, however, were important in filling gaps in our knowledge and correcting misinterpetations. None indicated that we were seriously in error.

From these corrected case studies of some 30–50 pages each, we wrote up shorter institutional vignettes for this book. These appear in Chapter 5. The long case studies provide the major source of information for succeeding chapters and allow comparison across the 13 institutions. The case studies report and analyze the events which led to increased black enrollments as well as responses in the administrative, faculty, academic, curricular, and student areas. They describe changes that were made in structures, roles, and typical job performance, and they assess impacts on institutional decision making, communication, resource allocation, and other important processes or patterns in the areas just mentioned.

Stage II: Four Institutional Surveys

In the second stage of our study, we conducted more extensive surveys on 4 of the 13 campuses. The questionnaire was designed for distribution to administrators, all arts and sciences faculty, black undergraduates, and a random sample of white undergraduates equal in number of the black student population surveyed. Findings from Stage I surveys aided us in the construction of the Stage II questionnaire, which was primarily designed to cover areas and topics defined by our original research questions not covered previously. Some questionnaire sections were common for all respondents; some were unique to each subgroup; and others were common to two of the three groups. The three questionnaires are presented in Appendix C. Table 4-2 identifies topics covered with each respondent group.

TABLE 4-2

Questionnaire Topics Addressed by Respondent Groups in Stage II Survey

Topics of Focus	Respondent Group		
	Administrators	Faculty	Students*
1. Role of Racial Minorities in Colleges and Universities	X	X	X
2. Institutional Goals for Blacks and Racial Minorities	X	X	
3. Institutional Racial Climate	X	X	X
4. Institutional Responsiveness	X	X	X
5. Institutional Impacts and Responses	X	X	
6. Future Institutional Commitments, Concerns	X	X	X
7. Impacts and Responses in Administrative Areas	X		
8. Impacts and Responses in Faculty and Departmental Activity		X	
9. Impacts on Student Life			X
10. Institutional Attractiveness for Black Students			X
11. Student Racial Climate			X
12. Black Students' Needs or Concerns			X
13. Personal Information	X	X	X

*Includes both black and white students.

It was not feasible to survey all 13 institutions included in Stage I. After a sorting process which eliminated some of the 13 because of controversies on those campuses that year, we were left with 9 institutions from which to choose our Stage II group. We then classified these 9 in terms of the responses and programs we had detected during Stage I. We decided to exclude the smallest institutions on the assumption that they were less likely than the larger ones to have an impact on higher education generally. This decision left us with four institutions in the second stage of the study—the University of Missouri–Kansas City; "State University" (in a midwestern state); State University of New York–Brockport; and "Metropolitan University" (a private school in a midwestern state). These universities differed widely in the comprehensiveness of their responses to increased black enrollments; the degree of separation versus intergration of minority programs; the degree of institutional commitment to minority concerns; and the degree of current racial tension. They also varied in public versus private control, size, and student selectivity.

Our visits to these campuses prior to the questionnaire distribution were critical for a number of reasons. We needed to convince representatives of key constituencies of the importance of our research and to establish ourselves as qualified colleagues. We had to insure individual anonymity so that the response rate would be adequate and the replies honest and valid. We needed faculty senate endorsement and the approval of key blacks. We found that acceptance and credibility were not the problem we thought they would be when we began our work. Perhaps our careful attention to questions of access—touching base with all relevant gate-keepers, offering to meet with anyone who had questions, promising feedback on our findings from the surveys—paid off. Equally important in assuring our credibility, we think, was the reception we received in the earlier institutional visits. We can say honestly that we saw people in the institutions as our colleagues—we were, after all, faculty members and graduate students at another institution struggling with similar questions—and we hope they shared that perception. Whatever the reason, entreé went smoothly at all four institutions.

"Cooperation" meant quite a bit of work from several people. We required names and addresses of all minority students. Acquiring these, along with a random sample of white students whose number equalled the minority population, meant that we needed clearance from the institutions' human subjects review committee as well as assistance from student and institutional research office personnel. (Although the student questionnaire asked the respondent to identify her or his race and/or ethnic identity, no such demographic questions were used on faculty or administrative instruments because, in most cases, the small numbers of blacks at each institution would have made maintaining anonymity impossible.) We needed accurate faculty and administrative staff lists. We were supplied with space, telephone, and a mail drop while we were on campus during the questionnaire distribution period so university people could approach us and have their questions answered. The institutional coordinator helped us find dependable students to conduct telephone follow-up calls to students.

One of the research assistants and a faculty member usually spent two days on a presurvey campus visit to arrange for administration of the questionnaires. Questionnaires were distributed through the campus mail to administrators and faculty and through the U. S. mail to students. This required that project staff spend approximately four days on each campus. Telephone follow-ups to faculty began on the third day. Second mailings provided stamped envelopes addressed to Ann Arbor.

In summary, a wide range of strategies was used to gain support and cooperation. The three essential ingredients were endorsement by the top administration, openness and candor on the part of the research team about the purpose and procedures of the research, and the intensive energy given to make the survey a success. As the next section will show, however, not even these ingredients worked for all constituencies.

RESPONSE TO THE SURVEY

There probably is not any "best" time to distribute questionnaires, especially to faculty. Perhaps the first day of a new academic year would be better than any other, but even that is doubtful. With the leverage of The Carnegie Council and the American Council on Education and a covering letter from Clark Kerr and Logan Wilson, a 1968 national survey of faculty achieved a nearly 60 percent response rate after follow-ups, about as high as has been achieved in a large faculty mailing. A 1972 survey of faculty conducted by Martin Trow barely reached a 50 percent response rate rate and more recent efforts just reached 40 percent on a third mailing.

Our returns are displayed in Appendix D. The response rate for administrators was high (an average of 76.1 percent), and the faculty response was acceptable (an average of 54.4 percent), especially in nine arts and science departments we had singled out for special attention. The overall response rate of 24.9 percent for students was low and leads us to limit our use of that data and to exercise extreme caution in the discussion of the student results.

Differences in response rates may reflect variations in commitment to black students and programs. (As we shall see, administrators as a group expressed a higher commitment than faculty as a group.) In any case, there were timing problems in our study which affected faculty and students more than administrators. As far as faculty were concerned, we could not have chosen a worse time—the very end of the term, just as finals were to begin and term papers were due. In one institution, two other major questionnaires reached the faculty in the same week.[3] There is no way to eliminate all of these hazards in a study of this type; the best one can do is minimize some and neutralize others.

METHODOLOGICAL TACTICS AND STRATEGIES: SOME INSIGHTS FROM RESEARCHING A SENSITIVE AREA

The delicate nature of our project introduced some complications beyond the usual concerns of field research and survey methods. Some we could anticipate, even if we could not deal with them in a completely satisfactory way. Others, however, caught us by surprise and we surmounted them with varying degrees of success. Since other researchers might encounter similar problems in the investigation of controversial and sensitive topics, we record some insights gained from our experience.

Data Inaccuracies and Deceptions

Institutional minority enrollment data—from national reports and from institutions themselves—were frequently difficult to obtain. Sometimes it seemed to be no more than a matter of poor record keeping; sometimes, too, blacks and other minorities were counted together with misleading results. For example, one institution had a fairly large group of Oriental faculty in its engineering and medical schools; minority staff were, thus, reported as high. Student self-reporting of race, as opposed to institutional tabulation (from financial aid offices or from a black student organization membership list), could produce quite different numbers.

Institutional records were most deficient in the sensitive area of black student retention. Support dollars were difficult to fix with certainty—how much came from what source (especially from the college itself) and from what part of the college's budget. There are many reasons for these gaps. Many institutions were under considerable pressure, internal as well as external, to demonstrate they had met goals to which they had committed themselves but which they sometimes could not achieve. This was especially trying when deadlines were short, financial conditions deteriorating, enrollments dropping, or staffing frozen. The temptation to exaggerate numbers of minority students or special programs are great when definitions of who and how to count are ambiguous.

Human Shortcomings

Immersed as we were in the history of the civil rights movement, we assumed that our interviewees would be able to give us accurate chronologies of events at their institutions which resulted in the increase in black enrollment. We discovered that many could not. They knew major events, but they were often confused about their sequence and, hence, causal connections. Such shortcomings were easily corrected with a little assistance from the interviewers, who had a chronology of occurrences and decisions relevant to black enrollments on campus from documented records.

However, the passage of time also frequently created a "good guy"/"bad guy" syndrome, especially at those institutions which there had been a significant confrontation. In many instances, the "bad guys" reportedly had left the college and so the range of persons we ended up interviewing may have been skewed. This was difficult for us to take into account in any systematic way. More often than not, a radical black leader on a campus had moved on to another institution and his side of the story could not be heard.

Closely related to the selective bias encountered by the participants who remained was what might be called "institutional defensiveness," a mixture of guilt and pride. We visited only colleges and universities which had succeeded in increasing their black enrollment. Faculty and administrators often displayed guilt at not having acted sooner, and yet they were also proud of their accomplishments—even when they judged them to be less than adequate. The subjects tended to view what the institution had done as being the best it could have done, and alternative decisions were no longer considered.

Perhaps the most dramatic example of this kind of retrospective accounting comes from Macalester College. Under the charismatic leadership of a new presient, Macalester made a dramatic and comprehensive commitment to bring in more blacks under the Expanded Educational Opportunities Program (EEO). Once it had made the commitment, many difficult and unanticipated events ensued. Below are accounts and interpretations drawn from our interviews about the events which led to and followed Macalester's decision to increase minority enrollments:

A Faculty Leader:

Under Arthur Flemming, as president, the faculty was asked for a program for the disadvantaged through the Faculty Advisory Council. . . . A program was approved by the Faculty Advisory Council for the college, if funding were available. The proposal was approved for black students who could pay their own way, but provisions were made for those who could not go for a full ride, $4,000 at that time . . .

EEO was originally a financial aid package for the economically disadvantaged—not necessarily the educationally disadvantaged since Macalester was a high quality liberal arts college, and saw itself as being very selective. Included in the proposal was a provision for an admissions recruiter and a counselor (one person for both), but the Admissions Office and the Counseling Center both saw an opportunity to gain a staff member, so it was agreed to approve two full-time staff for minority students. Also written in the proposal were provisions for additional staff in English and Math for possible remedial help for those who needed it as a support for their regular course load. Then Flemming wanted a coordinator for the program, and he brought in X. X was also charged with finding outside funding sources for the program. In the meantime, the Board of Trustees approved $900,000 in Endowment Funds as seed money, to be returned to the Endowment once the program was on its feet with outside funds. The seed money was to be used over a three-year period to give plenty of time for maturation. However, X arrived and asked for an assistant director, a financial aid counselor, and an office staff. . . .

In the fall of 1969, Puerto Rican, Native American, and Mexican American students were added to the EEO program as well as poor farm students from rural Minnesota. The nonblack minority students asked for equal staff and Flemming aproved that. It became much more expensive than anticipated. The Black House as well as the other houses were established at that time and more than a half million dollars were being spent on staff rather than programs. The money from outside did not pour in as promised. In the first three years, over $2 million dollars were spent by EEO, reportedly, and the college was at least $2 million dollars in the red. A new president was brought in.

It was during this time that the college's major donor discontinued his healthy annual contribution to the college. It was also during this time that it was decided to reduce the number of EEO students from 75–80 new students per year to 40 new students per year, so that there would be no more than 160 admitted over a period of four years. The EEO staff remained the same size.

Academic Administrator:

Flemming came and increased faculty salaries and student aid. He introduced an ambitious minority program. He, with the strong support and the help of the faculty, got the program going. There was a spirt of great optimism, but looking back, we went at it naively. Flemming was one of the most sanguine people I have every met. He refused to admit defeat. We are still seeing this legacy, even

though he left in 1971, when the balloon burst. The faculty feel
burned, disillusioned with the over-expansion. They experienced a
loss of nerve. . . . Flemming didn't produce the money.

Department Chairman:

The president and the new administration wanted more minorities on campus and were the major catalysts for the increased minority enrollment. The white student body supported this and the only
people who appeared to oppose it were a few individuals who were
more opposed to costs than anything else. . . .

Admissions Staff Member and Graduate of Macalester:

When Flemming came, it was an emotional era. Flemming gave
students quite a bit of power—coed dorms, Bill of Rights, Freedoms
and Responsibilities. Everyone was going at it in a naive, liberal
way. The college became mobilized around the minorities issue and
when students got here, people were surprised by how naive we
were. Mostly black students wanted to live closely together and they
didn't want to be spread around in the dorms. No one thought about
this ahead of time and some realities really hit us. . . .

Student Affairs Staff Member:

Tensions were high on campus, mainly because of the type of
black students who came; not the assimilating kind; most of them
from very urban, inner-city areas. Some whites hid from blacks (culture shock), some gave in as a result of being or feeling intimidated,
there were some housing contentions because of the close contact;
touchy adjustments all around. . . .
The first EEO director was a political activist who brought community presence and a nation-building philosophy to campus; would
rather work out in the community; did not hire a strong staff. Students in the program suffered from an effort which did not empha-
size the academics. . . .

Administrative Staff Member:

Faculty at Macalester and administration, too, have tended to
wait until a crisis arises before something is faced up to. There are
problems in the administration of admissions, i.e., agreeing on a
criteria for recruitment; grading problems for minority students de-

pend on the instructor's concern to work with students (but not on minority problems only). There are some faculty who cannot white-wash their racism, which produces fear among a very intellectual group of people. There are two communities at Macalester, with whites being very patronizing on the one hand and blacks not really caring on the other. Problems at or with EEO seem to override all other efforts to clear the air. There are strong personalities on both sides who call for a definite response.... Faculty are quite out-spoken now and the students are aware that something is wrong. The continuing controversy at Macalester is a motivating force for many people here....

A very complex picture of the past had become a clear story for each individual. It was our job to put individual perceptions and ac-counts together in such a way that they added up to a more complex, accurate picture.

Some Tactics and Strategies

We knew that race, status, age, and gender of interviewers might affect the accuracy of our results, so—to the extent possible—we tried to control these factors by assigning graduate students to interview students, senior researchers to senior administrators, blacks to blacks, women to women. Much more than these simple categories, of course, account for trust in an interview. But we had specific experi-ences which confirm the wisdom of this kind of matching. One ex-ample will give a flavor of what we mean. One of our graduate stu-dent assistants, a black, was having a hard time establishing an interview with a black counselor at one of the colleges:

He appeared to be very uncomfortable about my being there. He was very inquisitive about who sent me and what was going to be done with the report that we were writing. I told him that the college would get a copy of our report. He told me he could only talk for ten minutes because he had something to do. Later after we started talking, time did not appear to be a concern to him and he later told me that he thought that we were from the Internal Revenue Service. I think that he was testing me in the beginning since he asked several questions about Ann Arbor. He has a lot of friends in Ann Arbor and apparently has visited several times. After he really started talking, I tried to write as little as possible since it appeared to shake him up.

It turned out that this person was part of a group of moderate black faculty and staff who had been meeting secretly to develop a compromise plan that would save the college's minority program while at the same time meeting the objections of its critics. He had good reason to be suspicious of outsiders asking too many questions about that very issue. Once he established that the interview would not affect the outcome of the deliberations, he told the interviewer what had been happening. We think that he would not have been as open with a white interviewer.

Another issue was the effect of timing on our study. We believe we paid the price of lower response rate in Stage II because we asked people to respond candidly on a topic about which they had strong feelings just when the Buckley amendment was about to go into effect and when Watergate, the FBI, and the CIA were in the newspapers every day. This applied particularly to the second phase of our study. Our questionnaires had identifying numbers on them so that we could follow up nonrespondents. This standard procedure was explained to all respondents and, although we also explained that the lists were destroyed as soon as numbers were checked off, some respondents obviously remained uncomfortable and unconvinced.

Timing affected us in another way. Several of the colleges and universities in our study were just embarking on major evaluations of their minority programs and of their financial commitments. As long as we confined ourselves to interviews with selected individuals, and to fairly public facts, we were not threatening. However, as soon as we had tabulated results on a fairly broad range of questions asking for faculty, student, and administrator opinions, we were seen as possibly harmful.[4] This may explain why two of the four universities included in the Stage II surveys wanted not to be identified. In a way we did not anticipate, the more open-ended phase of our study was less of a threat than the survey phase.

Finally, we cannot close this review of our research experiences without saying somthing about the effect on us as researchers of delving into what continues to be a deep and painful issue for most Americans. In our interactions across race, age, and sex, we found ourselves debating interpretations of what we saw in our institutional visits and predictions for the future. The students on our team, particularly the black students, were more pessimistic than the faculty members. (An analysis of the ratings on the institutions by each team confirmed this sense.) Our own biases and presuppositions were tested by our late-night discussions. We also confronted subtle questions of manipulation: Did President X tell Marvin Peterson about that event to gain his sympathy? Why did the head of the Faculty Senate ask to see our report before it was published? Why did the affirmative action officer ask us about job possibilities in Ann Arbor?

Why did our liaison person set up meetings with some faculty rather than others? Why was it so difficult to make appointments with black students? Again, our team discussions helped to objectify these vague feelings of discomfort.

As interracial teams, we experienced some of the reaction that blacks alone or black-white groups face frequently in some part of America. We noticed the stares in the restaurants, particularly in some of the small towns we frequented during our trips.

Each of us had our own personal reactions to the people we encountered, and sometimes these reactions affected our individual assessments of a situation. Here, the team discussions and shared case studies were crucial in correcting blatant personal biases. But some personal reactions undoubtedly remain as the background against which we present our findings in the chapters to follow. In general, we pay less attention to personalities than to roles, structures, and events—although, in some sense, personalities are very much part of the stories of the 13 institutions.

Notes

[1]If overall enrollments were declining after 1970, the institution was dropped from consideration for it may have had an artificially high percentage of blacks.

[2]More often than not, some data we sought did not exist and, unfortunately, could not be compiled from the institutional records. Entrance test scores for minority students and retention rates were particularly difficult to document.

[3]We had minimum flexibility in our timing. A tight schedule made Stage I visits impossible to complete until well into January. Their analysis had to precede questionnaire construction, institution selection, and arrangements. Late spring was our only reasonable chance to conduct the survey (and it was a desperate rush) since we were working with a December 1975 deadline when funding terminated.

[4]Each of the four institutions in Stage II received tabulations of marginals.

Part II

The Determinants and Dynamics of Change

5

Stage I: The 13 Colleges and Universities

Marvin W. Peterson

The institutions in our study were selected from among the four-year colleges and universities in 14 states—Pennsylvania, New York, and the 12 north central states. Together these states are more representative of the nation as a whole than are other regions in the percentages of blacks both in the overall population and in colleges and universities. They are particularly more representative than either the southern states, which have a much larger black population and a very different history of black participation in higher education, or the western states (other than California), which have a very small black population.

As to the question of how typical our sample of 13 institutions was vis-à-vis other colleges and universities in the region, a number of observations can be made. First of all, it should be recalled that ours was not a random sample. We purposely excluded institutions which (a) had so very few blacks in 1968 that a percentage increase in 1972 would be essentially a statistical artifact rather than a large enough influx of new clients to impact on the organization, (b) did not appreciably increase their black enrollment over the time period, or (c) began with a high enough percentage of blacks that a further increase in the numbers of blacks would have no significant impact on these institutions. Each of these criteria gave a slightly different distortion to the "representativenesss" of our final sample of colleges and universities.

Nonetheless, some comparisons can be drawn between our selective sample and Arce's (1976) more inclusive sample of 150 four-year colleges and universities located in the 14 states in our study (see Chapter 2, pp. 4–9). As can be seen in Figure 5-1, both samples of institutions had average black enrollments of slightly less than two percent in 1968. But by 1972 the proportion of blacks in our sample increased at a greater rate and reached a higher level than did the average institution in the region. From 1972 to 1974, however, the average rates of increase were about the same for both samples.[1]

FIGURE 5-1

Black Enrollment Levels for Institutions in NIMH Sample and in Arce Sample (1976) Located in 14 Target States, 1968 to 1974

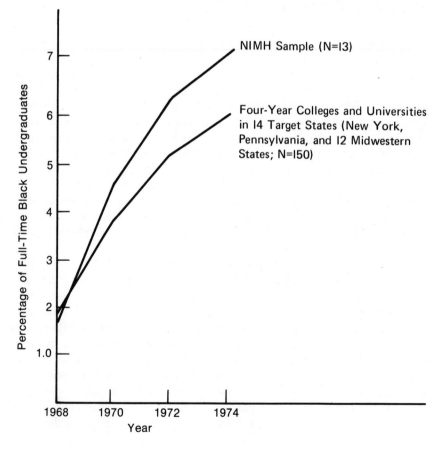

When the two samples are subdivided according to type of control, other kinds of differences are highlighted (Figure 5-2). The public universities in the two samples had similar proportions of blacks at both the beginning and end of the study period, and they had similar rates of increase. However, the public four-year colleges in our sample began and finished the study period with lower percentages than did those in the larger sample; nonetheless, the rates of increase, especially from 1968 to 1972, were nearly identical for both samples. The rate of increase of black enrollments is the more important factor for considering impact consequences and, thus, the typicality of our sample in this domain appears to be supportable.

FIGURE 5-2

Black Enrollment Levels for Public Institutions in NIMH Sample and in Arce Sample (1976) Located in 14 Target States, 1968 to 1974

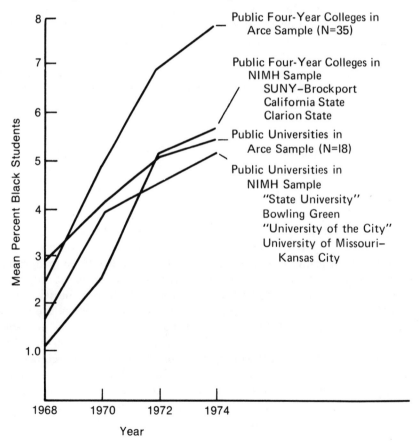

The differences between the private colleges and universities within the two samples are much more pronounced (Figure 5-3). In comparison to the larger sample, the private colleges and universities in our sample started with a lower percentage of blacks and ended with a higher percentage. The rates of increase, then, were appreciably greater in our sample. There was much greater variation in the private than in the public sector; some private institutions experienced an appreciable increase, whereas others showed little change. While there was also some variation in the rates of black enrollment increases among publicly controlled colleges and universities, it was relatively small, and the average rates of increase were the same for both samples. These differences are in accord with the expectation that private institutions would have more control over the decision to recruit or not recruit blacks than public schools could exercise, irrespective of desire.

In summary, while our earlier remarks about the limitations on generalizing from our findings still hold true, the publicly controlled colleges and universities in our sample had characteristics and experiences which were more typical of the larger population of institutions in the region than was the case for those schools under private sponsorship. We now turn to each institution's unique history during the period of our study.

THE LARGE PUBLIC INSTITUTIONS

Bowling Green State University

Bowling Green State University, in northwest Ohio, is a regional public university with four undergraduate colleges, a broad array of majors, and a growing reputation for innovative academic programs. From 1968 to 1974, the predominantly in-state student body increased from 11,485 to 13,613. Despite its location in a county with a less than 1 percent black population, black student enrollments increased from 156 in 1968 (1.4 percent) to 625 in 1974 (4.7 percent). During this period the institution was served by over 700 full-time faculty, of whom over half were in the College of Arts and Sciences; in 1974, 13 of the faculty members were black. Bowling Green made early and vigorous attempts to recruit black students during the period of intense conflict. It has had an extensive but often controversial set of programs for minorities.

FIGURE 5-3

Black Enrollment Levels for Private Institutions in NIMH Sample and in
Arce Sample (1976) Located in 14 Target States, 1968 to 1974

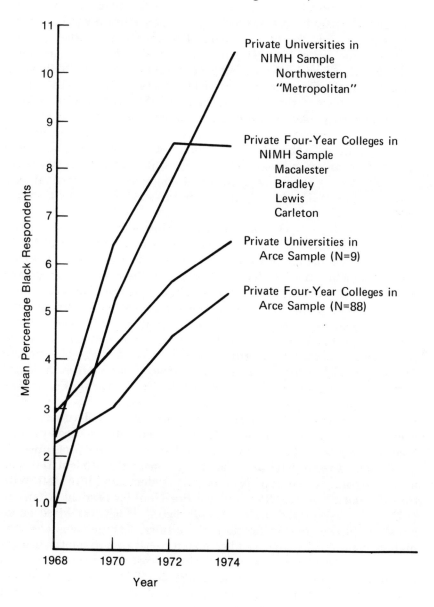

Prior to 1968, Bowling Green did not have an active history of involvement with minority issues. The institution's proximity to urban areas with substantial black populations, the general rise in black student enrollments nationwide, and the presence and quiet advocacy of a black vice president for student affairs were probably factors accounting for the numbers of black students who were on campus in the fall of 1968. During the 1968–69 school year, an informal tutorial, referral, and advising program for minority students—a precursor to the Student Development Program (SDP)—was started under the Office of the Vice President for Student Affairs, with a part-time staff person and university funds. The same year saw the emergence of an active Black Student Union (BSU), which submitted a list of requests to the administration in May 1969—requests which the administration subsequently discussed but did not act upon. On April 29, 1970, a comprehensive list of demands was presented by a more militant BSU with a call for administrative action within one week.

The shootings at Ohio's Kent State University on May 4, 1970, intervened. Bowling Green, like other campuses, was electrified; student groups immediately called for a strike. Black students, led by a black instructor, tried to focus attention on their own demands and pressured the administration for a public response. The president's answer, later modified by negotiations between black students and executive officers, culminated in an agreement on the following items: a goal of 500 black students for Fall 1970; a new financial aid package; a center for black or ethnic studies in the College of Arts and Sciences; a budget for recruiting black faculty and staff; a provision for a black culture collection; funds for the Black Student Union; and review of black student grievances by a special committee. On May 13 a new president, Hollis Moore, was named to replace departing President William Jerome, and Moore immediately endorsed his predecessor's agreement and moved to implement the new programs.

A black director who was brought in to head the Student Development Program moved quickly to recruit students and hire staff. With the elimination of the Office of Vice President for Student Affairs in 1971, SDP was placed under the provost. A black was hired as an assistant to the provost for minority affairs. Antagonisms over the management of SDP emerged between its active, charismatic director and the more moderate assistant to the provost, and a split developed among black staff and faculty members. In 1973, a new provost was selected who soon fired the SDP director. A black faculty and staff sit-in followed and the position of vice provost for minority affairs was created. The position was filled by a black in early 1974 and SDP was placed under him.

Internal conflict and general dissatisfaction with SDP led to a major evaluation and reorganization of the program as a multiservice agency. The reorganized SDP included: (1) the Developmental Education Program for academic support services to blacks and other students, including the federally supported Modular Achievement Learning Center; (2) the Educational Opportunity Program, including TRIO, Upward Bound, Project Search, and recruitment of and financial aid for disadvantaged students; and (3) the Personal Development Program for personal counseling and advising, promoting minority social and cultural activities, and community relations. The SDP recruitment officer and four student assistants worked closely with a black recruiter from the admissions office to recruit minority students from urban centers. One SDP staff member was in charge of financial aid and worked closely with a representative of the Financial Aids Office in distributing federal EOGs and BEOGs (Educational Opportunity Grants and Basic-EOGs), Ohio Instructional Grants, and university-funded Student Development grants and loans to SDP students.

In addition to providing academic tutoring and counseling for minorities through the SDP and the Modular Achievement Program, Bowling Green established the Center for Ethnic Studies in the summer of 1974. Although the center was the primary academic program for blacks, it lacked departmental status. With four full-time and three part-time faculty members, the center offered interdepartmental majors and minors in black studies in 1974–75 and sponsored a broad array of courses on other ethnic groups and issues. Several departments, primarily those with black faculty or joint appointments, were active supporters of the Center for Ethnic Studies.

BSU continued to be the central black student organization, which acted as the "umbrella" for other black student organizations and received funds from the student government. It also sponsored dances, social gatherings, and a few service projects. Four black fraternities and four black sororities were quite active and participated in the IFC and the Panhellenic Association. Other special interest groups such as the Black Athletes Coalition, the Black Graduate Students Association, and several cultural and artistic groups also existed at Bowling Green.

The major nonprogrammatic responses to blacks were the two new positions created—Vice President for Minority Affairs and Director of Human Resources, the latter with responsibility for affirmative action. Both positions were held by blacks. There was one other middle-level black administrator, an assistant dean of graduate studies.

The faculty as a whole did not play a major organizational role in these changes. However, the 13 black faculty members, together with black staff, did act at various times as a cohesive and effective force for black and minority concerns.

The situation at BGSU was complex. The SDP bore the brunt of the black student increase and, despite its internal problems, had an active array of programs. By 1975, declines in black freshmen enrollments and the danger of reductions in external funds for black programs and student aid were ominous signs. Recent administrative decisions have been in the direction of institutionalizing and centralizing the programs for minorities which have developed over the years.

"University of the City"

"University of the City," recently named as an A.A.U. member institution, is a large, well-known, complex urban university with 5 campuses, 15 schools and colleges on the main campus, and a highly respected faculty. About 18,600 undergraduate students (plus another 10,000 graduate students) were enrolled on the main campus is 1968. The undergraduate student body in the College of Arts and Sciences on the main campus is 96 percent in-state and academically strong (average SAT scores were above 1,070). From 1968 to 1974, undergraduate enrollments increased from around 7,000 to just over 8,000. Comparable black enrollment totals grew from about 150 (1.5 percent) to around 800 (9.8 percent) during that period. The faculty of the main campus remained relatively stable in number: there were 1,887 full-time equivalents, of whom 205 were black. The institution's experience with increasing black enrollments has reflected conscious effort to recruit black students and provide special programs and concomitant external pressures and demands. The size of the enrollment increase, the intensiveness of its impacts, and the comprehensiveness of the university's responses were perhaps the most extensive of any of the institutions in this study. The transition was marked by controversy, conflict, and some creative efforts.

Prior to 1965, City had experienced a decade of rapid development as a private, prestige-oriented institution. Following a financial crisis in 1965–66, it underwent a transition to state-supported status. This shift in control—together with the leadership of Chancellor Varden*, who arrived in 1967—led to a greater urban and regional emphasis which supported increased in-state and black attendance. Prior to 1968, the city in which the university is located was the scene of substantial civil rights activity, and the campus was the setting for extensive student activism. The 1967–68 year witnessed several events relevant to black concerns: the new chancellor sought ideas in the local black community for a "social justice" theme for the university; the university's Commission on Racism issued several reports; an administrative group developed a plan for the recruitment of minority students ("Project X"); the embryonic Black Action Society (BAS) presented a list of demands; and the Office for Community Educational Programs was formed and a black was hired as its first director. This activity was encouraged by the executive officers, who had been pressured to respond to minority concerns.

In the fall of 1968, "Project X"—which was headed by the director of the Community Education Programs, who reported to the provost—operated an informal program which admitted 50 minority students (primarily blacks) on an "experimental basis." Bolstered by this cadre of black students, on Martin Luther King's birthday the BAS renewed their demands in a confrontation with the chancellor and followed this with an occupation of the Computing Center. A tense conflict marked by threats of violence and finally by police intervention preceded a negotiated agreement. Black students pointed to this as a major victory; executive officers contended later that the agreement included commitments for activities already started or under discussion. Both sides agreed it served to accelerate responses and set a tone for ensuing controversies and demands associated with many activities and programs for blacks and other minorities at the university.

By the fall of 1969, Project X was expanded to three support programs for minority students. These grew rapidly and primarily served about one-third of the black and other racial minority undergraduate students. The institution provided staff for these programs, which also received student aid funds from institutional and federal programs and from an extensive state program.

On the academic side, in the fall of 1969 the Black Studies Program (the name approved by the faculty of Arts and Sciences), also known as the Black Community Educational Research and Development Program (the name used by the unit), was begun. It offered a

---

*Because this institution chose to remain anonymous for this study, the name of the individual mentioned here is fictitious.

broad array of courses, programs, and activities. The staff grew rapidly to about 30 members, but by 1974 it numbered about 15. The unit has been controversial. Struggles have focused on philosophy, direction, and, more recently, the selection of a new director and the evaluation of the unit.

Black student organizations expanded rapidly. BAS was the dominant black student group, guiding and coordinating many programs and activities. But seven black fraternities and sororities, with their own support organization, and numerous other black student organizations were also established to serve the varied interests of black students. An organization of black administrators, faculty, staff, and students was also formed and has occasionally been active in support of black issues, in attempts to mediate conflicts, and in support of other student concerns.

Less obvious nonprogrammatic impacts and responses also occurred. In the fall of 1969, the chancellor insisted that all top administrators participate in confrontation-oriented sensitivity sessions run by black psychiatric social workers. Since 1970, blacks have been appointed to several administrative positions, including those of vice chancellor and associate provost, and 3 of the 16 deans were blacks. A large number of black faculty members were hired after 1968, but not as a result of the institution's more recent affirmative action program. An interesting sidelight at the institution during this period was a resurgence in athletics and an improvement in the quality of the university's teams. The growing numbers of black and other minority athletes did lead to some friction which later resulted in actions to increase the number of black coaches and other staff.

Capturing the complexity of the university here is difficult. Clearly, financial constraints and changes in institutional control, black community and student pressures, and a supportive administration have all played important roles in the university's responses to black students. While there has been administrative commitment to programs, staffing, and funding, there has not been substantial faculty involvement in these changes. The pattern of response has been one of continuous pressure, negotiation, and conciliation which, in part, seemed to reflect this institution's governance style. Although black enrollment reached a substantial level by 1974–75 and programs were maturing, retrenchment was a strong possibility. That year witnessed major concerns about the institution's commitment to minority programs, expressed in controversies over several issues: the placement of the Community Education Program under the Dean of the Arts and Sciences College; the selection process for a new black studies director and evaluation of that unit; procedures for budgetary allocation; and guidelines for faculty promotion and salary increase review. These were, perhaps, precursors of questions which would soon face other institutions.

"State University"

"State University" is a highly respected, comprehensive, public university in a state with a black population of 1.2 percent in 1970. During the period from 1968 to 1974, the highly qualified undergraduate student body (ACT scores averaging approximately 25) increased from around 13,000 to over 14,000 (21,000 total). Black undergraduate enrollments increased from 84 (0.6 percent) in 1968 to around 570 (4.0 percent) in 1974. The institution's 1,200 very able full-time faculty included an estimated 15 blacks in 1974. The university's experience with increasing black enrollments was based on a comprehensive, clearly stated institutional policy commitment made in the spring of 1969 and was represented by the most extensive range of programs and activities of any institution in this study.

Before 1968, the university had numerous experiences that related to the later black undergraduate enrollment increase. State has been coeducational from the date of its founding, and it had an early reputation as a sympathetic place for southern blacks to pursue higher education. Sizable numbers of black Ph.D. students, predominantly from southern black institutions, were enrolled there in the 1930s through the 1950s. In the early 1960s, some white faculty were quite active in the southern civil rights activities and developed ties with faculty and students at predominantly black institutions. This led to formal exchange programs with two black colleges under a Developing Institutions Grant. In 1962, Joseph Lane* (who later became the institution's president) was appointed chairman of the active Human Rights Committee. From 1964 to 1969 President Harold Tyrone* was an active supporter of civil rights, and in 1966 he addressed the university on its obligation to provide access to groups who were underrepresented in the university. In 1967–68 he charged the Human Rights Committee to study the university's commitment to ethnic minorities and encouraged blacks in the student senate to develop recommendations in this area.

*Because this institution chose to remain anonymous for this study, the names of the individuals mentioned here are fictitious.

Against the backdrop of these activities, on April 9, 1968—five days after the King assassination—President Tyrone drew on the Human Rights Committee report in addressing the university. He recommended a major commitment to the recruitment of minority students and the development of social action studies programs; consideration of an Afro-American studies program and research activities on minority issues; strengthening the university's ties with southern black colleges; and the development of supportive services and fund-raising activities to provide programs and financial aid for minority students. These extensive proposals apparently elicited strong emotional support within the university, and in the fall of 1968 they received the official endorsement of the Academic Senate.

During that first year, 1968–69, great strides were made. In July 1968 a minority recruiter (who later became the director of the Support Services Program—SSP) was hired; the first Institute on Afro-American Studies was held, directed by a faculty member in the American Civilization Program; a Martin Luther King Scholarship Program was established; and a Ford Foundation grant to support minority program efforts was received. By the fall of 1969 the Support Services Program and the new Educational Opportunity Program (EOP) were in place, and in the summer of 1970 the first director of the Afro-American Studies Program was hired. Extensive institutional funding—supplemented by foundation grants, gifts, and federal support (there were no state funds to aid low-income or minority students)—assured the growth of these units and of black student enrollment.

The changes, however, were not without controversy. Spring 1969 witnessed a widely publicized black athletes' revolt. There were minor incidents in the community, and black-white dormitory problems were extensive in 1970–71. President Lane, who succeeded Tyrone in 1969, was personally involved in the resolution of these problems and approved special commissions to review them. A 1973 Civil Rights Compliance Review led to the establishment of the Affirmative Action Office and to the creation of the Affirmative Action Task Force. More recently, militant Chicano students have pressed for greater attention, and the murder of a coed—allegedly by a black student—became a focus of attention. Despite these incidents, State has been spared the major explosions that occurred on other large campuses during the period.

Programs for blacks and other minorities were substantial at State. The Afro-American Studies Program, with strong administrative support and budgetary allocation, was housed within the Department of English in the College of Letters. It offered degree programs at the bachelors, masters, and Ph.D. levels, continued the summer Institute on Afro-American Studies, and sponsored several cultural groups and activities. The program had a respected director, five full-time staff who held joint appointments with other departments, and an advisory committee with representatives from other departments. The Support Services Program was staffed by eight full-time professionals (six blacks, one Chicano, and one white) and as many as 60 part-time students. The work of the admissions and financial aid offices was closely coordinated with that of SSP. The latter program was responsible for recruitment, financial aid, and counseling and academic assistance to educationally and economically disadvantaged students. It also administered the Afro-American and the Chicano-Indian Cultural Centers, each with extensive activities. Both the SSP and the Afro-American Studies Program were highly respected on and off campus, were substantially autonomous, and were open to self-evaluation.

As on other campuses, the Black Student Union was the oldest black student organization at State and it attempted to serve all black students. A number of black student groups operated under BSU, which received funds from student government, while several others received direct funding. In total, 20 to 25 black student social, cultural, and performing groups or organizations were identified.

Less extensive informal changes were also reported to us. The Office of the Minority Ombudsman and the Office of Minority Student Activities were created for students (counterparts to the Affirmative Action Office). A number of ad hoc commissions had supplemented the Human Rights Committee's work in this area. Two minority vice presidents—a black man and a white woman—were included among the executive officers, a group which expressed a clear commitment to minority concerns. Yet there were few minority individuals among the faculty and staff, as already noted. While recruiting attempts had been made, there was little evidence of success. The faculty in general seemed little affected by these changes, except for those who were personally involved with the various black programs.

Recent issues and concerns at State University have focused on the limited number of black faculty and staff; the impact on the minority programs of possible program evaluations and financial retrenchment; the pressure of other minority groups (e.g., Chicanos) for greater attention; and the recruitment of and use of financial aid for out-of-state students by a public institution. However, State's minority problems seemed far less critical than those of the other institutions in our sample. A liberal and responsive administration, able black leaders, and carefully devised programs had been given strong institutional support and seemed more secure than most.

THE SMALL PUBLIC INSTITUTIONS

SUNY–Brockport

The State University of New York College at Brockport, a former Normal School and until 1961 a State Teachers College, is one of 13 public colleges of arts and sciences positioned between the four university centers and the network of 38 community colleges in the SUNY system. Faculties in seven academic divisions and three related units (Alternate College, Continuing Education, and the Educational Opportunity Center in Rochester) offered a wide range of undergraduate and masters degree programs. Students were primarily in-state and of average academic ability (SAT scores averaged 950, down from 1,100 four years earlier). From 1968 to 1974, full-time undergraduate enrollments increased from 4,187 to 7,763 (total enrollments exceeded 10,000). Black student enrollments increased from 57 in 1968 (1.4 percent) to 460 in 1974 (5.9 percent). The institution was served by a faculty of about 575 members, of whom 50 were identified as minority. The college's experience with increasing black enrollments has been marked by early and deliberate response to disadvantaged students, a high degree of continuous conflict and tension, and an extensive and visible set of response programs.

SUNY–Brockport, after 1964 under the strong leadership of President Brown, was a leading participant in SUNY's era of academic expansion. It was initially more dedicated to recruiting highly qualified faculty and building respectable academic programs than to conducting social experiments. But prior to 1968 and as early as 1966, the social and philosophical commitment of the president and a few others led to an informal attempt to identify small numbers of economically and academically disadvantaged students in the Rochester area. In the fall of 1967, the institution's Master Plan included the mission of "aiding the academically disadvantaged." An Educational Opportunity Center was being established in nearby Rochester and the admissions office was pushing for the formalization of "Summer Start," a program of recruitment, pre-enrollment summer courses, counseling, and a first year of transitional academic assistance. The latter program was initiated in the fall of 1968 when 41 disadvantaged students (about half of whom were black) were enrolled. These efforts received substantial publicity, and the president released a statement stressing concern for disadvantaged students. His stance was that of an integrationist. The fall of 1969 witnessed the opening of a cultural center for black students in response to the concerns of those who had felt "unwanted" and had formed the Afro-American Society (later replaced by the Black Student Liberation Front—BSLF).

But these early efforts and philosophies did not forestall the volatility of 1969–70. An early BSLF dormitory sit-in preceded a more formal set of demands, a series of intense but nonviolent "meet-ins" with the administration, and a spring protest of the burning of the Afro-American Culture Center. The latter event was merged with a larger student strike protesting the U.S. invasion of Cambodia. During that year a task force was at work developing a black studies department. A black was appointed as an assistant to the Dean of Undergraduate Academic Affairs to supervise Summer Start and other programs for disadvantaged students, and other changes were occurring which increased the scope of existing activities.

The programmatic responses emerging at Brockport began to be well established by 1974. The original Summer Start program was expanded and supplemented by the Educational Opportunity Program (EOP) for educationally and economically deprived students (70 percent were minority, mostly black). In addition to the regular program, EOP had counselor-interns to supplement its staff. The Department of Black Studies, established in September 1970, adopted a militant and separatist position under its first chairman and was the focus of considerable controversy. The new department became more stable under more recent leadership and established relationships with other departments. An interdisciplinary program in African studies was created, but it had limited enrollments. The admissions office continued to carry a primary role in recruiting black and disadvantaged students. The primary financial aid sources were from state and federal programs for the educationally and economically disadvantaged. BLSF remained the dominant black student organization; while less militant than it had been earlier, it continued to have a strong role in student government.

In sum, Brockport's response to black students was handled primarily by the administration, although the administrative structure was relatively untouched, except as already noted. The student organizations and patterns suggest continued racial separatism and some tension. The faculty had strong departmental ties and was represented by collective bargaining. In general, faculty members did not play key roles in program development; they resisted the separatist orientation of the Department of Black Studies and bemoaned the general reduction of student quality, although some departments worked with minority students in creative ways. Brockport's recruitment of minority staff was more successful than most. The high proportion of black faculty, however, was partially explained by the fact that 20 of Brockport's 50 black faculty were with the Educational Opportunity Center in Rochester. On the administrative side, a strong and concerned president has changed the institution's function and personnel and is the key to understanding Brockport's responses to blacks (and to most other major impacts on the institution).

California State College

California State College, a former teachers college, is one of the 14 state colleges in the Pennsylvania State College system. It acquired its state college status and expanded its offerings in 1959, although it has remained heavily oriented toward teacher preparation. The undergraduate student body was primarily in-state and reflected a diverse ability range (SAT scores averaged about 950). Between 1968 and 1974 enrollments declined from 4,547 to 4,188, after reaching over 5,000 in 1970. Black student enrollments increased from 62 in 1968 (1.4 percent) to 233 in 1974 (5.6 percent) in a county with a black population of about 3 percent. The institution's 300 faculty members were unionized and had a "no-cut" contract. Twelve of the faculty members were black. California State's experience with increasing its black enrollments has been characterized by evolutionary responses to a set of external forces.

Prior to 1968, California State had no distinctive history with blacks. The institution is located in an area of low-income small towns, each with its own European ethnic character, which has not been supportive of outsiders—particularly blacks from nearby Pittsburgh. Further, the institution's expansion during the 1960s onto state-condemned city property strained community relations. Proximity to Pittsburgh and the general national increase of black college enrollments appeared to account for the small but increasing numbers of black students who entered California by 1968. In the spring of 1969, newly appointed President George Roadman encouraged the hiring of an admissions staff member to increase the enrollment of minorities, although there was no evidence of an organized recruitment campaign. An Upward Bound program was also launched on campus that year. By that time a student group, the Black League of Afro-Americans at California State (BLACS), had already presented the president with a list of demands, without any significant incident or conflict. The following summer, perhaps as an outgrowth of the Upward Bound activity or as a response to one of the student demands, the Student Incentive Program (SIP) was initiated to provide transitional compensatory employment for entering minority students and a black was hired to direct the program.

Concurrent with these events, in the fall of 1969, the State of Pennsylvania (along with 10 other states) was ordered by HEW to develop plans to desegregate its colleges and universities. Shortly thereafter, the State Department of Education held a conference for state college administrators on the admissions of minority students. The state, however, did not appropriate any money to support educationally and economically disadvantaged students until the 1971–72 academic year with the passage of Pennsylvania's Higher Education Equal Opportunity Act 101. A state desegregation plan was submitted on June 1, 1974. Perhaps as a result of all these events, black enrollments increased sharply in 1970 and continued to increase through 1972. A part of the latter increase, however, may have been the result of the efforts of a white professor who organized a minicourse directed at identifying black students' needs. Offshoot activities led to the establishment of an Afro-American Culture Center (1972) and to the creation, with presidential support, of a recruiting program called Black Student Search that was organized by black students. The lack of a concerted, college-wide effort was given as the reason why this activity was not more extensive. After 1971, the recruitment effort was in the hands of the admissions office and black enrollments remained largely unchanged, although they increased somewhat in percentage because total enrollments declined.

The programmatic responses to the black student presence were not extensive. There were no academic programs for blacks, and while some courses were created, none gained obvious popularity. On the supportive service side, Act 101 money was used to convert SIP to the Office of Special Services under the Vice President for Student Affairs. While the office provided compensatory education, counseling, and tutoring services and was concerned with all students who were educationally disadvantaged or who were in academic difficulty, the clientele was reportedly primarily black. The admissions office had one black staff member and maintained a program of recruitment at high schools with large populations of black students. However, the increasingly open admissions policy of the institution limited selection. The financial aid office administered the state and federal student aid programs, including those established for disadvantaged students, but it had no institutional funds or monies for blacks exclusively. The Afro-American Culture Center was a focus of activity for BLACS, and the campus had a black fraternity and sorority.

On the nonprogrammatic side, visible administrative changes were few. There were two black administrators—the Director of Special Services and an assistant admissions officer. The faculty were not directly involved in the creation of most of the programs, except as individuals, and there was only a limited number of blacks on the faculty. Student life was marked by separatism and, earlier, by some hostility (for example, tensions and charges of discrimination in athletics led to the hiring of two black assistant coaches; tensions were further increased when shots were fired into a black residence, supposedly by a father who was irate over interracial dating). More recent issues focused on the lack of black enrollment increases, the need for minority programs and staffing, and student racial tensions—but these were subordinated to concerns about total enrollment declines, the strictures of a "no-cut" collective bargaining agreement, faculty job security, and the possible reduction of state financial support. In 1974, those who were concerned about the future of minority program efforts described the general campus tone as constraining and demoralizing.

Clarion State College

Clarion is one of 14 institutions in the Pennsylvania State College System. Formerly a teachers college, since 1960 it has developed a broadly based liberal arts program. From 1968 to 1974, the undergraduate student body, which was primarily regional and of average academic ability (SATs around 1050), increased from around 3,400 to just over 4,200. Despite its rural, small-town location, black student enrollments increased from around 15 in 1968 (.4 percent) to over 200 in 1974 (4.7 percent). A faculty of about 300 (under collective bargaining in 1974–75) served the institution. Clarion's experience with increasing black student enrollments has been one of careful, organized modifications of modest proportions.

Located in a county with less than a 1 percent black population and remote from most urban areas, Clarion had only limited experience with black students prior to 1968. It had attempted to respond to the increasingly diverse interests in its rapidly growing student body, which included many from relatively low income families. An early awareness of minority issues was reflected in a Fall 1968 faculty orientation topic: "The College and the Disadvantaged."

Clarion was relatively isolated from the pressures of the civil rights movement and from the events surrounding Martin Luther King's assassination. Not until the fall of 1969 did a group of black students urge the acting president to recruit more black students. He responded by developing a recruitment program, focused in the state's urban centers, which employed black students as recruiters and bussed black high school students to the campus for visits.

The initial recruitment effort was modestly successful. Through the efforts of key administrators, the fall of 1970 witnessed the beginnings of a supportive service activity (later called the Student Development Program—SDP) for disadvantaged students. The expanded recruitment efforts in 1970–71, which were primarily the responsibility of the new black director of SDP, produced a sharp increase in black enrollments through 1973.

The organization of SDP was the major programmatic response at Clarion. The program was later partially supported by the state's Act 101 funds. SDP, under the Office of Student Affairs, was responsible for black recruitment and advocacy and it provided remedial summer programs, counseling, academic retention advice, tutoring, and other social programs for disadvantaged students (about half of whom were black). The admissions program worked closely with SDP, and the financial aids office used a broad range of state and federal programs to assist needy students, but these two offices did not have specific activities focused on blacks and minorities. There was no black studies or other academic program focused primarily on blacks. The Black Student Union, founded in 1971, was the major black student organization and sought to provide a range of social, cultural, educational, and service programs. Other black student organizations, two or three performing or cultural groups, and a black sorority and fraternity provided additional black activities.

It was, perhaps, the informal pattern at Clarion which explained the relatively conflict-free experience during the period of increased black enrollments. In an isolated white community the black students established their own separate student organizations and life on the campus. Administrators were aware of minority concerns, responded to black groups, and encouraged programs directed toward disadvantaged students. The president encouraged recruitment of black faculty and administrators: five black administrators and nine black faculty members were on the Clarion staff at the time of our visit. Ad hoc committees dealt with issues of interracial education, desegregation, and affirmative action, and some faculty members were involved in these committees. Occasional new courses oriented to black concerns and the inclusion of appropriate black or minority content in courses indicated some faculty responsiveness. With a few exceptions, however, Clarion faculty were less involved than administrators in the initiation and implementation of the college's minority programs. In 1973–74, a state grant was used to fund a "human relations audit" by a black consulting firm.

Unlike some other institutions, Clarion's experience with increasing black enrollments was not highly controversial, nor did it bring a multitude of formal organizational changes or programs. There was a continuous, almost informal attempt to deal with blacks as part of a larger emphasis on disadvantaged students. The top administrators tried to anticipate or at least to respond realistically to issues as they arose. More recently, the advent of collective bargaining in the Pennsylvania State College system, enrollment leveling, and financial pressures received much attention and threatened to strain the support for minority programs. Other more recent concerns have focused on the recruitment and retention of black faculty and staff, the need for better integration of the Student Development Program within the regular academic program, and the nagging concern that the separatist student patterns mask deeper conflicts between low-income whites and blacks.

University of Missouri–Kansas City

The University of Missouri–Kansas City is a complex, urban university which espouses a concern for liberal education. There are upper division and graduate programs in three principal areas: the health sciences; the performing, visual, and interpretative arts; and urban concerns. From 1968 to 1974, the undergraduate student body was primarily regional (95 percent in-state; 75 percent commuters) and of moderate academic ability (average SAT scores were 950). Undergraduate enrollments increased from around 5,000 to over 8,000 (total enrollment was approximately 11,000), and black student enrollments increased from around 150 in 1968 (3.5 percent) to over 550 in 1974 (8.1 percent). Faculty in 1974 numbered around 460, of whom 2 were identified as black. The institution's experience with increased black enrollment has been evolutionary, but it has included some deliberate attempts to increase minority enrollments and to provide special programs. There has been little disruption or overt conflict.

Prior to 1968, the university had very limited experience with blacks. The institution's transition from a private to a public institution in 1963, with attendant lowering of tuition, and its location in a city that was 22 percent black and the site of civil rights activity in the mid-1960s may have accounted for much of its early black enrollment. A very active Division of Continuing Education and a few civil rights activists on the faculty (including the first Kansas City CORE chairman) were involved in minority-related community programs and issues. After 1968, under the leadership of a new chancellor, the institution focused more directly on defining its role as an urban public university serving a regional clientele. This direction was supportive, if not directly related, to the enrollment of blacks and other minority students. The initial efforts to increase black enrollments occurred in the spring of 1968 when a small number of faculty members and administrators, with top administrative endorsement, designed the Transitional Year Program (TYP) for low-income and minority students. This program, funded by a two-year state grant, followed the earlier Upward Bound and Talent Search programs, all of which were housed in the Division of Continuing Education.

The increase in black enrollments after 1968 was gradual and continuous. In 1968–69, a group of black students formed The Afro-American Student Union (TAASU) and engaged in high school "visitations" (Missouri does not allow "recruitment"). In the summer of 1969 a black was hired on the admissions staff, and also during that year a black was hired as an assistant to the chancellor. The continuing growth of black enrollments seemed to result from the increased visibility of blacks on campus and in the high school visitation teams, the availability of TYP, the accessibility of the institution to commuter students, evolving urban concerns in various academic areas, and the support of a small number of administrators and faculty.

The TYP program was a supportive service program concerned with contacting, identifying, enrolling, and providing a transitional support program for new students who were economically or educationally disadvantaged (predominantly blacks, but also Hispanic students and some whites). It was expanded in 1970 with the receipt of federal funds, and by early 1975 its staff included five full-time professionals. The TYP office worked closely with the admissions, financial aids, and student affairs offices to accomplish its objectives, but it was not closely integrated into the academic program. Partially for the latter reason, the program was transferred in 1974 from the purview of the Division of Continuing Education to that of the Dean of the College of Arts and Sciences. The director of TYP was also responsible for administering the Upward Bound Program, two federally funded Outreach Centers—one in a Mexican-American section of Kansas City, one in a predominantly black area (both developed originally under Continuing Education), and an embryonic community "Depolarization Project."

In 1971, through the encouragement of a black part-time faculty member, the Ethnic and Black Awareness Center (later the Ethnic Awareness Center) was established. Initially located within the provost's domain, then under the Dean of Students, and most recently under the Dean of Arts and Sciences, this cultural center sponsored several activities but had little budgetary support and only a part-time director.

On the academic side, there was no black or ethnic studies program (although there was a long-standing Judaic studies program). Several courses related to ethnic groups were available, however, and an interdisciplinary focus on the black or Latin American experience was offered through the American Culture Program. Some of the professional and graduate programs reportedly had specific minority emphases but were not included in this study.

In the student arena, there was TAASU (recognized by the All Student Government), the Black Exodus cultural group, and a black fraternity. The older and commuting nature of the student body, an extensive student affairs program, and limited evening facilities and offerings probably prevented student groups from becoming a dominant force on this campus as they were at some others.

On the less formal side, the institution initiated at the chancellor and provost level some special committees and studies focused on minority issues, but there were few identifiable results. While an extensive affirmative action structure was created (three offices—one each for academic, nonacademic, and student areas), staff recruitment of blacks was only marginally successful. By early 1975, there were newly hired black administrators in the School of Education, in the medical school, on the staff of the Dean of Students, and in the College of Arts and Science, but all were below the dean level. There was a long history of black professional staff in the Division of Continuing Education. In 1973–74, the Dean of the College of Arts and Sciences, a white man and a strong supporter of black and minority issues, had pressed for black faculty recruitment, but he left after one year. There was continued administrative pressure on this issue but with few results. Budgetary issues in the spring of 1975 were foremost for the institution—as well as for the minority programs. The lack of minority faculty, the limited staffing of the minority programs, and the lack of cohesive concern for minority problems (among minorities as well as among whites) remained as issues at the University of Missouri–Kansas City in 1974–75. The difficulties of relating to a minority population which spans state lines in this urban region and of coordinating minority student programs with nearby institutions were also identified as problems. The pattern of response on this campus, however, was clearly one of gradual institutional evolution in its perceived role, in minority enrollments, and in minority programs. The institution was not subjected to extensive internal conflict or external pressure. The response came from some administrators and a few key individuals; but the developments were sporadic, occasionally disjointed, and often subject to the availability of external state or federal funds.

THE LARGE PRIVATE INSTITUTIONS

"Metropolitan University"

"Metropolitan University" is a well-known private institution with extensive graduate and professional offerings. It is an institution sponsored and assisted but no longer fully controlled by the Jesuits. During the period from 1968 to 1974, the undergraduate student body became increasingly non-Catholic, career-oriented, and of declining but sound academic ability (average SAT scores over 1000). Enrollments decreased from over 6,300 to around 4,300 as whites were moving out of the deteriorating inner city and as less expensive public two- and four-year institutions were opening in the metropolitan area. Black student enrollments during the same period grew from 177 in 1968 (2.7 percent) to 572 in 1974 (13.2 percent). Metropolitan had a highly qualified faculty of 789, most of whom held appointments in the graduate and professional schools. The institution's experience with increasing black enrollments has been marked by strong administrative initiative, intense conflict, and—perhaps more than other institutions in our study—by constraints and forces largely beyond the control of the institution.

Metropolitan University has long had a reputation as an institution receptive to minorities. In the 1940s, one of its instructors advocated the integration of the public schools. The university apparently admitted blacks before the parochial schools did and continued to do so through the 1950s. In 1967–68—at least a year prior to similar

efforts by most other institutions—its president, Father Schmidt,*
started planning the university's Collegiate Help Program (CHP) for
black recruitment, financial aid, and academic support (later called
the Distinctive Academic Program—DAP). With initial support from
the Ford Foundation, a first group of 52 black students entered in the
fall of 1968. At that time a presidential report suggested a 10 percent
enrollment goal for Metropolitan. During this time, the president led
in the formation of a consortium, with foundation funding, which was
to recruit and support students for two-year periods at one of the local
community colleges and then assist them in transferring to one of the
area's participating four-year institutions.

The Despite these early steps, there was apparently little involvement
and awareness by others at Metropolitan University regarding these
initial efforts to bring minorities to the university. Problems began to
emerge during the 1968–69 school year as new black students formed
the Association of Black Students (ABS). Charging harassment by
white security officers, black students occupied the office of the Dean
of Arts and Sciences. Black security officers were hired as a result of
the incident, but a later failure to hire a black administrator may
have precipitated a more serious confrontation the following year.
May 1970 saw a prolonged and intense series of allegations, demands,
a student strike, court injunctions, and negotiations. Eventually, with
the help of an outside negotiator, an agreement was forged, including
the creation of a new vice presidency which was filled by a former
black dean.

The programs emanating from these early administrative initiatives and expressions of black student concerns included the CHP and
later the DAP, whose director and professional staff of seven reported
to the Vice President for Academic Affairs. The DAP staff, working
with the admissions office, recruited and selected the students for
whom it provided a variety of academic and personal support services.
Declining institutional sources of financial aid threatened the continuation of the DAP program since there was no special minority student aid, aside from federal student aid programs and a small state
program. The only academic program focusing specifically on blacks
was a one-person Institute for Afro-American Studies, located under
the Academic Vice President, which was begun in January 1974. The
institute coordinated an interdisciplinary program of courses in other
units but lacked visibility within and outside the university. In stu-

---

*Because this institution chose to remain anonymous for this study, the name of the
individual mentioned here is fictitious.

dent life, the initial efforts of ABS were superseded in 1971 by the Black Residence Union, reflecting concerns with housing. The dominant black student organization was the Black Student Alliance (BSA), which was formed in 1972 and received funds from the Student Government Association.

The creation of a new administrative position, Assistant Vice President for Student Development/Minority Affairs, and the establishment of the DAP represent the major administrative changes at the university that can be traced directly to minority concerns. Aside from a study of grading issues and the occasional creation of a course listed in the Institute for Afro-American Studies, faculty had little involvement in programs for black students. The lack of an affirmative action office, combined with declining enrollments, partially accounted for the limited black professional staff (two black faculty members).

By 1975, the future of the university's minority programs seemed to be tied to the enrollment declines and to financial stringency facing the institution. Fundamental questions concerning its viability in an urban setting and a possible "tipping point" for black/white enrollments confronted Metropolitan University. (The latter would have become a moot point if tuition outpaced available financial aid for blacks.) Lesser in comparison were problems of limited black program staff and funding, housing and social facilities for black students, the lack of black faculty, and black-white student tensions. Metropolitan University is an example of an institution in which early administrative initiative on minority issues was extensive but where responsiveness has been limited by the lack of involvement by other affected groups. The effects on the university's enrollment of changes in the surrounding city and of the competition from public colleges and universities, as well as severe limitations on financial resources, threatened to further constrain the institution's capacity to sustain its early initiatives.

Northwestern University

Northwestern University in Evanston, Illinois, is a distinguished, medium-sized, private university. During the period from 1968 to 1974, the institution's undergraduate student body—recruited nationally and of high academic quality (average SATs around 1200)—remained essentially stable in size, increasing from just under 6,700 to over 6,900. Black student enrollments increased from around 150 in 1968 (2.3 percent) to over 550 in 1974 (8.0 percent). The faculty on the Evanston undergraduate campus numbered about 790, of whom 42 were black. Northwestern's experience with increasing black enrollments has included early and deliberate (though not always widely publicized) attempts to recruit blacks, a period of intense conflict, and ultimately substantial success in the recruitment and retention of black students through graduation.

Northwestern was the only institution we visited that had embarked on concerted black student recruitment in a deliberate manner prior to 1968. However, this earlier start was evidently a response to pressures other than from blacks themselves. In the early 1960s, Northwestern's wealthy, white image was clear (if not accurate), for the university had received substantial publicity amid unsubstantiated charges of an anti-Semitic admissions policy. In 1964 and 1965, partially in response to these concerns, a small group of key administrators formed the Committee on Financial Aids which established as a goal "diversifying the student body." During 1965–66, with the receipt of a Wieboldt Foundation grant and the hiring of a new director of admissions, a black student recruitment campaign was launched. In the fall of 1966, 54 black students, most of whom had low SAT scores but strong recommendations, were admitted to Northwestern; this figure was up from the 5 out of 1,609 in the 1965 freshmen class. By the spring of 1968, Northwestern had well over 100 black students on campus, and it had already experienced early attempts by blacks to form student organizations, an emergent black student leadership, and a black-white fraternity controversy. The campus had also been the site of a symposium on violence, in which prominent black speakers participated, and black students had already presented an initial set of grievances.

Escalating frustrations, reinforced by campus disruptions elsewhere, led to a black student occupation of a Northwestern administration building and the presentation of "nonnegotiable" demands after Martin Luther King's assassination. The confrontation and negotiation between students and university administrators was tension-ridden, rhetoric-filled, and widely publicized. The threat of police intervention, Board pressure, and Board reluctance to accept what it saw as concessions on its own part heightened and prolonged the controversy. Interestingly, the principal administrative negotiator in this and following negotiations developed a reputation on campus as an open and fair but tough-minded individual; he later became president.

The recruitment, admissions, and financial aid efforts began before the 1968 crises, but they received additional impetus from the negotiated commitment to a 10–12 percent black admissions goal.

The addition of a black staff member in admissions and one in financial aids assisted Northwestern's competitive recruitment program and encouraged coordination with other black groups. The African-American Student Affairs (AASA) unit, administered by an associate dean of students, provided a diverse range of formal and informal cultural and social activities.

The primary academic program for blacks was the Department of African American Studies, established in 1971 as a nondegree program within the College of Arts and Sciences. The department was the focus of controversy on issues of academic direction, autonomy, and legitimacy. Related programs such as Upward Bound, a summer program for black students in science, and the efforts of various professional schools had been initiated earlier and supported Northwestern's recruitment efforts. Two black student organizations, the socially oriented For Members Only (FMO) and the more political Afro-American Student Union (AASU), originated in 1967–68 and provided the leadership for the early confrontation. FMO, which worked closely with AASA, became the dominant black student organization, not only in social and cultural events but also in monitoring the university's commitment to blacks. Numerous other black student organizations—six fraternities and sororities, two creative arts groups, and several professional or special interest groups—tended to diffuse black student influence but reflected the increasing numbers and diversity of the black student population.

The less formal patterns at Northwestern suggest marginal success in black staff recruitment. Of the 42 blacks on the staff, 16 were assistant professors or higher. Yet, many departments had no black faculty. In general, the faculty structure was not directly affected by the addition of the Afro-American Studies Department. Several lower level administrators were blacks and they had the trust of black students. Certain white administrators who were involved either in the initial efforts in black recruitment and/or the negotiations with black students had recently acceded to executive roles.

Northwestern has been less pressured than some of the other institutions in our sample by enrollment declines, financial stress, or affirmative action and civil rights activism. The recent issues of concern have included a leveling-off of black enrollments, reduced black cohesion, greater black-white separatism, dual black-white student structures, and the small number of blacks in higher level administrative and faculty positions. Compared to other institutions, Northwestern's response in 1974–75 to blacks seemed more secure, and its problems, though real, were not immediately threatening.

THE SMALL PRIVATE INSTITUTIONS

Bradley University

Bradley University in Peoria, Illinois, is a small, private university with a substantial range of traditional academic programs in five colleges and four schools. The student body was primarily in-state or regional and was of average academic ability (SAT scores averaged 1000). From 1968 to 1974, total enrollments decreased from just over 5,000 to under 4,000. Black student enrollments increased from around 150 in 1968 (3.0 percent) to 430 in 1974 (11.3 percent). The faculty in 1974–75 numbered around 275, representing a 20–25 percent decrease from the 1970–72 period when total enrollments began to decline. The institution's experience with increased black enrollments has been complicated by external factors and unintended consequences of institutional actions. The university's informal responses to the increase have reflected a nondiscriminatory stance.

Prior to 1968 Bradley had somewhat more experience with black students than many of the institutions in this study. Without any recruitment effort, black enrollment had reached 149 by 1968, a number which may be explained by certain attractions about the institution. In the late 1950s and early 1960s, Bradley had attracted black basketball players who led them to national visibility in the televised National Invitational Tournament (N.I.T.). Beginning in 1963, the college initiated a scholarship for black students from the Peoria area in the name of the institution's first black faculty member. A few of the white faculty members had been civil rights activists in Peoria in the 1960s and had encouraged able young blacks to attend Bradley University. All these factors, no doubt, made the low-tuition private school attractive to college-bound black students.

Unlike the other institutions in this study, Bradley developed no formal recruitment effort or other overt program to increase black student enrollments. Nevertheless, it experienced a steady increase in black enrollments from 1968 to 1974 which resulted from three factors. First was the availability of a need-based, state-funded, student aid program which could be used at private colleges and universities in Illinois. In 1974, this accounted for $1.8 million of Bradley's $2.5 million in student aid (most of the rest was federal aid) and made attendance feasible for low-income students.

The second factor was an intense period of student activism from 1968 to 1970 in which black issues were prominent. Prior to 1968, racial incidents involving Bradley blacks on or off the campus had been minor or isolated. But in the fall of 1968, the Students for a Democratic Society (SDS) and the emerging Black Student Association (BSA) initiated a sit-in against construction firms regarding the failure to hire minorities while erecting a new campus building. While a confrontation was avoided, Bradley did later establish the Special Building Committee comprised of students, faculty, administrators, and trustees to review future construction contracts. In the spring of 1969, the BSA presented a set of demands for a black cultural center, black activites, a black studies program, and the recruitment of black faculty. The administration made some commitments to move in these directions. These initial responses might have assured some trust had it not been for the treatment of black students after a building take-over in 1968–69 protesting a decision to increase tuition. Trustee intervention to modify a judicial hearing process that had been negotiated by administrators reportedly alienated black students who already felt they were being dealt with more severely than white students in a similar library sit-in. This activism prompted the start of some black programs and provided visible evidence of the black presence on campus.

The third factor supporting the black enrollment increase came about in response to the continued overall enrollment decline of 1970–72. An institutional self-study, a planning effort, and an ad hoc review of the financial situation at Bradley led to extensive administrative and financial changes, including a 25 percent reduction of faculty. Concomitant with this effort was an intensified campaign for funding and a revision of the financial aid program. Although there was no black recruitment effort per se, Bradley recruiters began to visit a greater number of urban high schools and the recruitment teams included black students.

The formal programming for blacks at Bradley has been quite limited due in part to retrenchment. The Black Studies Program, initiated in the fall of 1969, was basically run by one person with the help of part-time staff. It had only limited support from other departments for its interdisciplinary offerings, and by 1974 it had had four directors. The Black Culture House was also started in 1969 under the Black Studies director, but it lacked financial and staff support. The admissions and financial aid efforts were officially nondiscriminatory and did not focus on any minority groups per se, but they were expanded as noted. The major focus for black concerns was within the student affairs office, which responded informally and often successfully to increased student tensions and to new advising and counseling needs. In the fall of 1974, the student affairs staff created the first academic support service, Curriculum II, a program for students in academic difficulty which served many black students.

Less organized responses to blacks were reflected in the growth of black student organizations: nine black fraternities and sororities and two cultural clubs offered alternatives to BSA. The faculty in general and its Academic Senate were little affected by the black student increase but were more concerned about retrenchment and general institutional quality. While admissions standards were reportedly unchanged by the admission of more blacks, faculty members did express concern about admissions standards. Early attempts to hire black faculty were partially successful and there were seven blacks on the staff at the time of our study. The latter were reported as generally supportive of black students and some taught classes with black content, but they were not particularly active on campus. The major administrative concerns after the period of activism have been with the decline in enrollments, financial retrenchment, and reorganization—including a change of presidents in 1971. The only blacks in professional positions were with the student affairs office.

Thus, Bradley's black increase has been a matter of visible historical precedents, individual faculty initiatives, available state funds, black student pressures, and institutional responses to enrollment declines. Bradley's overall response to black students has been characterized by an active, informal policy of nondiscrimination, rather than any special recruitment activities for blacks or minorities. While the institution was responsive to early black demands, financial retrenchment limited special programs at the start. The informal efforts of black students, student affairs staff, and a few key black and white faculty and administrators provided the major mechanisms for dealing with black concerns. Issues in the fall of 1974 were the constraints of limited finances and inadequate staffing for black programs. Tensions existed between black and white students, but separate student organizations meant racial isolation. Student affairs staff tried to deal constructively with tensions as they arose. Other black student concerns revolved around inadequate social facilities and the limited off-campus activities in a city where local blacks looked to the college's black students for services and social activities which the latter were hard pressed to provide.

Carleton College

Carleton College in Northfield, Minnesota, is a well-known, private liberal arts college with a highly respected faculty, a reputation for a strong and traditional academic program, and an effective community governance system. Between 1968 and 1974 the student body, which was recruited nationally and was academically superior (combined SAT scores above 1300), increased gradually from predominantly full-time enrollments of about 1,450 to 1,650. Black student enrollments increased from around 50 in 1968 (3 percent) to over 130 in 1974 (8 percent). The faculty during this period grew from approximately 120 to 130 full-time equivalents, two of whom were black. The institution's experience with increasing black student enrollments was based on a clearly enunciated policy commitment made in early 1968. Carleton experienced the least amount of disruptive or overt conflict of any of the institutions in this study.

Prior to 1968, Carleton had only limited experience with blacks either in the student body or on the staff. In the early 1960s, there was a small group within the faculty who had raised questions concerning possible discrimination against Catholics and Jews. In 1964, Carleton was approached by the Rockefeller Foundation and eventually received a grant to participate in the foundation's ABC program (A Better Chance). This program consisted of a search for talented young blacks and a series of summer programs on college campuses to prepare them for attendance in private secondary schools. These initial efforts and issues no doubt sensitized some individuals at Carleton to the issues of the larger civil rights movement. In January 1968, the dean established the Ad Hoc Committee on Negro Affairs to study and make recommendations about the college's efforts on behalf of black students. In March 1968, the report of this group led to the establishment of the White Action Committee which was to implement some of the changes. Simultaneously, plans were underway to host black students from midwestern colleges later that spring. These activities and the assassination of Martin Luther King moved the retiring president to recommend a 10 percent black enrollment goal for the college (in a state with a black population below 1 percent); the recommendation was enthusiastically endorsed by the college's community governance body. This decision became a public commitment, was reported to the Board of Trustees, and received national coverage from *The Wall Street Journal* as an active, peaceful response to the tragic events of that spring.

In the first year, the recruitment of black students was accomplished through the regular admissions office; no separate admissions staff or selection procedure was established. The recruitment of blacks, like the recruitment of white students, was selective and on a national scale. Initially, the ABC program made Carleton attractive to some black students and allowed the college to identify a pool of able black secondary students for potential college enrollment.

In the spring of 1969, following charges of racism against the admissions staff by a black student organization (Students Organized for Unity and Liberation—SOUL), the Office of Minority Affairs was created. This office, which reported directly to the dean, was responsible for black student recruitment and admissions (with latitude to use different selection criteria), as well as for other minority concerns. Its efforts—combined with financial aid from private, institutional, and federal resources—accelerated the admissions of black students, and by the fall of 1972 over 10 percent of the freshmen class was black.

The primary academic response to black concerns at Carleton was the creation of an interdisciplinary black studies program, created as a result of the recommendations of the Committee on Negro Affairs. The program's development was slow. It had only one faculty member in 1974–75, it did not sponsor a major as did other interdisciplinary programs, and it provided only two courses of its own. In other areas, the Office of Minority Affairs was active in encouraging SOUL, continued to operate the ABC program for several years, established a black cultural center, and sponsored other activities and programs. Black student organizations that were formed included the Black Repertory Workshop Theater, the Gospel Choir, a dance group, a chapel group, a literary magazine, and some informal academic and professional groups.

Aside from these programmatic responses to the increased black student presence, the impacts of and responses to blacks at Carleton were limited. There has been no overt conflict. Some credit the community governance system, some the good faith effort, and still others the high academic ability of the black students for the lack of disruptions in dealing with problems and tensions. Since 1968, four blacks have been appointed to Carleton's Board of Trustees. Despite reported faculty recruitment efforts, there were only two black faculty members in 1974–75, and the director of the Office of Minority Affairs was the only black administrator. Recent issues at the institution have concerned the lack of role models for black students in responsible administrative positions, the increasing proportion of student aid going to black students (over 95 percent received some form of student aid and about one-third of total student aid funds went to blacks), and the lack of supportive staff for other minority groups (Hispanic, Indian, etc.). Due to the small numbers of black students and the predominantly white, rural nature of the community, black students had concerns about their limited off-campus social life and the multiple demands of the several active black student organizations. The problems and issues were not unique for a small college in a rural location, but they did provide a focus for continuing concern.

Lewis University

Lewis University (Lewis College prior to 1971), located outside Lockport and Joliet, Illinois, is a small, recently secularized, private institution which endeavors "to prepare students for useful careers and community service." During the period from 1968 to 1974, Lewis had a predominantly local, first generation, middle-to-low-income student body, which increased in number from just under 1,700 to over 2,700. Most of the increase resulted from the entry of women and minority students. Black enrollments increased from around 20 (1.3 percent) to 170 (6.7 percent). The number of full-time faculty serving this student body was around 100, of whom 3 were blacks. The experience with increased black enrollments at Lewis has been the result of internal and external pressure, has been shaped by other institutional changes, has been the subject of continuous tension and minor conflicts, and has produced a broad range of responses and controversies.

Prior to 1971, Lewis had been a small, Christian Brothers liberal arts college, with declining enrollments and a rural location. And prior to 1968, it had had few black students and, except for a 1968 disturbance, no racial incidents. There was a sizable low-income black and white population in nearby Joliet and South Chicago, but there were no four-year public institutions nearby. In June 1969 an Office of Civil Rights Compliance Review made explicit recommendations for creating more equal educational opportunity at Lewis. The college's exact responses were not made clear to us, although it was reported that there had been a partially successful inner-city recruitment effort, a 1969–70 Minority Task Force which produced no documented reports, and an informal, post-admissions support program directed by a new black counselor.

As black enrollments increased, the period from 1969 to 1970 witnessed the formation of the Black Student Union and continued racial tensions and demands. A black cultural center was established and a black was hired as an advisor to BSU. However, it was not until the spring of 1971 that a formal admissions program for black and minority students was created. That spring also witnessed a sit-in in which the president agreed to a wide range of demands, including the addition of black staff positions in counseling, recruitment, and financial aids. The years of 1969 to 1971 were also the period of declining overall enrollments, an abortive merger attempt with a neighboring college, and the final decision to secularize the institution.

In the summer of 1971, with the support of a new trustee structure, a new president expanded and revised the administrative and academic structure of Lewis, establishing it as a university with several colleges. Minorities did not go unnoticed: a special task force was created to clarify earlier commitments to minority programs and to identify important issues; Lewis received a federal grant to formalize a supportive services program for minorities—the Success Program; and a black was hired as Vice President for Community Services. In 1972, the trustees formally endorsed a "Policy of Equal Opportunity." The continued rise in black enrollments after 1971 was credited to more flexible student regulations, the change to coeducational status, an active intramural and intercollegiate sports program, two new professional colleges (Business and Nursing), and improved use of federal and student financial aid (Illinois has a need-based student aid program), as well as to the special programs for blacks.

The major programmatic response to blacks and minorities was the Success Program, which was directed by a former black counselor under the Dean of Arts and Sciences and supported primarily with Title III funds. It was the only supportive service program for all disadvantaged students (two-thirds of whom were black). With two part-time student assistants, the Success Program focused on course work to improve communication skills, on informal remedial and counseling services, and on referrals. The Black Cultural Center was an active headquarters for black student social affairs, cultural activities, enrichment programs, and collections of artifacts. With a limited budget and staff (a part-time director and nine part-time student assistants), the center was the focus of some enmity from predominantly low-income white students who saw it as "special treatment" for blacks. After Lewis's 1971 reorganization, the admissions and financial aid offices developed a clearer definition of "disadvantaged students" and a new recruitment strategy, added one black staff person, and developed an effective financial aid program relying on state and federal student aid. Working relationships between the admissions and financial aid offices and the Success Program were good. The student arena included BSU, which was recognized by the student government, and four black fraternity and sorority groups which were not part of IFC on campus. Lewis also had an interracial club, "The Seekers." The university did not have a black studies program, although this was a persistent issue and, in the fall of 1974, the focus of a student-trustee confrontation.

On the more informal side, the primary administrative activities have already been identified. The Lewis faculty and academic administration were not active forces in the black response programs. The crucial role played by student affairs staff and by the directors of the Success Program and the Black Cultural Center in continually dealing with racial tensions in virtually all campus areas and activities represented a major response pattern to minority student issues at Lewis. In late 1974, major issues included the funding uncertainty of the Success Program; the lack of a formal black studies program; the unresponsiveness of faculty and academic programs to blacks; the lack of success in recruiting black staff; tensions between low-income white students and blacks; increasing demands for attention from Chicanos in Joliet; and the anticipated resource demands of new units such as the proposed law school on limited institutional resources.

In summary, the institution had reacted with initial ad hoc decisions, which were focused under a new administration. Some later accommodation to minority concerns had developed in the areas of supportive services and student affairs, but the academic area had been relatively untouched. Informal response patterns and extensive reliance on external resources for minority programs left major issues regarding the future solvency and coordination of the programs unresolved.

Macalester College

Macalester College in St. Paul, Minnesota, is a well-known private liberal arts college with an excellent faculty and a good academic reputation. During the period from 1968 to 1974, the nationally recruited student body declined somewhat both in quality (although average SAT scores were still above 1150) and in numbers (from predominantly full-time enrollments of around 1,800 to 1,700). Black student enrollments increased from 40 in 1968 (2 percent) to 170 in 1974 (10 percent). The number of faculty during this period declined slightly to 131 full-time equivalents, 4 of whom were blacks. Of all the institutions in this study, Macalester made the most extensive commitment to black enrollments and drafted the most comprehensive initial plan for black and other minority programs. Its experience during this period was marked by intermittent controversy and conflict. The college recently attempted to assess its efforts in a serious, systematic way—something none of the other institutions in our sample had done.

Prior to 1968, Macalester's experience with blacks was very limited, despite the involvement of some of its faculty and students in civil rights activities. The arrival of Arthur Flemming as president in the summer of 1968 sparked Macalester's minority effort. A charismatic leader who had formerly been Secretary of HEW and President of the University of Oregon, Flemming became a catalyst for examining the college's social commitment. He encouraged an ad hoc group to develop a specific proposal and, in the ensuing months, there appeared a comprehensive set of recommendations for recruiting "educationally and economically deprived" students and for providing more extensive services. Known as the Expanded Educational Opportunities (EEO) proposal, it was widely reviewed, approved by the Faculty Advisory Council, and transmitted to the Board of Trustees. In January 1969, the Board endorsed the proposal and approved its financial support, including the expenditure of up to $900,000. During the remainder of the year a program was designed, students were recruited, and, in June 1969, a director of the EEO was hired. An aura of optimism surrounded this far-reaching program, and it was hoped that the new students and the programs planned for them would be integrated with the college's formal and informal patterns.

The first year shook many illusions. In the fall of 1969, 82 EEO students (including 63 blacks) arrived on the Macalester campus. Shortly thereafter, the newly formed student Black Liberation Affairs Committee (BLAC) pressed for and received funding for a black cultural center. Other minority students—Native Americans and Hispanics—demanded and received from President Flemming funds for their own staff and cultural centers. Mistrust and hostility began to build among the minority groups and between blacks and whites. The new EEO director, after a brief attempt to resolve differences, adopted a separatist stance for EEO. He argued vigorously and successfully for increased EEO staff, funds, and programs for recruitment, academic support, financial aid, and cultural activities. These were not closely integrated with other organizational units. It became apparent to the administration that the orientation of EEO would not only be separatist, but it would also be more toward high-risk students than had been anticipated. It also began to appear that EEO would cost more than planned since new external funds were not forthcoming.

The crucial event at Macalester, however, was the withdrawal of financial support by Macalester's major donor. Whether the withdrawal of this support was for reasons of financial mismanagement, dissatisfaction with the separatist orientation of EEO, or general disillusionment with higher education, it eventually precipitated President Flemming's resignation during the 1970–71 academic year. A new president was forced to make drastic cuts in the 1971–72 budget and also reduce the number of new students brought into EEO.

Resentment and alienation among blacks and whites continued unabated after Flemming's departure, and faculty who originally supported the EEO program began to question the financial burden of the program and its effectiveness. In the fall of 1973, a former black admissions counselor was named the second director of EEO. The continued declines in white enrollments which began in 1971–72 exacerbated financial pressure on the institution. In the summer of 1974, when it became clear that 1974–75 enrollments were overestimated, the new president cut the total budget by about $250,000 and EEO's budget by $80,000. This precipitated a confrontation in the fall of 1974 in which students occupied a major campus building. This intense conflict received wide media coverage and was eventually resolved with the help of a mediator from outside the college. In October 1974, the president announced he had accepted a position elsewhere, and the trustees announced the appointment of a special, multiracial committee to study the institution's commitment to minorities.

Despite the controversy, the reduced proportion of new students, and the propensity to go in its own direction, the EEO program prospered. By 1974–75, it had 16 full-time professionals plus student tutors, counselors, and advisors who were also responsible for minority recruitment, financial aid, remedial help, and extra-curricular programming. EEO had six separate staffs and coordinators—for four groups of minority students (blacks, native Americans, Hispanics, Puerto Ricans), for its Black Educational Institute, and for the Upward Bound program. EEO students grew from an initial group of 82 to 185 in 1972–73 and accounted for 157 of the 224 minority students at Macalester in 1974–75. EEO and its components were the primary formal programmatic response to blacks at Macalester. BLAC, the Native American Coalition, and the Hispanic Student Group, with the help of EEO and the student government, sponsored many campus activities representing their ethnic concerns and interests.

In other areas of campus life, the impacts of the minority commitment were considerable. The financial impact and cost of EEO was still under debate in 1974–75, and administrative pressures were substantial. Following its initial approval of EEO, the Board of Trustees became involved during the financial crisis of 1970–71 and after the events of the summer of 1974. An expected study and evaluation of the program was never completed. There were four black faculty members in 1974–75 (not including EEO staff), and the role of black faculty and staff has been critical in the evaluation of EEO and in the review of the college's commitment to minority student recruitment and support.

Increased minority enrollments at Macalester have had little impact either on the regular administrative or academic structures, since EEO and the various minority-oriented student organizations were separate entities. Yet in terms of decision making, staffing, institutional direction, and attitudes, minorities have had a tremendous impact at Macalester. Despite extensive and widely approved initial plans, occasional conflict and controversy seemed to be the result of overly optimistic and perhaps idealistic expectations by white administrators and staff, coupled with separatist minority leadership and loss of financial support. The college's self-examination—represented by the special trustee subcommittee on minorities and the selection of the third president of the "minority era"—may represent an important opportunity for confronting not only the costs and effectiveness of Macalester's minority program but also the many unresolved issues left from the Flemming period. These are the dilemmas of a well-planned but uncontrolled program for minorities—the conflict of integrationist versus separatist strategies and philosophies; the fickleness of funding sources; and the problem of finding the range of cultural and educational diversity that is tolerable in a small college community.

In the following chapters we examine the forces and events which influenced the increase in black enrollments and the nature of the events which precipitated the influx.

Notes

[1]Our institutions were larger, on the average, than those in the Arce sample, with full-time undergraduate enrollments of 5,914 vs. 3,947. Hence, the absolute numbers of blacks per institution were larger in our sample, again, on the average. The congressional districts in which our colleges and universities are located had a slightly lower percentage of blacks than the districts of the larger sample (6 percent vs. 7 percent), and they also had a somewhat higher average family income ($7,522 vs. $7,224).

6

Environmental Forces:
The Crucial Context

Marvin W. Peterson

Change rarely occurs in a college or university as a simple function of external forces. Rather, it is a complex process in which internal and external forces interact in ways that reflect both a particular organization and its particular setting. In this chapter, we examine the experiences of the 13 colleges and universities in our sample as they began to increase black enrollments, delineating how external and internal forces combined to set the stage for their responses, which we discuss in detail in the following chapters.

The initiating conditions for any organizational change are important to examine because the extent to which internal or external forces initially support or resist change provides some indication of both the salience of the issue and the ease with which it will be accomplished. Looking at the balance of internal versus external forces shows whether the organization has control over its destiny. The nature of the early events for change may reflect on the long-term legitimacy of decisions and on the commitment of those who later implement them. This chapter approaches these questions by examining the external forces or pressures impinging on each of the 13 institutions, the predispositions or earlier experiences relevant to the issue of black enrollment, the precipitating events and decisions, and the nature of the initial strategies for increasing black enrollments.

THE IMMEDIATE ENVIRONMENT

Few organizations experience major changes in their client populations without support or resistance from within their relevant environments—from the region and groups they serve and from those to whom they are accountable. These forces may be potent, direct, and require immediate and prolonged attention and consideration, or they may be less well-defined and have a more subtle influence. In Table 6-1 we have attempted to identify those external forces which supported or resisted the enrollment increases in the institutions under study. The table distinguishes the strong and active pressures for resistances to increased black enrollments from conditions which were more generally supportive or resistive. The external forces may originate from the demographic makeup of the region, community characteristics, competition, or governmental agencies.

The demography of each institution's recruiting region is shown in Table 6-2. The percentage of blacks in the state population and in the immediate SMSA (Standard Metropolitan Sampling Area) or county is an indirect measure of the potential availability of black students.[1] At most of the institutions in our study, the initial percentage of black students was well below the percentage of blacks in the region and state, indicating that a black student pool did exist. This factor was most important for Northwestern University, "Metropolitan University," the University of Missouri-Kansas City, and the "University of the City," which are all located in urban areas with large black populations. It was much less important for Macalester College and Carleton College in Minnesota and for "State University" located in a predominantly agricultural state.

These differences underscore the need to understand the institutions' recruiting regions, an issue that was raised at most of the institutions in our sample. Carleton and Macalester, which did not have large black populations near them, defined their recruiting areas nationally. This is typical of prestigious, private institutions and was true as well at Northwestern. State University defined its recruiting area for black students as essentially the entire Midwest, a practice that probably occurred at other selective institutions which were located in areas with small black populations but which had made commitments to increase minority enrollments.[2] For Clarion and California State Colleges in Pennsylvania, which serve a more local region, and to a certain extent for State, the low proportions of blacks in their locales were a resistive or at least a nonsupportive factor for increasing black enrollments.

TABLE 6-1

Supportive and Resistive Factors in Institutional Environments

Institution	Active Support	Supportive	Resistive	Active Resistance
Bowling Green		1. Commuting distance to Toledo 2. Regional black population	1. Conservative local community—no activism in 1960s	
Bradley		1. State financial aid program (1970) 2. Black population of state (13%)		
SUNY–Brockport		1. No competition for blacks in Rochester area 2. State grant program 3. Black population of State	1. Poor commuting from Rochester 2. Small community	
California State	1. Office of Civil Rights desegregation pressure 2. Penn. Board of Education pressure	1. State grant program (1972) 2. Act 101 program money from state (1971)	1. Isolated area—ethnic communities 2. Regional black population	1. Local community response to blacks and growth of institution
Carleton		1. Out of state black clientele	1. Rural small town 2. Low black population of state	

TABLE 6-1 continued

Institution	Active Support	Supportive	Resistive	Active Resistance
"University of the City"	1. Local black leaders	1. Civil rights activities in the city 2. Black population of city 3. State grant program		
Clarion State	1. Office of Civil Rights—HEW 2. Penn. Board of Education pressure	1. State grant program 2. ACT 101 program money (1971)	1. Rural area—no black population 2. Local housing problem—attitude of locals	
Lewis	1. Office of Civil Rights compliance review (June 1969 & May 1968)	1. State Grant Program 2. Black population of South Chicago and Joliet area 3. No nearby public institutions	1. Rural location	
Macalester		1. Liberal environment of Twin Cities area 2. Substantial donor support		1. Withdrawal of support by major donor

TABLE 6-1 continued

Institution	Active Support	Supportive	Resistive	Active Resistance
"Metropolitan University"		1. Growing black population of the city 2. Vatican II and social conscience of Jesuits	1. Catholic constituency of the city 2. White flight 3. Neighborhood of institution 4. Competition from public institutions with lower tuition	
University of Missouri–Kansas City		1. Urban area—22% black 2. Only public four-year colleges in area 3. State minority support program	1. Border problem—no Kansas-Missouri reciprocity agreements 2. Changing neighborhood 3. Community views as manipulative landlord	
Northwestern		1. Black population—Evanston, Chicago, state, and national	1. Lack of social gathering places for those who cannot travel	
"State University"		1. Location in liberal border state 2. Community involvement in civil rights	1. Small black population	

TABLE 6-2

Black Population Characteristics in Institutional Settings
(1970 Census Data)

Institution	Black Population (%)		Blacks in Elementary and Secondary Schools (%)		Median Family Income ($)	Median Black Family Income ($)
	County or SMSA	State	County or SMSA	State	County or SMSA	
Bowling Green	<.1	9.5	<0.5	10.8	10,878	—
Bradley	4.0	12.8	5.5	15.7	10,641	7,105
SUNY–Brockport	7.0	11.9	8.0	13.8	11,965	7,646
California	3.8	8.8	4.4	10.1	8,665	5,953
Carleton	<1.0	0.9	<0.5	1.0	9,486	—
"University of the City"	7.0	8.8	8.3	10.1	9,729	6,334
Clarion	<1.0	8.8	<0.5	10.1	7,635	—
Lewis	6.8	12.8	7.2	10.1	11,790	8,700
Macalester	2.0	0.9	2.9	1.0	11,679	7,665
"Metropolitan University"	40.8†	10.2	53.8	12.9	8,173	6,528
University of Missouri– Kansas City	22.0	10.2	28.1	12.9	9,904	7,241
Northwestern	6.1†	12.8	21.4	15.7	13,931	9,671
"State University"	<1.0	1.2	0.5	1.4	9,942	—

†Immediate city.

Other local community characteristics were also significant factors. Being located in small, rural towns with few blacks negatively affected attempts to increase minority enrollments at Bowling Green State University, California, Clarion, Carleton, Lewis University, State University, and SUNY-Brockport. There may not have been active community opposition to the entry of blacks at these institutions,[3] but because there was no local black community with which black students could feel at home, nor in many cases was there any available off-campus housing, an all-white location was a negative factor for recruiting black students unless there were other compensations. For example, at Lewis, Bowling Green, and Northwestern proximity to larger black population centers was a desirable feature to black students. Some institutions made an all-white location more acceptable by revising campus housing patterns, liberalizing social regulations, and offering a variety of social and cultural programs for blacks. State University's location, in a liberal border state with a long history of progressive educational opportunity and in a city with a reputation for early activism in the civil rights movement, was an important attraction for blacks who otherwise might not have been willing to go to school in an almost all-white community.

Location near black population centers was not without its dilemmas. Young blacks in Peoria, which lacked adequate social outlets for blacks, turned to the Bradley campus and to its black student activities. This brought a number of problems. Black students, in order to maintain a good relationship with young local blacks, tried to accommodate them—which meant they needed more space. Not being students, the local blacks were not subject to the same norms of behavior and university regulations and behaved in ways that intimidated white students. The result was a prolonged controversy over the use of space for social events which caught Bradley's black students in the middle.

Different complications occurred at Metropolitan, City, and Kansas City. All are in cities with large black populations, near changing or transitional neighborhoods with increasing crime rates that deter both black and white students. At Metropolitan, the flight of whites—particularly Metropolitan's old Catholic constituency—had a negative effect on total enrollments. Kansas City and the University of the City were increasingly pressed as public institutions to serve nearby black and other urban population groups. At City, it was clear that local black leaders were involved in early demands on the institution to increase black enrollments. At Kansas City, the pressure has been less direct, although many respondents suggested that active pressure from the NAACP on the public school system deflected pressure away from the university. Both City and Kansas City became the focus for extensive civil rights activities, and during the period from 1966 to 1968 the efforts of several black leaders—including King, Carmichael, Abernathy—served to sensitize some of the leaders of local white institutions to black concerns.

The availability of other higher education institutions is another external factor which can support or limit an institution's attempts to increase black enrollments. For the private institutions with high tuitions, this was crucial. Carleton, Macalester, and Northwestern each compete in a national market for able students and are subject to competition for other schools.

Bradley, Metropolitan, and Lewis, although also private institutions, have lower admissions standards than other private schools and more regional drawing power and, thus, face even more competition from private and public institutions. However, both Lewis and Bradley have an offsetting advantage since they are located in areas where there are no readily available public four-year colleges or universities and no similar private institutions. Of the three, Metropolitan University is the most vulnerable to competition from other schools. As a private, urban institution, its early interest in serving black students has been undermined by the expansion of the local community college system and the growth of branches in two state university systems. Public institutions, with their lower tuition rates, are less vulnerable to competition from private institutions except in one respect: individuals at all of the public institutions in our sample mentioned difficulty in attracting academically able black students because of the aggressive recruiting and financial aid programs of some prestigious private institutions.

The role of state and federal governmental agencies in supporting or pressuring for increased black enrollments was identified as a factor at many of the 13 institutions. The federal impact was felt in 1969 in Pennsylvania when the U.S. Office of Civil Rights notified Pennsylvania and ten other states that they were in violation of Title VI of the Civil Rights Act of 1964 and had to formulate plans to desegregate their colleges and universities. This order resulted in a 1969 conference run by the state's Department of Education for state college admissions personnel, which affected Clarion and California State. An Office of Civil Rights compliance review at Lewis in 1968 and 1969 was another example of a government agency applying direct pressure that supported increased black enrollments.

Perhaps less dramatic but equally influential in this respect were state student aid programs. All the states represented in this study had such programs by 1970. In Missouri, a supplemental appropriation in 1968 lasting for two years allowed the University of Missouri at Kansas City to launch its recruitment and support program for black students. In Illinois, state programs of financial aid made funds available in 1970 to students on the basis of need at private as well as public institutions. These state monies combined with federal programs for student aid were key factors in enabling private institutions such as Bradley and Lewis to attract increasing numbers of black students, despite their higher tuitions.

Two other environmental factors affecting private institutions are worthy of note. Macalester was the beneficiary of substantial support from a private donor which enabled its new president to increase black enrollments very quickly. The danger of having only a single source of support was underscored by the traumas at Macalester when that support was withdrawn. Lewis and Metropolitan, both institutions with strong religious heritage, each began a program of minority expansion following a period of secularization. At Lewis, the religious order had apparently been unable to cope with declining enrollments in the late 1960s. The Office of Civil Rights compliance review which suggested Lewis was not giving enough attention to minorities could be dealt with only after the institution was secularized in 1970. Secularization redirected Lewis's mission so that it was able to expand both its white and its black enrollments. At Metropolitan, however, although the process of secularization was begun earlier, the institution was still faced in 1975 with a declining total enrollment which affected its ability to support its commitment to blacks.

In sum, within the environmental context a wide array of factors act as conductors for larger societal forces affecting colleges and universities; these factors may include local community characteristics and groups, competitive conditions, federal legislation and executive or judicial rulings, state legislation or state agency direction, state and federal funding, and other institutional support groups. The specific pattern has varied for each of the institutions in our study, but, for the most part, supportive pressures were stronger and more prevalent than resistive pressures in the late 1960s. Resistive external forces were not much in evidence for these 13 institutions at that time.

INSTITUTIONAL PREDISPOSITIONS:
THE PERIOD JUST BEFORE
THE BLACK ENROLLMENT INCREASE

While external pressures may act as strong forces toward organizational change within an institution, the institution could nevertheless attempt to resist or neutralize such pressures. An institution's predisposition to accept or initiate a change is determined by its prior experience with elements of the proposed change or with the forces pressing for it. There were numerous internal factors or experiences within all 13 colleges in our sample which predisposed them to increase minority enrollments. These are summarized in Table 6-3.

First, we will examine the commitment and support given by the leaders of the institutions for increasing black enrollments. The presidents at six of the institutions were strong proponents of this shift in their institutions. These included President Brown of SUNY–Brockport, President Roadman of California State, President Tyrone at State University (who was succeeded by an equally committed president), President Flemming at Macalester, Chancellor Varden at the University of the City, and Father Schmidt at Metropolitan. President Brown, who had run an OEO Program in Michigan, stressed as early as 1966 that Brockport should begin a search for "disadvantaged" students; he spoke out strongly in favor of a policy of integration in SUNY–Brockport's program for minorities. President Roadman at California State was described as acting out of a moral consciousness and concern for the disadvantaged. President Tyrone's involvement in the civil rights movement was well-known and predated his address to State University in 1966 stressing its obligation to provide educational opportunities to underprivileged groups. Tyrone's successor, Joseph Lane, had earned a reputation at the university as the faculty chairman of the university's first Human Rights Committee in 1962. President Flemming came to Macalester in 1968; he was formerly Secretary of HEW and, as President of the University of Oregon, he had been known as a strong supporter of civil rights causes. Chancellor Varden, arriving at City in 1967 from a previous administrative post at one of the military academies, surprised some of his new staff with his statements on social justice and his willingness to meet with minority groups in nearby black communities to seek new ideas. Father Schmidt, president of Metropolitan University, was known within his community for his quiet commitment to civil rights. Later on, Hollis Moore (who arrived at Bowling Green in

TABLE 6-3

Predisposing Factors and Major Institutional Changes
Affecting Black Enrollment Increase

Institution	Supportive	Resistive	Other Major Changes
Bowling Green University	1. Quiet advocacy of Vice President for Student Affairs 2. Early Student Development Program (1968–70)		1. Institutional Growth 2. Addition of new faculty and graduate study move institution beyond local orientation
Bradley University	1. Basketball team's national reputation 2. Garrett Scholarship Program 3. Early black student activism (Fall 1968) 4. Faculty ACLU activists		1. Enrollment decline and release of 25% of faculty in 1970–72 2. Reorganization of administration 1970–72
SUNY–Brockport	1. President Brown's experience and social philosophy 2. "Summer Start Program" (1967) and active director of admissions	1. High selectivity up to 1972	1. SUNY Master Plan and Growth 2. Reorganization from teachers college to liberal arts college 3. "University center" aspirations
California State College	1. Commitment of a few liberal faculty 2. Commitment of new president 3. Early Upward Bound and SIP program		1. Hiring of substantial number of faculty from out-of-state in 1969 2. New president in 1969
Carleton College	1. Liberal faculty questioning (c. 1960) discrimination against Catholics and Jews 2. ABC Program 1966	1. Tradition of slow change 2. Low financial resources relative to other elites	1. Governance structure with constituency input on all issues

TABLE 6-3 continued

Institution	Supportive	Resistive	Other Major Changes
"University of the City"	1. Small number of black faculty pre-1968 2. Chancellor Varden's arrival and "social justice" emphasis 3. Project A (Spring 1968) 4. Early activism of black students (1968–69)		1. Change from municipal university to "quality institution" 2. Financial crisis of 1965 and state-related status of 1967 3. Urban orientation and limited growth of late 1960s and early 1970s.
Clarion State College	1. Forward-looking, anticipatory administration 2. Early activism of blacks—involvement in recruitment	1. Tradition of fairly high selectivity for public institution	1. Conversion from state teachers college (1962) 2. Growth in 1960s
Lewis University	1. Early black student pressure 2. Religious commitment 3. Declining enrollment of white males		1. Change from Christian, liberal arts to community & career focus 2. Administrative reorganization 3. Increase in female enrollment 4. Increase in lay influence
Macalester	1. 1961 long-range plan specified commitment to economically, socially, culturally diverse student body 2. Activism of faculty, students in civil rights, anti-war work 3. Arrival of President Flemming, 1968 4. Supportive private donor		1. Innovative nature of institution 2. Active recruitment of scholars 3. Growth of academic reputation 1950s–1960s
"Metropolitan University"	1. Mid 1940's—faculty member calls for end of segregation in parochial system 2. Father Schmidt's leadership in civil rights 3. Project AHEAD—1968		1. Secularization of institution-lay board 2. Declining enrollment—1967–72 3. More local student body—lower selectivity

TABLE 6-3 continued

Institution	Supportive	Resistive	Other Major Changes

University of Missouri–Kansas City	1. Public status allows reduction of tuition
	2. Small group of activist faculty—e.g., first chairman of CORE chapter in KC
	3. Activities of Continuing Education Center—1963–68
	  a. Upward Bound
	  b. Talent Search
	  c. Transitional Year Program
	4. Early activism & recruiting by black students (1968–70)
		1. Tradition and reputation as a private liberal arts institution	1. Change from private to public—1963
			2. New Chancellor—1968
			3. Autonomy struggle with state—Master Plan with regional professional orientation
			4. Loss of liberal education focus

Northwestern	1. 1965—Committee on Financial Aid to Students sets goal to "diversify" student body 2. Early black student activism	1. WASP image and anti-Semitic accusations.	
"State University"	1. 1930s, 40s, 50s black Ph.D. students 2. Civil rights activity from faculty—1960s 3. USOE Developing Institutions Project 4. Human Rights Committee 5. Presidential leadership of Tyrone and Lane		1. New President—1969 2. Turnover of other top administrators 3. Limited state appropriations—1972

1970) and Lester Carr (who became president of Lewis in 1971) were identified as important contributors to their institutions' initial efforts relating to minority concerns. Previous presidents at the latter two institutions—and those at Bradley, Carleton, Clarion, Kansas City, and Northwestern—were not as vocal in support of increases in minority enrollments, but neither did they oppose the increases. None of the presidents, of course, were viewed favorably by all constituencies and few escaped criticism from hostile whites within and outside their institutions—nor did they later avoid confrontation with militant blacks.

Other administrators were also crucial in sensitizing their institutions to their potential responsibilities to black and other minority students. As mid-level administrators, their efforts were important but not as visible as those of the presidents: there were admissions and financial aid officials who began informal minority recruiting before it was in vogue; there were student affairs staff who saw the early strains among the different groups of minority students and recognized the need for particular programs and services before they existed; there were athletic directors and coaches who not only recruited blacks for their athletic ability but hoped to see them succeed in other ways as well. For each administrator identified as supportive before the black increase began, however, there were far more who were either indifferent, unaware, or even opposed. Several presidents even removed white administrators who opposed the black enrollment increases. Interestingly, no top-level academic administrators (vice presidents or deans) were identified as playing highly visible leadership roles in the early years of minority enrollment.

During the early and mid-1960s, faculty efforts which might have supported the impending enrollment changes in these institutions were generally limited and were mostly focused off-campus. At Bradley, a few faculty who were ACLU activists encouraged some local Peoria blacks to attend the institution, assisted in finding them housing, and generally befriended them. One of these faculty members became a key negotiator when black students later presented a set of demands. At Carleton, a small group of faculty were raising questions about discrimination against Jews and Catholics, and they later became active in running an early summer program for black high school students. At Kansas City there was a small group of faculty activists, including the chairman of that city's first CORE chapter. At Macalester, a sizable group of young faculty activists was involved in civil rights activities off-campus. The most active faculty at any of the institutions were at State University, where there was extensive faculty involvement in civil liberties issues locally and in civil rights marches in the South. Ties between State and several southern black colleges eventually emerged from these activities.

Overall, however, off-campus involvement with civil rights and minority issues was not translated into an extensive or organized faculty initiative for minority programs at their own institutions. White students were more involved than faculty in campus demonstrations. Macalester, Northwestern, State, and City were all politically volatile in the 1960s, but most of the activism addressed the Vietnam War, political repression, and the draft—all issues which were not directly related to the institutions themselves. Campus governance was the only internal issue that received any extensive political attention. The growing numbers of black students at Bradley, Northwestern, and City were large enough to generate small disturbances by black students, but these went largely unnoticed in the heat of other events. But the names in the news at that time reflected the move of civil rights activism to the North. Even when Rap Brown, Ralph Abernathy, Martin Luther King, Eldridge Cleaver, and Stokely Carmichael visited campuses at that time, their message was directed outward to the nation at large rather than inward to the institutions themselves.

Black issues began to emerge relatively early on two of the campuses in our study. At the University of the City in 1967–68, a black faculty member in the Medical School charged the institution with racism. At Chancellor Varden's direction, the Commission on Racism was established to study the problem. At State University that same year President Tyrone asked for a review of a proposal for minority programs which had been developed by blacks in the Student Senate, and he directed the Commission on Human Rights to study and recommend directions for the university's minority commitment.

If leadership, faculty activity, student activity, and formal recognition of black or minority issues on campus were mildly supportive forces for increased black enrollments by 1968, institutional image or tradition were seen as constraints on several campuses. At Lewis, the religious service heritage of the Christian Brothers had focused on a traditional liberal arts education, scarcely encouraging to black students. At Carleton, the institution's complex governance system was described as limiting the speed with which the college could respond to a new clientele or adjust its selective admissions standards. Northwestern's WASP county club image and high selectivity were seen as inhibiting the initial influx of black students. Similarly, former private institutions like City and the University of Missouri at Kansas

City were not reputed for a concern with urban or minority problems—nor were public institutions like Brockport and Clarion, whose admissions criteria had become more selective during rapid growth periods in the later 1960s. Thus, dimensions of tradition and image—whether accurate or not—were viewed as factors which inhibited increased black enrollments.

Finally, some features of the 13 institutions prior to 1968 may provide clues to how change is initiated within other colleges and universities. The early and gradual development of early black or minority-oriented ancillary programs at some of the institutions had given certain individuals experience in dealing with minorities in a peripheral activity. Seven of the 13 institutions had such programs before 1968, when enrollments began to increase sharply. Bradley, for example, successfully recruited some outstanding black basketball players in the 1950s. When most major university teams were all white, several years in the National Invitational Tournament with national TV coverage no doubt gave Bradley a favorable image among blacks. Later, in 1963, Bradley began a scholarship fund (named for the institution's first black faculty member) for outstanding black students in the Peoria area.

State and City also had early experience with black athletes, and people at State were proud of their institution's tradition during the 1940s and 1950s of attracting graduate students from predominantly black undergraduate institutions. Several departments kept lists of their black Ph.D.s for future recruitment into faculty and staff positions. With the help of grants from the U.S. Office of Education, State entered into bilateral relationships with two black colleges.

As a result of a 1964 Rockefeller Foundation Grant, Carleton College became involved with A Better Chance (ABC), a summer program to help economically deprived 13- to 16-year-olds prepare for private secondary schools; later on Carleton recruited some of its black students and staff from among individuals in the ABC program. California State and Kansas City housed federally funded Upward Bound programs for disadvantaged high school students, and the latter institution also sponsored Talent Search and other minority-related courses and activities. Clarion, Bowling Green, and Brockport started their minority programs informally a year or two before the large influx of black students began.

Just as each of the 13 institutions had faced external pressures to increase black enrollments, each had had experiences prior to 1968 which predisposed them to support such a decision. Clearly, administrative leaders were sensitive to external changes and pressures. Although faculty and students were less involved in campus leadership, they were participating in civil rights activities on many of the campuses. Some of them were finding ways to start rudimentary programs that moved their schools into a quickened pace of involvement in civil rights at home.

SOME CONTEXTUAL CHANGES

Either immediately before or during the period of black enrollment increases, seemingly unrelated changes in institutional control, mission, student enrollment patterns, governance, and external support served either to enhance or to constrain the institutions' abilities to increase their black enrollments.

Four of them experienced a change in control during the period we examined. The University of Missouri in Kansas City, in 1963, and the University of the City, in 1965, changed from private to public status, which then set other changes in motion. Despite strong local support, Kansas City had long been underfinanced. At City as well, financial support had begun to wane. In both institutions, a prolonged struggle ensued over mission and autonomy and the top leadership changed. Kansas City became part of the University of Missouri system, while the University of the City changed to a "state supported" status. The immediate implication for increased black enrollments at both universities was lower tuition, which made them more accessible to lower income students. This accounted to some degree for the presence of a small number of black students on those campuses prior to active recruiting programs.

We have already mentioned the secularization of Metropolitan and Lewis. Formally, this meant that the boards of trustees for both schools shifted to lay status. At Metropolitan the change occurred officially in 1967. At Lewis, the shift to a lay board occurred in 1971. The immediate impact of secularization at Lewis and at Metropolitan was reflected in changes in both leadership and mission.

Changes in Institutional Mission

Eight of the institutions in our sample experienced a variety of changes in mission which then led to other changes having an impact on the recruitment of black students. California, Clarion, Bowling Green, and SUNY-Brockport—all former state teachers colleges—had each experienced rapid growth during the 1960s and expanded their offerings well beyond the traditional teacher education programs. As institutions located in small communities and counties with no substantial black populations, their transformations were accompanied by close examinations of their potential regions of service; in each case, these included areas with black populations. California and Clarion looked to Pittsburgh where there were no public four-year institutions. Bowling Green looked to northwest Ohio, Toledo particularly. Brockport, an aspiring university center in the new SUNY system, is near Rochester which did not have a public four-year institution.

Such expansion also meant the addition of new young faculty open to new ideas, programs, and student clienteles. Thus, for each of the four institutions a change in mission from teacher's college to general liberal arts college meant growth in the range of programs, a wider service area which included cities with black populations, and the addition of more cosmopolitan, often more liberal faculty.

Mission struggles at Kansas City and at the University of the City had similar elements. Attempts to resolve the question of autonomy and to develop an institutional master plan at Kansas City were only minimally successful during the period from 1963 to 1968. However, as a result of a change of leadership in 1968 and the gradual dissolution of older problems, the institution created a master plan coordinating the traditional arts and sciences college and several professional schools. However, a liberal education philosophy still predominated in the College of Arts and Sciences, a focus that was often strained by professional programs and by the urban, commuting nature of the student body. The mission struggle at City revolved around the conflict between its earlier identity as a prestigious national university and the pressure to respond to more local needs. It is clear that after a period of acting chancellors, the University of the City—like Kansas City—selected a chancellor whose primary role has been to move the institution to a clearer definition of itself as an urban institution. This has been reflected in changes in administrative leadership at both the executive and deanship levels, by the development of numerous programs for new student groups (not just black undergraduates), and by the addition of a large number of minority faculty. Both Kansas City and City have extensive continuing education and in-service programs. Thus, two former private institutions with high academic aspirations, not very attuned to their immediate surroundings, were in the process of redefining their purposes and programs in a way that made them more attractive to local students and more sensitive to local needs.

Lewis and Bradley are private institutions that changed their missions after having made some effort to increase black enrollments. Both institutions experienced enrollment declines in the late 1960s, a year or two before the general decline began in private institutions in Illinois and in the Midwest. The enrollment declines and accompanying secularization at Lewis led the institution, under its new president, to reject the traditional liberal arts program and become a "communiversity"—an institution dedicated to serve its community. In 1971, Lewis became coeducational and added the College of Continuing Education. Later years saw the addition of several other new units, a major academic/administrative reorganization, and a large influx of new funds. Enrollments began to increase substantially at the same time that enrollments in most non-elite private institutions were beginning to decline. With a relatively open admissions policy, financial aid programs, and the new emphasis on career curricula, Lewis became more attractive to blacks.

Bradley, on the other hand, responded to its enrollment declines by engaging in a thorough self-appraisal. The enrollment declines brought into question the proliferation of programs that had occurred in the more affluent early and mid-1960s. In 1970–71, an institutional self-study was undertaken, an administrative planning team was established to look at institutional goals and administrative structures, an ad hoc committee on faculty exigencies was formed, and a coordinated series of small group meetings involving all administrators and faculty was initiated; these efforts eventually led to a drastic administrative reorganization.

While Lewis's redirection and new growth enhanced its ability to attract blacks, such was not the case at Bradley. Clearly, Bradley's redirection and cutbacks hindered the expansion of embryonic black-related programs, and the experience at Bradley was a precursor of things to come at other institutions.

Shifting Student Body Patterns

The most pronounced institutional changes in student body patterns were declining enrollments. California State, Metropolitan University, Lewis University, and Bradley all experienced early enrollment declines. Enrollment declines began at Macalester after 1970.

Another key change in the student bodies was their increasingly local origins. This was particularly striking at Metropolitan, as well as at Kansas City and City. At Metropolitan, this pattern began in the late 1960s just when the local pool of students began to be drawn to the burgeoning community colleges and state university branches. At Kansas City and City, the increasingly local origins of the student bodies merely underlined the need for a more local focusing of mission—a circular and reinforcing set of pressures which tended to move the institutions more in consonance with the concerns of blacks and minorities living in the surrounding communities.

OVERALL PATTERNS OF CONTEXTUAL CHANGE

Tracing causal patterns in institutional histories is difficult. Yet the general changes experienced by these institutions do reflect several overall patterns. The first are those triggered by changes of control. The similar experiences of the University of the City, the University of Missouri–Kansas City, Metropolitan University and Lewis University are an example of one type of pattern. The shift from private to public control in the first two institutions led to a shift in mission which eventually transformed them into institutions with purposes and programs more attuned to their locales. At Metropolitan and Lewis, secularization was tied to other changes, such as overall enrollment declines, which in turn made the institutions more accessible and attractive to black students.

A second pattern revolves around declining enrollments at private, nonprestigious institutions like Bradley and Lewis. At each of these schools, the decline led to a re-evaluation of its mission. As a small private institution, Lewis's evaluation involved secularization, a change of leadership, and reorganization. The result was a new and wider view of the institution as directed toward the range of potential students in its region—a revision of mission that laid the groundwork for increased black enrollments. At Bradley, the self-evaluation precipitated by enrollment declines led to changes in administrative leadership, a refocusing of mission, and a reduction of staff—changes that were not directed at increasing black enrollments. Yet increasing numbers of black students continued to enroll while total enrollments declined.

The experiences of the state colleges—Bowling Green, Brockport, California, and Clarion—form a third pattern. The shift from teacher education to a liberal arts focus and growth during the 1960s led to expansions in course offerings, in staffing, and in definition of service regions which together facilitated the increase in black enrollments.

The prestigious institutions—Carleton, Macalester, State, and

Northwestern—showed few institutional changes that might have affected their capacities to increase black enrollments. Rather, a general climate of concern and commitment to minorities seems to have been important. A more democratic governance system at Carleton, new leadership at Macalester, concerned leadership at State, and a desire at Northwestern to eliminate its conservative image were minor institutional changes that supported attempts to increase black enrollments, although they were not as basic as the changes which occurred at the other institutions.

All 13 schools had either external environments that were supportive of increased black enrollments or favorable internal predisposing factors, sometimes both. No institution increased its black enrollments in the face of resistive internal and external forces, although clearly some had greater obstacles to overcome than others.

Notes

[1]Figures for black high school enrollments are better indicators but were not always available and were consistently a bit higher than the population statistics. Black family incomes in the institution's drawing region compared to white family incomes were examined as a measure of financial need. In all cases, these gross measures indicated the obvious—that family and per capita incomes were lower for blacks than for whites, showing the greater financial aid needs of black students. This, of course, negates the supportive character of the available pool, particularly at the higher cost private institutions.

[2]The practice of recruiting across state lines by public institutions produces conflicts. For example, some of the institutions said that competition from State for "good" black students in *their* regions was a negative or resistive factor for them. The issue of interstate recruiting by public institutions will probably be more controversial as budgets become tighter.

[3]One exception was California State where nearby white ethnic communities were openly hostile to the influx of black students. Negative attitudes, but no incidents of active resistance, were ascribed to "locals" in other rural or small town communities.

7

Precipitating Events and
Early Response Strategies

Marvin W. Peterson

Because the institutions in this study were in generally supportive environments and had experienced internal changes which tended
to predispose them to increase their black enrollments, it may be
instructive to look at the specific events associated with the first
attempts to enroll more black students. Table 7-1 identifies the precipitating events at each of the institutions, the parties involved in
them, and some initial results. The table provides some sense of
whether the events leading to formal attempts to increase black enrollments were internal (initiated by faculty or administrators), external, or a combination of the two.

It is clear that at Bowling Green, SUNY–Brockport, Carleton, the
University of Missouri–Kansas City, Macalester, "Metropolitan University," Northwestern, and "State University," the precipitating
events were initiated within the institutions. At California, Clarion,
and Lewis, they were external. However, at the "University of the
City" the precipitating events appeared to be both internally and
externally generated. Bradley—not included in Table 7-1 because it
had no formal recruitment activity—had also been subject to both
internal and external pressures.

The institutions' response strategies during the first year following the formal efforts to recruit blacks are summarized in Table 7-2.

TABLE 7-1

Events Precipitating First Formal Black Recruitment

Institution	Precipitating Events	Parties Involved	Immediate Result	Date of First Especially Recruited Black Group	Documented Largest % Black Increase	First Institutional Conflict
Bowling Green	Student Development Program; informal plans (Spring 1968)	VP student affairs	Student Development program (Fall 1968)	Fall 1968	1970–72	April 1975
SUNY-Brockport	Sought disadvantaged students (1966, 1967)	Director of admissions; president	Summer Start (Summer 1967–68)	None	1970–72	October 1969
California	Spring and Fall 1969 Pressures	President Roadman, BLACS demands on State Board of Education (HEW desegregation order)	Student Incentive Programs (Summer 1969)	Fall 1969	1968–70	March 1969
Carleton	Institutional activities and King assassination (Spring 1968)	Retiring president, Committee on Negro Affairs	Institutional Commitment (Spring 1968)	Fall 1968	1968–70	None
"University of the City"	Reports, recommendations, and demands after King assassination (May 1968)	Administration, University Committee on Racism Report, BAS demands	"Project X" and CEP (Summer 1968)	Fall 1968	1968–70	May 1968
Clarion	Design of recruitment drive (1969–70)	Acting president, black students	Educational Opportunity Program, later Student Development Program (Fall 1970)	Fall 1970	1970–72	1969

TABLE 7-1 continued

Institution	Precipitating Events	Parties Involved	Immediate Result	Date of First Especially Recruited Black Group	Documented Largest % Black Increase	First Institutional Conflict
Kansas City	Transitional Year Proposal (Spring 1968)	State Grant Program, some faculty, assistant dean, Continuing Education staff	Transitional Year Program (Fall 1968)	Fall 1968	1968–70	None
Lewis	OCR Review (Spring 1968–69)	OCR staff, president, other administrators	Recruitment effort (Spring 1969)	Fall 1969	1968–70	Fall 1969
Macalester	President Flemming's arrival (Summer 1968)	President Flemming, President of Student Community Council, Dean of Student's Ad Hoc Group, faculty, & trustees	Institutional approval of EEO (January 1969)	Fall 1969	1969–71	1970
"Metropolitan University"	Planning Collegiate Help Program (1967–68)	President, academic vice president, Ford Grant	Collegiate Help Program, (Fall 1968)	Fall 1968	1968–70	April 1969
Northwestern	Wieboldt Grant (Early 1966)	Admissions & financial aid, administration, dean, others	Recruitment (1966)	Fall 1966	1970–72	April 1968
"State University"	M.L. King Convocation (Spring 1968)	President Tyrone, Human Rights Committee, Student Senate Report	Formal institutional commitment, (Fall 1968)	Fall 1968	1970–72	None

TABLE 7-2

First Year Response Strategies

Institution	Enrollment Goal or Target	Recruitment	Identifiable Plan for Black/Minority Programs				Review of Plans by Regular Governance Structure	Evaluation Plan
			Admissions & Selection	Financial Aid	Support Services	Academic Program		
Bowling Green	no	informal	informal	no	informal	no	no	no
Bradley	no	informal	no	no	no	yes	no	no
SUNY-Brockport	unclear	yes	yes	informal	yes	no	no	no
California	no	yes	informal	informal	yes	no	no	no
Carleton	yes	yes	yes	yes	informal	yes	yes	no
"University of the City"	yes	yes	yes	yes	informal	informal	partial	no
Clarion	no	yes	informal	informal	yes	no	no	no
University of Missouri-Kansas City	no	informal*	informal	yes	yes	no	no	no
Lewis	no	yes	no	no	yes	no	no	no
Macalester	yes	yes	yes	yes	yes	informal	yes	yes
"Metropolitan"	unclear	yes	informal	yes	yes	no	no	no
Northwestern	unclear	yes	informal	yes	informal	no	no	no
"State University"	yes	yes	yes	yes	yes	yes	yes	no

Note: It should be emphasized that these are the *initial* response strategies (i.e., in first year following the formal initiating of black recruitment activities) and not the current situation.

*Recruitment in a formal sense is not allowed in the University of Missouri system.

The table indicates the extent to which each institution had developed a planned response strategy by the end of that first year. We have chosen to define "a planned response strategy" as the formal initiation, or the formal recognition by the institution, of at least one of four elements:

1. Aside from attempting to increase black enrollments, was an explicit goal or target established?
2. Were identifiable programs focusing on blacks initiated or formally anticipated in any of five areas: recruiting, admissions, and selection, financial aid, supportive services, or academic programming?
3. Was there formal review and approval of the black enrollment increase and related programs by a regular institutional governance body or process?
4. Was there a plan to evaluate the impact of the change in enrollment patterns or activities related to them?

As Table 7-2 reveals, four institutions—Carleton, Macalester, and State University, followed closely by the University of the City—were involved in substantial formal planning during the year following the first attempts to increase black enrollments; they all established enrollment goals, developed plans for renewal programs, and reviewed those goals and plans in their regular governance processes. Six institutions—Brockport, California, Clarion, Kansas City, Metropolitan, and Northwestern—made considerable efforts to formalize programs during the first year but were less concerned with goals and governance reviews of the plans. Bowling Green, Bradley, and Lewis made the fewest attempts to go beyond their initial recruitment efforts during the first year.

When we consider whether the precipitating forces for increased black enrollments were primarily *internal* or *external,* together with whether the first year's response strategy was *planned* or *unplanned,* we can identify four general patterns of response to black enrollment issues:

Adaptive: The efforts to increase black enrollments were primarily generated by parties within the institution and the planning elements and minority programs were generally anticipated or begun during the first year.

Responsive: The efforts to increase black enrollments were primarily generated by parties within the institution and planning and minority programs were undertaken but they were generally not anticipated or begun during the first year.

Reactive: The efforts to increase black enrollments were primarily generated or mandated from outside the institution and the planning elements and minority programs were generally anticipated or begun within the first year.

Evolutionary: The efforts to increase black enrollments were primarily generated or mandated from outside the institution and planning and programs were undertaken but they were generally not anticipated or begun within the first year.

Each of the 13 institutions can be categorized according to one of these four patterns (Figure 7-1).

Two other possible strategies were not reflected in this study—although if our sample had included institutions which had not increased their black enrollments during this period, we most likely would have witnessed such strategies as well:

Proactive: There is an external mandate for increased black enrollments, but the institution succeeds in changing the external mandate.

Resistive: There is an external mandate for increased black enrollments, but the institution resists or ignores it.

THE ADAPTIVE STRATEGY:
CARLETON, MACALESTER, AND STATE UNIVERSITY

Adaptive first-year strategies were developed at Carleton, Macalester, and State University, and all had institutional predispositions and/or environments which were at least somewhat supportive of increased black enrollments (see Chapter 6), but the precipitating events on these campuses were somewhat different. At both Carleton and State University, the precipitating events coincided with Martin Luther King's assassination, which seems to have been used by major institutional actors as an opportunity for introducing proposals to recruit more black students. The Committee on Negro Affairs at Carleton, chaired by the academic dean, had been meeting throughout the preceding winter and spring and had made an extensive report which had already been accepted by the community governance council. Following the King assassination, the retiring president recommended a commitment to a goal of a 10 percent black enrollment, which the faculty endorsed. But the institution's immediate response was not merely a commitment to a goal; it also included the formalization of a black recruitment effort, the establishment of an office of minority affairs which would provide financial aid and some support

Figure 7-1

Pressures for Black Enrollment Increases and Early Response Strategies—
Four General Patterns

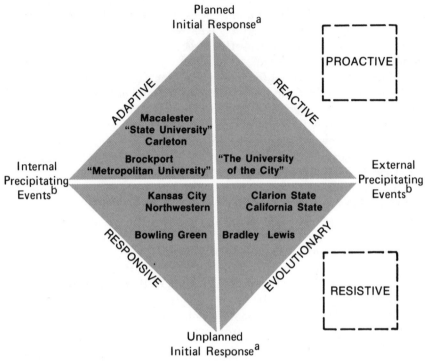

Planned
Initial Response[a]

PROACTIVE

ADAPTIVE

REACTIVE

Macalester
"State University"
Carleton

Internal
Precipitating
Events[b]

Brockport
"Metropolitan University"

"The University
of the City"

External
Precipitating
Events[b]

Kansas City
Northwestern

Clarion State
California State

RESPONSIVE

Bowling Green   Bradley Lewis

EVOLUTIONARY

RESISTIVE

Unplanned
Initial Response[a]

[a]See Table 7-2.
[b]Demands from black students during this period are defined as external pressures.

services, and an embryonic, interdisciplinary black studies program.

At State University, President Tyrone apparently drew on prior recommendations from blacks in the Student Senate, his own earlier address on the importance of equal access to higher education, and the hastily concluded efforts of the Human Rights Commission (which had spent the year studying the university's commitment to minorities) to make proposals at a convocation following Martin Luther King's assassination. He also initiated major programs for the recruitment of minorities, supportive services, financial aid, fund raising, related academic and research efforts, and increased university involvement in black-oriented service activities. Essentially, these same principles had been endorsed by the University Senate earlier in the year, although the Senate did not review the precise program proposals made at the convocation. Thus, administratively generated activities which stemmed from the ideas expressed at the convocation were immediate and far-reaching: a minority recruiter was hired (he later became the director of the support services program); the Martin Luther King Scholarship Fund was established; a Ford Foundation grant to support minority efforts was received; and a summer Afro-American Studies Institute—the precursor to the Afro-American Studies Program—was held.

Macalester's proposal for increasing black enrollments was by far the most far-reaching and comprehensive of any of those we reviewed in this study. The precipitating experience at Macalester occurred the summer after the King assassination and was associated with the arrival of a new president, Arthur Flemming. One of Flemming's primary concerns was an examination of the college's social commitment. With the support of both Flemming and the president of the Student Community Council, a preliminary proposal was drafted by an ad hoc group called together by the Dean of Students. This proposal, the "Expanded Educational Opportunities Report," not only pointed out Macalester's responsibility to develop a program to insure that students from all segments of society—including students from disadvantaged backgrounds—have an opportunity to attend the institution, it also concluded that "Macalester College badly needs those students in its student body."

Because Macalester's initial response was unique in its comprehensiveness, we have chosen to reproduce the general statement of the proposal below.

In order:
To improve the educational resources of Macalester College by expanding the diversity of the student body, faculty, and staff,

To provide opportunity for high quality liberal arts education to students who cannot attend a high tuition college,

And to enable Macalester to take a larger responsibility in the education of distinguished graduates who will play an important role in determining the destiny of our pluralistic society,

The Advisory Council of the faculty moves faculty support of a program to expand educational opportunities at Macalester College, this program to be developed and implemented by the Advisory Council in conjunction with appropriate faculty committees, academic departments, and administrative officers, and to comprise the following essential components:

1. Provision of total aid (tuition, fees, room and board) for 75 new students each year, including new students from racial minority groups.

2. Specific recruitment and admission of potentially successful students from racial minority groups and economically deprived background.

3. Enrichment of the curriculum, to broaden awareness and deepen appreciation of the contributions of diverse groups to our society and to our cultural heritage.

4. Exploitation of existing arrangements for individualized educational programs and of flexibility in present procedures for evaluation of academic performance; exploitation of needs and possibilities for greater individualization and flexibility.

5. Establishment of diagnostic and remedial programs in communications and mathematics, open to all students.

6. Full and imaginative use of the summer programs, to provide orientation to college life and compensatory educational experience for students recruited under this program and others who would benefit by them.

7. Development of a flexible individualized program of advising.

8. Improvement of co-curricular programs and development of new programs to meet the needs of students recruited under this program as well as the rest of the college community in relation to them.

9. Orientation of faculty, students, administrators, and other staff, to begin in the spring of 1969 and be available on a continuing basis throughout the year.

10. Continuous coordination and evaluation of all parts of the program.

Among the specific recommendations included in the report was the goal of enrolling 60 new students from racial minority groups, including 50 from "educationally and economically deprived" background, and 25 new white students from backgrounds of "severe economic and educational deprivation." Also recommended in the proposal were the following:

1. Separate admission evaluation process;
2. Compensatory educational programs;
3. Decreased reliance on test scores as admissions criteria;
4. Recruitment of students from a wide geographical area;
5. The addition of a minority group member to the admissions office staff;

6. The use of Macalester black students in recruiting and screening applicants;
7. A pre-admission summer program;
8. An expansion of the counseling and advising staff to work with the new students;
9. Greater flexibility in academic evaluation;
10. Tutorial and special skills program during the academic year.

The Expanded Educational Opportunities Report was approved by the college's internal governance structure; was reviewed by the Board of Trustee committees on Education, Finance, and Investment; and was finally recommended to the full Board. Up to $900,000 from the college's unrestricted funds were to be made available over a three-year period. The proposal was approved and a massive effort to implement the proposal—involving faculty, students, and staff under the coordination of the provost and the dean—began in the winter of 1969. During the following spring and summer separate staffs were established for recruiting and for administering financial aid and supportive services.

Of the 13 institutions in our study, Macalester, State, and Carleton not only had the clearest conceptions of goals or targets for their efforts and a comprehensive set of initial programs, but they also were the only institutions in which there was a wide review of the proposals by faculty and students (and, at Macalester, by the trustees as well).

The experiences of these three institutions reflect a pattern which may be typical of more prestigious institutions with basically supportive environments for social issues and strong institutional governance mechanisms. Increased minority enrollments were anticipated and their impacts were studied; programs were planned and reviewed by various governance groups; and sensitive administrative leadership acted in a timely fashion. The results of their adaptive responses were reflected in the comprehensiveness of their programs, which are described in Chapter 8.

PARTIAL ADAPTIVE:
BROCKPORT AND METROPOLITAN

The response strategies at Brockport and Metropolitan appeared to fall between the adaptive and responsive patterns. Like Macalester, State, and Carleton, these two institutions existed in supportive environments and experienced precipitating events which primarily involved internal parties, but their responses were slightly less planned.

The conception of goals for the initial black recruitment activity was less clear at Brockport and Metropolitan than at the three adaptive institutions, and neither of the two developed a plan for reviewing the proposed enrollment changes. Initial efforts related to minority concerns were entirely in administrative hands on both campuses and were not reviewed widely or favorably by other parties within the institutions. As early as 1966 and 1967, Brockport's director of admissions, with the support of the president and a few others in the institution, sought to identify small numbers of prospective students from disadvantaged backgrounds, particularly blacks in nearby Rochester. A "Summer Start" program for new students who did not meet Brockport's normal admissions standards operated informally in 1967 and was substantially formalized before the summer of 1968. This program—with its local and statewide recruitment efforts, special admissions criteria, financial aid, summer classes, and personal and academic counseling—was a precursor of later, more extensive programs and activities.

At Metropolitan University, Father Schmidt's encouragement and the support of the academic vice president were responsible for the development of a special admissions and academic support program for blacks, the Collegiate Help Program (CHP), which enrolled its first students in the fall of 1968. Ford Foundation money provided initial support for the program that was a combination of recruitment, financial aid, and academic support in a summer session and compensatory assistance during the first year. An interesting sidelight is that about a year later Father Schmidt succeeded in getting the coordinating body for the higher education institutions in the city to help recruit and support minority students during the first two years at a community college and then facilitated their transfer to four-year institutions participating in the plan, including Metropolitan.

THE RESPONSIVE STRATEGY: NORTHWESTERN, BOWLING GREEN, AND KANSAS CITY

The precipitating events at Northwestern, Bowling Green State University, and Kansas City, also predated or coincided with Martin Luther King's assassination and were internally generated. But these institutions were much less deliberate in their early planning.

Northwestern's initial lack of formal planning for increased black enrollments and related programs may have been the result of its early and gradual evolution of response to minority interests. For somewhat obscure reasons (perhaps the desire to escape charges of discrimination that had been leveled at Northwestern a decade before regarding the admission of Jewish students), as early as 1965–66 a few key administrators became concerned about the need to recruit black students. With the support of a Wieboldt Foundation Grant, Northwestern began a formal recruitment, selection, and financial aid program focused on black students. This effort was successful in bringing over 50 minority students to the institution in the fall of 1966.

In the spring of 1968, Bowling Green's black Vice President for Student Affairs encouraged a black recruitment effort through the admissions office and initiated the Student Development Program (SDP). SDP was formalized and expanded in 1970, but the first formally recruited black students arrived and received some institutional attention in the fall of 1968.

The situation at Kansas City was similar to that at Northwestern and Bowling Green. In early 1968, a small number of concerned administrators and faculty members in the College of Arts and Sciences, administrators in the Continuing Education Division (which was running inner-city programs), and one or two faculty members involved in civil rights activities created a proposal for a two-year program which sought funds from a special state grant program for disadvantaged students. The resulting Transitional Year Program (TYP) did not specifically provide for active recruitment of minorities since "recruiting" was forbidden by the University of Missouri system; nevertheless, TYP staff members—many of whom had had prior experience with the Upward Bound and Talent Search programs for high school students run by the Division of Continuing Education—spoke with students in those programs and with other black students in city high schools. The initial activities of TYP were primarily to explain the advantages of the University of Missouri–Kansas City to prospective students and to offer limited financial aid and some academic assistance. The first TYP students arrived in the fall of 1968.

These three institutions seem to have formed this *responsive* strategy when there was neither strong positive nor negative environmental pressure for change (see Chapter 6). While there was no overwhelming external mandate, a group of concerned individuals were able to generate recruitment activities and to take advantage of available resources. The absence of strong administrative support and limited resources made planning of extensive programs difficult during this early period.

THE EVOLUTIONARY STRATEGY:
CALIFORNIA, CLARION, AND LEWIS

Our typology of initial institutional response provides no examples of "proactive" institutions (i.e., ones that responded to and changed the direction of extensive demands). However, California, Clarion, and Lewis are examples of institutions whose initial black enrollment increases resulted from external precipitating forces and relatively unplanned response strategies. All three institutions had more limited financial means and were in environments which were less supportive of black enrollment increases compared to most of the other schools in our sample. Lewis had been suffering total enrollment declines in the late 1960s, and California and Clarion were in rural areas with very small black populations.

California State College received a set of demands from a black student group in March 1969. Simultaneously, the State of Pennsylvania had been given directives from HEW to desegregate its state colleges. These events, coupled with the involvement of California's president led to the establishment of the Student Incentive Program (SIP). A black director was appointed to head the program in the summer of 1969. In the fall, additional staff were added to the admissions office and the college began active recruitment activities for the first time. In addition to recruiting, the early activities of SIP were primarily in providing supportive services since state funds for "educationally and economically deprived students" did not become available until the passage of State Act 101 in August 1971.

Precipitating forces at Clarion State also began in the fall of 1969 with the HEW pressures on the State of Pennsylvania and with a state-sponsored conference on minority admissions and simultaneous requests from a small group of black students. The key institutional participant appeared to be the acting president, who responded by setting up a recruiting program focused in the state's urban centers. This campaign brought busloads of black students to visit the campus. During the 1969–70 academic year, the Office of Student Affairs and the Dean of Liberal Arts provided leadership in establishing the Educational Opportunities Program (later the Student Development Program), which was in operation when black students arrived in larger numbers in the fall of 1970 (a year before Pennsylvania's Act 101 made funds available for such activities).

At Lewis, the precipitating force seemed to be the Office of Civil Rights compliance reviews conducted in 1968 and 1969. The second review recommended the enunciation of a clear policy of equal educational opportunity, a review of recruitment efforts, the publication of a policy of "open admissions," and the development of other counseling and tutoring programs by which work toward nondiscrimination in student admissions would occur. The institution's immediate response to that review was not made clear to us, but it is apparent that in the late spring of 1969 a recruitment effort focused primarily on inner-city blacks in the Chicago area was successful in bringing a new group of students to the campus in the fall of 1969. The presence of educationally disadvantaged blacks within the predominantly low-income, white student body led to two years of chronic tension and demands from blacks. But the institution's religious heritage and declining status left the administration unprepared to cope with the blacks' demands. There were few programmatic attempts to respond to the new black students until 1971 when Lewis's control, leadership, and mission changed drastically.

California, Clarion, and Lewis each experienced an evolutionary pattern of change which may be typical of the way institutions with less able students and modest finances responded to the pressures and ideologies for equal opportunity. They initiated changes later than the other institutions in our sample—a full year after Martin Luther King's assassination. The changes on these campuses were less extensive and less planned than those in wealthier, more selective schools. One activity was introduced at a time. The responses were more dependent on legal mandates and on the availability of external funding. Decisions were primarily initiated and implemented by administrators without internal review by faculty or higher governance groups.

MIXED STRATEGIES:
THE UNIVERSITY OF THE CITY AND BRADLEY

The University of the City's initial response strategy was more complex and somewhat less focused than those of the other institutions—perhaps reflecting the reality of change in a large, complex university. By the spring of 1968, a number of parties were concerned with the institution's response to minority issues and causes. A sequence of events that shaped the university's initial response occurred in the month and a half following Martin Luther King's assassination. Chancellor Varden had made an early university address on social justice, he had been aware of the extensive civil rights activities in the city during that year, and he had had many conversations with black leaders and community groups during the 1967–68 academic year. As a result he began to encourage the development of a program to recruit minority students. Initially, the chancellor, the provost, and a few other administrators met to formulate "Project X," a plan which used the assistance of community leaders in recruiting 50 minority students who were to enter the institution in the fall of 1968 on an "experimental" basis.

All persons involved said the plan represented a commitment by the administration to a direction, but that it lacked a clear notion of form or program content. In May 1968, a newly formed student group, the Black Action Society (BAS), presented the chancellor with a list of demands, including official recognition of BAS as the representative of black students, BAS involvement in Project X, and a goal of 20 percent black enrollment. Shortly thereafter, the University Committee on Racism, appointed earlier by Chancellor Varden, delivered its report stressing abandonment of certain intelligence tests for minorities, cooperation with BAS on recruiting and admissions, the use of faculty as counselors to black students, and an examination of the curriculum in terms of its relevance to black culture. With this kind of support for active measures, the administration pressed forward in the spring and summer of 1968 with Project X and also hired one of the community's black leaders as director of the new Office of Community Education Programs (CEP). This office, reporting to the provost, was the first base for Project X and other new programs which were begun during the following year or two.

Thus, in the fall of 1968, 50 minority students (primarily blacks) who did not meet regular admissions standards entered the university and were given financial aid and some academic support. The program was the focus of much criticism by black students during the initial year, as was the institution in general. Indeed, a major confrontation in January 1969 involving a black student occupation of the computing center was a crucial event during the 1968–69 academic year and was an example of the constant pressure from black students to expand black and minority-oriented programs of all kinds. By the fall of 1969, there were three minority programs under CEP and a black studies program was beginning.

This brief review suggests the combination of internal pressures (primarily from administrators, with some faculty involvement) and external pressures (from community leaders and students) for the initiation of activities to increase black enrollments at City. While

142   BLACK STUDENTS ON WHITE CAMPUSES

the programs were not planned in a formal sense, the institution did respond to the various political demands and pressures and, within the first year, had begun a diverse set of programs and activities. Top administrative support for the new programs was strong. Faculty were involved early but only indirectly—for example, by encouraging the institution in the general direction of increased black enrollments through the report of the Committee on Racism; faculty were not involved in any substantial way in reviewing or developing the specific programs. There was no plan for evaluation of programs. This became a point of contention in 1974. Thus, City represents an institution whose initiating parties for this change were clearly both internal and external and whose strategy was both anticipatory and more gradually responsive. But its resources and administrative commitment were comprehensive enough to make the response appear more planned than unplanned.

Like City, Bradley developed mixed strategies—but at the other extreme. Although Bradley made no special or formal attempts to recruit black students, the institution's black enrollments increased steadily from 1968 through 1974 both in terms of numbers and percentage of the student body. A variety of factors seemed to account for this increase, including the presence of blacks on its basketball teams in the 1950s and 1960s, the efforts of an early black faculty member, the establishment of a scholarship program for black students, and informal recruitment efforts by individual faculty members involved in civil rights activism. A series of black student confrontations and conflicts in 1968 and 1969 kept the institution visible to blacks. In a reorganization at Bradley following its general enrollment decline, an intensified recruitment program in 1970–71 attracted more inner-city high school students. The presence of a state student aid program based on need, along with federal student aid funds, also meant that low-income students could attend a private, semi-urban institution with a reasonable reputation for giving attention to students as individuals.

Thus, both internal and external parties informally supported the black enrollment increase at Bradley, and the institution's responses were generally unplanned. Limited resources and a lack of strong institutional leadership in this area prevented the more substantial program development that the enrollment increase might have implied. Bradley's stance of "nondiscrimination" was reflected in a pattern that was somewhere between *responsive* and *evolutionary,* and the institution's past image and a varied set of continuing pressures and events continue to support increases in black enrollments.

ADDITIONAL INSIGHTS

A few other conclusions can be drawn from an overview of the specific precipitating events and institutional response strategies on the 13 campuses. First, the institutions differed in the timing of their initial efforts to recruit blacks. While several of the precipitating events on six of the campuses—Bowling Green, Carleton, State University, Kansas City, Macalester, and the University of the City— occurred during the spring or summer immediately after the Martin Luther King assassination, only Carleton and State responded to the news of the assassination by immediately launching major new activities to benefit blacks. At these six institutions and at four others—Bradley, Brockport, Northwestern, and Metropolitan—the precipitating events occurred or began prior to this tumultuous event. The more rural institutions with less academically able students— Lewis, California, Clarion, and State—seemed less affected by the civil rights era or by the King assassination. This pattern of timing also suggests another important dynamic: at those institutions whose recruitment and response activities started earlier, these activities were more likely to have been generated internally.

The role played by outside funding sources in precipitating institutional action is another important element in these stories. Without exception, all the private institutions—Bradley, Carleton, Macalester, Northwestern, and Metropolitan—turned to and received outside foundation funds to support their initial efforts. Among the public institutions, only State University sought and received outside foundation funds during its initial planning. Other public institutions—Kansas City, and Clarion and California at a later date— received state grants to begin their recruitment and response programs. While almost all of the institutions relied to some extent on internal institutional funds to generate recruitment and early response activities, this was less true among the public institutions. In the private sector, Macalester made a commitment to use a sizable amount of endowment, but this later caused problems for the institution. Federal student aid funds were relied upon at most of the institutions if they were available. Lewis and Bradley, both private institutions, benefited from the combination of state and federal student aid—a combination that the other private and public institutions in our sample did not have, at least until much later.

Conflict with black groups and demands, which is discussed later on, played a clear role in precipitating initial minority recruitment efforts only at California, City, and possibly Clarion. This is not to say that other institutions did not experience conflicts and demands that centered on black recruitment and enrollment issues; however, conflicts between the institutions and black students were not a crucial precipitating factor because they came later after black students had already been recruited. As we shall see, conflict served a variety of purposes later on, including keeping up the pressure to increase black enrollments.

The parties involved in the precipitating events indicate some of the early dynamics of white institutions' responses to black students. Administrators predominated in these events: the presidents were directly involved at Brockport, California, Carleton, Clarion, State, Lewis, Macalester, City, and Metropolitan; academic vice presidents or deans played key roles at City and at Northwestern. Also crucially involved in the early events were the student affairs vice president at Bowling Green and a dean at Macalester, the admissions directors at Brockport and Northwestern, and an assistant dean and the Continuing Education staff at Kansas City.

Aside from the involvement of particular individuals, the faculties did not play a major role in these events. Only at Carleton and State did faculty members play some initiating roles on committees, although several faculty members were involved informally as individuals at Bradley and at Kansas City. Faculty bodies actually reviewed or approved proposals only at Carleton, State, and Macalester. To some extent, students played key roles in the conflict situations at California, Clarion, and City and also in formulating recommendations at State, Macalester, and Carleton. Black students and staff were among the initiating parties at six of the institutions: City, Bowling Green, Macalester, California, Clarion, and State.

The patterns of participation in the precipitating events tell a great deal about institutional style. Carleton, State, and Macalester were the only schools with extensive student and faculty involvement. Enrollment increases and response programs were discussed widely, and internal review of decisions by nonadministrative governance bodies was *de rigueur*. Collegial or community decision making and attention to wide commitment was consistent with the academic culture at these three selective institutions. While at most of the remaining institutions administrators dominated the initial discussion and implementation of programs, the University of the City deserves a special note. Its style in dealing with black minority recruitment and initial programs involved several parties. A variety of demands and high levels of controversy were exhibited in the 1967–69 period. Never enough to prevent implementation of major recruitment activities or programs but always keeping them highly visible, this political style was a precursor to the pattern of later minority events at that institution and seems to reflect its governance style on other issues as well.

Planning for this important social change—even in these specially selected institutions—was evidently limited. Anticipatory or planned responses which predated black enrollment increases were extremely limited. Explicit statements of enrollment goals and anticipated programs were apparent in only the three adaptive institutions—Macalester, State, and Carleton. There were conflicting reports about the existence of initial goals at Brockport, Northwestern, and Metropolitan. A substantial range of programs focused on blacks or minorities in selection, financial aid, supportive services, and academic programming—but these occurred in the year after the recruitment effort began. Only Macalester foresaw at the beginning the need to plan an evaluation of its critical new institutional direction. Another element of planning, an initial assessment of resource implications or needs, was totally absent from the discussions at all of the 13 institutions in the first year of their commitments to minorities. Macalester did provide substantial institutional funds; others launched fund drives or sought new external sources, and some even added new staff immediately. But no serious assessment of human, physical, or financial resource needs for this new direction was attempted. This is not surprising, for the late 1960s was not a time when serious planning efforts were undertaken. In higher education generally, financial and enrollment crises were only beginning. Colleges and universities made commitments to a direction or cause either because they were "right" or because they were "mandated." It was assumed that resources would continue to be available for higher education as they had been throughout the decade. And there was a naive confidence that the adjustments to the enrollment change would be relatively painless.

8

Conflict Dynamics of Institutional Response

Marvin W. Peterson

THE ROLE OF CONFLICT

The impact of the civil rights movement was more extensive and troublesome on the 13 campuses than any of the institutions had anticipated. Although many of them did have some prior experience with civil rights activism, as described in Chapters 6 and 7, it was primarily an off-campus issue before 1968. Liberal administrators, faculty, and students were often emotionally committed to advancing equality for blacks and to opening their campuses to greater numbers of black students. However, many of these individuals admitted in interviews that they had failed to anticipate that others in their institution might not remain as deeply committed as they were after the emotions following the King assassination had subsided. Nor did they expect that their own "good faith" gestures might be perceived by black students as untrustworthy or inadequate. Because blacks did not always adhere to nonviolent tactics, even those individuals who were early initiators or supporters of increased black student enrollments admitted that they had difficulty supporting the demands of black separatists and militants. They were ready for increased black enrollments and new minority-oriented programs, but they were not prepared for the political process which almost inevitably followed.

Several factors contributed to setting the stage for many of the early conflicts. One was the presence on each campus of a "critical mass" of about 50 black students who provided the nucleus for a student group in which blacks could share concerns and support mutual interests and demands. A second was the existence of a special recruitment effort and an at least embryonic supportive service activity which served as a center of activity for the new group of black students. An organizational base combined with a critical number of supporters was often reinforced by the social distance between new black students and other sectors of the institution. Except at Carleton and "State University," early recruitment efforts were not selective or well-focused. There was a common assumption that if admissions requirements were eliminated or softened, the moral commitment to equality would be fulfilled. But the new students often did not "fit" the institutions' expectations in academic preparation, financial means, social interests, or cultural styles. It is not surprising that black students felt alien to their new campuses and sought friendly faces and a supportive center of activity. Such conditions were an ideal spawning ground for the Black Power movement which had already influenced the young black students recruited between 1969 and 1971. In retrospect, the emergence on each campus of politically oriented black student groups seems to have been inevitable.

THE EARLY INCIDENCE AND FOCUS OF CONFLICT

Table 8-1 identifies the major conflicts involving blacks on each of the 13 campuses in which clear sets of demands were presented by blacks and the institutions gave formal recognition to the demands. Table 8-2 summarizes the incidence of on-campus conflicts and the associated demands and responses. The conflict incidents began to occur after the very first attempts to increase black enrollments. The events were also quite telescoped in time: 20 of 24 incidents occurred between the spring of 1968 and the summer of 1971. Only Bradley experienced a conflict prior to this period, and it focused on an external issue (the hiring practices of construction firms working on campus). Later conflict incidents at Lewis, Macalester, and "the University of the City" all occurred in the fall of 1974. Between 1968 and 1971, all the demands were concerned with the need for new programs or services. Conflicts after that time were more likely to be directed toward protecting earlier gains and preserving the autonomy of black programs.

The number and intensity of conflict incidents are indicators of the degree of impact of increased black enrollments. Only two institutions, Carleton and the University of Missouri–Kansas City, avoided any notable incidents. At Carleton, this may be explained by the college's well-planned program that included recruiting blacks with good academic preparation, the availability of adequate financial aid, and a review by a community governance decision-making system that apparently enhanced the commitment of both students and faculty to the enrollment increase. The Kansas City situation seems to be explained by the fact that it had a primarily non-residential, commuting student body in which it was extremely difficult to coalesce active student pressure groups, black or white. Eight of the institutions experienced a major conflict and seven experienced more than one. Even Macalester and State University, which had the most adaptive initial increase strategies and the most comprehensive programs, had major incidents. Some of the underlying reasons for conflict are discussed later; it is clear that the large number of incidents (24 at 11 institutions) and the severity of conflict (22 incidents were major) were two of the virtually unavoidable impacts of bringing in more black students.

The types of demands presented during these conflicts (Table 8-2) indicate the ways in which the institutions were being asked to respond. On the 11 campuses which experienced conflict incidents, a total of 72 demands relating to a variety of issues were presented, including 31 demands involving black-oriented activities or programs for increasing black enrollments, improved financial aid, supportive services, black studies, and black cultural facilities and activities.

The most common program demands were for black studies (10) and black cultural programs (5), indicating that these were areas in which the institutions were slowest to respond. Demands for increased black enrollments (9) all followed initial institutional recruitment efforts and spurred expansion of those efforts. That financial aid (2 demands) and supportive services (5 demands) were the two least common focuses of demands may reflect the fact that these were already viewed by the institutions as necessary areas for which external funds were more readily available.

Ten demands were focused on increasing black faculty and staff. Interestingly, these were not associated with affirmative action regulations since eight of the ten occurred prior to Executive Order 11246.

TABLE 8-1

Institution-Black Conflicts: Parties, Tactics, and Outcomes

Institution	Date and Focus	Parties	Tactics	Immediate Outcome
Bowling Green	Spring 1970 "Kent State"	1. Black Student Union 2. White students 3. Black faculty 4. VP Student Affairs 5. Other administrators 6. City officials	Demands to refocus Kent State disruptions on black issues. Demands negotiated.	Formal agreement with administration on most demands. Implicit faculty and trustee support.
Bradley	Fall 1968 "Union Discrimination"	1. Black Student Assoc. 2. Students for a Democratic Society 3. Faculty member 4. Other administrators 5. City police	Occupation of construction site. "Planned arrests."	Confrontation avoided. University established Special Building Committee. Administrators, faculty, and students reviewed contract and compliance.
	Spring 1969 "Black Demands"	1. Black Student Assoc. 2. Faculty members 3. Various administrators	Intense negotiations.	Agreement on several demands.
	Spring 1970 "Tuition Increase"	1. Black & white students 2. Administrators 3. City police 4. Trustees	Library takeover.	Damage costs assessed and disciplinary action taken.
SUNY-Brockport	Fall 1969 "Residence Hall and Black Demands"	1. Black Student Liberation Front 2. President	Formal presentation of demands & official response in two months.	President wrote public letter of response to each demand.
	Winter 1970 "Black Demands"	1. Black Student Liberation Front	Meetings to discuss demands, some intimidation	Further agreements and additional movement,

TABLE 8-1 continued

Institution	Date and Focus	Parties	Tactics	Immediate Outcome
		2. White faculty 3. President 4. Other administrators	and physical damage.	as in earlier efforts.
	Spring 1970 "Cambodia" and "Afro-America Center Fire"	1. White students 2. Black Student Liberation Front 3. Administrators	Focus on black issues, not Cambodia. Initial Student Center occupation and strike resistance.	Political coalition of BSLF issues in general student strike and joint participation in demands and strike.
California State	Spring 1969 "Black Demands"	1. Black League of Afro-Americans of California State 2. President	Presentation of demands.	Agreement to consider them.
	1970–71 "Black Athletes"	1. Black athletes 2. Coaching staff 3. Other administrators	Confrontation and disruptions.	Agreement to hire black assistant coach.
	1970–71 "Shooting Incident"	1. Black athletes 2. Local citizens 3. Administrators 4. City authorities	Blacks report incident. On- and off-campus incidents.	Investigation by authorities.
"University of the City"	Spring 1968 "Black Demands"	1. Black Action Society 2. Chancellor 3. Other administrators	Presentation of demands and threats.	Informal agreement to move in number of areas (some already started, others new).
	January 1969 "Black Demands"	1. Black Action Society, Black Panthers, and other black students 2. Chancellor 3. Students for a Democratic Society	Presentation of demands, occupation of Computer Center, and negotiation. Potential of police intervention.	Signed agreement by Chancellor.

TABLE 8-1 continued

Institution	Date and Focus	Parties	Tactics	Immediate Outcome
		4. Local community blacks 5. Other administrators		
	1970–71 "Black Demands"	1. Black athletes 2. Athletic staff 3. Other administrators	Presentation of demands, sit-in, negotiations.	Informal agreement and addition of black athletic staff member.
	Fall 1974 "Black Studies"	1. Acting director of Black Studies 2. Black Studies staff 3. Black students 4. Chancellor & Provost 5. Other administrators	Demands and confrontation.	Hiring of black studies director.
Clarion State	Fall 1969 "Recruitment" (minor incident)	1. Black student group 2. Acting president	Blacks request meeting and urge recruitment.	Recruitment program established.
Lewis	Winter 1969 "Black Demands" (minor incident)	1. Black Student Union 2. President	Presentation of demands.	Unclear, some changes forthcoming.
	Spring 1971 "Black Demands"	1. Black Student Union 2. President 3. Other administrators	"Sit-in" in student lounge.	Series of presidential commitments.
	Fall 1974 "Black Demands"	1. Black Student Union 2. President 3. Trustees 4. Other administrators	Presentation of demands.	Meeting of black students with Board committee.
Macalester	Fall 1974 "Budget Cuts"	1. Equal Educational Opportunity students and some white students 2. President 3. Other administrators	Faculty blocked from leaving chapel meeting. Demands for open review. Later occupation of Administration Building.	"Binding" agreement restoring some budget cuts signed by President and presented mutually at public press conference.

TABLE 8-1 continued

Institution	Date and Focus	Parties	Tactics	Immediate Outcome
		4. Trustees 5. Faculty 6. Civil rights groups 7. Outside negotiator	Demands, discussions, eventual negotiations, and external mediation.	
"Metropolitan University"	Spring 1969 "Black Demands"	1. Black students 2. Executive Vice President and Dean 3. Executive Committee of University Council 4. Student Council president (White)	Demands, sit-in, and negotiations.	Agreement to act on issues.
	Spring 1970 "Kent State" "Black Demands"	1. Director of Collegiate Help Program 2. Black students 3. President 4. Executive officers 5. Other black students & faculty 6. Outside negotiator	Assertion of black demands, not just Kent State, meeting take-overs, strike, sit-ins, isolated violence, negotiations, external mediation.	Future agreements and creation of new vice presidency.
Northwestern	Spring 1968 "Black Demands"	1. Black students 2. Executive officers (not president) 3. Black professor 4. Chicago Black group 5. Concerned trustees 6. City authorities	Demands, building occupation, and negotiations. Potential of police intervention.	Negotiated agreement signed by administration and endorsed in part by Trustees.
"State University"	Spring 1969 "Athletics"	1. Black athletes 2. Coaches 3. Other black students 4. President	Confrontation and revolt.	Presidential commission appointed to investigate.
	1970–71 "Discrimination Reports"	1. Black students 2. White students 3. President 4. Other administrators	Numerous conflicts, incidents, and demands.	Presidential commission appointed to investigate.

TABLE 8-2

Institutional Black Conflicts: Documented Demands and Responses*

Institution	Date of Conflict	Black Student Organization				Institutional Black Program					Staffing			Other Issues					
		Recognition	Information Control	Program Involvement	Miscellaneous*	Enrollment & Recruitment	Financial Aid	Supportive Services	Black Studies	Cultural Facilities or Activities	Black Faculty Recruitment	Black Staff Recruitment	White Staff †	Housing (On-Campus)	Social Space	Athletics	Black Holidays	Discrimination (Off-Campus)‡	Miscellaneous §
Bowling Green	Spring 1970			X	X	X	X	X	X	X	X	X	X			X		X	
Bradley University	Fall 1968								X	X	X							X	
	Spring 1969																	X	
	Spring 1970											X			X				
SUNY–Brockport	Fall 1969					X		X	X					X					
	Winter 1970					X		X	X										
	Spring 1970					X				X									
California State	Spring 1969	X		X		X													
	1970–71															X			
	1970–71																X		
Carleton College	None																		
"University of the City"	Spring 1968	X	X	X		X													
	Winter 1969		X	X					X	X		X	X						
	1970–71								X				X			X	X		
Clarion State	Fall 1974					X													
Lewis University	Fall 1969									X		X							X
	Winter 1969								X										
	Spring 1971								X										
	Fall 1974													X					

TABLE 8-2 continued

Institution	Date of Conflict	Black Student Organization				Institutional Black Program					Staffing			Other Issues					
		Recognition	Information Control	Program Involvement	Miscellaneous*	Enrollment & Recruitment	Financial Aid	Supportive Services	Black Studies	Cultural Facilities or Activities	Black Faculty Recruitment	Black Staff Recruitment	White Staff †	Housing (On-Campus)	Social Space	Athletics	Black Holidays	Discrimination (Off-Campus)‡	Miscellaneous §
Macalester	Fall 1974	X				x		X	X			X	X						xx
"Metropolitan University"	Spring 1969						x					X	X						
University of Missouri-Kansas City	May 1970											X							
Northwestern	None																		
"State University"	Spring 1968					X		X	X		x			X					
	Spring 1969													X		X			
	1970-71																		
22 Major Incidents		10 Demands / 5 Responses				31 Demands / 24 Responses					14 Demands / 12 Responses			17 Demands / 12 Responses					

Total Documented Demands: 72
Total Documented Responses: 53

2 Minor Incidents (many undocumented minor incidents were also reported)

Note: *Major incident* involves a documented set of demands and either physical violence, building or office occupation, or substantial disruption of regular activity. *Minor incident* involves a clear set of demands and formal acknowledgement of them. Major incidents occurred at eight institutions, minor incidents occurred at one institution, and two institutions reported no incidents at all. A *documented demand* is indicated by x. A *response*, X, includes either an official promise to act or action that occurred *after* demand.
*Includes (1) grievance procedure for black students following conflict, (2) recognition of funds for black student organization (these were informal, often continuing, issues on several campuses).
†Related to campus police issues.
‡Includes housing (Bowling Green); construction (Bradley); interracial dating (California).
§Includes tuition increase (Bradley); budget reduction (Bradley); affirmative action (Macalester); black program evaluation policy ("University of the City").

The two which occurred later were also not affirmative action issues. Indeed, affirmative action was the focus of only one demand—at Macalester in the fall of 1974. Four instances involving demands focused on white staff resulted from incidents between black students and campus police.

Nine demands were related to black student organizations: the issue of recognition for a primary black student organization (three demands) and the availability of institutional funds for the organization (one demand) was a serious issue on most campuses but was most often a continuous informal concern rather than a clear demand promulgated during an incident of conflict. Black student involvement in and control of black programs was a demand on five occasions. Finally, the 17 "other issues" were primarily related to student interracial questions—demands for separate housing or social facilities and for off-campus housing; specific complaints about discriminatory treatment in athletics; and demands dealing with campus policy on interracial dating. In sum, few areas of college and university life were ignored by this new group of black students.

On the response side, for 53 of the 72 demands we were able to identify specific institutional responses during or shortly after the conflicts—a rather high proportion. Many responses, of course, were merely promises or minor changes. But on the whole, it appears that conflict did elicit institutional responses, even though the responses may not have been adequate from the blacks' point of view. One reason that responses were not always viewed as sufficient or effective is that in every conflict incident the demands were addressed to administrators. These were individuals who were able to make an official response; however, they were often unable to deliver on the agreement—particularly when it necessitated faculty response.

THE DYNAMICS OF INSTITUTIONAL CONFLICT

The motives behind institutional conflict on each campus were confusing and complex, even in the eyes of the actors. Young, politically active blacks on the campuses saw causes and issues everywhere. Perhaps for this reason, there was little connection between the incidences of conflict and the initial institutional strategies for the black enrollment increases. Nor does it seem that the specific events which triggered the eruptions were of great consequence. In retrospect, conflicts in those early years seem to have been inevitable since demands almost always were extended well beyond an initiating incident.

The early conflicts indicated perhaps most of all that black students intended to be recognized, to stay, and to become part of the institution. Although particular demands and styles of presentation were given more attention than the motives behind them, black students were demanding real resources and commitments, including control over programs for blacks. The latter demand was anathema particularly to faculty members, who felt that the Black Power rhetoric was inappropriate for academic decision making. (Interestingly, the same faculty members apparently failed to see that, behind the rhetoric, the blacks' basic argument for academic autonomy was one to which they usually subscribed.)

In virtually all of the conflict incidents, black students followed the strategy of confronting the administration at the highest level possible with their demands, on the assumption that that was where power and resources were centered. In most situations, the presidents accepted the spotlight and attempted to negotiate for their institutions. Faculty showed little interest in getting involved in negotiations, although they expected to be kept informed. The difficulty with this strategy was that academic programs either were not promised or were slow to evolve, although more peripheral support programs were initiated rapidly.

The attempt to bring other parties into the negotiations is a tactic of interest. Black students used a variety of groups to gain support and legitimacy (black faculty, the NAACP, and occasionally white faculty or student groups) or to exert pressure (Black Panthers, activist community leaders, and large numbers of blacks). Yet black student leaders were careful to keep control of the conflict. Indeed, the reorientation of white student conflicts by black students at "Metropolitan University," Bowling Green, and Bradley to the blacks' own interests attests to their political sophistication and discipline. On the other hand, the presidents tried to bring more institutional representation into negotiations, a tactic which the blacks usually tried to resist. Some presidents resorted to force in the form of disciplinary action, calling the police and obtaining court orders.

In order to gain bargaining power, blacks tended to foster confrontation and heighten tension in a variety of ways. In the struggles over control, administrators admitted that their own shows of force were motivated as much by their concern that they not be viewed as "capitulating" as by their fear of the consequences of black student activity. On the other hand, black student leaders needed to gain institutional concessions to maintain credibility with their constituents. White administrators wanted to defuse conflicts and were usually willing to make concessions to keep the peace, but they were often caught between black groups and other constituencies whose views varied considerably.

ROLE OF KEY PERSONALITIES IN CONFLICT

Throughout the initial decision making regarding increased black enrollments and the period of conflict, most institutions had the presence of forceful, concerned, and even activist presidents, a few key faculty or administrative leaders, and one or more black leaders. Black student leaders and top administrators played a visible and pivotal role in conflict situations. Yet the brief portrayals offered here do not do justice to the impact of many of the individuals—present on all 13 campuses—whose activities were less visible. These were the black and white faculty members who negotiated informally during intense institutional crises; the white faculty members who knew black student leaders and could talk to them; the black faculty or staff members who inspired the respect of black students and yet were trusted by whites. On any one campus, four to six individuals—black or white; administrator, faculty member, or student; antagonist or protagonist—were clearly identifiable as key actors in the initial black student increases, the development of programs, and the resolution of conflicts. The fact that a few people were regularly singled out suggests the very important role of personalities in this traumatic period of institutional change.

SYMBOLISM AND GAME PLAYING

Because of the sensitive nature of the social issue represented by the entry of black students to predominantly white institutions, it is not surprising that symbolic behavior and gamesmanship were in the forefront during the early stages and became prominent during the conflict period. Examples are numerous; a few will suffice.

Names were important. The black students, perhaps reflecting the Black Power movement, selected names like Black Student Union or Association to imply a solidarity that may have been tenuous. The more creative acronyms—BLACS, BSLF, SOUL—used the imagery of liberation and cultural identity. The sensitivity to and negative connotations of names as symbols was seen in the shifting terms ("deprived" to "disadvantaged" to "minority") used to identify these newly admitted students. Even academic and support services programs sought titles which reinforced their sense of difference from ordinary structures and offices. Perhaps the classic example comes from the unit at the University of the City which had two names, an academic-sounding title used by university officials—Black Studies Program—and an activist, community-oriented title used by members of the unit—Black Community Educational Research and Development Program. The two names reflect differences in philosophy and in implied functional orientation and a struggle over autonomy.

The symbolism became part of the gamesmanship and brinkmanship which were most obvious during a conflict. The four-letter words, which became almost commonplace during the period of intense conflict, expressed blacks' disdain as well as attempts at intimidation. But blacks' threats and incidents of building occupation in many instances masked the reported fears among black students for their own safety in some of the confrontations. Similarly, administrators' insistence on orderly negotiations and the threat or occasional use of police and court intervention distorted their uncertainty about how to handle black protest.

"Taking credit" was one of the most familiar games once a settlement had been worked out. Finding ways for both black and white leaders to announce they had been responsible for a treaty was important for building support with the constituencies of both sides. For the whites, the agreement was a triumph for "reason" and "order"; for the blacks, a victory for "solidarity" and "struggle." This game was most vividly enacted at Macalester in the fall of 1974 after a widely publicized building occupation. The settlement received national press and television coverage after a long series of negotiations which involved an outside arbitrator. Both sides claimed victory and both took credit for the publicity accompanying the settlement. These subtle games are understandable if we recognize that black groups were seeking identity and legitimacy in a situation where they had little real power and autonomy, while white leaders did not know how to deal either individually or institutionally with blacks nor did they know where their commitments might take them or how much real support the settlements would receive from other concerned parties.

CONCLUSION

It is obvious that the dynamics of increased black enrollments were occasionally unique. The nature and extent of the conflict was something for which the institutions were unprepared, and the effects lingered. It is difficult to assess whether the confrontations had significant institutional impact beyond the initial increases in black enrollments or the results of conflict. It is obvious that many new programs and activities followed black demands, and new efforts to sustain or legitimize the changes had to follow. Certainly most blacks saw these as resulting from the confrontation tactics. White administrators were more likely to argue that many of the programs had already begun or were under consideration at the time the confrontations occurred. The prudent position on which both blacks and whites agreed is that conflict was effective in keeping the institutions' focus on their original commitments and was often influential in speeding up the rate of enrollment increase and program development. Chapters 9, 10, and 11 examine some of these programmatic and organizational changes in greater depth.

Part III

Institutional Impacts
and Responses

9

Programs for Black Students, 1968–1974

Zelda F. Gamson

Regardless of how they arrived on the campuses, once black students began attending predominantly white colleges and universities in large enough numbers to form a critical mass, new institutional problems began to present themselves. How would the black students be supported—academically, financially, and socially? Were the staff experienced enough or willing enough to work with students who came from different cultural and economic backgrounds and whose academic preparation was severely lacking in some cases, or at least not at the level expected of white students? What were the implications for admissions criteria, grading policy, and retention? How could black students achieve the sense of identity and security which would allow them to cope with what was an alien environment for many of them? It was not enough, as many white administrators and faculty quickly learned, merely to bring black students on campus and assume they would survive, let alone thrive. This was especially true for the black students recruited in the early period we are examining. For the most part, the black students recruited to the 13 institutions were not from the middle or upper class backgrounds typical of the small numbers of black students who had been on predominantly white campuses in previous eras.

Most of the new students came from working class families, and some were from highly deprived families in urban ghettos. In most cases, they were the first in their families to attend college. College recruiters and others at the institutions talked of getting the "best" black students—but there were not enough to go around. With competition from the more affluent colleges and universities, the moderately and minimally selective campuses had to take whomever they could get. The "busload" approach, by which recruiters would bring scores of new students to the campus from predominantly black urban high schools, seemed the only solution for institutions pressed internally and externally to increase their black enrollments rapidly. Some of the admissions officials to whom we spoke joked about stumbling over other college recruiters in some of the more popular high schools. The competition sometimes became fierce. For economic, political, and perhaps ideological reasons, the schools in our sample tended to focus their attention on northern cities. The South, which might have provided a larger pool of better prepared students, was pretty much ignored by all the institutions other than "State University."

In the past, higher education could respond to new clienteles by either selecting them to match existing student bodies or by integrating them in small enough numbers over a long enough period so as not to threaten the existing structures. These tactics were generally inadequate for the large numbers of underprepared black students recruited in the late 1960s. One response, of course, was not to recruit them in the first place; since institutions of this sort were not in our sample, we cannot comment on them. Another response, exhibited by a few schools in our sample, was to recruit from the pool of highly talented black youths and assume that the usual academic and social patterns would work. Some schools would recruit but not become overly concerned about what happened to students afterward—the state university pattern of earlier decades. But most institutions, whether intentionally or unintentionally, reactively or responsively, had to find ways to deal with the new students in their midst.

In this chapter, we examine the varieties of formal programs developed by the 13 institutions as more black students began to enroll. First, we look at support programs—recruitment aimed specifically at black students, changes in admissions criteria, financial aid programs for minorities, counseling, and tutoring. Generally speaking, these support programs were initiated and carried out by administrative staff and not by regular faculty. Academic programs, to be examined next in this chapter, came later. Here we will be talking about black or ethnic studies programs or courses as they developed over the period of our study.

Institutions can implement new programs in a variety of ways. Most obviously, the programs can vary in the degree of institutional commitment they receive—in terms of money, people, and recognized status. They can vary in the comprehensiveness of their activities, from a single focus to multiple foci. They can be incorporated into existing organizational structures or they can be added on as new structures; in either case, they can be located at the periphery of the institution or at its core. Finally, they can vary in the extent to which they are coordinated with other related activities. To some degree, these are all measures of the degree of integration versus separation of the programmatic responses. As we go through the chronology and character of these responses to black students, we will attempt to understand them in terms of these general organizational strategies for dealing with new programs.

SUPPORT PROGRAMS

We include a range of programs under this heading. With a few exceptions, the 13 institutions in our sample did not have formal support programs for minority students prior to 1968. The exceptions have been mentioned already in Chapters 6 and 7; these generally took the form of precollege programs (at Northwestern, Brockport, Kansas City, and Carleton), athletic programs (at Bradley and State), or a history of attracting black graduate students (State, Bowling Green, and "Metropolitan University"). These earlier programs then became conduits for attracting the new generation of black students. It was not until formal recruitment programs came in 1968–69, however, that these institutions began to implement a variety of other minority-related activities. In the chronicles of these schools, recruitment programs came first.

Recruitment of Black Students

Once the commitment was made to increase the enrollment of blacks, the question then became how to find the new students. Metropolitan University, "the University of the City," and the University of Missouri–Kansas City, which drew undergraduates from the cities in which they are located and maintained some off-campus programs, had an easier time than other institutions located farther away from urban areas. For them, announcing their newfound receptivity to minority students did not automatically guarantee that large numbers of black students would apply for admission. It became apparent, even at a time of an overall increase in college attendance, that colleges and universities would have to recruit black students in an active way. Northwestern University began to recruit early, in the fall of 1966, primarily from Chicago inner-city high schools. In 1966–67, SUNY-Brockport's Summer Start program, initiated by the director of admissions, began to identify small numbers of disadvantaged students, particularly in Rochester. The recruitment programs at Brockport and Northwestern came a year or two earlier than those developed at the other institutions in our sample (six of them began formal recruitment in 1968; five started in 1969).

The typical pattern was for the institutions to turn the black recruitment programs over to the regular admissions offices. It soon became apparent, however, that white admissions officers had limited experience in this area; some were even opposed to the whole effort. (Although we did not keep a careful record of this, we did hear about a considerable degree of turnover on admissions staffs, including the replacement of admissions office directors.) One way of handling this problem initially was to use black students to help recruit. At Clarion, for example, a delegation of students who went to the acting president to press for an increase in black enrollments was enlisted into Clarion's recruitment campaigns in Pittsburgh and other cities in Pennsylvania.

All but one of the institutions in our sample eventually hired at least one black admissions officer or coordinator. In 1974, 8 of the 13 placed primary responsibility for recruitment of minorities within their regular admissions offices, although almost all of these offices worked more or less closely with campus minority programs by involving staff members in visits to high schools, in screening applicants, and in developing contacts with black communities and organizations. Table 9-1 summarizes where the primary responsibility for recruitment existed on the campuses in 1974.

Another distinguishable pattern at Bowling Green, Carleton, Clarion, State, and Macalester was the recruitment of minority students primarily through a minority program. It is perhaps too strong to say that these were "separate" programs since from the beginning some did coordinate their efforts to varying degrees with the admissions offices (notably State, and others more recently). Indeed, all but one of the five following this route had a black admissions officer on the regular admissions staff.

Historically, these arrangements came about when full-blown mi-

TABLE 9-1

Recruitment Program Patterns as of 1974

Recruitment primarily through regular Admissions Office	Recruitment primarily through minority program (with some degree of coordination with Admissions Office)
Bradley	Bowling Green
SUNY-Brockport	Carleton
California State	Clarion
"University of the City"	Macalester
Lewis	"State University"
"Metropolitan University"	
University of Missouri–	
Kansas City	
Northwestern	

nority programs for academic and support services were beginning to be developed. Minority program recruiters often also had discretionary latitude over admissions as well—at least with respect to "opportunity" students—and strains between regular admissions people and the special program staffs began to surface. Macalester's Expanded Education Opportunity Program, for example, was vested with a great deal of authority over admissions decisions for minority students during its first years, despite initial plans to recruit through the regular admissions office. The first director of the EEO program recruited students who were more "high-risk" than was intended in the original blueprint for Macalester's minority effort. With the departure of this director, recruitment of black students was carried out in a more coordinated way—although there remained some competition between the admissions office and the EEO recruiters.

The trend toward joint recruitment programs was apparent on several of our campuses. This was often motivated by a desire on the part of the administrators and faculty members (and in a couple of cases, on the part of the boards of trustees) to regain the control over admissions they had relinquished in the flush of the activist years when they had turned recruitment responsibility over to minority programs. Bowling Green's history in minority recruitment is typical of this pattern. Prior to May 1970, the admissions office was making some recruiting trips to predominantly black high schools in urban centers of Ohio. The recruiters were white and they met with little success. After the spring of 1970, the university began sending out teams of black students to recruit in high schools. Within a short time, however, the Student Development Program (SDP), Bowling Green's multipurpose minority program, took over all minority recruitment. Following the president's commitment to double the enrollment of blacks over the summer, recruitment followed the "busload approach." A number of our informants admitted in retrospect that the initial goal had been unrealistic; several felt that it had brought serious problems to the university and to the students recruited at the time. The newly hired director of the Student Development Program, who had been given high recruitment quotas, operated with a free hand, often admitting students on his own authority. In recent years, Bowling Green's admissions office and its Student Development Program have been working together more closely, with SDP handling recruitment and the admissions office sharing responsibility for the selection of students. There was a significant decline in minority enrollments at Bowling Green in the fall of 1974, following a national trend in that direction, and efforts were begun to recruit from a wider variety of high schools in the state and to attract more highly achieving blacks.

Admissions Criteria

College admissions criteria, like academic standards, are apparently a sacrosanct topic. It was extremely difficult for us to get an accurate picture from those we interviewed about how the criteria used for admitting minority students compared with normal admissions criteria. We asked, but the answers were, to say the least, circumspect. Part of the problem lies with lack of adequate data comparing black and white students' entering scores on the ACT or SAT tests or on high school averages. On only seven of the campuses were we able to ascertain any comparative entrance scores—and even these were spotty. All of the available data showed that the black students scored lower than the white students (Table 9-2).

Even with the available figures it is difficult to interpret racial differences, since four of the seven institutions for which we have data lumped together "special admissions" students with minority students admitted under standard criteria. On the other hand, the two institutions which gave only special admissions entrance data also included some white students who were not eligible under the regular criteria.

Some of the institutions devised a formally recognized special admissions category, building in and legitimizing different admissions criteria. This was true with State's Special Support Services Department, City's Community Education Program, the University of Missouri–Kansas City's Transitional Year Program, SUNY-Brockport's Educational Opportunities Program, and Lewis's Success Program.

TABLE 9-2

Entrance Scores of Black and White Students

Institution	1968		1970		1972		1974	
	B	W	B	W	B	W	B	W
Bowling Green (ACT)	13	21	—	—	—	—	—	—
SUNY–Brockport (SAT)	—	—	—	—	—	—	622*	952
Carleton (SAT)	1241	1325	932	1307	936	1246	—	—
Lewis (ACT)	14	21	—	—	—	—	—	—
"Metropolitan" (SAT)	—	—	—	—	—	—	800	1025
Northwestern (SAT)	—	—	989	1236	1016	1235	990	1220
"State" (ACT)	19*	25	—	—	16*	24	—	—

Note: Data missing for Bradley, California, Clarion, Macalester, University of Missouri–Kansas City, "University of the City."
*Opportunity students only.

Special admissions categories, although not officially recognized, also existed more or less formally on the other campuses. This was especially true in those institutions which recruited black students through their primary minority programs: Bowling Green, Carleton, Clarion, and Macalester. At Bowling Green, for example, the proportion of black students admitted was higher than that of white students for a period of time. The closing time for applications was extended for black students beyond the regular deadline. Special forms and a waiver of the application fee were available for students admitted through SDP.

The other institutions claimed that traditional admissions criteria were applied equally, although a gap in average test scores between white and black students was still present. Schools with essentially open admissions—California, Clarion, and Brockport—could honestly say that the same criteria were being applied with all students. Other schools making this claim were more likely to be questioned by their own faculty and students.

After the first hurried attempts to recruit large numbers of black students, many of the institutions in our study became concerned about their ability to respond to the students' special academic needs. On some campuses, attrition became a serious problem. Early in the period the more selective institutions had been able to attract a number of black students who met their traditional admissions standards. But by 1974 when we began our study, even these institutions were beginning to talk about the need to recruit larger numbers of students who were better prepared.

Among the less selective colleges and universities, this concern also existed, although it was not always clear that they would succeed in attracting more able black students in a competitive and shrinking market. Lewis, for example, recruited black students in 1969 and 1970 with little concern for their credentials. Beginning in the academic year 1971–72, in response to faculty concern about student quality and attrition, Lewis's new director of admissions began efforts to recruit more selectively. Specific, but still flexible, criteria were developed in collaboration with each school or college.

Other campuses attacked this problem in different ways. Bowling Green was beginning to identify a pool of talented black high school students who might be offered achievement scholarships. Macalester increased the coordination of recruitment between its admissions office and its EEO program to upgrade the total pool of minority students, making use of its contacts with high school counselors and minority organizations around the country to identify talented students. Carleton built on its associations with prep schools through the ABC program.

Financial Aid

Closely related to recruitment and admissions is the question of financial aid. As we have already indicated, the existence of federal and state aid programs attracted black students who would not have gone to college otherwise. Grants enabled black students to enroll, once accepted, at a higher rate than white students on some campuses. (This was a factor which may have contributed to the lower academic profiles for black students.)

All of the institutions in our study eventually offered some form of financial aid—either from federal, state, or institutional funds, or from some combination of these. Not surprisingly, the wealthier colleges and universities used more of their own funds while the poorer institutions relied heavily upon external sources. The schools differed also in the alacrity with which they were able to gear up their financial aid staffs to make use of federal and state programs. Bowling Green, Bradley, and Lewis had no financial aid programs in the early period of minority increases; all of the other institutions did have some identifiable program in place early in the period. But at all the institutions it became clear that their ability to recruit minority students depended on their ability to offer substantial financial support.

Lewis, for example, prior to 1970 funded its financial aid program primarily from a limited amount of informally administered institutional funds. The use of institutional funds for student aid reportedly caused some budgetary strains at the time. Starting in 1971–72, however—under a new president and a new financial aid director—financial aid policies were codified, the staff grew, and efforts to utilize state and federal aid programs to support Lewis's increasing numbers of low and lower-middle income students (both whites and minorities) became more organized. In 1974–75 nearly 70 percent of the total student body was supported by more than $1,700,000 in all forms of aid. Of that total, about $1,300,000 came from the Illinois state aid program and over $300,000 from federal sources.

Although the quality of our data is variable, it is clear that very high proportions of the minority students at the 13 colleges and universities—in some cases, close to 100 percent—received financial aid.

The degree and sources of support varied across these institutions. The institutions which relied almost completely on external sources—Clarion, California, Bradley, and Lewis—offered smaller aid packages than those which drew on institutional sources. The wealthier private institutions expended higher proportions of their total aid on minority students (of course, their tuition and living costs were also higher). Macalester, for example, drew heavily on foundation grants and endowment funds to support black and other minority students. Students in the EEO program received between one-quarter and one-third of the total unspecified financial aid expenditures between 1970 and 1974. The percentage of total aid monies from internal sources going to Macalester's EEO students stood at 90 percent in 1970–71 and at almost 50 percent in 1973–74. In the latter year, it was estimated that the average aid received by EEO students was about two to three times greater than the average aid received by non-EEO students.

The less affluent universities in our sample also contributed their own institutional resources to the support of minority students, although the proportion of funds which came from internal sources was not as great as in the wealthier institutions. In 1973–74, almost 30 percent of the University of the City's total aid for students came from institutional funds; the figure was slightly over 20 percent at Bowling Green and at the University of Missouri–Kansas City, and almost 20 percent at Metropolitan University. These contrast with over 40 percent at Macalester and over 60 percent at Northwestern.

Northwestern's comprehensive financial aid program was fully tied into the recruitment of black students. Prior to 1965, only a small proportion of Northwestern's student body received financial aid. Between 1965 and 1968, it was reported that close to 100 percent of the black students received financial aid. University expenditures on financial aid grew almost fourfold in the nine years following its commitment to enroll substantial numbers of black and other minority students. Forty-three percent of all Northwestern students, but virtually every black student, received financial aid in 1974–75. The financial aid office had one black staff member who was responsible for working with black and low-income students.

The University of Missouri–Kansas City, although to a lesser extent than Northwestern, carried out a financial aid effort that was quite comprehensive from the beginning. When Kansas City began to increase its black enrollments substantially, the primary role of the financial aid office was to coordinate its decisions with other offices, particularly the Transitional Year Program and Talent Search. The office offered an evening financial aid service with on-the-spot needs analysis, although this part of the program was not very successful. Primary financial aid attention to minorities was channeled through federal programs targeted for low-income students. Kansas City also had three specific financial commitments to minority students: (1) institutional funds from outside donors which were targeted for blacks, (2) some scholarships which began after Martin Luther King's assassination, (3) and more recently a "special circumstances" fund.

Financial aid was relatively important to black students at the University of Missouri–Kansas City, and the majority of applicants who completed the financial aid forms received aid. Black students received substantial amounts of financial aid, as reflected in the 1973–74 statistics:

1. Total aid packages for blacks were 19 percent higher than for other students.
2. Thirty-one percent of the total number of students receiving aid were black; 35 percent of the total amount of money given out went to blacks.
3. Forty-eight percent of the total SEOG recipients were black; 52 percent of the total SEOG money went to blacks.
4. Forty-one percent of the total College Work-Study recipients were black; 38 percent of the total CWS money went to blacks.
5. Twenty-nine percent of the total NDSL recipients were black; 26 percent of the total NDSL money went to blacks.

California State drew almost its entire financial aid fund from federal and state sources; there was practically no internal money for financial aid. (In 1973–74, only $1,100 in institutional funds were available for student aid.) Increasingly, programs such as the Basic Educational Opportunity Grants and the PHEAA state aid program were making awards directly to the student recipient. The financial aid office acted primarily as a processor of forms rather than as a judge of who should receive aid. California State was able to meet the needs of its students through financial aid packages combining federal and state grants, work-study, and loans.

Several persistent problems emerged in the financial aids areas in a number of institutions. These were, first and last, economic. For the private institutions facing serious financial stringencies—Metropolitan University and Macalester College—fundamental questions were being raised within all sectors of the institutions about the degree of commitment of institutional funds to minority students. Faced with declining enrollments, Metropolitan eliminated institutional grant money for new freshmen in the Distinctive Academic Program. At Macalester, a major confrontation took place in the fall of 1974 over budget cuts between EEO students and the president. Similar confrontations over the same issue occurred on a number of campuses in the nation during 1974–75—most notably at Brandeis and Brown.

Even those campuses which were not facing immediate financial problems were beginning to re-evaluate the extent of their financial aid commitments to minorities. Carleton's president announced that a maximum of 40 percent of the student aid funds would be available to minority students. This, and similar decisions, had important implications for the number of minority students who would be attracted and held in the future.

Of course, those institutions which initially invested institutional funds could later draw on federal and state aid programs to maintain their minority enrollments. But for them, as for the institutions in our study which relied heavily on these external sources all along, the continuation of these sources at levels high enough to support needy students has become a major issue. With the elimination of the Ohio State Loan Program in 1972, Bowling Green had to establish relationships with local banks to provide some loans to students. But problems with student defaults, which were apparently higher for blacks than white students, made the local banks wary of continuing the loan program.

On campuses whose students were not from wealthy families—

such as Clarion, Metropolitan, Bowling Green, Lewis, and California State—students and, in some cases, faculty began to raise the question of "reverse discrimination" in financial aid allocations and other areas. There had not been direct confrontations between black and white students on this issue by the time of this study, but we did detect some hostility. This was less of an issue at the wealthier institutions, which may continue to be able to supply grants from institutional funds to the smaller numbers of non-minority students who need them; but at most schools it was a major question. With a continuing economic recession, middle-income families are beginning to question what they see as the disproportionate support given to students from lower-income families. These are all issues which are quite likely to continue—particularly in those colleges and universities which face long-term enrollment declines.

Academic Support Services

Black students needed not only financial support, but academic and social support as well. Such support took a variety of forms in the 13 institutions: one-to-one tutoring; special courses or sections of regular courses; pre-college courses; academic, career, and personal counseling; day-care provisions; medical and dental services; and cultural programs. Rudimentary support programs were introduced at the time of the initial enrollment increases or soon after when pressures from black students for more support began to be felt. All but 2 of the 13 institutions had clearly identifiable support programs during the initial period. Bradley and Lewis, which had no such programs initially, later amended that oversight: Lewis introduced its Success Program in 1973 and Bradley began its Curriculum II in 1974.

All of the 13 institutions had named programs which were responsible for some aspect of support services. As we have noted, some of these programs were responsible for recruiting and administering financial aid as well. Bowling Green, Macalester, Kansas City, City, State, and Clarion offered the widest range of activities in their support programs. Metropolitan, Brockport, Bradley, Carleton, California State, Lewis, and Northwestern were more limited. All focused some efforts on counseling or tutoring but varied in their activities. Table 9-3 lists the support programs at each institution, when they were initiated, and our best information about their range of activities. There was great variation in the content and comprehensiveness of the special programs offered.

TABLE 9-3

Major Support Services Units and Their Functions, 1974–75

Institution	Name and Date Initiated	Recruit- ment	Financial Aid	Functions Remedial Work	Tutoring	Counseling
Bowling Green	Student Development Program, 1968	yes	yes	yes	yes	yes
Bradley	Curriculum II, 1974	no	no	no	yes	yes
SUNY–Brockport	Summer Start Educational Opportunities Program, 1969	no	no	no	yes	yes
California State	Student Incentive program, 1969–71 Office of Special Services, 1972	no	no	yes	yes	no
Carleton	Office of Minority Affairs Minority Admissions Office, 1969	yes	no	no	no	yes
"University of the City"	Community Education Program, 1968–69	yes	yes	no	yes	yes
Clarion State	Educational Opportunity Program, 1970–71 Student Development Program, 1971	yes	no	yes	yes	yes

TABLE 9-3 continued

Institution	Name and Date Initiated	Recruitment	Financial Aid	Functions Remedial Work	Tutoring	Counseling
Lewis	Success Program, 1973	no	no	yes	no	yes
Macalester	Expanded Educational Opportunities Program, 1969	yes	yes	yes	yes	yes
"Metropolitan University"	Collegiate Help Program, 1968–70 Distinctive Academic Program, 1970	yes	no	no	yes	yes
University of Missouri–Kansas City	Transitional year Program, 1968	yes	yes	no	yes	yes
Northwestern	Afro-American Student Affairs, 1968	no	no	no	yes	yes
"State University"	Support Services Program, 1968	yes	yes	yes	yes	yes

Let us look first at two institutions with support programs that were quite comprehensive, Macalester and State. Macalester's program was probably the most wide-ranging, in terms of the services it provided, the financial support it received, and the types of students involved. The core of Macalester's program for minorities was the EEO program, which took on the responsibilities of recruiting, administering financial aid, providing counseling, tutorial and remedial help, and organizing extracurricular activities. Each of EEO's major components—including those for blacks, Native Americans, Hispanics, and Puerto Ricans—had its own coordinator and staff. In 1974–75 EEO had a staff of 16 full-time professionals, in addition to student tutors, counselors, and advisors. Approximate overall expenditures for the program were $900,000 in 1971–72, $957,000 in 1972–73, and $747,000 in 1973–74. Since the beginning of the program, EEO has received $966,000 in gifts and pledges from individuals, corporations, and foundations, including grants from the Special Services Program of the U.S. Office of Education and a three-year grant from the Rockefeller Foundation for a Native American project, as well as a grant from a small foundation and from the Office of Education TRIO Program.

Total enrollments in the EEO program grew from 82 in 1968 to 151 in 1970, 166 in 1971, 185 in 1972, and 157 in 1974. The primary academic activities of EEO were directed toward tutorial work on basic skills in various academic areas, but these efforts were not successfully coordinated with either the relevant departments or with the study skills counselors who worked on the staff of the Dean of Students. The English Department offered sections of a basic literature and writing course designed to help students with writing problems, and there were new approaches to teaching which attracted minority students to the introductory biology course. Two other programs which might have contributed to remediation were later dropped.

A major activity of the EEO program was counseling. Each student in the program had a counselor to help with academic and personal adjustment to the college. The EEO counselor also attempted to maintain contact with each student's instructors to keep track of progress and to pinpoint any problems the student may have been encountering. Some counselors acted as advocates for students when they were having academic problems. The extent to which counselors actually did work with faculty was not clear, although some faculty members complained of a lack of contact with EEO counselors. There was apparently some duplication between the counseling services

offered through EEO and those available through the Office of the
Dean of Students, and many minority students—including EEO students—made use of these services. Perhaps EEO's greatest strength,
but one which received less recognition because of its separatist over-
tones, was the development of extensive cultural, social, and community programs. These are described in a later chapter.

State University's Support Services Program (SSP) was also quite
comprehensive. Evolving out of the Educational Opportunities Program (EOP) established in 1968, the SSP was staffed in 1974–75 with
eight full-time equivalent professionals and approximately 60 part-
time student employees. The principal purpose of SSP did not change
from that stated for EOP in 1968: to locate, recruit, and provide
financial aid and economic assistance to students from educationally
and economically disadvantaged backgrounds. Low-income and ethnic minority students who did not meet the traditional entrance requirements to the university could be admitted through SSP, and
they were eligible to receive EOP grants if they could document financial need. In either case, these students were eligible for all academic support services of SSP.

SSP provided academic assistance, financial aid and financial
management counseling, personal counseling, social services, and career advising for enrolled students. In addition, SSP was responsible
for recruiting and admitting disadvantaged students and for administering financial aid. SSP also administered the Afro-American and
the Chicano-Indian cultural centers.

The academic support and counseling services of SSP were supervised by its associate director. The three major efforts in this area
were: (1) counseling through a system of assigned and supervised
peer advisors, called Your Special Friend (YSF); (2) academic tutoring using graduate and upper-division tutors, coordinated by a counselor for academic affairs; and (3) career counseling, a relatively recent addition to the services of SSP. The Academic Affairs Section of
SSP could also request an Instructor's Evaluation Form from the
instructors of freshman SSP students or those who were on probation;
the evaluations dealt with eight areas of academic work (attendance,
class participation, reading skills, test taking, etc.). The SSP and the
student both received a copy of the evaluation and the information
was used to provide specific assistance.

Another interesting innovation was the attempt to evaluate, both
objectively and subjectively, the extent to which each student was
making "reasonable progress toward completion of the degree." The

program made an allowance of five years for completion of the bacca-
laureate and included a rising minimum cumulative grade point
average requirement. The criteria of "reasonable progress" were
clearly spelled out to the student and the precise minimum performance necessary to remain in good standing was identified. Individual academic allowances could also be granted at the discretion of the
academic affairs staff of SSP.

In addition to academic support services, SSP has provided numerous cultural enrichment programs, social services such as baby-
sitting and day care, short-term or incidental off-campus employment, housing information and assistance, and health care counseling
and referral. SSP staff also advised students about the availability of
food stamps and other social services.

This program has been viewed favorably outside of the university
and has attracted attention from other institutions. The SSP director
has been active in national training programs for EOP staff. Clearly,
State University's Support Services Program has been widely viewed
as a model for programs of this type.

A newer, less comprehensive program was Lewis University's
Success Program. On a limited basis, Lewis has provided a support
program for black and other minority students since its initiation in
1969–70 of a small "special student, post admission program" for
students who were expected to "have a difficult time succeeding in
college." The criteria for selection were ACT scores (lower than 15).
Although the program was designed to include 50 percent white and
50 percent minority students, we were told that at least two-thirds of
the students were blacks or Chicanos. The primary emphasis of the
program was on individual counseling, provided by the director and
two part-time student assistants, and students were assigned to one
or more of three courses for improving communication skills. These
courses offered regular credit and focused on reading, public speaking, and writing. Under the Success Program, students could elect to
receive a study skills workshop and special tutoring by faculty who
had a reputation for their willingness to work with students on an
individual basis in place of one course during the first semester.
Other services and activities of the program included assistance in
obtaining medical, dental, and eye examinations and other services
for students through community agencies. With minimal staff, Lewis's Success Program served principally as a referral and informal
counseling support program with emphasis on insuring academic survival for first-year students.

SUNY-Brockport provided counseling and advising to the educationally and economically disadvantaged students enrolled in its Educational Opportunity Program. The approach was an unusual one. The faculty of the education and psychology departments operated a master's degree program in counseling for 12 graduate students which began with an orientation to the institution and to the kinds of counseling they could be expected to conduct. The master's students worked with the EOP in a one-year internship, under the supervision of faculty and other service units. Counselors-in-training were responsible for finding those EOP students assigned to them and for maintaining relatively close contact with each student. In addition, three full-time counselors were available to assist students with special needs.

In effect, then, even the institutions' with more limited support service programs for minority students offered either special counseling or tutoring. SUNY-Brockport, Northwestern, Carleton, and California State—all institutions with strong commitments to not making distinctions between majority and minority students—developed some special supportive programs for minorities. The other institutions did considerably more, and the comprehensiveness of minority programs did not seem to be related either to institutional wealth or to selectivity.

Although in the early years a number of the support service programs received outside funds for staff salaries, by 1974 all but one of the 13 institutions were paying at least some of the staff salaries with internal funds. (The exception was Lewis, which had Title III monies for its Success Program.) The size of the staffs varied considerably among the programs and did not seem to follow either a size or wealth distinction among the institutions. The largest support staffs were at Bowling Green, Brockport, State, Macalester, and Kansas City. Moderate-sized staffs were found at Clarion, Northwestern, the University of the City, and Metropolitan University. The smallest staffs—some of them relying on the part-time participation of individuals from academic departments and other offices—were at Bradley, California State, Carleton, and Lewis.

The support service programs differed also in their location and status within the 13 institutions. Typically, the programs were located initially under a high administrative officer and/or within the student affairs area. By 1974, seven of the support programs were placed in the academic area, one (State's) was located under the Vice President for Student Services and Dean for Academic Affairs, and only four remained in the student affairs area.

Summary of Comprehensiveness and Commitment to Support Programs

Regardless of the way support services were positioned and structured, it is possible to give a rough rating of the 13 institutions in terms of the degree of comprehensiveness of their overall efforts. It is also possible to rate them on the degree of commitment they gave to support services, based on the number of staff and student aid programs drawn from institutional funds. It is clear that almost half of the institutions made a committed and comprehensive effort to offer support programs to minority students. Only 3 of the 13 fell into the low categories on both commitment and comprehensiveness. (Table 9-4.)

TABLE 9-4

Comprehensive and Institutional Commitment to
All Support Services for Minorities

Commitment	Comprehensiveness		
	High	Medium	Low
High	Bowling Green Brockport Kansas City Macalester Northwestern "State" "University of the City"		
Medium	"Metropolitan"	Carleton Clarion	
Low			California Lewis Bradley

Note: Includes recruitment; financial aid; and academic, social and cultural support.

ACADEMIC PROGRAMS

All 13 institutions offered some courses with black-related content, such as Black history, Afro-American literature, and race relations (see Table 9-5). Some of these courses were being taught before the large influx of minority students, but many more began to be offered by both black and white faculty after the period of increased

TABLE 9-5

Academic Programs

Institution	Name and Date Initiated	Program Structure	Degree	Interdisciplinary Program
Bowling Green	Center for Ethnic Studies, 1970	Center	BA	yes
Bradley	Black Studies, 1969	Program	no	no
Brockport	Afro & American Studies Department, 1970	Department	BA	yes
California	Courses only			
Carleton	Black Studies Program, 1973	Program	no	yes
"University of the City"	Black Studies Department, 1969	Institute/Department	BA	no
Clarion	Courses only			
Lewis	Courses only			
Macalester	Courses only			
"Metropolitan"	Institute for Afro-American Studies, 1974	Institute	no	no
University of Missouri-Kansas City	Courses only			
Northwestern	African-American Studies, 1971	Department	BA*	no
"State"	Afro-American Studies Program, 1968	Program	BA, MA, Ph.D, concentration through American Civilization	yes

*The faculty approved the creation of this new department but did not empower it to award a degree. Students received a BA from Northwestern only.

black enrollments. Academic responses at the course level were somewhat invisible since individual faculty members may have incorporated materials related to minorities in courses not directly focused on those minorities. In addition, through independent study, special topics courses, field projects and the like, students were able to pursue topics related to minorities.

Eight of the 13 institutions developed formal academic programs focused on minorities, and 6 of these 8 were universities. Bowling Green's program had a multi-ethnic focus; the others focused specifically on black or Afro-American studies. Only one of the universities in our study, the University of Missouri–Kansas City, did not have a formal academic program, although it did offer the option of an interdisciplinary major with special emphasis on black America. The formal programs took a variety of forms: three were full-fledged departments (at Brockport, Northwestern, and the University of the City); the rest were programs or centers. Half were clearly interdisciplinary in content and approach; half were not. Half gave the B.A. (State University had M.A. and Ph.D. programs as well); half did not.

Black or Afro-American studies programs got a later start than support services programs nationally. In our sample of institutions, this was also generally the case, although there are several notable exceptions. State's Afro-American Studies Program began in 1968—when the first such program in a predominantly white college was opened at San Francisco State—and was planned about the same time State's Educational Opportunities Program was being planned. Bradley, which did not have a formalized support services program until 1974, initiated its Black Studies Program in 1969 in response to black student demands. Bowling Green, Northwestern, City, Brockport, Carleton, and Metropolitan all began their academic programs after the period of initial recruitment of black students and after the founding of supportive services units.

The institutions varied a great deal in the degree of support they gave to the programs (see Table 9-6). All were supported at least partially with internal funds, although the amount differed greatly. Professional staff size ranged from one person (a director) to 14. The best-supported programs were at Bowling Green, Brockport, State, Northwestern, and City. The programs at Bradley, Carleton, and Metropolitan University (the latter two began in 1973 and 1974) were poorly supported, limited programs.

Table 9-6 details the variety of ways in which the eight programs were tied into the academic structures of their institutions. Some of the programs were served by joint advisory committees and were

TABLE 9-6

Institutional Commitment and Integration of Major Academic Programs, 1974–75

Institution	Size of Professional Staff	Source of Funding	Program Supervision	Joint Advisory Committee	Joint Appointments	Degree of Director	Tenure of Faculty
Bowling Green	4 full-time faculty 3 part-time faculty, 5 graduate assistants	internal	Vice Provost for Minority Affairs	yes	NA	NA	NA
Bradley	1	internal	Vice President for Instruction	yes	yes	MA	no
Brockport	8	internal	Dean of College of Social Science	no	yes	Ph.D	yes
Carleton	1	internal	Interdisciplinary committee	yes	yes	MA	no
"City"	14	internal & external	Provost/Dean of College of Arts & Sciences	yes	generally no	NA	no
"Metropolitan"	1	internal & external	Vice President for Academic Administration	yes	yes	NA	yes
Northwestern	3–4	internal	Dean of College of Arts and Sciences	no	NA	NA	NA
"State"	4	internal & external	Chairman of English Department	yes	yes	Ph.D	yes

staffed by individuals in other academic departments. Bowling Green's Ethnic Studies Center was located under the new Vice Provost for Minority Affairs; it had a joint advisory committee and its staff members had joint appointments in other academic departments. Bradley's Black Studies Program was placed under the Vice President for Instruction and also had a joint advisory committee; it did not, however, offer joint appointments. Brockport's Department of Afro-American Studies was located under the Dean of the College of Social Sciences, with joint appointments but not a joint advisory committee. Carleton's Black Studies Program was under an interdisciplinary committee and could make joint appointments. State's Afro-American Studies Program was located in the English Department in the American Civilization program and had a joint advisory committee and joint appointments. Northwestern's African-American Studies Department was placed under the Dean of the College of Arts and Sciences. City's Black Studies Department was under the Provost and Dean of the College of Arts and Sciences, had a joint advisory committee and generally did not have joint appointment faculty. Metropolitan's Institute for Afro-American Studies was a unit under the Vice President for Academic Administration and had a joint advisory committee and joint appointments.

One key difference among the programs was the degree to which they could offer courses of their own. City's program offered courses of its own in four divisions: Black Humanities; Black Social Science; African Studies; and Caribbean Studies. At the other extreme was Metropolitan University, whose Institute for Afro-American Studies gave no courses but instead acted as a listing and dissemination office for courses taught in other departments. The more typical pattern for the well-developed programs was to offer a combination of courses, some specifically developed for the program (usually part of a "core" program or set of introductory courses) and some offered within the disciplinary departments. State, for example, from the beginning emphasized an interdisciplinary approach in which the Afro-American Studies Program offered some basic courses and a wide variety of departments were encouraged to offer related courses. Bradley's Black Studies Program offered two introductory survey history courses, and additional courses taught in other departments. Bowling Green's Center for Ethnic Studies offered courses through an experimental course program and through special topics courses in departments.

Only City's program did not make extensive use of the joint appointment mechanism. However, the programs varied in the extent to which they could make appointments, either exclusively or jointly.

Bowling Green only began making faculty appointments in Ethnic Studies—all of which were to be accompanied by appointments in departments—in 1974–75. State's faculty in Afro-American Studies also made departmental appointments. Northwestern, Brockport, Carleton, Metropolitan, and Bradley, on the other hand, did not offer appointments in their black studies programs.

Lack of consensus about direction has plagued the Black Studies programs at Northwestern, Brockport, and City. At Brockport, for example, the first black studies chairman, a Nigerian, championed a militantly critical view of the social sciences. The social science departments reacted against this, and relations between the black studies program and the departments grew exceedingly tense. In 1971, the political science department circulated a petition among its members opposing any form of cooperation, particularly in the granting of joint appointments. Real cooperation between white social science faculty and the black studies department did not occur until a new chairman, more moderate and academic in style, was brought in. Since then, strong relationships with the social science departments have been formed.

Conflicts took a different form at Northwestern. From its inception, the Department of African-American Studies faced opposition from black students. The chairmanship was not filled for the department's first year; later, a respected black scholar was appointed to that position. Students began to press for stronger participation in decision making within the department, but black faculty resisted giving them decisive control. The conflict reflected persistent differences in conception, found on other campuses as well, between those who wanted a scholarly department and those who wanted a more activist, community-centered orientation.

This dispute was also a continuing one at the University of the City. The department was weakened by a leadership struggle when its first chairman resigned in 1973. (Later, in 1975, it was headed by an individual who, while a student at City, had been involved in the Computer Center take-over.) There was a continuing conflict over the name of the department. The title originally approved by the faculty was "Black Studies Program," but the department used the title "Black Educational Community Research Department." Indeed, the university literature used the former name and the department used the latter. The struggle, again, was between an activist orientation on the part of the members of the department and a more academic one on the part of the administration and faculty outside the department.

In general, the stronger and more stable programs were directed by individuals with solid academic credentials and were able to offer tenure to their faculty. From the beginning, State recruited staff with good academic backgrounds; the two directors of its Afro-American Studies Program were respected scholars. Northwestern and Brockport, despite their more volatile histories, also recruited respected scholars to direct their black studies programs. City's Black Studies Department, while well-supported financially, could offer no tenure on its own and, since most of the faculty of the Black Studies Department had appointments only in that department, their security was far from assured.

The same could be said for most black studies programs, with the possible exception of the more institutionalized programs at State and Brockport. The programs at Bowling Green and at Northwestern, although both well-supported, did not offer degrees. Bradley's non-degree program had four directors since it began, was undersupported, and lacked consistency and direction. Carleton's program was new and marginal in 1975. And Metropolitan University's new program was poorly supported and, in the midst of a period of fiscal urgency for the institution, it was unlikely to receive more funds from internal sources.

THE DYNAMICS OF MINORITY PROGRAM DEVELOPMENT

We have observed some recurrent patterns in the timing, types, and range of programs developed in response to black students: (1) the early appearance of a formal recruitment program; (2) the use of special admissions criteria, either formally recognized in a special admissions category or informally practiced; (3) the early provision of financial aid in substantial amounts from internal monies, external sources, or a combination; (4) the development of a variety of supportive services through a defined minority program which was eventually developed on each of the campuses and initiated early at most of them; (5) the variety of ways these services could be organizationally structured, from highly centralized to decentralized patterns; (6) the recent trend to incorporate support services activities into the regular academic structure after initial implementation in the student affairs area or under another non-academic administrative office; (7) the later appearance of black studies programs and black-oriented courses; and (8) the variety of ways these academic programs could be structured and supported.

How did this all come about after the initial commitments were made to increase black enrollments? There was no single process; each of the colleges and universities had its own particular history, although many of them were responding to the same types of forces.

Timing seems to have been a crucial element in the history of program development on these campuses. In general, the earlier the response—particularly if it was well-supported initially—the more comprehensive the program was by 1974. This was evidenced in those institutions which moved quickly to establish an identifiable minority support program early in the period of increased enrollments: State, Macalester, City, Bowling Green, Northwestern, Brockport, Clarion, Metropolitan, and Kansas City. Programs which were initiated later, when financial resources were tight, were less comprehensive.

Leadership was crucial, as we noted in Chapter 7, in initiating responses. But it was also important in the continuation of those responses. Some institutions with strong presidential leadership in the initial phases failed to carry that leadership into the implementation stage—with negative consequences. At Macalester, the departure of President Flemming meant that the EEO program lost its strongest administrative advocate. The Chancellor at City, after initiating a recruitment program, responded only when black students and community people pressed the institution for further efforts. The new president at Metropolitan University, a person who did not share the former president's commitment to minorities, repeatedly expressed concern about the university's investment of institutional dollars.

With the exception of Macalester and State, support service activities and, in some cases, even academic programs, were introduced and implemented by administrators and not by faculty. The support service programs were carried out almost exclusively by student services people or by other staff brought in especially for those tasks. As these programs became institutionalized, particularly in the academic area, leadership from the top becomes less important.

External forces were important in the development of the programs at a number of institutions. The availability of state funds for supportive services was crucial in the programs at Clarion and California State. Title III funds supported the Success Program at Lewis. Federal and foundation grants helped all of the other institutions initiate and, in some cases, maintain their academic and supportive services programs at some point in their histories. And of course, federal and state aid programs helped support many of the minority students.

Conflict was a critical element in the development of programs after a sizable number of blacks had been recruited. There is no question that, once blacks were on campus, they brought heightened demands for further institutional responses. Typically led by a black student organization and often advised by staff members of the visible minority program on campus, the black students at eight of the institutions initiated major confrontations with administrators that led quite directly to new support service and academic programs.

To quickly review the conflicts and their consequences again: At Bowling Green a confrontation led by the Black Student Union brought an intensive recruitment program, the extension of the Student Development Program, expansion of financial aid to minorities, and an ethnic studies center. At Bradley, the 1969 demands of the Black Student Association led to the establishment of a black studies program. At Brockport, the Black Student Liberation Front presented a lengthy set of demands which led to the establishment of the African-American Studies Department and the addition of a black assistant to the Dean for Undergraduate Academic Affairs to supervise Summer Start and other programs for the disadvantaged. At Northwestern, as a result of a building occupation in 1969 which received national attention, the African-American Student Affairs Program was begun. At City the development of comprehensive programs resulted from a series of confrontations between black students and white administrators; the Community Education Program was expanded and a black studies program was founded after black students occupied the Computer Center. At Metropolitan University, black student militancy during a week of student strikes in 1970 (which also involved protests over ROTC) led to the creation of a new vice presidency staffed by a black and to the extension of already existing academic programs. And at Macalester, although conflict did not lead to any new programs, a building occupation by EEO students in the fall of 1974 resulted in the restoration of some of the program funds which had been cut by the new president.

Conflict, however, did not guarantee a substantial response. At Lewis, despite major confrontations between 1969 and 1971, there was no major academic support program until 1973 and no black studies program. In general, the more extensive the demands, the more extensive the response (again, with the exception of Lewis). Conversely, two universities—State and Kansas City—had comprehensive programs without having experienced major conflicts. Both of these institutions moved early to recruit black students and to provide them with a wide range of services.

Further, a full response to black student demands did not guarantee success or stability for the programs which were introduced. A number of the institutions, as we have noted, placed most of their minority programs within one major office. This device often engendered problems. Bowling Green's Student Development Program, hastily staffed and funded, quickly became a separatist program. Under its first director, a charismatic but difficult person, financial and management problems began to appear. Large numbers of poorly prepared students were recruited. Conflicts between SDP and moderate, more academic black administrators and faculty members developed; and, somewhat later, internal conflicts within the SDP staff began to surface. A new provost fired the director of SDP, with tacit support from non-SDP black staff. But later these black staff members staged a sit-in to press for the creation of the position of Vice-Provost for Minority Affairs, to which an individual was appointed the following year. Although the vice-provost was beginning to exert control over SDP and to more fully integrate the program into the mainstream of the university, the old schisms still persisted in 1974. When we visited the Bowling Green campus, the faculty remained suspicious of the program, and relations between SDP and the Ethnic Studies Program were problematic.

A similar scenario occurred at Macalester. Although the EEO program was approved by the Faculty Advisory Council, the student government, and the Board of Trustees, it too became a separatist program. The first director of EEO moved quickly to build an autonomous unit and increasingly recruited high-risk students. The program cost a great deal more than had been originally budgeted, and conflicts began to appear within the EEO staff. Following the withdrawal of support from Macalester's major donor in 1969 and President Flemming's resignation, the director of EEO departed also. Drastic budget cuts were made in 1971–72, and the EEO freshman enrollment was cut from 75 per year to 40. Further budget cuts were made in 1974. EEO students and their supporters staged a takeover of a college building, drawing national attention to the college. A detailed review of the EEO program, initiated by the Board, was begun that year. At the time of our visit, previously sympathetic white faculty and black staff were openly criticizing the separatist nature of the program, its academic quality, and its high cost. There was some indication that moderate black faculty, like those at Bowling Green after the departure of SDP's first director, were organizing to prevent a wholesale retreat from the college's minority commitment.

INSTITUTIONALIZATION AND FACULTY SUPPORT

As financial stringencies became more urgent, faculty support for the minority programs became more crucial. Yet since faculty, on the whole, were not involved in the initiation or implementation of such programs, they knew little about them. Support services programs in general were viewed with suspicion by the faculties. Attempts at coordination came late in most of the institutions we studied, even in those which had not developed a separatist tone.

In the history of the support programs for minorities, recruiting and financial aid came before academic services. As the latter became more elaborated, concern about questions of coordination, possible duplication, and separation from the regular academic activities began to be expressed. In all but one case among programs located in the academic area we were able to document a reorganization. Bowling Green's Student Development Program was originally placed under the Vice President for Student Affairs; it was later located under a new Vice Provost for Minority Affairs under the academic provost. Macalester's EEO program moved from the Vice President's purview to that of the Dean of the Faculty. City's CEP program was formerly located under the Provost's office and was recently placed under the Dean of the College of Arts and Sciences. Kansas City's Transitional Year Program moved in 1974 from the Division for Continuing Education, where it was initiated, to a position under the Assistant Dean in the College of Arts and Sciences. Only the support services programs at Clarion, Carleton, Lewis, and Northwestern remained in the student affairs area.

In one sense, this trend put the programs at a lower level in the administrative hierarchy: programs which were either located under a high administrative officer or under a vice president or dean of students were closer to the top administrative leadership. In the academic area, the minority programs typically appeared at the fourth echelon in the academic hierarchy.

On the other hand, the incorporation of support services into the academic bureaucracy was an indication that the program was being brought into the mainstream of the educational activities of the institution and was, potentially at least, more likely to be integrated into and coordinated with those activities than they had been when they were located in the nonacademic sphere. Since the academic hierarchy has more levels and greater decentralization, there may have been some trade-off in the degree of access these programs would have to executive officers and in the speed with which they could initiate new activities.

State's dual structure is worth examining closely. Located under a single office headed by an individual with the title "Vice President for Student Services and Dean of Academic Affairs," the Support Services Program had links with a number of related campus units. SSP staff members worked in the offices of Admissions and Financial Aids. There were additional direct ties between SSP and Educational Opportunity Program committees in the School of Law, Dentistry, and Medicine. The Director of SSP had ongoing involvement with these EOP committees and the SSP liaison people. A similar relationship existed with the graduate school. Coordination with academic units on the development of curriculum was more tenuous. Although the SSP director was on the Afro-American Studies Committee, most of the contact between him and Afro-American Studies centered on graduate programs. While interwoven into the fabric of the university, SSP was given considerable autonomy by the administration, especially by the Vice President for Student Services.

State's support program was the most highly coordinated of the 13 institutions in our study. Although we have noted the tendency in the last few years to move support services into the academic area, this did not guarantee coordination. Formal mechanisms were needed to insure such ties, and they did not happen automatically, especially if the support unit previously had a history of great autonomy. Coordination could be achieved by building a recognizable minority office into the institution under a major administrator and then guaranteeing liaison, review, and formal linkage. Coordination could also be achieved by locating minority concerns in a variety of existing offices. The 13 institutions followed different strategies of incorporation. State, Bowling Green, Kansas City, Metropolitan University, the University of the City, Macalester, Lewis, and Clarion drew all or almost all of their support services activities under one administrative office (either in the student area or the academic area). Bowling Green was most self-conscious about this device when it introduced the position of Vice Provost for Minority Affairs in 1973, under whom all minority-related programs were placed. At the other extreme were Bradley, Carleton, and Northwestern, which had decentralized minority concerns in several offices located in different parts of the organizational structure. Bradley handled minority issues in the housing office, in the financial aids office, and through Curriculum II. Northwestern, which had a comprehensive though highly decentralized operation, had black staff in admissions and financial aids, counseling, and housing, in addition to the more limited staff in Afro-American Student Affairs.

There is a paradox in these different efforts to integrate and coordinate. In order to present a set of unified services to students and to maintain access to top administrators, a single minority program would seem beneficial. But it would also run the danger of becoming a "runaway" program and of being viewed as separatist and illegitimate. The potential for engendering internal and external conflict is high in such a structure. A more decentralized approach would have the advantages of minimizing opposition and increasing integration. But it would also be less visible and have lower access to central decision-makers. Resources, both monetary and human, would be more diffused.

Black studies programs suffered from similar problems. Even though black studies have a closer connection to the academic structure—or perhaps especially because they do—it is likely to be questioned as an academic field. Several of the black studies programs in this study were understaffed and poorly supported. Even those which received greater financial support had not achieved control over faculty recruitment or promotion. Although a number of these programs had their origins in confrontation between black students and administrators, and were initiated in some cases without faculty review, their full acceptance and institutionalization, unlike supportive services, rested with faculties. Those introduced early with solid support (State, Brockport, Northwestern, City, and Bowling Green) had a better chance of surviving as of 1974–75 than those begun late and half-heartedly.

But, as we have already noted, even the early, well-supported programs faced trouble in times of budget cuts—particularly those which were lacking clear direction. Many of the programs reviewed in this chapter clearly reached a stable state and may even enter a period of decline. At a time when black enrollment reached a substantial level and new minority programs were just beginning to mature, all but a few of the wealthier institutions were being faced with retrenchment.

10

Student Organizations
and Student Life

Marvin W. Peterson and Roselle W. Davenport

During only a brief visit to a campus it was difficult to get an accurate picture of how its student cultures affected and were affected by issues related to increased black enrollments. However, we were able to learn a great deal about the public, formal side of student life by looking at extracurricular organizations and key events in which students were involved, particularly those connected with decisions to increase black enrollments.

THE STUDENT ROLE IN
INCREASING BLACK ENROLLMENTS

There seemed to be a relationship between general student protest activity in the 1960s and student support of black enrollment increases. While some white students on all of the 13 campuses in our sample were active in civil rights and other protest activity during the mid-1960s, the most intense student activity was at Macalester, State University, the University of the City, and, to a lesser degree, Carleton, and Northwestern. These were primarily residential campuses with bright students and highly organized student activities, including active student governments. At three of these five campuses, white students played an important role in the events leading to the initial black enrollment increases.

In 1968, student activists at Macalester were involved in designing, drafting, and approving the Expanded Educational Opportunities Program. At State University, the student government had been instrumental in organizing student participation in southern civil rights marches in the mid-1960s and had responded favorably to student exchange programs with black colleges. President Tyrone, following his convocation address after Martin Luther King's assassination, sought the involvement of State's key black students—in drafting proposals for minority programs and in reviewing them the following fall. At Carleton, although students did not initiate the black enrollment increase, they were insured involvement in that institution's community governance process.

The limited white student involvement in the events and decisions leading to increased black student enrollments at other campuses seemed due not so much to lack of interest as to the way those events were structured by black spokespersons and white administrators. There was no evidence of negative reactions among white students to the early decisions.

The concern of black students enrolled at the time of the first commitments to recruit large numbers of other black students undoubtedly preceded official recruitment decisions. Informal black student activity was reported on 4 of the 13 campuses. At State University, two blacks in the student government were instrumental in drafting a program for black student recruitment and related programs which were presented by the president during the convocation following the King assassination. At Clarion, a small delegation of black students found the acting president receptive to their ideas. At California State and the University of the City, black students made formal demands at the same time that initial recruitment plans were being designed by administrators. These early groups of black students helped to shape their campuses' early actions.

But the initiating role of students, both black and white, was limited. Students were most active on campuses where the existing governance structures or leadership philosophies already allowed their involvement. White students, while usually supportive of civil rights protests and the initial black enrollment increases, were not key instigators of change. Black students were more influential at this stage, but their greatest impact came later when their numbers increased.

THE STUDENT ROLE IN INSTITUTIONAL CONFLICT

In Chapter 8, we looked in detail at the dynamics of conflict in the 13 institutions. Here, we will focus only on the role of students in major incidents of conflict involving minority issues. We identified 24 such incidents on 11 of the 13 campuses. In all of these, black students were major participants. Fourteen of these incidents were instigated by a black student organization claiming to represent all black students on campus. Four additional incidents were initiated by white students, but black student organizations intervened to divert the conflict to their own issues (e.g., the SDS-instigated "union discrimination" issue at Bradley in 1968; the "Kent State" issue at Bowling Green and at Metropolitan in 1970; the "Cambodia" issue at Brockport in 1970). The remaining incidents involved black athletes or other black students not represented by a particular organization. These incidents for the most part did not occur until after the initial increase in black enrollments, but they did reflect the early formation of politically active black student organizations on the campuses.

Black student groups followed the tactics of separating their issues from those of white students and of focusing their efforts toward the institutions' top-level administrators, the presidents and executive officers. White student participation in most of the early incidents was limited. The four incidents in which black issues were added onto other issues were exceptions. Only at Bradley did black and white students join forces, in opposition to a proposed tuition hike. In incidents at State University and at Macalester white students actively supported black demands, and at Metropolitan University the white president of the student body served as a negotiator during conflicts involving black students.

The general separation between black and white students indicated tensions on campus, not just tactical decisions. Formal demands also reflected these tensions. For example, some of the black demands asked for recognition of black student organizations. Other demands covered matters such as: housing (reflecting racial tensions in the dorms or the desire for separate black dorms); social space (conflicts over use of facilities); athletics (discrimination in intercollegiate and intramural programs); and interracial dating. Racial incidents stemmed from issues relating to lack of black cheerleaders; rejection by white students of off-campus blacks invited by black students; reports of threats, intimidation, and personal violence; interracial dating; lack of white student support for black events; concerns over student government resource allocation; and demands for black student representation in student government.

INTERRACIAL PATTERNS AND CLIMATE

The list of racial tensions was extensive on each campus. On all four campuses in Stage II of the study—SUNY–Brockport, Metropolitan, the University of Missouri–Kansas City, and State University—students saw higher levels of racial tension within the student body than did faculty or administrators, and interracial tension among students continued to be substantial in the spring of 1975. The charges and countercharges between black and white students became a familiar litany on all the campuses (and some of it continues even today): white students described black students as cliquish and as having a "different lifestyle." The former characterization referred to black students' preference for black-only social gatherings, organizations, teams, and friendships. Included within the latter were the playing of loud music, interest in different styles of interpersonal relations (the handshake, jargon, etc.), different study patterns (late at night or irregularly scheduled), and different cultural, academic, and social interests. Blacks, on the other hand, saw white students as not wishing to mix except superficially with blacks and as not being willing to accept or experience some of their own interests or ways of doing things. On the antagonistic extremes, whites feared violence by blacks, and blacks believed their own interests were being subverted by white students.

Although our data are limited, they do give us the impression that certain conditions exaggerated tensions among students. Where the gap in economic and social backgrounds was large—for example, at Macalester and at Northwestern—early tensions were greatest. Interracial tensions were less strong at two other selective institutions—Carleton and State University—whose white and black students were not from radically different backgrounds. Perceptions of inequities in the allocation of resources also produced hostility toward blacks among white students. In institutions with large proportions of students from lower income families, such as Lewis, white students resented the provision of what they saw as expensive, possibly exclusionary special services and programs for minorities. Finally, the absence of nearby black residential or social communities also exacerbated tensions among black and white students.

BLACK STUDENT ORGANIZATIONS:
EMERGENT SEPARATISM

An important component of the impact of black students on each of the 13 campuses was the emergence of a black student organization that claimed to represent all of the black students on campus (Table 10-1). These groups typically emerged within one year after the first cohorts of specially recruited black students arrived on the campuses. For most of the institutions, this was in 1968 or 1969, shortly after the assassination of Martin Luther King.

The new group of students had been brought to white campuses with high expectations and a post–civil rights era consciousness, but they found few planned programs ready to deal with their interests, concerns, and needs. On seven of the campuses, the black students immediately made their presence felt by initiating major confrontations. By the time of our campus visits, informants on most of the campuses could no longer recall the exact nature of the student groups which had organized the first confrontations. However, some characteristics are clear. Most had been formed by the specially recruited black students. Less well prepared academically and more economically disadvantaged than the white students or earlier black students, they were poorly socialized to the norms of change in academe. Nevertheless, black student leaders were effective in their efforts in spite of, or perhaps because of, that gap. Most of the groups had spokespersons who were often effective in building support among fellow black students and among sympathetic whites, in spotting institutional weaknesses, and in using conflict strategies.

Black student leaders represented a group that the institutions were trying to assist and—unlike the white student radicals of the 1960s—were complaining about conditions the institutions could more easily do something about. Yet for institutional leaders to give in to black students' demands, in the face of personal insults and bitter condemnations, was not easy. The limits of confrontation and force were often overstepped on both sides. Black students, fueled by a sense of righteousness and injury and lacking the sophistication and experience of academic politics, made it difficult for white leaders to distinguish rhetoric from bargaining ploys. Group spirit and unity were easy to whip up in the early years, and the blacks' initial success in getting presidents and executive officers to negotiate was exhilarating to them.

TABLE 10-1

Black Student Organizations

Institution	Intensive Black Student Organization* (Year Founded)	Fraternities and Sororities§	Other Organizations//
Bowling Green	Black Student Union—BSU (1968)	8	5
Bradley	Black Student Alliance—BSA (1968)	8	4
SUNY–Brockport	Black Student Liberation Front—BSLF (1969)	NA	NA
California State	Black League of Afro-Americans at California State—BLACS (1969)	2	
Carleton	Students Organized for Unity and Liberation—SOUL (1968)		9
"University of the City"	Black Action Society—BAS† (1968)	7	2*
Clarion State	Black Student Union—BSU (1971)	2	2
Lewis	Black Student Union—BSU (1969)	1, plus 2 interest groups	
Macalester	Black Liberation Affairs Committee—BLAC (19--)		2*
"Metropolitan University"	Black Student Alliance—BSA‡ (1972) [formerly Black Residence Union (1971)]	City-wide intercollege chapters	
University of Missouri– Kansas City	The Afro-American Student Union—TAASU (1968)	1	1
Northwestern	For Members Only—FMO (1967) Afro-American Student Union—AASU (1968)	6	4*
"State University"	Black Student Union—BSU (1969)	5	10*

*This category includes recognized organizations representing all black students on a campus.
†This organization was a part of an intercollegiate black organization: Black Action Student Intercollegiate Struggle (statewide).
‡This organization was part of an intercollegiate black organization: Association of Black Collegians (citywide).
§This category includes those formally organized. Other informal black social groups existed on several campuses.
//Includes organizations with formal institutional recognition; other informal groups may have existed. The asterisk (*) indicates that the primary black student organization operated equivalent suborganizations.

By 1974 the situation had changed: The black student organizations had become legitimate. Some focused on narrow purposes and others retained a broader scope. Some of the primary groups focused on coordinating all black student organizations on their own campuses; some preferred to act primarily as political pressure groups; and still others wished to run all black programs. The range of functions espoused, but not necessarily practiced, included: to unify black student interests; to be recognized as blacks' official representatives on the campuses; to educate, or confront, the institutions about inadequacies of their programs for black students; to provide black cultural programs and experiences for their members and the campuses; to provide service programs to the local black or minority communities and give black students an opportunity to participate in them; to provide educational or support services for black students; to sponsor social and other special interest activities for black students; to raise funds (or obtain allocations) for black programs or activities; and to relate to blacks in the community and black students at other colleges and universities. This was a heady list, even if only partially pursued.

Some of the black student groups had organized ways of accomplishing a broad range of purposes. The Black Action Society (BAS) at the University of the City is an example. In 1974 BAS was a well-organized student organization with diverse activities and concerns. The major purpose of BAS was to articulate the needs of black and minority students at the university, which was accomplished by a number of different mechanisms. A steering committee included representatives from all of the organization's major committees. Standing committees included the Political Action Committee, the Black Action News Committee, the BAS Theater, the Programming Committee, the Social Committee, and the Public Relations Committee. Each of these sponsored major activities in its area of concern. Activities of the BAS also included organizing a Black Week, community service projects, and social and cultural events. The BAS also maintained a close working relationship with City's Department of Black Studies and Community Educational Programs. The organization was a member of the Black Action Student InterCollegiate Struggle (BAS-ICS), an embryonic group which linked the black student groups from all of the state's colleges and universities. A most interesting recent development in the evolution of black student organizations is the growth of such networks.

While some of the black organizations enhanced their influence both among black students and within their institutions, most were reported to be somewhat less effective and attractive in the mid-1970s than they had been in their early years. The varied reasons for this included: the growing diversity of black students and the concomitant diversity of black student organizations; rapid turnover in black student leadership; poor funding; decreased support from white student groups; geographically dispersed living accommodations; the lack of good issues to rally around. The web of internal and external relationships with other student groups, with community groups, with administrative offices, and with black or minority programs necessary for a stable organization had become increasingly complex and difficult to control.

The institutionalization of intensive black student organizations was just beginning to be faced on the 13 campuses in 1974. On most campuses, these groups came under the control of the official student government, at least for allocations of student activity funds. This arrangement was a source of conflict on most of the campuses, since in earlier years some of the funds for black student organizations had come from high-level administrative offices or from minority support services programs. In 1974, the exact patterns of funding varied. In some institutions, funds were given to the intensive black student organization for almost all "recognized" black student activities, but this created problems of internal distribution for the black student group. On each of several other campuses, the intensive black student group was just one of several black organizations seeking funds from the student government—which placed them, to some degree, in competition with one another. The situation was further complicated by the fact that some black student activities, whether run through the intensive organization or not, were funded through additional sources: cultural activities may have been partially supported through the black studies program under an academic officer; student social activities may have received funds from the student government or the student affairs office; and service and other activities may have been under the aegis of a minority program administrator.

From this complexity, four clear student organization patterns emerged. In the first, the intensive black student organization ran all black student organizations and activities and was placed under the student government or within the student affairs sector. In the second, numerous black student organizations existed and reported independently through student government. The third and fourth patterns are variants of the first two, with the differences being that the organizations were responsible to more than one administrative officer. In essence then, the intensive black student organization and many of the other black student organizations were ultimately incorporated into the official bureaucratic structures for funding and recognition, if not for programming and politicking.

In addition to funding, the relationship of the intensive black student organizations to student government and the issue of black student representation became sources of substantial problems on most of the campuses. Here again, four patterns emerged. In the first, the student government made a provision for electing a black student representative. In the second, the intensive black student organization elected or appointed a representative to the student government—or, as in the case of Metropolitan University, it appointed the student government vice-president. In the third, provision was made for appointing black students to student government committees. In the last pattern, no provisions were made for the representation of blacks. On each of several campuses, a black had been elected by the student body as either president or vice-president of the student government.

Over the period since the emergence of an intensive black student organization on each campus, several other black student organizations were also formed (see Table 10-1). These were developed primarily in response to black student needs and interests, with the encouragement of black faculty and staff, student affairs staff, and/or student government. Some represented special black interests, and others reflected the inability or unwillingness of groups of blacks to become a part of pre-existing white student organizations. Except at Macalester and Carleton, which had neither fraternities nor sororities—blacks at all of the institutions formed active fraternities and sororities, occasionally local but often chapters of national black Greek-letter organizations. But on the campuses where a Panhellenic or Inter-fraternity Council existed, the black fraternities and sororities were not affiliated with them. Indeed, at the University of the City, a coordinating unit was formed to help black fraternities and sororities deal with common problems.

Equally numerous were special interest black organizations. The most elaborated were cultural and performance organizations for drama, dance, and music. The names reflect the black culture emphasis of these groups: Mojo Theater; the Gospeliers; Black Genesis; Voices of Soul. Some were athletic groups: Black Athletes Coalition; Black Karate Club; a varsity pep squad. Some were primarily social or residential units. Several off-campus service groups were active: Ebony Sisters; Brothers Inc.; Sisters, Inc. Some groups of black students, primarily at the more elite institutions, formed professional interest groups (e.g., law; pre-med; psychology). The number of black organizations was probably greater than we were able to detect, since at some institutions they may have existed as part of an intensive black organization and may not have been identified separately (e.g., State, Macalester, Northwestern, the University of the City).

The size and diversity of black groups on the 13 campuses led to new problems, such as finding black faculty and staff advisors in institutions where few were available and attracting enough members on campuses where the numbers or interest of black students were not great enough. Coordination of scheduling with white organizations to equalize the use of limited facilities was often a problem which, in some institutions, led to the establishment of special student government or Dean of Students committees to resolve them.

At the heart of the matter was a more basic issue. A sizable number of predominantly black student organizations replicated the functions of existing white student organizations. Students and staff continually reported little or no white student involvement (other than by the student government) in black student organizations and clubs, and vice versa. This pattern of separate student organizations gave validity to the reports of separate housing choices and infrequent interracial socializing. On only one campus, Lewis University, did we find an active interracial student group, "The Seekers."

A PARADIGM: BLACK-WHITE STUDENT RELATIONS

Student attitudes towards interracial relations, identified in our Stage II survey when combined with these patterns of student organizations, suggest a two-dimensional pattern of black-white student relations. First, on an organizational dimension, one can describe a campus according to a separate versus integrated pattern of its student organizations. On an attitudinal dimension, it is possible to construct a continuum from acceptance through disinterest or indifference to rejection or antagonism in black-white student relations. These two dimensions together produce four possible patterns of the racial climate on a campus (see Figure 10-1):

Fully Integrated: The organizational and activity patterns of black and white student groups involve mixing of races and accepting of the other race's interests and concerns.

Racially Tense: The organizational and activity patterns of black and white student groups assure mixing of the races, but attitudes between the races are antagonistic.

Pluralistic: The organizational and activity patterns of black and white student groups involve separate racial patterns, but attitudes between the races are positive and accepting.

Racist: The organization and activity patterns of black and white student groups involve separate racial patterns, and attitudes between the races are negative and/or antagonistic.

FIGURE 10-1

Organizational Patterns and Student Interracial Attitudes

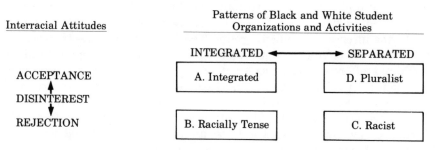

There were some identifiable differences on the 13 campuses we visited, but, unfortunately, we have systematic attitudinal measures only for students at the four campuses where survey data was collected. Thus, we cannot identify all 13 institutions to fill in the paradigm. Both our visits and the question responses at four of the institutions indicated a clear sense of mutual disinterest or distrust among students of both races on the attitudinal dimension. Organizational activities, as we have described them, followed an essentially separate racial pattern.

Despite this rather pessimistic picture of the student racial climate, we can trace some critical transitions and venture a prediction or two. Initially, the campuses recruited black students on the assumption that student activities and relationships would be essentially integrated (Pattern A in Figure 10-1). The liberal attitudes among faculty and students led them to show their commitment to black students on campus just as they had off-campus in supporting the civil rights movement. However, the new black students brought their own lifestyles, interests, and activities, which often clashed with those of white students. Black special interest groups formed. Incidents of conflict, at the institutional level as well as in the informal life on campus, began to split white and black students. The white student body began to develop negative reactions toward blacks, who were simultaneously adopting a separate political and organizational stance. The campus atmosphere became *racially tense* (Pattern B) or *racist* (Pattern C). The assumption of integrated patterns of activity and positive interracial attitudes was weakened and, in some situations, destroyed.

By the time of our visits to the 13 campuses, the general atmosphere had shifted from rejection to mutual disinterest between black and white students, while organizational activities continued to be separate. In the absence of strong forces working for improved racial acceptance among black and white students, there seemed little likelihood that any of these institutions would move toward either a *pluralist* student body (Pattern D) or an *integrated* one (Pattern A). We found only one interracial student group, "The Seekers" at Lewis University, which was working to improve racial relations on campus. Student affairs staff were often active in promoting interracial acceptance, while faculty as a group were less involved. Top administrators did not seem as concerned with this goal as they had been earlier. With budgetary declines threatening minority programs and student affairs programs on most campuses, there was an increasing likelihood of conflict between black and white students over priorities.

INSTITUTIONAL ATTRACTIVENESS FOR BLACK STUDENTS

One interesting paradox emerged in our study. Most of the 13 institutions recognized the patterns of student organizations just portrayed and recognized the tense interracial climate which was confirmed in our Stage II surveys. They also saw themselves as taking positive, if inadequate, steps to deal with these problems. They noted the variety of activities they were conducting or supporting in an attempt to make themselves more attractive to black students. In addition to setting up formal minority academic and support programs, they said they were providing more space for black social and cultural activities, expanding intramural programs, providing black residence advisors or black student residence areas, and hiring black staff, among other things. The paradox is that, despite this reported concern, not one of the institutions attempted to ascertain in a systematic way what made it more or less attractive to black students or how black students' perceptions of the institutions differed from those of white students. Data from our Stage II student survey on "Institutional Attractiveness for Black Students" show measurable differences between what black students said attracted them to an institution and what white students believed attracted the blacks.

Nine out of 12 institutional features were rated lower as factors attractive to blacks by the black students themselves than by white students on the Stage II campuses. This difference in itself is an indication of sources of friction or misunderstanding between the races (Table 10-2)—particularly if white faculty or administrators had the same misperceptions. The exceptions are even more instructive: black students rated "good academic reputation" and "availability of a good program in preferred major" as the two most important attractions for them, while white students perceived the black students as placing less emphasis on these features. The other most attractive aspect of their institutions for blacks was the availability of financial aid—an item white students rated lower (perhaps they felt that minority students received a proportionally larger share of the aid dollars). The blacks rated everything else—particularly athletics, location, availability of black social and cultural activities, and the presence of black faculty and active black students—at the middle or lower end of the scale.

The implication, of course, is that greater attention to black students' academic interests should be a major concern. This requires a response from faculty and department-level academic programs—a level at which, as discussed in Chapter 13, the institutions have not been particularly responsive. The institutional responses appeared to be in areas that black students rate lower—either because they already existed or because they truly are of less importance.

CONCLUSION

In sum, the picture of the response to black students within the student body has not been encouraging. White students, along with the faculties and administrations, initially anticipated integration, but they found that the first groups of black students were different and more militant than they had expected. The newly recruited black students reacted with frustration, defensiveness, and mistrust. A period of activism, after which white students largely withdrew from leadership roles and even participation, was followed by substantial black-white hostility and tension. The creation of separate black clubs, organizations, and living patterns later dissipated some of the early overt conflicts over facilities, space, and funds. The colleges and universities themselves have not been systematically attempting to find out why black students are attending the institutions. However, this pattern of separatism was scarcely a stable situation for black or white students who were soon to be competing for declining resources in their institutions and for declining job opportunities for college graduates.

TABLE 10-2

Institutional Attractiveness for Black Students, by Race

Attractive Institutional Attribute	Mean for Black Students	Mean for White Students	Mean for All Students
Desire to be near home or live at home	2.7	2.7	2.7
Good academic reputation of institution	3.9	3.1	3.3
Availability of a good program in preferred major	4.0	3.6	3.7
Black or minority recruitment and admission program	3.1	3.4	3.3
Presence of black faculty and/or active, visible black students on campus	2.8	3.6	3.3
Location in an urban area or presence of nearby black communities	2.6	3.0	2.8
Availability of black social life and cultural activities oriented to black people on campus	2.7	3.5	3.3
Acquaintance with students who attended the institution or its reputation among blacks	2.7	3.5	3.2
Availability of financial support	3.9	4.7	4.1
Opportunity to participate in intramural or intercollegiate athletics	2.2	3.4	3.0
Desire to be away from home	2.4	2.9	2.7
Existence of black or ethnic studies program	2.7	3.4	3.2
N =	181	339	591†

Note: The question was as follows: "The enrollment of black students at this institution has been increasing. In your opinion, how significant are each of the factors listed below in *attracting black students? Black students*: Rate the significance of these factors for *your* being attracted to this institution. *Other students*: Rate how significant *you think these are for black students* at this institution. (Check one response for each item.)"

The 12 items were rated on a five-point scale as follows: (1) of no significance; (2) slight; (3) some; (4) substantial; (5) of very great significance.

†Total N is more than for black plus white column because some students did not answer the racial identification question.

11

Impacts on Administrative, Faculty, and Organizational Structures and Processes

Marvin W. Peterson

This study anticipated that attempts to increase black student enrollments would have an impact on the administration, the faculty, and some other organizational patterns. While explicit administrative and faculty perceptions of role impact are identified more precisely in the Stage II survey data (Part IV), our Stage I interviews and documentary analysis identified significant changes in organizational structures and processes.

ADMINISTRATIVE STRUCTURES AND PROCESSES

Our earlier discussions of environmental forces and institutional experiences (Chapter 6), of precipitating events and response strategies (Chapter 7), and of conflict (Chapter 8) identified the key role played by administrative leadership as some of these institutions began to enroll black students. Administrators, particularly the institutions' presidents and key executive officers, were primary participants in early responses and they often became targets of black students' anger. They were usually the main negotiators in conflicts when a list of demands was presented, and administrators continued to be major actors once agreements were forged. Therefore, it is important to ask what effects the entry of blacks had on administrative and governance structures. We turn first to the impact of black issues on the trustees.

Trustees: Involvement and Reaction

The 13 institutions in our sample are of varied sizes and differ in the types of governing boards they have. The six private institutions have autonomous boards whose members are appointed. Two institutions report to public university system boards: Brockport is part of the SUNY system under the New York Board of Regents, and Kansas City is part of the University of Missouri system under the university's Board of Curators. California State and Clarion State have local boards but are part of the Pennsylvania State College System under the state's Commission on Higher Education. Bowling Green and "State University," as large public institutions, have their own governing boards. "The University of the City," a quasi-public institution, represents yet another pattern: 24 members of its board are appointed by the institution and 12 are public representatives. Despite this variety the racial composition of these boards was essentially homogeneous—only two had black members prior to 1968.

There was no indication in any of the 13 institutions that the trustees as a group or as individuals were instrumental in initiating the increase of black students. Neither were any of the changes in board memberships the result of student demands. Blacks were appointed to several of the boards either during the civil rights period or after the initial increase of black students and programs. The governing boards played similar roles in the black enrollment increases at nearly all of the institutions—and their involvement was minimal. It was typical for the boards to be aware or informed of the initial attempts to increase black enrollments but not to be involved in any formal decisions. However, the presidents at Carleton and Macalester sought the involvement of the governing boards in the discussion and approval of the initial minority programs.

The pattern was repeated at later stages when formal programs for minorities began to emerge. At Carleton and Macalester, the boards were involved in programmatic decisions from the time of the decisions to increase black enrollments, and in the public institutions new programs sometimes had to be approved by the governing boards. In other instances, new programs may have been reported but the records are unclear as to when or how that occurred. In no instance was there board resistance to the initiation of any of the emergent programs for blacks. Some boards reviewed budgets for particular minority programs, but these did not become controversial until the more recent conflicts over financial retrenchment.

In incidents of conflict between black students and the administration, the boards of trustees tended to adopt a hands-off posture, thus giving latitude to administrators to negotiate a settlement. Administrators in turn had a sense of the limits which the trustees would accept. On occasion an individual board member with strong feelings might attempt to influence the president or other board members. Several presidents reported that they had been subject to such pressure from individual board members as well as from students; they each knew what the black student demands were and they knew the views of certain board members, but they did not have a clear picture of the acceptable range of agreement for the board as a whole.

Following negotiations, the boards often reviewed agreements and occasionally were asked to endorse them. At this stage, uncomfortable situations sometimes arose. In one case, the board endorsed an agreement but refused to endorse the preamble in which the institution was asked to acknowledge its "racist" history. In another, the board was said to have intervened to establish punitive procedures against participants in a sit-in. In many of the conflicts, a black board member (usually recently appointed) was cited as effective in mediating the internal divisions on a board or between the board and the president following a conflict. In one incident, a black board member served as a mediator between a president and a black student group; in another case, a black who served as an outside negotiator during a conflict at an institution was later appointed to the institution's board.

Even when board members were drawn indirectly into the black student conflicts, this did not result in any new board policies or practices. It appeared that this general non-involvement stance was merely a reflection of their role in other student conflicts. However, in two more recent events, the governing boards at Macalester and Lewis became more directly involved in reviews of minority programs. This may be a trend at the other institutions as well; in our judgment, increased involvement has more to do with the increasing openness of boards generally and with the difficult resource decisions facing them.

Impacts on Administrative Roles

While both the impacts on and the responses of the institutions' governing boards resulting from the changes in black student enrollments were limited, such was not the case for administrators—particularly presidents and those in certain areas of administration. Administrative roles were changed appreciably both by design and by necessity. Presidents, student affairs staff, and admissions and financial officers were most affected by these changes. The impacts on academic administrators—vice presidents, deans, and department chairmen—while perhaps as personally intense, were not as visible and occurred later. Some of the reasons for these differential impacts are obvious.

Presidents are expected to lead, and the important roles played by several of them in predisposing their institutions to accept and even initiate the black enrollment increases has already been noted (Chapter 7). They were also the focal institutional representatives for public conflicts with black students (Chapter 8), as well as for the informal confrontations and unregistered conflicts. In the late 1960s, both white and black student demands were predicated on the assumption that the president (or other executive officers) personified "The Man" who could change things.

Admissions and financial aids offices were often the first point of contact between the black student and the institution and, consequently, were the first offices to add black staff members. The rapidly changing nature of state and federal programs for student financial aid—which mixed grants, loans, and work arrangements and required some needs analysis—further complicated the life of the financial aids staff. Expanded student aid funds not only provided visibility for financial aids directors, but also meant a much larger financial aid staff had to be hired and managed.

Student affairs staff were generally acknowledged to have experienced the greatest impact from the entry of black students. Somewhat belatedly, concerns about academic standards, test scores, and remedial needs added new burdens on the admissions or the counseling offices. Problems of dealing with tensions between black and white students, while they varied at different campuses, were usually focused in these offices—at least until major conflicts arose. Additional work loads fell on student services offices which had to deal with new black student organizations and committees for interracial problems. Concerns included black-white tensions in housing, increased demand for intramural sports, the need for more formalized social activities for blacks, scheduling conflicts between black and white groups, and complications in community relations. In addition, coordination between new supportive service programs for blacks and minorities and academic components usually became the responsibility of the student affairs offices.

Academic administrators, on the other hand, focused on problems of recruiting and hiring black faculty and staff, dealing with their professional concerns and prerogatives, and developing academic and/ or supportive services for black students. Yet there were few black faculty on most of the campuses and their professional concerns appeared mainly as a result of affirmative action and retrenchment. Even for department chairpersons—on whom many academic issues and black student/white faculty issues naturally would be expected to focus—the tensions may have been extensive, but the changes were few. (See Chapter 13 for a discussion of departmental changes.)

The visible impacts on administrators certainly appeared greater than those for faculty. The reasons for the disparity are subtle. The 13 institutions usually added more minority members to their administrative staffs than to their faculties. The presence of new black staff members meant that white administrators had increased contact with black administrative colleagues. While this may have eased the direct demands from black students on white administrators, there were many instances where the impact was reported to be the opposite. Whether in student affairs, academic affairs, admissions, financial aids, or elsewhere, black administrators tended to attract black students both as friends and as resources. Directly or indirectly, black administrators became advocates who pressured the white administration to change. This is reflected in the survey data presented in Chapter 12 which show that the institutions' responses and commitments to blacks were perceived as higher by administrators than by faculty, and the demands of black students on their own roles were seen as greater by administrators. Yet administrators also saw the personal impacts of the presence of blacks more positively than did faculty.

Administrative Style

Administrators played out their roles vis-à-vis black issues in a variety of ways. The "social reformers"—most often high level administrators who were relatively new to the institutions—tended to see the colleges or universities as places to ameliorate the condition of blacks in the larger society. Charismatic and energetic, the reformers usually operated with an emphasis on wide participation but moved quickly and had little patience with laggards. Administrators of this type, including a couple of presidents in this study, initially attracted strong support and evoked high expectations within their institutions but faced the risk of disillusionment when efforts failed or when the pace of change slackened.

The "liberal conscience" style was typical of administrators who believed in the goals of civil rights and were adept at both "doing" and "leading." These people were aware of the inner workings of college and university life. While constantly pressing for change, they had a good sense of timing and of institutional readiness to move. At least two of the presidents in our sample institutions and a number of student affairs people fit this pattern. Respected by both blacks and whites, they were still subject to student pressure—in part because they were seen as highly effective.

The "positive pragmatists" were also committed to civil rights, but provided less of a push and direction than either the "social reformers" or the "liberal conscience" types. Rather, these administrators showed early awareness of minority pressures and of the need to deal with them. They were more willing to try a variety of things, to risk failure, and entered more willingly into conflict than either the "reformers" who rode roughshod over conflict, or the "liberals" who tried to avoid it. The "positive pragmatists" were respected and feared both by blacks and whites. Their sense of timing, results, and overall record were the things for which they were judged. At least two presidents fit this leadership style.

There were also the "cautious compromisers," who were less flamboyant than the "positive pragmatists." Good managers who were generally supportive of blacks' concerns, they were unwilling to move boldly or rapidly. Almost always, administrators of this persuasion had substantial experience in higher education and in their own institutions. They were neither revered nor feared by blacks or whites, but because of their comparative inaction they were assailed by the extremes of both groups. Some of the presidents in our sample of institutions and many second- and third-echelon white administrators appeared to fit this style.

The "competent critics" were the administrators who seldom expressed opposition to blacks but always knew their weaknesses and spoke openly about them. These individuals were seldom directly involved with minority activity and their competence in their own areas protected them. They were respected by whites and occasionally attracted a following on black issues. More important, blacks feared and disliked them because they were individuals who could subtly but effectively undermine their programs and interests.

The "resistant reactionaries" were opposed to the black presence—if not for racial reasons then on academic or programmatic grounds. They were more openly critical than the "critics" and would actively seek opportunities to express their opposition. These individuals were generally ignored by many whites. Although viewed as "racists" by blacks, they were not as feared as the critics. This type was most often found in administrative areas not directly involved with minority programs.

New Offices for Blacks

It is also important to look at the ways administrators responded by creating positions for black administrators. New academic and supportive programs for blacks usually meant hiring black administrators to oversee the programs directly. Occasionally new positions concerned with a broad range of minority affairs activities might be created as "umbrella" offices which did not directly operate any minority academic programs but instead coordinated the nonacademic programs for minorities. A third approach was to create new second and third echelon "assistant to" positions not designated for minority persons or explicitly responsible for minority programs but to hire black staff members to fill them. This practice was most prevalent in admissions and financial aids, although it occurred with some regularity in other areas such as student affairs and at the assistant or associate dean levels in academic affairs. In practice, individuals in these administrative positions often dealt primarily with black or minority people and issues. Such lower echelon positions were occasionally assigned informal responsibility for minority students within their nonminority office (e.g., black or minority recruiter, Associate Dean for Afro-American Student Affairs, minority student counselor). A fourth pattern was to promote the director of a minority program to a position with a more general title. For example, at Kansas City the director of the Transitional Year Program became an assistant dean of the College of Arts and Sciences but still retained minority program responsibility.

It was rare to find a black person occupying a top-level administrative position or a middle-level functional position not explicitly responsible for minority programs and affairs. Only five institutions had second echelon officers: the vice president for student affairs at State University, at Bowling Green, and at the University of the

City; the dean of students at Macalester; and the vice president for personnel at Metropolitan University. At Lewis a black served as vice president for community relations until 1972, but the position was discontinued when he left. Other high ranking black administrative officers not explicitly responsible for minority affairs included an associate provost and three academic deans at the University of the City. No other institution had a black academic dean, although several had one or more black assistant or associate deans. At Brockport a black served as assistant to the president for community relations, and at Kansas City a black was assistant to the chancellor.

The presence of top-level minority administrators with other than minority responsibilities was seen by both blacks and whites as evidence of serious commitment to minorities. That black individuals were selected for the five top administrative posts identified above is suggestive of some important dynamics. The vice presidents at State University and Metropolitan University had been respected professors and academic deans at those institutions before being named vice presidents. Metropolitan's vice president was hired after a conflict incident. The vice president at Bowling Green had prior administrative experience there, while the one at the University of the City was a former faculty member at that institution. The dean of students at Macalester, a graduate of that college, had already been serving as an administrator there. It appears these top-level positions went to blacks who were known and respected in their institutions.

Surprisingly, there was little apparent relationship between the presence of black administrators, either for minority or nonminority positions, and the presence of black faculty. Institutions with top-level black administrators like State University, Macalester, and Metropolitan University were among the group of institutions with fewer than 3 percent black faculty. Brockport, with over 9 percent black faculty, did have a black assistant to the president and several other black administrators. However, only the University of the City stood out as having both a substantial number of black executive officers (one vice president, one associate provost, and three deans) and a high percentage of black faculty (Table 11-1).

The dynamics of this latter situation are worth reporting. City not only had a good reputation, an urban location with a nearby black community, early efforts to recruit black students, and a decent salary level with which to attract black faculty and administrators, but it also had a chancellor who took a strong leadership position on the minority issue at a relatively early date. In the fall of 1969, following the occupation of the computer center, the chancellor and most of the top-level administrators attended regular "confrontation-sensitivity sessions" run by black psychiatric social workers. It is apparent that the chancellor encouraged (some said demanded) attendance at those sessions. Shortly thereafter, some white administrators reportedly left the institution and the numbers of black faculty and administrators began to increase.

The Black Administrators

As we have noted, blacks were hired to fill positions primarily in minority programs or areas of responsibility. White administrators, interestingly, did not seem to feel that these new appointments implied any status differences—in contrast to the tendency among white faculty to view blacks in minority programs as holding more marginal faculty positions. Neither were black administrators viewed by their white colleagues as having higher or lower status because of the degrees they held or because of positions they had had before taking on their new jobs. The white administrators seemed to take a pragmatic view: they noted the blacks' performance in their current jobs and their degree of militancy. Yet failure to recognize cultural differences and their own naiveté did lead white administrators to recruit some blacks who were later seen as "mistakes"—people who were long on rhetoric but short on experience and performance. White administrators, nonetheless, were more comfortable with moderate blacks who pressed for change within the confines of the institutions' mores than they were with the more militant blacks. In addition, blacks who were promoted to nonminority positions from within their institutions tended to be more moderate and gained greater respect than blacks who held positions in minority programs, at least in the early years.

The directors of minority programs had varied qualifications. Some had excellent prior experiences, but others had very limited backgrounds for the jobs they were doing. Some were viewed by whites as competent, while others were widely criticized for incompetence. Minority program directors themselves viewed their own roles differently; some wanted their programs to be well integrated with similar nonminority programs and others preferred a more separate role.

Not surprisingly, then, blacks in minority administrative positions faced some difficult obstacles. Their programs were new. They were typically either underfinanced by their institutions or supported by a federal contract with heavy reporting requirements and limited or uncertain duration. Active support from white faculty and administrators in related units was limited. Many minority program administrators found that support and legitimacy had to be earned constantly, particularly as other minority and women's groups began to siphon off support. As the novelty of black studies programs began to wear off, the problem of producing enough credit hours became urgent both to guarantee survival and to maintain interest among black students and white supporters. At the other extreme, if admissions standards dropped and the number of students increased, the work load of support programs multiplied rapidly, but budgetary formulas seldom kept pace. The position of the black administrators in minority programs was fraught with all of these tensions and dangers. That many adopted a variety of strategies to keep themselves and their programs going was to be expected. Several of these individuals were in contact with a network of administrators in similar units at other institutions—an important source of ideas and support, and occasionally an avenue of escape.

The situation of the black administrators in nonminority positions was also complex, but in different ways. As Moore and Wagstaff (1974) found in their survey of black administrators, work overload was intense. The official role demands were always those of the position; these were no more or less complex than for white administrators. However, being black made any administrator an obvious target for black students seeking a friend to help with problems. Because there were so few black faculty, black administrators were often sought out by students in these institutions for personal advice and academic help. They served as advisors to black student groups and were asked to participate in cultural programs. Departments sought them out to be unofficial lecturers or student advisors. There were endless meetings with visitors or deputations of concerned minority groups which required a "black presence." For these administrators, the workload became virtually impossible.

Other Administrative Structures

There were other temporary patterns of administrative response. At one point or another, most of the presidents created some committee, commission, or task force to study and make recommendations on a variety of issues: racism at the University of the City; minority commitment, athletic disruptions, and dormitory problems at State University; Negro affairs at Carleton; student financial needs at Kansas City; human relations at Clarion; and so on. The academic vice presidents or provosts occasionally created special committees to deal with minority issues such as admissions criteria, the role of black faculty and support staff, and other questions which faculty governance bodies tended to skirt. Interestingly, this approach seldom was used by deans or department chairpersons in arts and science departments we examined. In student affairs, special committees were created to deal with interracial incidents, minority problems, and activity scheduling. A less formal mechanism, common in student affairs and to a lesser degree in other areas, was an interracial group which would coalesce to deal with minority problems whenever they occurred. The pattern became a familiar one: the dean or vice president for student affairs, two to four student affairs staff (black and white), one or more black or minority program staff members, and perhaps interested faculty members would become a group whenever black-white tensions emerged. At places like Bradley, Lewis, and Kansas City, this method appeared to be the primary mechanism for dealing with minority issues in student affairs, in creating supportive services, and even in initiating curricular changes.

Another administrative problem which fostered new administrative structures was in the area of external relations. At University of the City, the attempts by the new chancellor to get acquainted with the black community near the university led in part to the creation of the Community Education Program. At Metropolitan University, Father Schmidt's activities led to the formation of an inter-institutional program for recruiting black students. In Kansas City, the absence of interstate compacts in an institution located near the state line presented the institution with problems of relating to a minority community which crossed state lines. The University of Missouri–Kansas City had other external relations problems. As a growing institution, it had continued to acquire nearby property through a private foundation which held the property and eventually made a gift of it to the university. In a transitional neighborhood, this activity was often seen as an attempt by the university to manipulate the neighborhood racial balance.

FACULTY ORGANIZATION AND PATTERNS

The impact on and response of undergraduate faculty to the increasing black student clientele was almost as difficult to trace and document as the patterns in student life and culture described in

Chapter 10. The formal involvement of faculty with the new academic and support programs for black students was described briefly in Chapter 9, and some departmental level changes are highlighted in Chapter 13. The purpose of this discussion is to highlight the more visible faculty patterns of involvement in the initial increase of black students; the faculty role in institutional conflicts; changes in faculty governance structure; and the recruitment and role of black faculty.

Faculty Role in the Enrollment Increase

We have seen that faculty played a limited role in the early stages in each institution's change in its black student clientele. Prior to the enrollment increase, some faculty members participated as individuals in civil rights groups locally or in the South. White faculty members expressed concern about discrimination against minorities on campus, examined the relationship of their classroom subject matter to the experience of blacks, informally recruited black students, participated in early black or minority related programs such as Upward Bound, Talent Search, A Better Chance, black scholarship selection committees, and so forth. At State University organized faculty activity was expressed not only through their involvement in civil rights in the South, but also through institutional ties to two southern black colleges, their Human Rights Committee reports, and a history of working with black graduate students in earlier decades. While they were generally supportive of increased black enrollments, the faculty did not express their predispositions in any organized way on their campuses prior to 1968.

A review of the events leading to the initial black student increase suggests a continuation of this pattern. Only at Carleton, Metropolitan, and State University were there faculty committees on "Negro Affairs," "Racism," and "Human Rights" (respectively) which drafted reports and/or recommendations regarding appropriate institutional responses to blacks or minorities. But even here the faculty did not initiate those activities. At Macalester, President Flemming involved some faculty members in drafting the initial proposal. At Kansas City, individual faculty members were also active but without any official faculty sanction. Only at Carleton, State University, and Macalester were faculty governance bodies formally included in the review and approval of the proposals to increase black enrollments. The involvement of faculty in developing the academic and support programs for blacks discussed in Chapter 9 was also limited. This pattern of limited involvement does not suggest disapproval—merely that faculty were not involved. Indeed, there is evidence on most campuses that faculty organizations and groups were initially supportive of increased black enrollments and the early minority programs.

Institutional Conflicts Between Faculty and Black Students

While there were reports of early tensions between black students and white faculty members in all of the 13 institutions, they were not extensive or as vivid as the reports of tensions between black and white students. The pattern of black-related institutional conflict incidents reported in Chapter 8 supports this contention. The faculty, like the white student body, was seldom a party to these institutional conflicts. In the 24 incidents reported in this study white faculty were not among the major participants, except at Bradley where a single white faculty member served as a mediator between students, administrators, and city police, and at Metropolitan where the white chairman of the Faculty Senate was involved in the negotiation during the occupation of the computing center in 1969. While initial confrontations occasionally included faculty (e.g., the Macalester protest started when EEO students blocked faculty in their meeting room to present their demands) or indirectly affected them (the occupation of buildings or a computer center), they did not become involved in direct confrontations. Even black faculty were usually not actively involved. (Directors of minority-support programs were the exception.) The role of faculty in conflict negotiations on most campuses was also largely peripheral—either they were informed of progress by an official faculty representative, were asked to "advise and confirm" decisions already made, or were informed later and left to react.

Officers of faculty governance bodies, recalling negotiations between black students and white administrators, complained that faculty had little or no opportunity to approve the settlements that resulted from the negotiations. Most faculty respondents recognized that to try to recover faculty prerogatives by rejecting some of the agreements after the negotiations had been completed would have been politically unwise and realistically impossible. Some administrators were aware of the dilemma and only agreed to "recommend" the establishment of academic programs (e.g., black studies at Metropolitan). Limited consultation with faculty and irregular decision making may explain why some of the programs were established as units which were independent or outside of the faculty governance system.

Black students had their own ways of getting around the faculty. On all campuses some departments were identified as supportive and others as antagonistic. The choice of majors among black students reflected these judgments. Faculty suffered tensions, too, but they were more indirectly expressed as concerns for declining student quality (which usually applied to the entire student body), lack of student interest in subject material, poor study habits among the "new special students," and the need for better remedial and service programs and staff. Occasionally, more personal faculty frustrations were reported: difficulties in relating to "the new student"; lack of knowledge of the material about blacks; perceived threats from black students; and additional demands on faculty members' time.

Faculty Governance: Impacts and Responses

In most colleges and universities, faculty have an accepted structure for conducting their affairs which, no matter how effective or ineffective, they guard jealously. The impact on and responses of some of these structures was a major concern in this study. The limited involvement of faculty in the initial increase of black enrollments (Chapter 7), in the formation of academic and support programs for blacks (Chapter 9), and in the institutional conflicts (Chapter 8) accounted for the almost nonexistent impact on faculty governance patterns.

The 13 institutions exhibited some variation in the structure of faculty governance. Carleton's College Council, involving students, faculty, administrators, and trustees, was an example of a participatory senate structure. Macalester retained a more traditional faculty Academic Council. Lewis University, growing and in a state of transition, had no formal faculty governance structure and depended on academic committees and informal consultation with deans and the academic vice president. Brockport, California, and Clarion had faculty unions but also retained their older academic or faculty senates. The remaining institutions reflected the pattern of medium to large institutions, having some form of university-wide faculty or academic senate and some form of college-wide governing faculty or representative council in the college of arts and science.

Despite these variations in structure, several conclusions emerge about the impact on faculty governance. First, none of the institutions established a procedure to insure the representation of black faculty (admittedly sometimes few in number), students, or staff members. Second, in some instances black faculty were members of college or university-wide governance bodies, but these individuals were usually cited as being nonactivists on black or minority issues. Just as activist students decided to circumvent faculty and press demands on top-level administrators, so activist black faculty chose not to participate as members of these faculty governance bodies or were not elected to them. (Only at Macalester in 1974 did black students focus their initial demands on the Faculty Advisory Council.) Third, none of the faculty governance officers at the 13 institutions could identify permanent or ad hoc committees which studied minority supportive service programs, demands, or related issues. Faculty governance bodies did occasionally review black faculty recruitment and issues related to tenure and promotion status, and they also considered special student admission criteria and some proposals for black studies programs or degrees. But these topics were usually merely discussed and rarely came to a vote. Implementation was always left to others. Finally, faculty governance groups on several campuses were reported to have been supportive of some of the black changes, to have never actively blocked their implementation (although there were procedural attempts to do so), and to have never formally evaluated such programs. However, on most campuses there was a growing tendency for the faculty governance bodies to be interested in the process of institutional resource allocation and to suggest the need for evaluation of academic and supportive service programs, including black and minority programs.

Thus, we saw relatively little involvement of faculty governance bodies with black issues or programs. Most of the significant decisions and implementation were being handled by administrators outside of faculty governance channels or on a limited basis at departmental levels (see Chapter 13). The major problems reported by faculty governance representatives concerned general issues of enrollment and financial declines, declining quality of the student body, resource allocation and possible reductions, tenure and promotion policies, faculty recruitment, collective bargaining, or institutional mission changes. In all the institutions, these issues had a higher priority for faculty governance bodies than minorities did.

Recruitment of and Role for Black Faculty

All 13 institutions were faced with the need to increase the number of black faculty members, either because of the needs of the increased numbers of black students, because of a commitment to do so, or because of affirmative action requirements. Yet in three institutions it was not clear that there had been even an effort to recruit black faculty. However, in those instances where there had been documented recruitment efforts, it is clear that these efforts were most successful from 1970 to about 1972—prior to the advent of affirmative action and to the enrollment declines in most of these institutions.

In the fall of 1974 the number of black faculty in each of these 13 institutions ranged from one to over 200. The percentage breakdowns are shown in Table 11-1.

TABLE 11-1

Percentage Black Faculty by Institution

Under 3%	3–6%	Over 6%
Bowling Green	Bradley	Brockport
Carleton	California State	"University of the City"
Macalester	Clarion	
"Metropolitan"	Northwestern	
University of Missouri–	Lewis	
Kansas City		
"State University"		

At Brockport and the University of the City, the percentage of black faculty actually exceeded the percentage of black undergraduate students. However, at City, a large number of black faculty members were in professional schools, while at Brockport about 21 black staff members were in its Rochester center, an inner-city unit. The strategies for recruiting black faculty at the 13 institutions varied from minimal to extensive efforts: (1) a presidential promise to recruit black faculty and staff, reinforced by verbal encouragement of deans and department chairmen to do so; (2) decentralized (department level) but clearly delineated strategies for identifying black faculty, with the acknowledgement that any department would hire minority candidates who met institutional standards; (3) a centralized (dean or academic vice president) version of #2; (4) attempts to create goals and search procedures; (5) no program but unusual effort by a department chairperson or higher level administrator; (6) hiring of supportive service staff without faculty appointments—usually by a dean or vice president—who later obtained academic appointments for them either in a support service unit or in an academic department.

The tactics for recruiting black faculty were often quite inventive. State University updated addresses of its former black Ph.D.'s and tried to recruit them; the University of the City first recruited black administrators (academic and nonacademic) and involved white administrators in sensitivity sessions while launching an early recruitment program. The forces affecting recruitment efforts included the availability of a nearby black community; the presence of black faculty, administrators, and programs; adequacy of salary offers; prestige of the institution; faculty expansion; and the willingness of the institution to bend or change its faculty appointment criteria.

Variations in appointment practices contributed to the uncertainties experienced by black faculty members. Some black faculty with all the normal credentials received normal appointments with high status and legitimacy. Others received normal appointments without normal credentials; that is, they were awarded first class status but had lower legitimacy. Some in black or Afro-American studies were unclear about their faculty status and legitimacy. They had a formal faculty appointment to a recognized unit with all the appropriate faculty prerogatives, but—depending on the academic and administrative recognition of the department and the strength of its members' credentials—status and legitimacy could vary substantially. In other instances, appointments to supportive service units were clearly nonacademic, but they sometimes carried academic perquisites: a form of second-class faculty status with first- or second-class legitimacy depending on the individual's credentials.

The difficulty of ascertaining actual status was compounded by joint appointments between black studies and academic departments; between black studies and supportive service units; between supportive services and academic departments; and between an administrative office and either a department or black studies unit. A further complication was the fact that many black faculty members had only part-time appointments. Many combinations existed on a single campus, so it was little wonder that both black faculty members and the institutions were sometimes confused and frustrated over the ambiguous nature of the black faculty members' official status and perquisites.

Beyond the vagaries of the official side of the black faculty member's role, unofficial expectations could expand it appreciably. Many administrative and faculty committees needed black (and more currently, women) representatives; black student organizations needed black faculty advisors; black community groups sought receptive black faculty members to make the universities more responsive to their needs; black academic professional associations desired full participation; and a never-ending stream of researchers wanted to talk to these new faculty members (as we were often told). Role overload and stress frustrated many of the black faculty members to whom we spoke. Their official roles were often unclear and the performance expected of them in the regular academic setting was additionally confused by the unofficial and unspecified set of expectations placed upon them.

It is little wonder, then, that the primary concerns of black faculty focused on recruitment (the need for colleagues); clarification of official recognition of their faculty position; access to the tenure track; and use of promotional criteria which recognized their special role and the demands placed on them. Compounding these concerns were very real ideological differences among black faculty within any given institution. In some of the institutions, for example, one subgroup of blacks in a black studies program would favor a politically active community or service oriented program, while others would favor an academic and scholarly approach to black studies. Black faculty also differed about whether supportive services for black students should be a remedial, noncredit activity or should be integrated into the curriculum. Some black faculty enjoyed working with black student groups, while others preferred to focus on their own scholarly work. The picture of black faculty in those institutions where there were a sizable number of black staff was somewhat similar to that of black students: they represented a diverse set of interests and concerns and were frustrated by the demands placed on them. However, black faculty usually were not as outwardly hostile in their relationships with white colleagues as black students were with white students.

Given the realities of the black faculty role in these institutions which were attempting to respond to increased numbers of black students, it is little wonder that they reported attempts to organize. However, given their limited numbers, their heterogeneity, and the extensive role demands on them, it is not surprising that such efforts usually resulted in no more than occasional social gatherings. The exception was the University of the City, where an organization of black administrators, faculty, students, and staff was formed.

Faculty Overview

This review of the impact on and the response of faculty patterns and structures to the increased black enrollments suggests that little has taken place and that there has been limited faculty leadership. In large part, this may be due to the fact that most faculty behavior occurs at the departmental level and in interpersonal relationships with students and other departmental colleagues. Yet the introduction of black faculty has been probably the most significant change in the pattern of faculty life in recent decades. The problems for and the pressures on black faculty members in their conflicted, overloaded, and ambiguous roles were greater than those on white faculty, who only had to deal with the black students in class and with the recruitment, hiring, promotion, and perquisite issues raised by the new cadre of black faculty colleagues. The white faculty have been fortunate that, at least to date, their black colleagues have not organized and rebelled as did the first group of black students.

OTHER ORGANIZATIONAL CONCERNS

Aside from the impacts on administrative and faculty roles and patterns, there were several other organizational responses which the increase of black students evoked. The organizational process for legitimizing and sustaining change, the shifting role of leadership, and emergent problems of resource allocation and program evaluation were crucial to the responses to black students. In addition, some unique dynamics in affirmative action, collective bargaining, and networks for blacks also deserve comment.

Legitimizing Change

The institutions in this study used several strategies to legitimize and gain acceptance for the increase in black enrollments and the development of black programs. Reliance on personal influence or charisma and appeal to moral values were very important in building support. The combination of personal influence and moral support from administrators, particularly presidents, and respected white faculty was a powerful early source of legitimacy. The danger of overemphasizing this approach was exemplified at Macalester, where a strong, charismatic president advocated the college's extensive commitment to minority programs. Yet when he lost the support of a major donor and as the costs of the program increased, the programs he had helped to establish lost legitimacy within the college. The president at the University of the City was more action-oriented and sought support in the black community. A statesmanlike retiring president at Carleton and two liberal presidents at State University capitalized on their concern for minorities at the time of Martin Luther King's death by spurring their institutions' governance bodies to obtain a broad commitment. At other institutions, presidential legitimization was less visible, often taking the form of administrative decree and allocation of resources to black programs. Here in particular there was the implicit assumption that presidential support *was* institutional commitment.

A more complex form of legitimization was the public commitment of a variety of constituencies to a broad policy mandate to increase black enrollments and provide necessary support programs. This occurred at State University, Macalester, and Carleton. At other institutions, widely discussed public commitments were not forthcoming, often because there was no governance forum or procedure for making such commitments.

External support was a crucial legitimizer. State and federal student aid programs supported low-income students and special service programs at little or no cost to the colleges. Several institutions used them early and extensively. Lewis even brought in a new financial aid director to improve access to this source of funds. The availability of external resources made it possible for administrators to begin programs with minimal expenditure of institutional monies and to circumvent institution-wide reviews or approval. The programs so constituted were "officially" legitimate. Because of the external funding, they were not especially threatening to the rest of the institution. More threatening external mandates such as HEW's suit against the State of Pennsylvania or the Office of Civil Rights' review at Lewis, or the fear of such reviews at other institutions, provided another "official" form of legitimation. Administrators could point to those mandates as requiring minority enrollment increases.

A variety of administrative devices served to legitimate the commitment to blacks by keeping it quiet. Several administrators rationalized or downplayed the impact of new minority programs and the internal resources they required. Others redirected resources quietly and without public review, a ploy which finessed internal resistance and at the same time allowed the institutions to claim a commitment to blacks and other minorities.

The patterns of black enrollment increases and minority programs in colleges and universities were not unique for the time. While the decisions about blacks were typically not approved by high-level governance bodies, few reported to us that there had been any particular irregularity or illegitimacy in the way those decisions were made. Rather, in the late 1960s, this was the way most new programs were started. An idea with reasonable internal interest and external funds to support it was almost always acceptable.

The Role of Leadership: Essentials and Limits

Leadership is always a key variable in any substantial organizational change. In these 13 institutions, both black and white leadership was crucial. We have seen how important the commitment of white leaders was to initiating the recruitment of blacks. A few black students and an occasional black faculty member or administrator played an early "sensitizing" role—raising issues about and concerns for minorities. But they did not have a black constituency in the early stages. We have seen that a new, frequently militant black leadership emerged as more black students began to arrive. Black protest and pressure changed the role of white leaders—still mainly white executive officers—from initiators to mediators or negotiators during the conflict era.

As the conflict period ended, the issue of leadership either became less significant or shifted to black staff. Black leadership emerged in various places—from the faculty, minority administrators, or black students. Leadership depended less on building a student constituency and more on gaining personal respect, enhancing the credibility of minority programs, and establishing relationships with other units. White leadership at this point was also less dramatic, more often taking the form of placating whites who were beginning to complain about the "concessions" of earlier years and of attempting to build credibility with other disaffected white groups both internally and externally.

The critical concern on the 13 campuses when we visited them in 1974–75 was with the types of leadership that would emerge among blacks and whites as retrenchment, resource reallocation, and program evaluation threatened to affect commitments to blacks and other minorities. Would blacks turn again to activist black leaders to protest their losses, as at Macalester in 1974, or would they turn to leaders who would operate within current academic norms? Would white leaders stand by the earlier commitments made to blacks and other minorities or would they follow the will of the white critics who were beginning to surface? In addition to leadership, the future courses of these institutions depend to a large extent on how problems of resource allocation are solved.

Resource Allocation and Program Review: Emergent Issues

We have seen that all of the 13 colleges and universities devoted some internal funds to support programs for minorities. However, the availability of external monies in the late 1960s and early 1970s was a critical factor in bringing in large numbers of black students. The reality, of course, was that external sources began to disappear—precipitously at Macalester, predictably at the institutions with federal grants with fixed time periods, or gradually as funding agency interest waned. None of the institutions was making any explicit, visible attempt to plan a financial transition to shift minority program support from external sources to internal operating budget sources. Not surprisingly, at all the institutions and particularly at those with very little internal funding of minority programs, black students and staff pointed to this as a lack of institutional commitment. Faced with declining budgets and lacking clearly accepted patterns for reviewing resource allocation reductions, administrators were uncertain about how to handle the issue. The growth mentality of the 1960s which sought added new programs with external funds, the failure to review resource allocation patterns, and the lack of a planned transition were causing substantial concern on all of these campuses.

Administrative domination of financial resource allocations meant that administrators supportive of the expansion of black programs had increased allocations to those programs without an open review, even at the more prestigious institutions with strong traditions of departmental and faculty autonomy. This pattern allowed minority programs to grow without program review and without clarification of appointment procedures for staff. This was more acceptable in a period of expansion, but it becomes more problematic in periods of retrenchment. Minority staff recognized the problem by the time we interviewed them: they wanted the protection of faculty status and resisted reviews which did not offer some reassurances about the continuation of their programs. While several institutions were attempting to develop resource allocation and program evaluation processes during our visits, all admitted that it would have been easier to have done so earlier when there was more flexibility. The changes that had been fostered and hastened by administratively dominated resource allocations set up the situation for current problems.

The Role of Collective Bargaining

Collective bargaining was not directly related to minority issues, yet it did affect the dynamics of the response to minorities at three of the campuses.

At Clarion and California, the unionized faculties had negotiated three-year contracts with a clause guaranteeing no staff reductions. In the face of declining enrollments, such agreements not only increased financial problems but may also have negated affirmative action programs to increase black or minority hiring. This impasse came between white faculty and black students on those campuses and placed administrators in a difficult position.

Another issue surfaced at University of the City, where a bargaining election was pending. Because many of the black faculty at City were either not on the tenure track or still untenured, a sizable proportion reportedly supported unionization. While the options on the ballot were unclear at the time of the study, a number of people noted that blacks might constitute as much as 20 percent of the faculty (depending on the definition of the bargaining unit). If they were to operate as an effective coalition, they were capable of influencing the outcome of the vote and potentially the priority of the bargaining issues. Thus, unionization has become an organizational factor in institutional response to minorities.

Affirmative Action and Pressure from Other Groups

It is clear that the advent of affirmative action programs in the 13 institutions was quite separate from the decision to increase black enrollments. None of the institutions had anything like an affirmative action program prior to the issuance of Executive Order 11246, although some had actively recruited black faculty and staff previously. Since most faculty openings had been filled before the advent of affirmative action, black faculty and staff saw affirmative action only as having increased non-academic black staff. The activities of the affirmative action officers tended to be focused on preparing reports; studying and reviewing personnel procedures, salary structures, and recruitment and hiring practices; hearing grievances mostly from the non-academic staff; and assisting in recruitment programs and efforts. There was little formal contact between the affirmative action office and the various programs for black students, except in data gathering and analysis.

Affirmative action, by definition, has led to the rise of other minority groups and of women as pressures on colleges and universities. At several of the institutions in our study, efforts initially focused on blacks have been broadened to include all economically and educationally disadvantaged students. However, since blacks were the focus of the initial efforts and were the largest minority group in these states, blacks were the primary beneficiaries. The expansion to include other under-represented groups has caused some problems and tensions as these other groups seized on affirmative action.

Only Macalester set up supportive units for different racial groups. In some of the institutions, the minority admissions effort has brought in small numbers of other minorities, particularly Chicanos. New student groups were founded—at Lewis, State University, Kansas City, and University of the City—which pressed for recognition, for institutional resources, and for special programs. While not as visible as the initial black presence, Chicanos have pressed their own interests. At State University, Lewis, and Kansas City, conflict during the mid-1970s has centered on Chicano demands. One interesting sidelight is that several of the institutions whose initial focus was on blacks have only recently become aware that the concentrations of Chicanos in their recruitment areas may approach that of blacks. At State University the issue raised by Chicano students was whether a public institution should recruit blacks from outside the state when it did not actively recruit Chicanos from within the state.

The more recent addition of women as a pressure group affected blacks as well. While the institutions saw the two issues quite differently, blacks feared that activist women would get more attention and more of the scarce resources. On at least one campus, the black women students who were pressured by both black and women's groups elected to form a separate organization. Whether demands from other minority and women's groups would lead to a diffusion of institutional response was a concern to the minority groups themselves. While there was talk of a Third World Coalition on several campuses, none had emerged substantially by the time of our visits.

The Role of Black Networks

Another unique organizational aspect of the impact of black students on white campuses was the formal and informal networks of individuals involved in black-related programs and activities. Within each institution, an informal network of black and white staff formed around black-related problems or minority questions. This was a particularly important mechanism for supporting and mobilizing blacks during crises at the smaller colleges. It was more difficult to detect such networks at the universities, although at least at one of them— the University of the City—a black network was formalized into an organization of black administrators, faculty, students, and staff.

There were also identifiable inter-institutional networks. Black staff from different institutions—particularly those individuals in

charge of minority support, financial aid, and recruitment programs—occasionally met on a state or regional basis. The directors of
minority programs receiving federal grants met regularly to share
problems and information. Affirmative action and student aid officers
were likely to meet in regional meetings sponsored by the regional
offices of U.S. Office of Education. Heads of black studies programs
met regularly on a national basis. There was also an informal recruiting network for black studies faculty in which persons teaching at
one institution were well-known to those at other institutions, an
advantage not possible in larger associations. Black faculty in some
disciplines had their own associations or caucuses which served typical faculty concerns for self-development and job information. They
also had other purposes such as providing an exchange of many of the
black speakers whose names we saw repeated at the institutions we
visited.

CONCLUSION

This chapter highlights the fact that the institutional impacts of
and responses to black students were not limited to the student life
and new programs for black students described in Part III. No seg-
ment of the institution—faculty, administrative, or other organizational structures and processes—went unaffected. Some areas were
changed more than others and some responses were more visible than
others. However, the ways in which changes affected individuals and
how they were perceived is yet another dimension of impact. The
survey data discussed in Part IV highlights this important dimension
of institutional life.

Part IV

The 1975 Perspective:
Integration, Segregation, or Pluralism

12

Administrative and Faculty Perceptions

Robert T. Blackburn and Marvin W. Peterson

INTRODUCTION

Thus far we have been concerned with the institutional responses of the 13 colleges and universities to the increase of black students. We were equally interested in how such events affected and were perceived by individuals in the institutions—administrators, faculty, and students. (Due to limited response rates the student data are not dealt with extensively.) Because administrators were more directly involved in initiating enrollment increases and negotiating with black students during crises, was the impact different on them than it was on faculty? Did the commitments of leaders differ from those of other administrators who served in support roles? Did departmental faculty respond differently because of the nature of their discipline or because differential responses were called for? Did personal attributes (age, for example) account for how individual faculty perceived the impact of the increased black enrollments? Were there differences between institutions that showed different degrees of conflict? These and other questions were ones the second phase of our study attempted to answer. Our discussion deals with the results of an in-depth survey of administration and faculty on 4 of the 13 campuses—Brockport, "Metropolitan University," The University of Missouri–Kansas City, and "State University."

This chapter first presents a brief methodological section describing the analysis techniques employed in this portion of the study. We then turn to a comparison of administrative and faculty responses and also examine differential administrative responses by level and by function. Although some overall faculty data are discussed in this chapter, a more detailed faculty analysis which includes contextual, disciplinary, and personal variables is presented in Chapter 13.

THE INDICES

The survey instruments, sampling procedure, and response rates were discussed in Chapter 4. The actual questionnaires administered to students, faculty, and administrators are shown in Appendix C. As was indicated in Table 4-2, some sets of questions were presented to all groups (e.g., about racial climate) and some to only faculty and administrators (e.g., about institutional goals). Some sets of questions were unique to each constituency (e.g., about impact on each constituency).

For the sake of data reduction and preliminary analysis, items within questionnaire sections were factor analyzed. Indices were identified from item clusters and given names depicting the theme common to the group of items. Most individual items were dropped from further analysis if they did not achieve a minimum factor loading of .40. However, some individual items which dealt with issues that the case studies had shown to be of critical nature were retained for systematic treatment.

Table 12-1 describes each index reported in this and the following two chapters. Additional information about each index can be obtained in Appendix E, where the actual questionnaire items used to comprise each index and their factor loadings are identified, along with the respondent groups answering them. The direction of the high scores and the range for each index are included in parentheses at the end of each index description.

TABLE 12-1

The Indices

Topic 1. Role of Racial Minorities in Colleges and Universities

Universal-Particular Standards. Three items expressing that admissions and performance standards should be the same for minorities as for all other students (H = Universal; 0–9).

Long-Term Minority Impact. Three items dealing with the long-range positive outcomes of affirmative action and increasing numbers of minority students and programs (H = Positive; 0–9).

Institutional Integration-Pluralism. Three items describing the advantages of pluralism over integration in lifestyles, educational and social activities, and separate programs for minorities (H = Integration; 0–9).

Topic 2. Institutional Goals for Blacks and Racial Minorities

Institutional Black Priority. Eight items supporting recruitment and admissions of blacks; provision of remedial academic, social, and cultural services; creation and continuation of black and/or ethnic programs; recruitment and hiring of black faculty; recruitment and hiring of minority staff outside of minority affairs; commitment of institutional financial resources for programs; commitment of institutional financial aid; and creation of top administrative office concerned with minority issues (H = Important; 0–32).

Non-Academic Support (a subset of the *Institutional Black Priority Index*). Four items supporting recruitment and admissions of blacks; provision of remedial, academic, social, and cultural services; commitment of institutional financial resources for programs; and commitment of institutional financial aid (H = Important; 0–16).

Affirmative Action (a subset of the *Institutional Black Priority Index*). Two items supporting the recruitment and hiring of black faculty and also minority staff outside of minority affairs (H = Important; 0–8).

Integrating Concerns for Blacks. Three items supporting the recruitment and hiring of black and/or minority staff for administrative positions outside of minority affairs, the inclusion of black content in all courses related to American life, and the development of strong institutional ties with community black groups (H = Important; 0–12).

Topic 3. Institutional Racial Climate

Black-White Trust. Three items dealing with degree of trust between black students and white constituencies—for students, faculty, and administrators (H =Trust; 0–12).

Openness and Inclusiveness. Three items dealing with concern for black issues, the open discussion of racial issues, and the seeking of black representation (H = Open; 0–12).

Administration, Faculty, Staff Interaction. Two items dealing with the degree of social and professional interaction between black and white personnel (H = Positive; 0–8).

Black Visibility and Influence. Three items dealing with the extent to which blacks are visible and influential—in the student body, faculty, and administration (H = Visible; 0–12).

TABLE 12-1 continued

Topic 4. Institutional Reponsiveness

Willingness. Five items dealing with the institution's willingness to establish and/
  or develop programs or services for blacks in the areas of student recruitment, admissions, financial aid; tutoring, counseling, advising; black/ethnic
  studies; social and cultural activities; and black faculty and staff recruitment
  (H = Willing; 0–20).
Adequacy. Five items dealing with the adequacy of the institution's effort in providing programs and services for blacks in the areas of student recruitment,
  admissions, financial aid; tutoring, counseling, advising; black/ethnic studies;
  social and cultural activities, and black faculty and staff recruitment (H =
  Adequate; 0–20).
White Commitment to Blacks. Eight items dealing with the current commitment to
  minority programs by different constituencies (H = Active Support; 0–32).
  Administrative Commitment (a subset of *White Commitment to Blacks*). Four
    items dealing with the current commitment of executive officers, aca-
    demic administrators, department chairpersons, and student affairs staff
    (H = Active Support; 0–16).
  Faculty Commitment. Three items dealing with the commitment of governing
    faculty, the faculty, and black faculty and staff (H = Active Support; 0–
    12).
  Student Commitment. Two items dealing with the current commitment of the
    student government and white students (H = Active Support; 0–8).

Black Commitment. Two items dealing with the current commitment of the black
  faculty and staff and black students (H = Active Support; 0–8).

Topic 5. Institutional Impacts and Responses

Black Influence Exertion. Six items dealing with the degree to which blacks exert
  institutional influence at various levels—trustees, executive officers, school
  or college, departments, faculty, and student body (H = Great Deal; 0–24).
Total Black Influence. Four items dealing with the degree to which black groups
  have institutional influence—administrators and staff, faculty, students, and
  coalitions of these three groups (H = Great Deal; 0–16).
Authoritarian Treatment. Three items dealing with the institutional level at
  which racial issues get settled, the manner in which the administration im-
  plements decisions on racial issues, and the attention racial issues receive (H
  =Authoritarian; 0–12).

Topic 6. Future Institutional Commitments, Concerns, and Issues

Future Commitments. Five items dealing with the institution's future commitments to black student recruitment and financial aid, tutoring, and advising;
  black focused curricula; social and cultural activities; and recruitment of
  black faculty and staff (H = Reduced; 0–20).

Topic 7. Impacts and Responses in Administrative Areas (Administrators Only)

Black and Minority Enrollment Impact. Two items dealing with the impact of
  increased black and minority enrollments on the functioning of an administrative office (H = A Great Deal; 0–8).

TABLE 12-1 continued

Black Staff and Program Impact. Six items dealing with the impact of the addition of black faculty, administrators, and staff, of affirmative action practices, and of the creation of minority programs and groups on or off campus on the functioning of an administrative office (H = Great Deal; 0–24).

Positive-Negative Relationships. Eight items dealing with how black and white administrator, faculty, and staff relations are perceived and assessed by administrators—on factors of respectfulness, openness, personalness, supportiveness, union, concerned, and significance (H = Positive; 0–28).

Personal Openness. Six items dealing with how an administrator's personal role has been affected by the presence of more black students, faculty, and staff—on the dimensions of personal satisfaction, concern for minority issues, flexibility, job challenge, personal effectiveness, and commitment to the institution (H = Increased; 0–24).

Topic 8. Impacts and Responses in Faculty and Departmental Activity (Faculty Respondents Only)

Help and Accommodation. Five items dealing with teaching techniques and practices—provide extra help, extend deadlines, refer students to tutors, allow a wide range of assignments to meet requirements, permit paper and/or exam rewrites (H = Helpful; 0–20).

Subjective Evaluation. Two items dealing with using class participation and other subjective judgements when evaluating students (H = Subjective; 0–8).

Time Demand. Four items dealing with reallocation of time use—more for teaching and preparation, less for scholarship, more for counseling, and more with student service people (H = Decreased; 0–12).

Black Curriculum Impact. Two items dealing with increased black content in courses and more class discussions on racial issues (H = Increased; 0–8).

Personal Interaction. Four items dealing with the degree to which blacks discuss career and/or graduate school plans, seek counsel regarding personal problems, speak to respondent on campus, and participate in class (H = More; 0–16).

Departmental Black Concern. Two items dealing with special faculty efforts to insure success of blacks and to present materials which appeal and interest them (H = Concern; 0–6).

Topic 9. Impacts and Responses in Student Areas (Student Respondents Only)

Tense/Hostile Student Racial Climate. Six items dealing with views of racial relations characterized by tense v. relaxed, hostile v. friendly, competitive v. cooperative, separate v. integrated, disrespectful v. respectful, and pessimistic v. optimistic (H = Tense; 0–24).

Student Separation/Integration. Five items dealing with the importance of black/white student relationship problems or issues on campus—separate seating patterns in dining facilities, interracial dating and friendships, conflicts over areas for socializing, white participation in black-oriented events, and black participation in all-campus events (H = Problem Area; 0–20).

OVERVIEW OF THE INDICES
AND THE MEANING OF RESPONSE

As Table 12-1 shows, the factor analysis of items within the major sections of the questionnaires produced a number of meaningful indices. We will refer to these indices in our discussion of the responses of faculty and administrators as well as in making comparisons between faculty and administrators where common indices exist in this chapter. However, before turning to these more particular findings, it is interesting first to inspect the more general patterns of responses of administrators and faculty. In order to achieve this overview, the mean scores on the indices of Table 12-1 were themselves subjected to a second factor analysis.

The composite level of the mean scores on these indices by the predominantly white faculty and administrative respondents in these four institutions provides a sense of how they viewed their institutions' experiences with black students. (See Appendix G for actual scores.) In viewing the "role of institutions of higher education" in dealing with minorities, faculty and administrators were fairly evenly divided over whether to employ particular or universal standards and whether to form separate or integrated arrangements, but they tended to see the long-term impact of increased black enrollments as positive.

In assessing their own "institutional goals for blacks and racial minorities," they saw this concern as having a somewhat important priority. Their view of the institutions' "racial climate" suggested there was some degree of interracial trust, openness, positive interaction, and visibility for blacks. In viewing their institutions' "responsiveness" to blacks they saw themselves as somewhat willing (as opposed to very willing) to develop programs; they viewed administrators, faculty, and students as being passively supportive of black and minority programs and blacks as being actively supportive. In terms of institutional "impacts," they perceived blacks as having some but not a great deal of influence and reported that there was some tendency for decisions on black issues to be handled somewhat more from the top down or at higher levels. They felt that "future institutional" commitments to blacks would be either the same or greater than present commitments. Thus, the perspective of the combined respondents in these four institutions was guardedly favorable or optimistic.

Perhaps of greater interest than these general patterns is the manner in which these indices clustered when they were factor analyzed. The loadings of the indices on this secondary factor analysis are presented in Appendix F; however, we will focus in this discussion on the second order factors and the correlations of the indices comprising them. Five second order factors emerged and appear to have some significance.

The first of these, "Breadth of Goals for Blacks," contains all four indices (and only those four) from the questionnaire category of institutional goals for black or racial minorities (Topic 2 in Table 12-1). Table 12-2 presents the zero-order correlations among the indices, which are all quite high. This factor expressed an *institutional ideology* which asserts that there should be a high institutional priority on black issues, an emphasis on more academic support programs, and a commitment to affirmative action.

TABLE 12-2

Factor 1: Breadth of Goals for Blacks

	Institutional Black Priority	Non-Academic Support	Affirmative Action	Integrating Concern for Blacks
Institutional Black Priority	—	.92	.83	.70
Non-Academic Support		—	.64	.60
Affirmative Action			—	.73
Integrating Concern for Blacks				—

The second factor, "Willingness and Commitment," comes from five of the six indices in the questionnaire category of institutional responsiveness (Topic 4 in Table 12-1). Again the zero-order intercorrelation matrix in Table 12-3 shows moderate to high correlations. However, an "adequacy" index from this same set of questions did not attain the minimum .40 loading weight and instead emerged with another second order factor. The Willingness and Commitment factor seems to suggest the *intentions* of the administrator and faculty respondents toward blacks and their perception of their own and other groups' commitments to blacks. This intent to support black concerns should not be confused with an assessment of actual behavior, however, since the index measuring the perceived adequacy of response did not load heavily on this factor.

Separate from institutional ideology and intent is *perceived behavior*. The third factor, "Racial Climate and Activity," contains two of the three indices in the questionnaire category of institutional impact

TABLE 12-3

Factor 2: Willingness and Commitment

	Willing-ness	Commit-ment to Blacks	Adminis-trative Commit-ment	Faculty Commit-ment	Student Commit-ment	Black Commit-ment
Willingness	—	.66	.64	.61	.45	.39
WhiteCommitment to Blacks		—	.93	.87	.80	.55
Administrative Commitment			—	.74	.59	.51
Faculty Commitment				—	.66	.70
Student Commitment					—	.46
Black Commitment						—

(Topic 5 in Table 12-1), two of the five indices from institutional responsiveness category (Topic 4 in Table 12-1, including the index on Adequacy of Response), and three of the four indices in the institutional racial climate area (Topic 3 in Table 12-1). In addition, individual items on black activism, pluralism versus separatism, student racial patterns, and black representation also have loadings that are greater than .40. In all, seven indices and four separate items comprise the Racial Climate and Activity factor. The zero order correlation matrix in Table 12-4 shows low to moderate correlations. This factor appears to reflect the respondents' perception of behavior in racial climate and activity patterns.

The fourth factor is a corollary of the third which we have labeled "Interracial Trust/Conflict." Its components are one index from the Racial Climate section of the questionnaire (Topic 3 in Table 12-1) and two items dealing with black trust and the level of racial conflict on campus. The zero order correlation matrix is shown in Table 12-5. One of the correlations is low and another only moderate. The factor seems to measure the *perceived psychological* (as opposed to behavioral) element of trust and interracial conflict.

The fifth and final factor is conceptually less clear than the others but seems to reflect the respondents' *values* or *beliefs* and we have called it "Higher Education Pluralism-Integration." It contains all three indices from the Role of Racial Minorities Section of the questionnaire (Topic 1 in Table 12-1). Table 12-6 shows the relatively low correlation coefficients among the indices. Some interpretation is necessary. It appears that those who favor acceptance of differing styles,

TABLE 12-4

Factor 3: Racial Climate and Activity

	Openness	Administration/Faculty/Student Interaction	Black Visibility & Influence	Willingness	Adequacy	Black Influence Exertion	Total Black Influence	Black Activism*	Pluralism or Separatism*	Student Interracial Patterns*	Black Representation*
Openness and Inclusiveness	—										
Administration/Faculty/Student Interaction	.51	—									
Black Visibility and Influence	.59	.55	—								
Willingness	.49	.39	.44	—							
Adequacy	.42	.34	.45	.58	—						
Black Influence Exertion	.54	.39	.58	.42	.50	—					
Total Black Influence	.52	.47	.66	.47	.50	.70	—				
Extent of Black Activism*	.42	.22	.38	.29	.26	.35	.41	—			
Extent of Pluralism (Over Separatism)*	.40	.33	.32	.24	.25	.30	.34	.14	—		
Active Student Interracial Patterns*	.41	.43	.43	.22	.21	.33	.36	.14	.24	—	
Involved Black Representation*	.31	.30	.46	.31	.37	.39	.44	.25	.19	.21	—

*Questionnaire item rather than index.

TABLE 12-5

Factor 4: Interracial Trust/Conflict

	Black/White Trust	Black Trust of Other Minorities*	Campus Racial Conflict*
Black/White Trust	—	.56	−.33
Black Trust of Other Minorities*		—	−.15
Campus Racial Conflict*			—

*Item rather than index.

TABLE 12-6

Factor 5: Higher Educational Pluralism-Integration

	Long Term Minority Impact	Institutional Integration-Pluralism
Universal-Particular Standards	−.31	.30
Long-Term Minority Impact		−.28

programs, and activities for blacks or minorities (pluralism) also favor particularistic standards for different groups—a pluralist perspective—and tend to view the long-term minority impacts more favorably. Conversely, those who favor more integrated (less separate) patterns also favor more universal standards—an integrationist perspective—and view the long-term minority impact less favorably.

The difference in long-term impact, however, is one of degree since most all respondents tended to place that on the positive end of the spectrum. Our earlier description of the separate nature of student-related activities and academic and support programs may suggest that the integrationist perspective has not succeeded—accounting for their more negative view of long-term impacts. This fifth second order factor does suggest that a *belief system* or *set of values* along a pluralistic-integrationist dimension does exist. It is doubtful that these indices would measure an extreme segregationist position, since few of the respondents expected negative long-term impacts of the increased black enrollments.

As we examine the responses of faculty and administrators, it is important to keep in mind differences in the levels and meanings of response reported in the survey data. Some indices reflect on institutional *ideology;* others express *intent;* others are reports of actual *behavior;* others include a *psychological* sense of trust; and others reflect a *set of values* or a *belief system.* Thus, "response" as represented in this analysis of the indices from the faculty and administrators survey has a complex, multidimensional meaning reflected in these five second order factors or clusters of the indices in Table 12-1.

ADMINISTRATOR/FACULTY COMPARISONS

In general, the postures of faculty and administrators toward the larger issue of blacks in higher education were similar—both groups were moderately concerned, responsive, and committed. There still remains, however, the question of possible differences between the two populations. Long-run success and goal accomplishment require that these two constituencies hold positions compatible enough to work together; either group by itself could not succeed without the endorsement and support of the other. However, universities typically have a "we-they" schism between faculty and administration. The gap between the two groups varies from college to college and sometimes is more rhetorical than substantive. Nonetheless, more often than not differences of opinion and ideas for action can surface on sensitive issues.

Table 12-7 shows that on several indices related to role, goals, institutional responsiveness, and impact on the institution, statistically significant administrative-faculty differences did exist. However, for the most part the differences were ones of degree, although a few indicate that the two groups held different interpretations and/or priorities. For example, administrators had higher scores on all four goal indices. That is, administrators more strongly endorsed integration, affirmative action, financial support, and high institutional priority for black concerns. Since faculty also showed some support of these same goals, the differences were in degree rather than direction. Administrators also scored higher on five impact and responsiveness indices, seeing those as more favorable than did faculty. On the other hand, as administrators strived to achieve their goal commitments, they believed particularistic standards were sometimes necessary—an issue with which faculty disagree. In addition, despite the number of indices which show a more active administrative concern and level of activity, the administrative groups declared their institutions' responses to be less adequate than faculties believed them to be.

TABLE 12-7

Faculty and Administrator Comparisons on Selected Indices: Index Scores, F Values, and P Levels

Indices	Administrators	Faculty	F	p(<)
Role of Racial Minorities				
Universalistic-Particularistic Standard				
(H = Universal; 0–9)	4.25	4.72	6.03	.02
Long-Term Minority Impact				
(H = Positive; 0–9)	6.51	5.93	14.48	.03
Institutional Goals for Blacks or				
Racial Minorities				
Institutional Black Priority				
(H = Important; 0–32)	20.19	18.07	16.01	.01
Non-Academic Support				
(H = Important; 0–16)	10.65	9.66	12.62	.01
Affirmative Action				
(H = Important; 0–8)	4.98	4.28	15.74	.01
Integrating Concern for Blacks				
(H = Important; 0–12)	6.70	5.55	24.97	.01
Institutional Responsiveness				
Adequacy				
(H = Adequate; 0–20)	9.66	10.50	4.72	.04
Administrative Commitment				
(H = Active Support; 0–16)	12.70	12.06	4.86	.04
Black Commitment				
(H = Active Support; 0–8)	7.04	6.58	11.25	.01
Institutional Impacts				
Total Black Influence				
(H = A Great Deal; 0–16)	7.83	7.21	6.11	.02
Authoritarian Treatment				
(H = Authoritarian; 0–12)	8.24	7.31	27.12	.01

Additional evidence supports the stronger stand taken by administrators. Table 12-8 shows the individual items from the section of the questionnaire dealing with the role of racial minorities in colleges and universities. These are 8 of the 12 items not used in any index but which reached a significance level of .05 or less in differentiating administrators from faculty.

While there was basic agreement between administrators and faculty in the direction of their answers, in every case administrators took the stronger position with respect to minority concerns. Administrators advocated a more activist stance (items 7, 9, and 10) and particularistic practices (items 12, 14, 15, 19, and 20) than did faculty. When an item was favored by both groups, administrators expressed a higher level of agreement; when an item received an overall vote of disagreement, administrators disagreed less strongly. When there was a genuine difference in direction between the two groups, administrators came out on the side more favorable to minorities.

In earlier chapters we saw that, most often, any decision to take a strong position toward increasing black enrollments was made at the top. Even administrators admit this fact, one that normally is contrary to the collegial form of governance these institutions espouse (note the last index in Table 12-7). Once a decision is made and the necessary machinery set into action, administrators act to accomplish the goals they set; they give the support and loyalty an organization needs to function smoothly. On the other hand, faculty tend to have multiple loyalties and endorse a set of professional canons of conduct, including the right and duty to criticize the employing organization. "The university right or wrong" will not be endorsed by faculty to the same extent that it will be by administrators. These data certainly suggest faculty were less prone to endorse the minority position in these four institutions.

ADMINISTRATIVE RESPONSES

Having seen that, on the average, administrators and faculty expressed a similar moderate-to-supportive set of positions on minority issues, we now examine subgroups within the administrative respondents. As our campus visits in Stage I had shown, the top administrative echelon was usually the target during confrontations. Also, individuals in different administrative offices interacted with black students on quite different matters. We wanted to see, then, if differ-

TABLE 12-8

Administrative-Faculty Differences on Role of Racial Minorities on Items Not Used in Indices: Mean Scores, T Values, and P Levels

Item	Faculty	Administration	t	p(<)	Interpretation
7.* Colleges and universities have an obligation to encourage racial interaction in all areas of campus life.	1.94	1.76	2.64	.01	Administrators agree more strongly
9. Black or ethnic studies programs should have a strong focus on activist and/or community service activities.	2.77	2.59	2.86	.01	Administrators don't disagree as strongly
10. Despite our concern over racial injustices, colleges and universities *do not* have a primary responsibility to rectify that situation.	2.71	3.03	3.97	.01	Administrators disagree more strongly
12. Remedial education should not be offered for academic credits.	2.03	2.33	3.74	.01	Administrators agree less strongly
14. Racial minority students are best served by continued stress on traditional standards of academic performance.	2.23	2.47	3.33	.01	While both groups are split (scores mean 2.5), administrators disagree a bit more
15. In light of current and projected enrollment declines, colleges should move toward open admissions.	2.85	2.65	2.64	.01	Administrators don't disagree quite as strongly
19. Colleges and universities should insure the inclusion of Blacks and other racial minorities in faculty and administrative positions not specifically responsible for those groups.	2.01	1.75	3.81	.01	Administrators agree more strongly
20. Despite concern for past discrimination, hiring and promotion decisions must favor the most qualified individual in colleges and universities.	1.66	1.81	2.30	.05	Administrators agree less strongly

*Item numbers in first section of questionnaires. See Appendix B. Scores range from 1 (Strongly agree) to 4 (Strongly disagree), with mean agree scores being less than 2.5 and mean disagree scores being greater than 2.5.

ences appeared when respondents were grouped by appointment level and by administrative functional area.

Responses by Appointment Level

The chief executive officers had to deal with questions from the trustees or from the state legislatures on how the institutions were being run. Assistant or associate personnel more frequently confronted issues like lounge space or accusations of racism against security staff. From a "room-at-the-top" perspective, one might expect those at different administrative levels to both value and view minority issues differently.

The sample size made possible comparisons between mean scores of administrators at three levels of appointment—(1) executive officers (president and vice-presidents), (2) deans and directors, and (3) assistants and associates to individuals in the first two categories. The principal findings from these analyses was the lack of any significant difference among the administrative levels. In fact, the similarities between the administrative hierarchies were so great that on only one index did the p value drop to .05—a result which would be expected to happen by chance when comparisons are made on as many as 29 variables. Hierarchies may exist, and values and perceptions may differ up and down an organizational ladder, but in these institutions administrative stratification did not exist with respect to beliefs and views about blacks or minority concerns.

Responses by Administrative Area of Appointment

Reclassifying the administrative respondents by four areas of appointment—(1) academic affairs, (2) business/finance, (3) student affairs, and (4) black/minority affairs—yielded quite a different picture. Sixteen of the 29 indices were significant at less than the .05 level and 11 of those were at less than the .01 level. Table 12-9 shows the mean index scores, F values, and significance levels.

It was the black/minority affairs personnel who were always farthest away from the other three groups. In addition, in almost every case the business/finance group was at the other pole. To the extent that there was an additional consistency to the pattern, more often than not academic affairs staff were closer to business/finance administrators, and student affairs personnel were closer to black/minority affairs staff. Again, the unusual group was black/minority affairs staff.

Table 12-9 reveals more than statistical differences among these groups. It shows that administrators who worked in the black/minority area—and this was where the highest proportion of black administrators and sympathetic white staff were located—perceived the rapid increase in black student enrollments quite differently than did their colleagues in other administrative offices. Those in minority affairs saw the long-term impact to be much greater than did typical individuals in the other organizational areas. At the same time, the minority office staff viewed the racial climate to be considerably less favorable than did the others; they saw less black/white trust, less black visibility, less openness to problems, and less interaction between campus groups. In addition, the minority affairs personnel viewed the institutions' responses to black student entry as the least adequate, and they judged the willingness and commitments of all whites—administrators, faculty, and students—to be the weakest. In fact, minority affairs staff saw black influence to be much lower than did all others. (The last four indices in the Impacts and Responses in Administrative category reflect the same differences.)

While it is understandable that those most intimately involved in a cause, as those in black/minority affairs obviously were, would tend to have more extreme views (and in the direction found in each instance in Table 12-9), it was not immediately apparent why administrators in business and financial roles were at the other extreme. Two factors help explain their position. First, increased black enrollments entailed an appreciable rise in financial aid. Large numbers of previously unhandled dollars were now processed—and not always smoothly, despite the good intentions of those involved. Moreover, the money was secured and dispersed only after considerable effort and difficulty. From the perspective of activity and effort, it is understandable that financial administrators saw a strong institutional response.

Second, not infrequently administrators in the business/finance area are most removed from "the life of academe." They are less likely to have been members of the faculty than are those administrators in academic affairs offices. Business officers are more apt to have closer relationships with bankers and merchants than are people in either student or academic affairs. If racial biases exist off-campus (or vis-à-vis students in general), business personnel will be confronted with it. They cannot escape the campus strains even when they are away from it.

In summary, the numerous differences that existed between administrative areas, which were not reflected in different levels of

TABLE 12-9

Administrator Differences as Related to Areas of Appointment: Index Scores, F Values, and P Levels

Indices	Academic Affairs	Business and/or Finance	Student Affairs	Black/Minority Affairs	F	$p(<)$
Role						
Long-Term Minority Impact (H = Positive; 0–9)	9.50	8.63	9.67	11.11	5.30	.01
Racial Climate						
Black/White Trust (H = Trust; 0–12)	6.35	7.38	5.46	4.11	7.58	.01
Openness and Inclusiveness (H = Open; 0–12)	6.76	6.69	5.81	4.78	3.15	.04
Administration/Faculty/Student Interaction (H = Positive; 0–8)	4.91	4.63	3.62	2.56	7.67	.01
Black Visibility and Influence (H = Visible; 0–12)	5.71	6.38	4.52	4.00	3.60	.03
Institutional Responsiveness						
Willingness (H = Willing; 0–20)	16.53	17.88	15.15	14.00	2.90	.05
Adequacy (H = Adequate; 0–20)	10.12	13.00	8.70	7.11	5.45	.01
White Commitment to Blacks (H = Active Support; 0–32)	24.62	26.94	22.11	17.11	8.75	.01
Administrative Commitment (H = Active Support; 0–16)	13.38	14.38	11.98	10.22	7.05	.01
Faculty Commitment (H = Active Support; 0–12)	9.53	10.25	8.73	7.11	6.88	.01
Student Commitment (H = Active Support; 0–8)	5.59	5.94	5.17	3.44	5.53	.01

TABLE 12-9 continued

Indices	Academic Affairs	Business and/or Finance	Student Affairs	Black/Minority Affairs	F	p(<)
Institutional impacts						
Black Influence-Exertion	10.91	12.31	9.42	7.33	4.81	.01
(H = A Great Deal; 0–24)						
Impacts and Responses-Administration						
Black & Minority Enrollment Impact	2.41	1.63	2.96	4.11	3.58	.03
(H = A Great Deal; 0–8)						
Black Staff & Program Impact	7.32	1.63	5.71	9.33	6.27	.01
(H = A Great Deal; 0–24)						
Positive-Negative Relationships	19.91	20.62	19.12	15.33	2.69	.06
(H = Positive; 0–28)						
Personal Openness	15.29	13.25	16.02	18.00	5.71	.01
(H = Increased; 0–24)						

appointment, suggest that black administrators (and whites who had similar aims and values) were dispersed vertically throughout the organization even though they were segregated by functional areas. The average response at all administrative levels was much the same. Attitudes, beliefs, and perceptions, however, differed markedly from one administrative area to another.

FACULTY RESPONSES

Faculty members to a lesser degree believed that they had a social commitment to minority issues, that the entrance of minorities into their institutions would be healthful in the long run, and that segregation was not desirable. They had some questions about such matters as activism, open admissions, and performance standards. However, the overall tone was one which was in accord with the hopes and aspirations of the new student clientele.

Similarly, while there were some differences between the four institutions participating in the survey on perceptions of institutional goals for blacks (see Chapter 14), again a moderate to positive response prevailed toward such objectives as strong black and/or ethnic studies programs and the recruitment and hiring of minority faculty and administrators. While faculty members expressed a personal commitment to altruistic goals and believed that their institutions had shown real signs of concern, they remained critical on a number of points. For example, they said that their universities' responses to blacks had been less than adequate. Faculty were sensitive to the impacts that increased black enrollments were having on departmental matters, but most stated that their professional lives had not been altered to any large extent.

While the above remarks characterize the faculty collectively, we were interested in what differences might exist between academic subgroups. For example, to the extent that "liberalism-conservatism" on minority issues entered the picture, we suspected that there might be differences among faculty members of different age groups. In addition, job security was becoming a more important issue on campuses and, hence, rank and tenure could have affected their views. As a corollary of this, activity to increase the number of women on the faculties might have led this underrepresented group to view plans to increase black staff as threatening.

Differences by Rank

Academic rank carries status and influence in academic communities when it comes to matters of governance, program approval, recruitment, hiring, and promotion. In addition, rank as a variable is a proxy for age and for tenure. Therefore, we would expect to find differences between full and associate professors (older, tenured, and more powerful) and assistant professors and instructors (younger, less secure, and with little influence).

Table 12-10 displays all indices for which the F value attained statistical significance. The absence of any goal indices in Table 12-10 is important to note at the outset. The absences show that all four ranks perceived the four institutional goal indices similarly. Also, two of the three role indices had insignificant F scores, again showing the homogeneity of the faculty, regardless of age, rank, or tenure status. Only the long-term minority impact index was judged differently ($p < .10$) by the faculty in different ranks. Here, in a steady progression through the ranks, full professors saw the long-term minority impact to be significantly lower than each of the other three groups. Although the full professors did not view that impact to be inconsequential, they did not believe it would be as great as instructors believed it would be.

Turning to matters of climate and responsiveness, three of the four racial climate indices and all seven of the institutional responsiveness indices generated statistically significant F ratios. With the exception of only one other index—authoritarian treatment (i.e., the tendency for black issues, in contrast to other university issues, to be dealt with in a more closed fashion and for decisions on black issues to come from the top down)—there were no differences between ranks. With regard to their views of future institutional commitments to minorities and a host of activities that deal with instruction, curriculum, and governance matters, instructors and all three professorial ranks replied in essentially the same way.

When statistically significant differences did occur, the pattern was a highly consistent one either up or down the ranks. That is, with some slight exceptions, full professors and instructors were on opposite ends with their responses and the two intermediate ranks were in between and in progression.

Some inferences seem to follow from these results and give a glimpse of internal faculty dynamics vis-à-vis the new student clientele they faced. First, the outcomes seemed to be less a consequence of the manifest variables of rank and tenure than they were of the

TABLE 12-10

Faculty Differences as Related to Academic Power: Index Scores, F Value, and P Level

Indices	Professor	Associate	Assistant	Instructor	F	p($<$)
Role						
Long-Term Minority Impact (H = Positive; 0–9)	6.68	6.92	7.11	7.33	3.62	.02
Climate						
Black/White Trust (H = Trust; 0–12)	6.26	5.74	5.89	5.50	2.82	.05
Openness and Indecisiveness (H = Open; 0–12)	6.18	6.10	5.70	5.67	2.64	.06
Black Visibility and Influence (H = Visible; 0–12)	6.93	5.40	4.62	4.30	4.39	.01
Institutional Responsiveness						
Willingness (H = Willing; 0–20)	16.04	15.85	15.42	13.86	8.70	.01
Adequacy (H = Adequate; 0–20)	11.17	10.43	10.17	9.24	4.73	.01
White Commitment to Blacks (H = Active Support; 0–32)	23.71	23.28	22.01	20.64	8.41	.01
Administrative Commitment (H = Active Support; 0–16)	12.60	12.45	11.55	10.62	10.87	.01
Faculty Commitment (H = Active Support; 0–12)	9.12	9.08	8.70	8.33	3.79	.02
Student Commitment (H = Active Support; 0–8)	5.44	5.18	5.07	4.86	4.21	.01
Black Commitment (H = Active Support; 0–8)	6.74	6.67	6.46	6.22	2.77	.05
Impact						
Authoritarian Treatment (H = Authoritarian; 0–12)	7.77	7.44	6.90	6.64	10.27	.01

correlated characteristics of age and years in the profession. The older and more experienced academics perceived events differently than younger people. The older faculty were probably more removed from conflicts which took place and from direct interaction with minority students. The senior members gave credit to their institutions' responses, willingness to provide opportunities to minorities, and the commitment of all constituencies. They saw high and positive interaction between their universities and the students. At the same time, from their greater experience, they did not appear to expect the long-run impacts of increased minority enrollments to be as great as did those individuals who were more directly involved and who had less experience in higher education. Older faculty members judged black entry to be more administratively dominated and to be handled outside of regular faculty channels than were other issues affecting the universities.

The responses of younger faculty members were consistent with an interpretation based on age. More idealistic and directly involved, they saw more inadequacies in their universities' responses. They personally thought blacks were having an impact, one that would last. They were doubtful that the necessary commitments for the successful treatment of the new clientele were as strong as they needed to be.

There were some aberrations in the pattern of young to old and they occurred within the associate professor group. As studies by Schuman and Laumann (1967), Blackburn (1972), and Sherman (1973) have demonstrated, faculty at this career stage sometimes display more "conservative" characteristics than do their colleagues in the ranks above or below them, or, for that matter, than they will themselves show if they are promoted to full professor. Associate professors possess the fewest career options. They recognize that they must first earn promotion at home. Associate professors are especially sensitive to the internal power of their institutions. As is shown in Table 12-9, the associate professors gave lower ratings than either full or assistant professors on black/white trust but higher ratings than those two groups on black visibility and influence.

When matters came closer to the faculty roles of teaching, evaluating students, course content, and the like—age, rank, and tenure mattered very little. In these areas of day-to-day job performance, the effects were pretty much the same for faculty at all levels. They asserted that their teaching techniques and evaluation practices were the same for black as for white students; that the new clientele had increased the time they gave to teaching, counseling, and other instructional matters; and that this additional time had come from a slighting of scholarly work. In addition, in the view of faculty at all ranks, minority issues did affect departmental hiring and promotion matters, but the overall impact was between "very little" and "somewhat."

Sex Differences

There were only very slight differences between women and men in their responses. The women saw more positive long-term minority impact, less authoritarian (or top down) decisions about minority matters, and greater departmental concern for blacks than did men. In only three instances did F ratios exceed the .05 level (see Table 12-11). Two of these—the Long-Term Minority Impact and Authoritarian Treatment indices—were the same ones that occurred in the comparisons by rank and may well be a function of the same latent factor—that of age—which operated there. In general, the women were newer to academic posts and therefore more concentrated in the lower echelons. The idea that women may have viewed blacks as competitors for scarce positions was not supported by the data.

TABLE 12-11

Faculty Differences as Related to Sex: Index Scores, F Value, and P Level

| Indices and Items | Faculty | | F | p(<) |
	Female	Male		
Role				
Long-Term Minority Impact	7.32	6.87	6.37	.01
Impact				
Authoritarianism	9.85	10.39	6.76	.01
Departmental Black Concern	5.04	4.66	7.08	.01

In summary, then, age and experience were factors which distinguished faculty perceptions of how their universities responded to black issues, what the racial climate was on campus, how such issues were dealt with, and what their long-range impact would be. At the same time, when it came to day-to-day behavior on the job—teaching, departmental governance, and the like—age, rank, and sex did not seem to matter. We turn to a more detailed faculty analysis in Chapter 13 which includes disciplinary and personal variables.

SUMMARY

In general, administrators and faculty demonstrated essentially the same moderate social values, with administrators expressing stronger or more favorable views about minority issues. While variations did exist, on the average administrators responded with concern for racial issues and believed that they and their institutions had given a positive response to an important social matter. In the main, faculty views paralleled those of administrators, and the differences were more of degree than of kind.

The principal differences among administrators occurred across functional lines, not by level of appointment. Those working in minority affairs held the most critical views of their institutions' success. The differences which occurred among faculty were almost exclusively related to age and stage in career. The younger faculty, with the occasional exception of associate professors, held a more critical posture. But regardless of age or academic discipline, their day-to-day behavior changed very little. Chapter 13 examines faculty roles and departments in greater detail.

13

Faculty and Departmental Response Patterns: Individual and Contextual Predictors

James R. Mingle

Faculty are the principal operatives and departments are the principal organizational units of colleges and universities. An assessment of the impact of blacks on higher education must look closely at what happens in the daily relations between students and faculty in the various academic departments. The Stage I interviews identified institutional responses such as special programs in admissions, academic counseling, and student organizations. These interviews, however, were less appropriate for understanding what went on in classrooms and faculty offices.[1]

Stage II of our study, therefore, concentrated on tapping the dimensions of faculty and departmental response. Nine departments (English, history, biology, chemistry, mathematics, economics, political science, psychology, and sociology) were selected for special attention. While these are not departments that necessarily have large numbers of black majors, they do typically provide required general education courses and, hence, have high black enrollments, especially at the introductory level. In each of the four universities included in the Stage II survey—SUNY-Brockport, "Metropolitan," University of

Missouri-Kansas City, and "State University"—these departments were faced with a more than an average amount of pressure related to minority concerns.

In our survey of faculty and interviews with 36 department chairpersons (nine disciplines at each of four institutions), we sought answers to two central questions: (1) What has been the impact of increased black enrollment on departments and what are departmental characteristics which predict those impacts and responses? (2) What has been the response of faculty members to increased black student enrollments and what are the individual and departmental contextual characteristics which predict that response? An important aspect of the faculty member's response was expected to be the normative climate found in the faculty member's department. The conceptual framework in Figure 13-1 presents graphically the design of this analysis.

FIGURE 13-1

Conceptual Framework

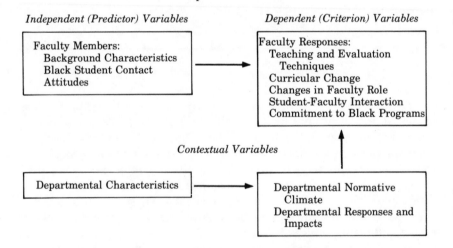

DEPARTMENTAL RESPONSES

While much of the response to black students was centered at the institutional level, the department is nevertheless an important organizational unit to examine. If black faculty were to be hired to form a new department, existing departments would participate in making the selections; likewise, if new courses were to be offered within the traditional disciplines, existing departments would be the focal point for the debates regarding the content of and authority over those courses. Furthermore, the normative climate of the department was suspected to have significant impact on individual faculty responses within the classroom.

The interviews conducted with department chairpersons sought to identify the major aspects of blacks' impact on departmental structure and procedures. Their responses to questions about the existence of courses with a predominant focus on black issues and departmental provision of remedial and tutorial programs are reported in Table 13-2. Questions directed to faculty asking about the impact of black enrollment on and the academic climate of the department are reported in Tables 13-2 and 13-3.

Courses, Remedial Help, Black Faculty, and Committees

Courses concerned with black issues existed on the four campuses in 14 of the 36 departments, including 7 of 8 humanities departments (English and history) and 7 of 16 social science departments (sociology, economics, and political science). (Table 13-1.) Most common were courses in Afro-American literature and black history. Some social science departments offered an occasional course in which black issues were a portion of the curricula (e.g., urban economics, minority group politics). The department chairpersons perceived a general feeling of declining interest in these courses, especially among white students. As might be expected, none of the natural

TABLE 13-1

Departmental Structural Responses:
Number of Departments by Discipline Reporting Responses

Discipline	Number of Departments	Black Courses	Tutorial Programs	Remedial Courses
English	4	4	3	1
History	4	3	0	0
Biology	4	0	2	2
Chemistry	4	0	4	2
Mathematics	4	0	3	3
Economics	4	2	1	0
Political Science	4	2	0	0
Psychology	4	0	1	0
Sociology	4	3	1	0
Totals	36	14/36	15/36	8/36

TABLE 13-2

Faculty Perception of Departmental Impacts: Percentage Distribution
(N = 363)

Impact of Increased Black Enrollment on Department	Less Difficult	Unchanged	More Difficult
Hiring and appointment decisions	1.8	43.4	54.8
Relationship with the central administration	9.0	78.3	20.9
Promotional and salary decisions	0.3	82.6	17.1
Maintenance of academic reputation	0.9	82.6	16.5

TABLE 13-3

Departmental Black Concern: Rank Ordered by Discipline

	Discipline	Mean*	Minimum	Maximum	Standard Deviation
Humanities	History	3.28	3.10	3.05	.15
	English	3.04	2.53	3.82	.50
	Economics	2.84	2.40	3.33	.33
Social Sciences	Political Science	2.81	2.33	3.50	.48
	Psychology	2.52	1.67	3.58	.68
	Math	2.40	1.33	3.33	.76
Natural Sciences	Sociology	2.38	1.67	3.20	.59
	Biology	2.06	1.73	2.40	.27
	Chemistry	1.77	0.86	3.00	.78

*Maximum possible score is 6.00, minimum is 0.

science departments had courses with a principal focus on black issues. But neither did 10 of the 24 social science and humanities departments.

Arrangements for tutorial help were found in 15 of 36 departments and were common in disciplines concerned with basic skills such as English, mathematics, and chemistry. These arrangements, however, were quite informal. Typically, graduate students provided free help to struggling undergraduates, with departments acting as a referral service. Department chairpersons were generally unaware of the extent of tutorial services or the kind of students who received tutoring.

Remedial courses were least common. Less than one-quarter of the departments offered such courses. Those that did could be found almost exclusively in the natural science departments of biology, chemistry, and mathematics. Only one of the four English departments (and none of the history or social science departments) offered a remedial course. However, all four of the universities had developed some form of special support program at the institutional level. The anecdotal reports from chairpersons and faculty of the English departments suggested that blacks and other new students had significant effects on the level at which introductory courses were being taught. Rather than add special remedial courses, departments chose to absorb ill-prepared students into the regular courses.

As for committee activity directed specifically to minority issues, the department chairpersons reported very little. None of the 36 departments had committees with a minority focus, although there were a few reports of ad hoc committees which later disbanded. Five of the 36 departments did report minority issues as a sometime interest of standing committees—usually those concerned with graduate admissions.

Hiring and Promotion

Few of the departments had responded to the increased black student enrollments by hiring black faculty. Each of six departments had one black faculty member; one department had two blacks on its faculty. Four of the eight black faculty members were in English and history; two were in the social sciences and two in the natural sciences. Blacks, then, represented 1.2 percent of the 667 total members of the 36 departments.

Faculty and department chairpersons strongly associated affirmative action with black student issues, although it was an issue not directly related to increased black student enrollments. As Table 13-2 indicates, 55 percent of the faculty believed that hiring and appointment decisions had become more difficult as the result of "minority issues, pressures, or considerations." The same degree of impact was not evident in the area of promotion and salary decisions, however. Fewer than one in five of the faculty respondents believed that these decisions had been complicated by minority considerations.

Several department chairpersons noted their concern with affirmative action programs, but in 1974–75 they felt little direct pressure to hire black faculty. One department head expressed the belief that money was more readily available to departments that could produce a black or a woman candidate. Almost universally, however, department chairpersons felt there was strong departmental autonomy over the hiring of new faculty. Direct pressure from administrators on this issue would have been viewed as highly inappropriate.

This is not to say that considerable procedural changes had not taken place in hiring minorities. Departments had substantially formalized their search and appointment procedures, utilizing written guidelines and attempting to reach minorities through advertisements and extensive informal contacts. Nearly 70 percent of the departments had a formalized policy on faculty recruitment. The natural science departments, however, were considerably less formal on this matter than the humanities or social science departments.

In general, then, while outcomes have been little affected in hiring and promotion, procedures appear to have changed substantially. Minorities and women were being sought and reportedly considered, but relatively few were being hired. If nothing else, department chairpersons were acutely aware of the affirmative action issue.

Faculty Attitudes about Black and Minority Issues

The calm of the post-confrontation period was reflected in the attitudes of department chairpersons, who expressed low levels of anxiety over black student dissatisfaction. If polarization existed openly during the earlier period, it had almost totally disappeared from view by the spring of 1975. When faculty were asked if different opinions on black and minority issues had caused polarization in their departments, over 90 percent responded negatively.

ACADEMIC CLIMATE AND CONCERN FOR BLACK STUDENTS

Another important aspect of departmental response to black students is the normative climate of the departments. Faculty were asked a number of questions concerning the racial and academic climate of their departments, including an index of supportiveness or Departmental Black Concern (Table 12-1). The two items making up this factor are:

1. Faculty make special efforts to ensure the success of black students.
2. Faculty present curriculum in order to have an appeal and interest to black students.

Table 13-3 presents the departmental scores on this index, averaged by disciplines and rank ordered. Discipline area differences are apparent—with the humanities at the top and the natural sciences at the bottom. The variance within discipline is significant, however, with individual natural science departments, for example, scoring quite high and some psychology and sociology departments comparatively low. Even the highest single department (English in one university) scored less than 4 out of a possible 6. This disciplinary difference can be seen in another way. There were significant differences (p < .02) in faculty responses to an item which asked them the extent to which the increased number of black students at their university had affected the content of their courses (Item 3e, "Impacts and Responses in Faculty and Departmental Activity," Appendix C). The humanities faculty reported the greatest effects, natural sciences faculty the least, and social sciences faculty were in between.

Two item measures of departmental academic climate were also examined for their relationship to supportiveness for black students—rigor and universalism. The two questionnaire items[2] which measure these concepts were:

1. *Rigor:* Faculty place greater demands on departmental majors than is the norm for the institution as a whole.

2. *Universalism:* Faculty in my department make the same academic demands on blacks and whites.

Both rigor and universalism were found to be negatively related to the Departmental Black Concern index (r = −.40 for rigor; −.64 for universalism). While the relationship between the academic climate items and Departmental Black Concern is substantial, these variables are also closely associated with discipline. The natural sciences and quantitatively oriented social sciences have the reputation of making greater demands on their students than the humanities and the "softer" social sciences. The relationship between these measures of disciplinary academic climate and black concern were tested by Multiple Classification Analysis.[3]

Table 13-4 presents the results of predicting Departmental Black Concern from the academic climate measures and area of discipline.[4] The table reveals a strong relationship between discipline area and Departmental Black Concern (Eta = .57) and a moderate downward adjustment when the climate predictors are considered (Beta = .42). From another perspective, the table reveals the small (but statistically significant) independent effects of the academic climate measures. The unique or net effect of the universalism measure is 3.5 percent of the total variance explained by this model.

The response, then, of departments to increased black enrollment can be characterized as inconsequential. The impact on the structure and processes of departmental activities has been minimal. The majority of faculty felt the overall impact had been quite negligible. Only 4 percent of the respondents saw a great deal of impact at this level of organization.

TABLE 13-4

Multiple Classification Analysis of Academic Climate Measures and
Disciplinary Area Predicting to Departmental Supportiveness

Departmental Characteristics	Predicting from Each Separately		Predicting from All Simultaneously	
	Eta	Eta^2	Beta	Beta^2
Discipline Area	.57	.321	.42	.178
Academic Climate— Rigor	.32	.103	.12	.016
Academic Climate— Universalism	.45	.211	.19	.035
			R = .532	
Percentage of Variance Explained = 36.5.			R^2 = .283	

Only half of the social science and humanities departments had
courses with a black focus (some of which were endangered because of
lack of interest). Fewer than half of the departments had tutorial
programs, and most of these involved only graduate students and not
faculty members. While 8 of the 36 departments had remedial
courses, these were viewed more as responses to a general decline in
student ability in the institution than as special responses to black
students.

There was no evidence of conflict within departments or with the
central administration over black-related issues. Nor was there any
committee concern with these issues, except in the area of graduate
admissions. There was an increased concern with hiring. Faculty believed that affirmative action considerations had made departmental
hiring more difficult. Procedures had been substantially formalized,
but few of these departments had hired black faculty.

Perception of the normative climate of a department relative to
blacks differed among the disciplines. A climate of concern for blacks
in a department was negatively related to an academically demanding climate. Faculty seemed to believe that it is not compatible to be
demanding of students, provide equal treatment for all, and still be
supportive of blacks.

In short, the arts and science departments of this study have been
only slightly affected by increased black student enrollments. They
remain the traditional models of university departments with basic
organizational structure, goals, and processes essentially unaltered.
Departmental climate however, appeared to vary significantly from
discipline to discipline and, in some cases, from department to department within the same disciplinary area. This climate of response will

serve as an important context in examining the individual faculty responses discussed next.

INDIVIDUAL FACULTY RESPONSE

The Dimensions of Response

The questionnaire distributed to faculty members measured their perceptions of their own role change as a consequence of increased black enrollments, as well as their attitudes toward and commitment to institutional programs developed for minorities. From the data reduction techniques applied to the questionnaire, six indices of response (described in Table 12-1) emerged which are of interest here. The first five are from the section dealing with Impacts and Responses in Faculty Activity and the last is from the section on Institutional Responsiveness:

Help and Accommodation: This is a fairly complex dimension which represents the responses most closely associated with the teaching role of faculty. Faculty scoring high on this index provided special help (or directed students to it) and demonstrated greater flexibility as well as a willingness to deviate from traditional practices and standards when dealing with blacks. Faculty scoring low provided no special treatment for black students (i.e., different from that for whites).

Time Demand: This index measures the impact on a faculty member's allocation of his own time to various activities. Time spent in response to black students was viewed as detracting from that devoted to creative and scholarly work.

Subjective Evaluation: A high score represents more frequent use of subjective evaluation with blacks and whites.

Black Curriculum Impact: A high score on this dimension indicates increased black content and class discussion of racial issues.

Personal Interaction: This dimension measures the degree of personal interaction (relative to other students) between black students and faculty. High scorers had a greater amount of personal contact and exchange with black students both in and out of the classroom.

Faculty Commitment: Faculty were asked to evaluate their current level of commitment to institutional minority programs on a scale from active opposition to active support.

The Degree of Response

As Table 13-5 indicates, the arts and science faculty believed they had made few special responses to black students, whether in the allocation of their time, in the way they graded, in the manner in which they taught their classes, or in the content of their curriculum. When faculty were asked to indicate the degree to which black minority issues, pressures, or considerations had altered their role as faculty members, about seven of ten responded "very little."

The greatest impact appeared to be in the time spent counseling students, with 43 percent of the faculty indicating that increased time spent in this activity has been the consequence of increased black student enrollments in their institutions.

TABLE 13-5

Faculty Impact/Response to Increased Black Enrollment
(N=363)

Help and Accommodation	Use with Blacks as Compared to Other Students		
	Less	Same	More
Provide extra help	0.9%	72.1%	29.0%
Extend deadlines	0.3	74.6	25.0
Refer to tutors	—	58.6	41.4
Allow wider range of topics in assignments	0.9	79.8	19.3
Permit rewrites of exams/papers	0.3	76.6	23.0
Subjective Evaluation			
Subjective evaluation of student effort	0.6	83.6	15.7
Evaluation of class participation	2.1	91.4	6.5

Black Curriculum Impact	Decreased	Remained the Same	Increased
Black content in courses	0.3%	72.7%	27.0%
Class discussions of racial issues	1.5	73.3	25.1
Time Demand			
Teaching and class preparation	—	87.1	12.9
Counseling of students	0.3	56.6	43.1
Interaction with support personnel	0.3	68.6	31.1
Creative and scholarly work accomplished	10.3	87.6	2.1

Personal Interaction	Less	Same	More
Blacks, compared to other students			
... Participate in class discussion	38.7%	54.2%	7.0%
... Speak to me on campus	16.0	72.9	11.1
... See me about personal problems	31.5	57.3	11.3
... Discuss career plans	29.1	62.4	8.6

Faculty Commitment to Black Programs	Opposition	Indifference	Passive Support	Active Support
	3.8%	13.3%	57.5%	25.4%

The measures which make up the personal interaction index showed the most variation. The average faculty member characterized his or her interaction with black students as being somewhat lower than with the other students.

As for the commitment to the institution-wide programs for black students, faculty expressed general support for them (83 percent). While there was little overt opposition, support for their universities' commitment to black programs was more likely to be passive (58 percent) than active (25 percent).

Predicting Faculty Response

In exploring faculty response to increased black enrollments the questionnaire gathered information on faculty attitudes, background characteristics, individual contact with black students, and the climate of the respondent's department. These were then employed in a linear regression model using Multiple Classification Analysis and categorical variables to predict faculty response.

Attitude Predictors: Faculty were asked a variety of attitude questions about blacks and black issues in higher education. From factor analysis, three indices were found relevant—Universal-Particular Standards, Long-Term Minority Impact, and Institutional Pluralism-Integration (see Table 12-1). In addition, a single item was used as a measure of faculty racial ideology: "Despite our concern over racial injustice, colleges and universities *do not* have a primary responsibility to rectify that situation." For example, it would be possible for an individual to hold "liberal" values and simultaneously believe that the chances for accomplishing desired goals are endangered rather than enhanced by the university entering the political arena.

Universal-Particular Standards: To use Parson's terminology, "particularistic" faculty viewed race as a valid criterion in judging admission and performance standards. "Universalistic" or "meritocratic" faculty did not; for them, race was not to be considered.

Long-Term Minority Impact: Faculty were asked a number of interrelated questions about the long-term impact of minorities on colleges and universities. The index covers perception of both the impact of black student enrollment and affirmative action, which faculty view as closely related.

Institutional Pluralism-Integration: This index measures attitudes concerning the relationship of minority programs to institutional structure and the integration of minority groups into the mainstream of the institution.

Institutional Responsibility: Faculty were asked about their attitude toward the responsibilities of colleges and universities to rectify
racial injustice.

Faculty showed varying degrees of agreement and disagreement
in their attitudes. (See Table 13-6.) On the more generalized statements about the impact of blacks on higher education or the effect of

TABLE 13-6

Percentage Distribution of Faculty Responses to Attitude Measures

Attitude Measure	Agree 1 2	Disagree 3 4
Particular-Universal		
Black and racial minorities should meet the same academic admissions standards as all other students.	57.0	43.0
Different performance standards are probably required for some racial minority students.	51.3	48.7
Different admissions criteria and standards may be justified for some racial minority groups.	65.0	35.0
Long-Term Minority Impact		
Increases in black and other racial minority enrollments and special programs for them reduce academic standards.	31.2	68.8
In the long run the entrance of racial minority students and the development of related programs will strengthen our colleges and universities.	88.4	11.6
Affirmative action, despite its underlying concern for equality, is detrimental to the viability of our colleges and universities.	23.5	76.5
Institutional Pluralism-Integration		
Diversity of life styles and separate living patterns among blacks and other racial groups should be encouraged in colleges and universities.	38.0	62.0
Pluralism can be diverse and colleges and universities should not support separate educational, cultural, and social activities by various racial groups.	40.9	59.1
Programs for blacks and other racial minorities will be more effective if they are given a separate departmental identity.	14.5	85.5
Institutional Responsibility		
Despite our concern over racial injustice, colleges and universities *do not* have a primary responsibility to rectify that situation.	43.0	57.0

affirmative action, faculty were overwhelmingly positive. On more specific roles for institutions vis-à-vis blacks, there was far less agreement. On the questions concerning admissions and performance standards which make up the Universal-Particular index, the faculty split nearly evenly on these questions. The most agreement was found in the question about the long-term impact of minorities on colleges and universities: 88 percent of the faculty believed that the impact would be positive.

The correlations among these attitude measures found in Table 13-7 provide insight into the interconnectedness of the attitudes. Faculty holding universal values about standards (no special exceptions for race) tended to view the long-range impact of minorities in negative terms (r = −.35). They also tended to be less inclined to assign their institution responsibility on race issues (r = −.29). Universalism was also related to a belief that blacks should become fully integrated into the culture and organization of the institution (r = .37). Expressed in another direction, particularistic faculty (those who would apply different criteria to blacks and whites) tended to view the long-range impact in positive terms, view separate programs and lifestyles as beneficial, and consider colleges responsible for solving problems of racial injustice. The relationships, however, are not strong in any instance. (See Table 13-7.)

TABLE 13-7

Intercorrelations among Attitude Measures

	Universal-Particular (H=Universal)	Long-Term Minority Impact (H=Positive)	Institutional Pluralism-Integration (H=Integration)
Long-Term Minority Impact	−.35	—	—
Pluralism-Integration (+)	−.37	−.32	—
Institutional Responsibility	−.29	.38	−.18

Variables which reflect the departmental context in which individual response has taken place were also used as predictors. Those included the presence of black faculty and the index of the department's climate of black concern discussed earlier. Mean scores were calculated on the index for each department and then assigned to all faculty in the department. This is similar to other research employing contextual analysis where the focus remains on the individual but group variables are employed as characteristics of individuals.[5] The multivariate analysis also employed background characteristics such as age, tenure status, sex, discipline, and the degree of lower division contact with blacks in the classroom as predictors of response.

Predicting Teacher Role Response

The three interrelated dimensions (Help and Accommodation, Subjective Evaluation, and Time Demand) discussed earlier were combined into a composite, additive index of teacher role response.[6] Table 13-8 presents the unadjusted relationships (Eta's) between the faculty attitude, background, contact, and departmental context predictor variables and the composite role response index and also the adjusted relationships (Beta's) which consider the unique relationships of the predictor variables and the response index.

Lower Division Contact. By far the best predictor of response is contact with undergraduate students at the lower division level. Faculty with a higher percentage of blacks in introductory courses felt the greatest impact on the allocation of their time and in the way they teach. High contact at the upper division levels is not similarly related.

Attitudes. The strongest attitude predictor is the index of Universalism-Particularism.

TABLE 13-8

Multiple Classification Analysis of Individual and Contextual Variables
Predicting to Teacher Role Response

Variable	Predicting from Each Separately		Predicting from All Simultaneously	
	Eta	Eta^2	Beta	Beta^2
Background Characteristics				
Age	.20	.041	.16	.027
Tenure*	.01	.000		
Sex*	.02	.000		
Discipline	.12	.014	.15	.021
Institution	.24	.055	.02	.000
Attitudes				
Universal-Particular Standards	.18	.032	.21	.045
Long-Term Minority Impact (Negative)	.18	.033	.15	.021
Pluralism-Integration*	.01	.000		
Institutional Responsibility*	.11	.012		
Contact				
Lower Division	.37	.139	.33	.107
Departmental Context				
Black Concern	.17	.028	.17	.031
Black Faculty (Negative)	.07	.005	.16	.026
			R = .437	
Percentage of Variance Explained = 26.3			R^2 = .191	

*Beta^2 less than .015 in preliminary models.

Not only were universalistic values related to a reluctance to provide special help or to devote greater amounts of time to black students, but they were negatively related to commitment to institutional programs and curriculum changes. When faculty members believed that black students should meet the same standards as whites, they also tended to show an unwillingness to alter traditional teaching styles to meet the needs of these students.

On the other hand, the study does not address directly the concept of the impact of responsiveness versus just response. No information exists on student performance outcomes related to various kinds of "special help and accommodation" or universalistic standards.

The Importance of Context. Two contextual variables were important predictors of Teacher Role Response. Departmental Black Concern demonstrated a modest effect on individual faculty behavior, even after accounting for its interrelationship with other variables in the model. The normative climate of the department did appear to influence individual faculty in the classroom. Given the private nature of faculty work and the minimum amount of peer observation which takes place, even the modest influence demonstrated seems important.

Membership in integrated departments (those with black faculty) *negatively* affected Teacher Role Response. Since no identifiable subgroup of black faculty was available for analysis (there were too few to guarantee anonymity), we are handicapped in our explanation of this anomalous finding. Do white faculty who have an opportunity to observe the responses of black colleagues view their own responses as less "special" than do faculty who have only other whites as a frame of reference? Or do black faculty have the effect of relieving white faculty members' need to respond to blacks? Future research needs to examine whether black faculty and faculty in integrated departments are more resistent to appeals for special treatment from black students.

Perception of the long-term impact of blacks shows a modest negative relationship to response. Those who felt the greatest impact (reported the greatest response) tended to view the long-term impact of blacks on higher education in more negative terms. This suggests that responsive faculty—who are also more likely to teach introductory courses—are pessimistic about the future.

Background Characteristics. The only background characteristic which demonstrated significant predictive power was age (Beta = .16). It was the older faculty member who reported greater role response. Differences between universities (which were significant before accounting for other variables) disappeared when such variables as age and degree of contact with black students were taken into account.

The Meaning of Response at the Departmental Level

Conclusions from a study which attempted to explore such a variety of impacts at different levels are by their nature tentative. However, the findings on faculty and departments indicate a pervasive ambivalence.

When faculty members were asked general questions about the impact of blacks on higher education and their attitudes toward racial issues, the overwhelming majority responded moderately but favorably (Chapter 12). But when the role-specific attitudes and behaviors of those who might have felt the greatest impact of blacks were examined, there was a distinct shift toward nonresponsive attitudes and even expressed perceptions of negative impacts. Faculty teaching large numbers of black undergraduates in introductory courses were obviously key people. Yet they appeared to be frustrated and pessimistic about the impact of their efforts.

One of the more encouraging developments in higher education in recent years has been the emergence of teacher effectiveness programs and research on the teaching and learning process, an activity which Cross believes was brought about by the presence of "new students" in higher education. "Without knowing it," Cross says, "students with poor academic backgrounds have challenged college instructors to look at their ability to teach. Traditional college students who are selected for their motivation and skill for academic work are no challenge to pedagogy."[7] The findings of this research suggest strongly the need for such programs for faculty. We know little about the relationship between response and outcome, but we do know that the faculty and departments in this study have been relatively unaffected by and unresponsive to the increases in black enrollments in their institutions.

Unfortunately, we were unable to examine the response of black faculty to black students. A comparison of their responses with those of white faculty would provide valuable information. We suspect that black faculty, to a greater degree than white faculty, are able to respond with special help while keeping their expectations high. On the other hand, there is no reason to believe that their formal pedagogical training is any different from that of their white colleagues.

The effects demonstrated by the contextual variables also have implications for faculty development programs. The normative climate of the departments did influence faculty behavior in the class-rooms. Faculty development programs which are departmentally based or which involve significant numbers of faculty from the same department would appear to have additional reinforcement power.

Finally, a discussion of an institution's goals and purposes and their compatibility with the abilities and aspirations of the student body is essential. As the emphasis in some institutions shifts to the undergraduate levels and toward more open admissions, increasing numbers of faculty will be faced with the disparity between their expectations for students and their own role and reality. While a clearer conception of institutional goals will help, a reward and incentive system which would direct faculty energies toward creative and effective responses to this new clientele is essential. Information on what those responses are is a prerequisite.

Notes

[1] The analysis presented here is from James R. Mingle, "Faculty and Departmental Response to Increased Black Student Enrollment: Individual and Contextual Predictors," unpublished Ph. D. dissertation.

[2] Items 9i and 9c, respectively, in the Faculty Questionnaire. See page Appendix C.

[3] Frank Andrews, et al. *Multiple Classification Analysis: A Report on a Computer Program for Multiple Regression Using Categorical Predictors.* 2nd Edition. (Ann Arbor: Institute for Social Research, The University of Michigan, 1973).

[4] Due to the small number of departments per discipline, the number of predictor categories was limited to the three larger areas—humanities, natural sciences, and social sciences.

[5] See, for example, Ted K. Bradshaw, "The Impact of Peers on Student Orientation to College: A Contextual Analysis," in Martin Trow (ed.), *Teachers and Students* (New York: McGraw Hill, 1975).

[6] Pearson R's between indexes: Help and Accommodation and Subjective Evaluation ($R = .42$); Help and Accommodation and Time Response ($R = .58$); Time Response and Subjective Evaluation ($R = .33$). Curriculum Response was also moderately related with these three indexes ($R = .25$ with Help and Accommodation and Time Response) but was excluded from the conceptual reasons.

[7] K. Patricia Cross, "The Instructional Revolution," a paper presented at a meeting of the American Association of Higher Education (AAHE), Chicago, March 8, 1976.

14

Four Institutions: Racial Climates, Responses, and the Future

Zelda F. Gamson

In this chapter we give detailed attention to the four universities—SUNY-Brockport, "State University," "Metropolitan University," and the University of Missouri-Kansas City—selected for our intensive surveys in the spring of 1975. All of these universities made early efforts to recruit black students and to provide extensive services for them. All invested a fair amount of institutional funds and time into this commitment. All had clearly identifiable programs associated with minorities. All of them, particularly State and Brockport, have had strong, consistent advocacy for their minority commitments from their presidents and from other administrators.

They differed, however, in several important respects. Two—Metropolitan and the University of Missouri-Kansas City—are located in major urban centers; two are not (although Brockport serves a nearby city, Rochester). Three of the four experienced major shifts in control or mission just prior to the rise in black enrollments. Metropolitan University secularized rapidly during the 1960s and became more oriented toward its urban location. Brockport expanded rapidly after becoming a liberal arts college in the SUNY system. Kansas City became a state institution after having been a private municipal college and began to seek a unique mission for itself. Only State University did not undergo a major redirection during the period we are examining.

The four institutions differed also in the degree of conflict which accompanied their minority efforts. Although all four universities initiated their minority programs in response to internal forces, two of them—Brockport and Metropolitan University—experienced major confrontations with black students.

Our field visits and analysis of documents led us to conclude that by 1975 State University had the most fully developed, mature, institutionalized response programs for black students. It was one of the three "adaptive" institutions in the sample of 13 colleges and universities. At the other extreme, we found that the University of Missouri-Kansas City did not begin until 1975 to institutionalize the minority programs which had been developed at its periphery (within the Division of Continuing Education) and which had only recently been shifted into the College of Arts and Science. SUNY-Brockport, while it resembled State in the comprehensiveness of and support for its minority-oriented programs, lacked a clear focus and plan for all of its efforts; much depended on the leadership of the president in a situation that continued to be volatile. Finally, Metropolitan University moved early and for internally motivated reasons to recruit black students, but by 1975—primarily because of general financial problems—it appeared to have reached the limit of its response to minority concerns.

We can classify the four institutions according to (1) the degree of conflict experienced since the introduction of large numbers of black students, and (2) the institutionalized responsiveness to the minority commitment by 1975 (Table 14-1).

TABLE 14-1

The Four Institutions by Degree of Conflict
and Institutionalized Responsiveness

Institutionalized Responsiveness	Degree of Minority-Related Conflict	
	High	Low
More	Brockport	State
Less	Metropolitan	University of Missouri–Kansas City

In this chapter, we want to look at the extent to which these judgments based on field work are reinforced by data from interviews with a larger and more representative sample of administrators, faculty, and students. Given what we have already learned from Stage I of this study about the histories and responses of these universities to black students, we examine in this chapter how the individuals who were involved perceived, experienced, and contributed to those histories and responses. For example, how did those at universities which experienced a great deal of conflict surrounding blacks view the climate, commitments, and responsiveness of their institutions? How did these institutions differ in their across-the-board commitments to blacks, and what were the particular circumstances that brought increased numbers of blacks to each campus? What would be an accurate perspective on the question of integration versus segregation versus pluralism at those four institutions? What were the hopes and fears for the future among the people in our study?

Our Stage II survey confronted most of these issues as directly as was possible in a questionnaire format. While we have been cautious about interpreting responses to any single item, the use of indices and attention to patterns of response has increased our confidence in the validity of the questions. As in Chapter 12, we present the combined responses for administrators and faculty members, summarized as indices measuring the following topics: the role of racial minorities in colleges and universities (Table 14-2); the breadth of goals for blacks (Table 14-3); racial climate and activity (Table 14-4); institutional responsiveness and commitment (Table 14-5); and impacts and responses at the administrative and faculty levels (Table 14-6). In addition, we compare the four institutions on the extent to which their members believed they would continue their commitment to blacks in the future (Table 14-7). As we shall see below, while the four universities were above the average on most indices, there were consistently significant differences among them. We have eliminated from the tables the few indices on which there were no statistically significant differences.

THE IDEOLOGY OF INCLUDING RACIAL MINORITIES IN COLLEGES AND UNIVERSITIES: THE GENERAL ROLE AND SPECIFIC INSTITUTIONAL GOALS

As we saw in Chapter 12, respondents were more likely to endorse universalistic standards (as opposed to particularistic) and racial integration; they saw the impact of minorities in higher education as positive in the long run. Among the four universities, respondents at the University of Missouri-Kansas City showed the highest mean scores on these issues (Table 14-2). Respondents at State University stood out

TABLE 14-2

Role of Racial Minorities in Colleges and Universities (Mean Scores for the Four Universities)

Measure	University of Missouri–Kansas City	"Metro-politan"	"State University"	SUNY-Brockport	All	Overall Significance of Difference
Particular-Universal Standards (H = Universalism; 0–9)	5.04	4.50	4.67	4.46	4.64	<.05
Long-Term Minority Impact (H = Positive; 0–9)	6.25	5.41	6.21	6.03	6.03	<.001
Institutional Pluralism-Integration (H = Integration; 0–9)	5.46	5.19	4.91	5.27	5.17	<.001

TABLE 14-3

Institutional Goals for Blacks and Racial Minorities (Mean Scores for the Four Universities)

Measure	University of Missouri–Kansas City	"Metro-politan"	"State University"	SUNY-Brockport	All	Overall Significance of Difference
Institutional Black Priority (H = Important; 0–32)	16.16	17.54	18.90	19.95	18.44	<.001
Non-Academic Support (H = Important; 0–16)	8.63	8.95	10.07	10.58	9.83	<.001
Affirmative Action (H = Important; 0–8)	4.33	3.60	4.53	4.67	4.40	<.001

TABLE 14-4

Racial Climate and Activity (Mean Scores for the Four Universities)

Measure	University of Missouri–Kansas City	"Metropolitan"	"State University"	SUNY-Brockport	All	Overall Significance of Difference
Openness and Inclusiveness (H = Openness; 0–12)	5.06	5.29	5.93	5.83	5.64	<.001
Administration/Faculty/Student Interaction (H = Positive; 0–8)	3.14	3.00	4.11	4.10	3.74	<.001
Black Visibility and Influence (H = Visible; 0–12)	3.00	3.47	4.66	5.63	4.45	<.001
Total Black Influence* (H = A Great Deal; 0–24)	5.70	7.17	7.53	7.98	7.31	<.001
Black/White Trust (H = Trust; 0–12)	5.55	5.42	6.03	5.18	5.58	<.001
Black Influence Exertion (H = Exertion; 0–24)	7.96	10.16	9.51	10.46	9.66	<.001
Campus Racial Conflict* (H = Substantial; 0–4)	.69	1.14	.84	1.75	1.14	<.05

*Item rather than index.

as being the least concerned with institutional integration, while those at Metropolitan saw the least amount of long-term impact from minorities in higher education—a pessimism which also surfaced in some of the other questions in the survey. Thus, it appears that the University of Missouri-Kansas City, which had more limited programs and activities for black students (and, if we are correct in our assessments, the lowest levels of institutionalized responsiveness and conflict), held the most optimistic view of the role of racial minorities in higher education.

However, when the questions focused on particular goals for their own institutions, the administrators and faculty at the four universities clustered differently (Table 14-3). Specifically, respondents at the four institutions differed substantially in their ratings of institutional priority placed on recruiting and serving blacks, the provision for non-academic support, and commitment to affirmative action. SUNY-Brockport was rated highest on all of the goals, State was consistently second, and Metropolitan and Kansas City received the lowest overall ratings. Metropolitan received particularly low ratings on affirmative action, while Kansas City was rated low on the extent to which it had placed a high priority on black concerns. Respondents at State and Brockport—which we had already judged to have made the most institutionalized responses—expressed the greatest commitment to broad institutional goals for blacks; individuals at Metropolitan and Kansas City—both judged to have less institutionalized responses—reported lower institutional commitment. There was a notable disjunction between Kansas City respondents' strong endorsement of an abstract commitment of higher education to minorities and their perception of a lower institutional commitment.

RACIAL CLIMATE: INFLUENCE AND CONFLICT

How did faculty and administrators describe the atmosphere in which blacks were introduced into their universities? What was the degree and quality of interaction between blacks and whites? We tried to get at these questions in a number of ways—by asking about the degree of trust between blacks and whites; about the amount of campus racial conflict; about the openness of the institution to black participation; about the degree of interaction between blacks and whites; and about the visibility and influence of blacks (see Table 14-4). Although the combined scores for the four institutions were below the midpoint for each of the measures, all of the racial climate indices did show strong, statistically significant differences among the institutions. The institutions differed particularly in two dimensions of racial climate, an influence dimension and a conflict dimension. On questions tapping black influence (black visibility and influence; administrator/faculty/student interaction; openness and inclusiveness), SUNY-Brockport and State University were rated considerably higher than either Metropolitan University or the University of Missouri-Kansas City. Again, our earlier judgments about the greater institutionalized responsiveness at Brockport and State are clearly validated.

So are our ratings of conflict. Crosscutting the influence dimension, responses to questions on conflict and degree of trust between the races (e.g., black-white trust, black influence exertion, and racial conflict) produced a different ordering among the four universities: Brockport and Metropolitan showed the lowest levels of trust and more racial conflict than either State or Kansas City.

It is clear, then, that conflict between the races and the influence of blacks are not necessarily correlated. State seemed to typify a situation of mutual acceptance among the races, with its pattern of higher than average black influence and low conflict. At the other extreme, the University of Missouri-Kansas City reflected a situation of mutual isolation—lower than average black influence and low conflict. The patterns of racial climate at Brockport and Metropolitan— both high in conflict but with different degrees of black influence— were also reflected in the institutional responsiveness to blacks.

INSTITUTIONAL RESPONSIVENESS AND COMMITMENT

All of the universities rated themselves above the midpoint on the various indices of responsiveness—the current willingness of the institution to develop programs or services for blacks; the adequacy of these efforts; the overall commitment of various white groups to the development of black programs and services; the specific commitment of white administrators and faculty; and the commitment of blacks (Table 14-5).

With the variety of ways we addressed the question of responsiveness, it is striking how consistently the four institutions were ordered. On five of the six indices, SUNY-Brockport ranked first, and on the sixth it tied for first place with State. State was consistently in

TABLE 14-5

Institutional Responsiveness and Commitment (Mean Scores for the Four Universities)

Measure	University of Missouri–Kansas City	"Metro-politan"	"State University"	SUNY-Brockport	All	Overall Significance of Differences
Willingness (H = Willing; 0–20)	13.39	13.45	14.88	15.88	14.67	<.001
Adequacy (H = Adequate; 0–20)	8.57	9.36	9.84	11.35	9.99	<.001
White Commitment to Blacks (H = Active Support; 0–32)	20.03	20.36	21.80	21.80	21.06	<.001
Administrative Commitment (H = Active Support; 0–16)	10.50	10.66	11.23	11.57	11.10	<.001
Faculty Commitment (H = Active Support; 0–12)	7.84	8.11	8.46	8.91	8.43	<.001
Black Commitment (H = Active Support; 0–8)	6.23	6.53	6.63	6.75	6.58	<.001

second place, and Metropolitan was in third place. The University of Missouri-Kansas City was clearly the least responsive of the four by any measure.

IMPACTS ON AND RESPONSES AMONG ADMINISTRATORS AND FACULTY

There were also interesting differences in the way administrators and faculty members in these four universities reported the impacts of increased black enrollments on their particular activities and domains. (See Table 14-6.) While administrators overall did not see high levels of impact from black staff and programs, they were above the mean on the degree to which they saw their relationships with blacks as positive and open. Administrators at Brockport reported the largest degree of impact from black staff and programs, while those at Metropolitan described a more negative picture: the impact of black staff and programs was significantly lower and relationships were more negative.

There was a reversal of this pattern among faculty at Metropolitan, who consistently reported more impact on their teaching than did faculty at the three other universities: they reported accommodations in teaching style, used subjective evaluation, interacted more with black students, and reported more departmental concern with black students. Faculty at the three other universities did not differ sharply from one another.

OVERALL PATTERNS AND IMPLICATIONS FOR THE FUTURE

The picture of the four institutions that emerged from the survey was consistent with the patterns set out in Table 14-1. Brockport and Metropolitan were seen by faculty members and administrators as being high in conflict; State and Kansas City were seen as more peaceful. However, arrayed along a variety of impact measures, Brockport and State resembled each other more, while Kansas City and Metropolitan looked similar.

Clearly, the most volatile racial climate was at Brockport. While respondents there perceived the highest level of conflict and the lowest racial trust, they also reported a great deal of influence from, interac-

TABLE 14-6

Impacts on and Responses by Administrators and Faculty (Mean Scores for the Four Universities)

Impacts and Responses	University of Missouri–Kansas City	"Metropolitan"	"State University"	SUNY-Brockport	All	Overall Significance of Differences
Administration						
Black Staff and Program Impact (H = A Great Deal; 0–24)	7.81	4.91	5.55	8.06	6.65	<.05
Positive-Negative Relationships (H = Positive; 0–28)	19.42	16.76	21.29	18.29	19.39	<.001
Personal Openness (H = Increased; 0–24)	16.25	14.86	14.84	15.94	15.48	<.10
Faculty and Departmental						
Help and Accommodation (H = Helpful; 0–20)	11.37	11.96	11.10	11.45	11.40	<.001
Subjective Evaluation (H = More Subjective; 0–8)	4.12	4.34	4.13	4.18	4.18	<.01
Personal Interaction (H = More; 0–16)	10.86	11.58	11.25	10.84	11.09	<.01
Time Demand (H = Increased; 0–16)	14.86	15.00	14.54	14.97	14.81	<.001
Departmental Black Concern (H = Concern; 0–6)	2.35	3.25	2.64	2.72	2.72	<.001

tion with, and involvement by blacks on campus. The least volatile racial climate, but also the one with the least amount of black impact, was at Kansas City. The most open, trusting, and pluralistic racial climate was at State. The picture for Metropolitan University was the most problemmatic and pessimistic. There was a great deal of conflict and black activism at Metropolitan, low levels of interracial trust and interaction, no strongly endorsed goals centered around black issues, and no evidence of high or positive impacts on administrative roles. Yet faculty at Metropolitan reported the greatest effects of black students on their teaching. There was an obvious contradiction at Metropolitan between how the faculty said they responded to black students and administrators' lower levels of responsiveness.

Other inconsistencies emerged from the surveys at the other three campuses. At Kansas City, we found a contradiction between the general ideological support for the role of racial minorities in colleges and universities and the low impact and responsiveness within the institution itself. At State, the steady responsiveness to blacks on the part of the university as a whole was not reflected much in faculty responses. At Brockport, high commitment and responsiveness did not mitigate distrust between blacks and whites.

It is significant that the one private institution in this group of four was the most pessimistic about its future commitment to minority students. As we have noted several times, Metropolitan had large financial deficits when we conducted our study and had experienced significant enrollment declines just as black students were enrolling in large numbers. Despite early comprehensive efforts, strong leadership from the top, pressure from black students, and support from the surrounding black community, Metropolitan University had made a lesser overall response than either Brockport or State. The impact perceived by faculty on their own teaching roles may have helped to absorb and diffuse the effects of increased black enrollments at Metropolitan. However, there was no indication that the faculty who may have responded to the blacks in their own classrooms influenced the activities of either of Metropolitan's two minority programs, the Special Help Program and the Afro-American Institute. Nor does it appear that the Metropolitan faculty were able to provide the resources to support and attract black students.

Brockport seems to have been on the verge of consolidating its high levels of support and responsiveness to black students. Its problems seemed to lie primarily in interpersonal relationships on campus and in low levels of trust between blacks and whites.

State clearly had the most solidly developed responses to black

290 BLACK STUDENTS ON WHITE CAMPUSES

students and had obviously reached a level of acceptance for its efforts and a quality of mutual respect between the races that were enviable. If anything, the danger at State may lurk in too smug a view of its success. Faculty, for example, did not report high levels of impact on their own roles.

Finally, at the University of Missouri-Kansas City as a whole the racial climate was one of placid isolation. Since minority programs at the university were developed and implemented in the Division of Continuing Education, their impact in the wider university has been minimal. There was little pressure either from blacks or from other sectors of the institution to broaden its commitment, nor were there overwhelmingly powerful student concerns or problems which distinguished Kansas City. What did distinguish it were an ideological commitment to universalism and integration and a view of the long-term impact of minorities in higher education. Either the need for or pressure to push further will determine the University of Missouri-Kansas City's future minority involvements.

In summary, we have learned from this examination of the responses to our survey at the four universities that there were, indeed, high levels of responsiveness to black students. Responsiveness did not seem to be related to high levels of early conflict at the time of our survey, five or six years after the initial entry of large numbers of black students. Rather, the institutions' responses to black students were related to an overall climate of concern with and commitment to dealing with racial issues. Commitment and responsiveness go together regardless of their history and sources, whether due to high levels of activism and pressure from blacks, as at Brockport, or because of consistent and early leadership from whites, as at State.

There is no easy transition from experience with responding to blacks to endorsement of goals for other colleges and universities; in fact, the greater the amount of on-campus experience, the more sober the view for higher education in general. Nor is there an easy transition from institutionalized response structures to the integration of the races or to consistency between the attitudes and behavior of faculty, administrators, and students.

Our study, of course, has looked at institutions that were still in transition. For all the difficulties they had in responding to blacks and for all the unanticipated problems this new student group brought, the respondents in our survey allowed themselves some measure of optimism in thinking about the future. In answering questions about their institutions' future commitment—to providing financial aid, recruitment, and admissions programs for blacks; to tutoring, counseling, and advising; to black or ethnic studies and other black-oriented curricula; to social and cultural activities; and to recruitment of black faculty and staff—most of the respondents at the four universities thought that in the future there would be as much, or even greater, commitment to blacks. (See Table 14-7.) Brockport was seen as having the greatest overall future commitment to blacks, the University of Missouri-Kansas City and State followed closely, and Metropolitan came last. Variations in the degree of optimism among the four universities reflect both how far they have come and how far they think they need—and can afford—to go in responding to the black students on their campuses. Whether these abstract reports of future commitment and support can or will be tapped in the difficult years ahead is a critical issue. The next chapter takes this longer perspective.

TABLE 14-7

Future Institutional Commitment to Blacks (Mean Scores for the Four Universities)

Commitment	University of Missouri–Kansas City	"Metro-politan"	"State University"	SUNY-Brockport	All
Overall Future Commitment (H = Reduced; 0–20)	8.90	9.96	9.09	8.73	9.11
*Specific Areas**					
Student Recruitment, Admissions, Financial Aid (H = Reduced; 0–4)	1.70	2.08	1.87	1.67	1.82
Tutoring, Counseling, Advising, Services (H = Reduced; 0–4)	1.73	2.03	1.83	1.63	1.79
Black Studies, Other Black-Focused Curricula (H = Reduced; 0–4)	1.96	2.03	1.82	1.87	1.90
Social and Cultural Activities (H = Reduced; 0–4)	1.98	1.98	1.87	1.86	1.91
Black Faculty and Staff Recruitment (H = Reduced; 0–4)	1.48	1.86	1.63	1.64	1.65

*Items rather than indices.

Part V

Evolution or Revolution:
The Process Reviewed

15

A Model of Institutional Response to Increased Black Enrollments

Marvin W. Peterson

While we have seen that the 13 institutions responded to a new black student clientele in a variety of ways, they also had certain common experiences. This chapter identifies these similarities across five phases of response to the increased enrollments of black students (see Table 15-1):

1. A period in which certain conditions *predisposed* the institution toward the impending black enrollment increase.
2. A period of *precipitating events* in which initial attempts to recruit black students were launched.
3. A period of *transitional trauma* as black students reacted to, made demands on, and created conflicts within their new institutional settings.
4. A period of *active accommodation* in which black students, their new programs and staff, and the college or university made some accommodations to one another.
5. A period of *reassessment.*

Within each phase, certain issues or dilemmas predominated in the institutional impact of the presence of black students on campus (top half of Table 15-1). The institutions, in turn, employed a variety of strategies in responding to these issues and dilemmas (bottom half of Table 15-1). The impacts and the response strategies occurred

TABLE 15-1

A Model of Institutional Response to Increased Black Enrollments

	Predisposing Conditions	→ Precipitating Events	→ Transitional Trauma	→ Active Accommodation	→ Reassessment: Institutionalization or Retrenchment
Institutional Impact: Issues and Dilemmas	External Pressures: Relevant segments • demographic • legal/political • interest groups • other institutions Strength or cohesion Intensity Predictability Direction and strength • active support • supportive • resistive • active resistance	Internal/external initiation Planned/unplanned response Voluntariness or control of response Source and style of white leadership Conflict level • internal • boundary Resource availability Timing	Comprehensiveness of response Commitment; adequacy and level of support Black/white conflict Black identity Black control of black programs Black/white leadership relations	Black/white acceptance or trust Separate/integrated black structures Institutional responsiveness or commitment	Priority of black programs • staff appointment and program status • program locus Legitimacy of institutional review process (rational/political) • order of review • representation • data utilization • criteria Minority interest group relations Black/white leadership relations
Institutional Strategies of Response	Internal Pressures: Leadership Proactive/reactive Competitive/cooperative Prior experience • sensitivity • concern • readiness	Adaptive Responsive Reactive Evolutionary	Power politics Negotiation Creative disturbance Bureaucratic or paternalistic Cooperation Capitulation	Degree of trust Pattern of separation/integration/coordination Degree of responsiveness	Full institutionalization Partial institutionalization Instability Retrenchment Termination
Societal and Institutional Contexts	Shifting societal values and governmental interventions on black/minority issues. Changing institutional conditions: mission, direction, and purpose; governance; leadership; resources.				

within a context shaped by societal and institutional conditions. This chapter reviews the nature of these contextual conditions and then examines the impact issues and response strategies during each of the five phases.

THE ROLE OF INSTITUTIONAL AND SOCIETAL CONTEXT

The Societal Context

Several contextual factors in the wider society influenced the responses of the 13 colleges and universities to black students. First, the shift in the civil rights movement from a focus on nonviolence and integration to militant separatism was a crucial factor that affected many whites. Administrators and faculty, some of whom had been involved in the early civil rights movement, had influenced their institutions to admit more black students. They were then confronted with black students who were more in tune with black nationalism than with the spirit of integration. This created a difficult transition for many liberal whites; psychologically, as well as organizationally, they were unprepared for the conflicts that were to occur on their campuses.

Second, federal and state intervention on behalf of minorities had profound effects on higher education. The civil rights movement of the 1950s and 1960s led to governmentally supported financial aid and other special programs which eased the initial burden on colleges and universities that attempted to bring in large numbers of blacks during the late 1960s. A short time later, the expanded powers of the Office of Civil Rights for data gathering and review, executive orders on affirmative action, and court actions made it clear that equality was a legal as well as a moral issue. The definition of who was to be served by these federal programs broadened to include not only blacks but other minority groups, women, and the culturally, economically, and educationally deprived in general.

Third, as the definition of a minority group shifted, so did the concept of fairness. The 1960s were marked by an emphasis on nondiscrimination—equal treatment for all, equal opportunity, "color blindness" in record keeping and decision making. The 1970s have seen a shift to "affirmative action"—special plans and programs for minorities to eliminate inequities, identification of the "disadvantaged," the development of programs to assure successful completion of higher education and not just access to it, efforts to keep track of progress in removing inequities.

The Institutional Context

During the period from 1968 to 1975, the 13 institutions in this study were experiencing changes which affected their ability to respond to these larger social issues. Changes in governance, mission, and leadership patterns were often intertwined. The shift from private to public status and a more local orientation reinforced the University of Missouri-Kansas City's and the University of the City's ability to respond to black populations in their regions. Secularization and redirection of mission moved Lewis and Metropolitan to accept new clienteles, including blacks. An expanded service region and the broadening of educational programs of former state teachers colleges like Clarion, California, Brockport, and Bowling Green enabled them to respond to the needs of blacks. Changes in leadership were also crucial. At State University, a new president carried on the commitment of his predecessor to bring in more blacks. Northwestern, the University of the City, and Macalester appointed presidents who were early proponents of a commitment to minorities.

Several institutions were suffering from enrollment declines. At Bradley and Lewis, financial difficulties led to a redefinition of purpose and an expansion in recruitment efforts which in turn led to increases in black enrollments. Recent enrollment declines in other institutions have had mixed effects, sometimes leading to lower admissions standards and increased recruitment of minorities, sometimes raising serious questions about the future of existing minority programs. The force of institutional context was further complicated by changes in the local environment, particularly for urban institutions like Metropolitan, Kansas City, and the University of the City, where demands for services by minorities, "white flight," and inner-city problems enhanced the need for minority programs but made the provision of them in traditional forms difficult and demanding.

PERIOD OF PREDISPOSING CONDITIONS

Prior to the period of increasing black enrollments, all 13 institutions had been subject to a variety of predisposing internal and external forces. These can be divided into several different dimensions. First, the institutions' environments influenced the recruitment of black students in either a positive or negative way. Demographic conditions—the number of blacks in the recruitment area and the presence of other racial or ethnic groups—was one important factor. Governmental and legal bodies which brought their influence to bear either in the form of available funds or legal mandates were another. Interest groups—civil rights organizations and community groups— and other colleges and universities in the region were important environmental forces.

We saw that during the early phases the environments of these 13 institutions were more supportive than resistive. In at least three cases, legal mandates played a substantial role in influencing the decision to recruit more black students. The only initial resistive factors were geographical and demographic—isolation and distance from black population centers.

Although the supportive factors in the contexts of the 13 institutions continued to be important through all the phases of responses to black enrollments, they were most powerful at the beginning. In a basically supportive environment, the institutions could increase black enrollments on their own terms; numerous internal activities paved the way. White students, faculty, and administrators were all sensitized to the issue of racial equality by early civil rights activities; strong administrative support for black concerns; some active black students and faculty; occasional programs and activities oriented toward minorities. In some institutions—State University and Carleton, for example—a dramatic event like Martin Luther King's assassination accelerated activities that were already being planned. Other institutions were not as prepared to start programs for blacks, which meant that initial responses were tentative and less adequate.

The Institutional Responses

Strategic responses at this early stage depended heavily on institutional leadership, particularly on the president and/or other respected faculty or administrators who saw a need for the institution to respond to blacks. These responses could be either proactive or reactive. Some institutions actively sought to redefine and extend their service regions, to become involved in changing community housing discrimination patterns (State University), or to solicit ideas from community groups (the University of the City). Others merely reacted to legal directives.

For the most part, these colleges and universities ignored environmental forces, perhaps because they were usually supportive.

With the exception of the leadership taken by Metropolitan University in forming a consortium with local community colleges, the other institutions acted alone in recruiting black students. The more selective institutions could afford to recruit and compete for the most able black students; the less selective ones competed as far as their resources would take them. Some could draw on prior experience and reputation with blacks. A few others with pre-college programs, and Bradley and State through athletics, had a head start in the competition for both black students and staff.

THE PRECIPITATING EVENTS

For 12 of the 13 institutions we were able to identify the exact year when they actively began to recruit black students. The decision to recruit blacks and the preparation of a recruiting program typically took one year, but in some cases it took even less time. This phase was followed by approximately a year of the first influxes of new students and the implementation of the first special programs.

The impact issues during this period varied with the strength and direction of the external influence and the proactive or reactive strategy of the institution and its leadership during the prior period. Whether the decision to initiate the enrollment increase was made internally was determined mainly by the degree to which it was voluntary. To some extent, the degree of voluntariness reflected the sensitivity and readiness of key leaders during the predisposing period. More important, the voluntary nature of the decision seemed to enhance the commitment of the institution to follow through on the implications of the enrollment increase.

Another important issue at this time was the planned versus unplanned nature of the response. A planned response, either initially or within the first year of the black enrollment increase, included an enrollment target, a comprehensive range of programs, formal approval of the decision to increase black enrollments and offer new programs, and an evaluation plan. None of the institutions, however, anticipated the consequences of their initial attempts to increase black enrollments.

Leadership during this period took a variety of forms, from the encouragement of wide support and open review ("participatory"), to the avoidance of public discussion of administrative decisions ("bureaucratic"), to involvement in open controversy ("political"). These styles of leadership stemmed from the governance traditions of the institutions and from a recognition on the part of top administrators that potential internal resistance dictated careful timing.

The level of conflict during the precipitating phase was relatively low. Almost all of the initial attempts to increase the enrollment of blacks occurred immediately or very shortly after the King assassination, when concern about civil rights and racial discrimination was high. In the context of the late 1960s, the decision to recruit more blacks was seen as morally correct. Adroit leadership, positive predisposing experiences, and the availability of outside resources paved the way. Nascent internal resistance was neutralized by moral fervor and new sources of funds.

The Institutional Response Strategy

Four response strategies can be defined on the basis of the source of initiation (internal *v.* external) and the degree of planning involved (planned *v.* unplanned). These patterns are: (1) *adaptive* (internally initiated and planned); (2) *responsive* (internally initiated and unplanned); (3) *reactive* (externally initiated and planned—none of the institutions in our study fit this pattern); and (4) *evolutionary* (externally initiated and unplanned).

The adaptive and responsive institutions were all marked by supportive external conditions, internal patterns supporting the change, and strong leadership—a combination not found in the evolutionary institutions. It is clear, however, that the initial response strategy did not prevent the occurrence of conflict later on, nor did it predict the later comprehensiveness of programs. (For example, many institutions broadened their responses after incidents of conflict.) In general, however, early adaptive responses dampened high levels of subsequent conflict and contributed to the maintenance of the original commitment to blacks. This was true of two of the three adaptive institutions, State and Carleton. The exception—Macalester—experienced a good deal of conflict in trying to reduce its allocations to minorities during a financial crisis which occurred soon after it introduced an ambitious program for blacks and other minorities.

PERIOD OF TRANSITIONAL TRAUMA

The next phase, which lasted for about two years, followed the initial enrollment increase. During this period, the number of black students (and occasionally black staff and faculty) reached a "critical mass"—large enough to mobilize for political action. Blacks raised a number of challenging questions: Was there a comprehensive range of response programs to meet black student needs in recruitment and admissions, financial aid, supportive services, academic programming, and cultural and social facilities? What was the adequacy and level of support for these programs? In the period of transitional trauma, an understanding of how black needs were to be voiced and heard in the governance structure had not yet crystallized. Declining trust between black and white students, racial conflict in many areas of student life, increasing black visibility on campus, and the issue of black control of black programs formed a backdrop to confrontations in this period. The period from 1969 to 1971 was a time of severe conflict and increasing breakdown in the relationships between blacks and whites.

Crucial during this period were the interactions between black and white leaders, in particular between the leaders of the major black organization on campus and the president. Demands, responses, and negotiations during incidents of conflict passed through these key individuals. The black leadership needed to show results. The president, usually able to exercise less control over his institution than blacks recognized, could not appear to cave in, but he also could not resort to overwhelming force. In confrontations between the two sides, a combination of negotiating skill, respect for the adversary, and an ability to cut through rhetoric and institutional protocol was necessary—but it was a combination that was rare.

The Institutional Response Strategy

Two key variables seemed to encompass the responses during this period of high conflict. The first was the institution's (or the administration's) tolerance for conflict, and the second was the institution's (or the administration's) concern for maintaining control of black programs. The strategies are displayed in Table 15-2.

TABLE 15-2

Institutional Strategies of Response to Conflict

Institutional Concern for Control of Black Programs	Tolerance for Conflict	
	Low	High
Low	Capitulation	Disturbance
Moderate	Cooperation	Negotiation
High	Bureaucracy or Paternalism	Power Politics

Capitulation: There is low tolerance for conflict and low concern for institutional control. There were allegations that this occurred at several of the campuses. (In the one or two instances in which it appeared that such charges of capitulation were justified, there were no resources or commitment to back up the demands that had been officially conceded. This usually led to further frustration and conflict.)

Cooperation: There is low tolerance for conflict and moderate concern for institutional control. This strategy emphasized the need of blacks and whites to work together. It attempted to resolve issues in the context of traditional patterns or community needs.

Bureaucracy or Paternalism: There is low tolerance for conflict and high concern for institutional control. This approach relies on threats and insists on disciplining disrupters. There is concern that bringing in outside force is a sign of institutional weakness. (This approach was apparent in several incidents and seemed to have the effect of keeping the president as the target for future demands.)

Disturbance: There is high tolerance for conflict and low concern for institutional control. In this setting, the institutional representative attempts to exaggerate the demands and the real conflict, by either justifying the concessions or by encouraging recalcitrant members of the institution to go along with a settlement.

Negotiation: There is high tolerance for conflict and moderate concern for institutional control. In this strategy, resort to external force or threat is limited but tolerable levels of conflict are usually clearly stated.

Power Politics: There is high tolerance for conflict and high concern about institutional control. Responses involve bringing in "whatever force is necessary," usually external, to retain or regain control before negotiating. (This strategy led to prolonged antagonism at two institutions.)

The strategies of response during this period depended a good deal on the personalities of the president and other key institutional actors. They often had to deal with constituencies who had differing views regarding the presence of blacks, their specific demands, and their tactics. Both sides tried a variety of tactics to gain advantages, to control publicity, and to claim "credit" for the positive results.

THE PERIOD OF ACTIVE ACCOMMODATION

Once the trauma of the major conflicts had subsided, most of the campuses actively began trying to accommodate to black students by focusing on building programs with whatever support the institution provided or could be pressured to provide. White faculty and staff, sometimes eagerly and sometimes grudgingly, accepted the fact that the increase in black enrollments and related response programs, whether initiated by acceptable or unacceptable means, were on the campus to stay. It was during this period that several new impact issues emerged.

The Impact Issues of Accommodation

The three important issues of this period evolved naturally from the prior period and from the realities of making an accommodation. Whites' perceptions of the prior period of conflict, blacks' early disappointment with the early institutional response, and the growing awareness of the conflicting lifestyles and educational expectations of black and white students brought the issue of trust and acceptance to the fore. During this period, whites were suspicious of the motives of blacks, and vice versa. Yet, in the wake of earlier protests and institutional commitments, it was difficult for whites to ignore the presence of black students. Having received some recognition, blacks had to some degree become part of the institution and seemed less willing to risk whatever gains they had won. Each group viewed the other from an uneasy distance with attitudes that ranged from acceptance to rejection, from trust to mistrust with many in the middle position of mutual disinterest.

The extent to which programs for blacks were intended to be separated from, coordinated with, or integrated with nonminority programs was unclear during the accommodation period. Hopes for formal and informal integration in student relations had been shattered by then. The tendency to start separate black support services, either after initiating the increase in black enrollments or in response to protests, produced strains with existing services, and, consequently, that practice was beginning to be questioned. White faculty and some departments showed decreased willingness to offer black studies courses. Black studies programs began to develop their own orientations and ideologies. Strains continued as separate black activities and programs developed in the face of demands for integration and coordination between minority and nonminority units.

Finally, the meaning of institutional commitment to blacks began to be raised during this period. The answer was not simple, since it implied institutional, programmatic, and interpersonal levels of response in daily campus life. Blacks recognized that obtaining political victories guaranteed little beyond admission, financial aid, and some tacit recognition of a black presence. Real commitment had to come from faculty and students as well as from administrators. Whites, on their side, were becoming aware that emotional responses to civil rights or to the tragedy of Martin Luther King's death meant that a return to life as usual was impossible. A new group of students, new programs, and the resource demands these implied would continue to affect their lives in unanticipated ways. Thus, the meaning of responsiveness and the nature of the institutions' commitment to blacks began to be debated and understood in a more complex, perhaps more realistic way.

The Response Strategy

Responses to the dilemmas of accommodation varied at different times and in different areas—student affairs, support services, and academic programming—within the same institution. The following paradigm, based on the nature of the relationship of organized programs for blacks to similar nonminority programs and interracial attitudes, produces six possible patterns of accommodation (Table 15-3).

TABLE 15-3

Institutional Accommodation Strategy

Interracial Attitudes	Nature of Relationship of Organized Programs for Blacks to Similar Non-Minority Programs	
	Integrated	Separated
Mutual Acceptance or Trust	Fully Integrated Community	Pluralistic
Disinterest or Tolerance	Laissez Faire Nondiscrimination	Isolationist
Mutual Rejection or Mistrust	Bureaucratic Paternalism	Racist Bureaucracy

Fully Integrated Community: There is mutual acceptance or trust and programs for blacks are fully integrated into the institution's regular programs. (This was an early ideal but not one observed at any of the 13 institutions.)

Laissez Faire Nondiscrimination: There is mutual disinterest or tolerance, and programs for blacks are fully integrated with regular structures. (This pattern appeared in institutions that maintained that they neither discriminated against nor gave special attention to any group. The pattern was observed most often in attempts by white faculty to offer Black Studies as a multidisciplinary program without a departmental base.)

Bureaucratic Paternalism: There is mutual distrust and programs for blacks are fully integrated with regular programs. While blacks occasionally reported this response strategy for their institutions, it was most frequently observed in student affairs offices which ran support services for all students through the same structure.)

Pluralistic: There is mutual acceptance and separate organizational units for black programs. (The best examples had developed reasonably effective coordination between the minority and nonminority units. This pattern was observed in some of the institutions in the supportive services and in black studies programs.)

Isolationist: There is mutual disinterest or tolerance and separate organizational structures for black programs. (This pattern seemed to fit student organizations in many of
the institutions. Examples also were found in supportive services and black studies
programs where the black faculty and staff had few relationships with regular faculty
and staff.)

Racist Bureaucracy: There is mutual rejection and separate organizational units for
black programs. (While this pattern was reported, there was low consensus at these
institutions about this pattern. Some early supportive service programs with activist or
separatist ideologies were most representative of this pattern.)

THE PERIOD OF REASSESSMENT: INSTITUTIONALIZATION OR RETRENCHMENT

This final phase reflected conditions facing higher education generally. Ideally, a period of reassessment should occur after programs
for blacks have had an opportunity to mature and be absorbed into
the institutional mainstream, thus providing a fair basis for assessing
effectiveness, acceptance, and commitment. The results of such an
assessment could then guide the institutionalization of responses to
black students. Unfortunately, however, a reassessment was required
at some institutions before they had gone much beyond the period of
precipitating events—for example, at Macalester in 1971 when it lost
the support of a key donor, or at Lewis and Metropolitan when their
overall enrollments began to decline. Reassessments at an early stage
generated conflicts which then merged with the demands of the period of transitional trauma. Because of declining resources, many
institutions were proposing overall program evaluations, including
minority programs—particularly those whose outside funding was
running out. Such a situation raised the question about whether reassessment had as its ultimate purpose further accommodation or institutionalization of the commitment to minorities, or whether it was
merely a rationalization for cutbacks. Conflicts at Macalester and at
the University of the City, as well as fears at other institutions,
suggested that carrying out such reviews was not going to be a simple
matter.

Retrenchment Issues

Perhaps the foremost issue in the period of retrenchment was the
priority of black programs vis-à-vis other programs. In the past, this
question was not raised in a comparative sense. In 1968–70, concern
for blacks could usually be accommodated without denying other in-

stitutional needs. (Indeed, at some institutions the outside financial aid which accompanied the entry of new students may have kept other priorities afloat.) In periods of decline, while white administrators were not anxious to approach the priority issue directly and did not relish a return to confrontation and conflict, black staff and students nevertheless feared the results. Both sides had a tendency to focus on secondary issues rather than seriously reassess what had been accomplished and why. Black staff pressed the issues of appointment status for minority faculty and staff. White administrators experimented with "relocating" black studies programs to bring them closer into the mainstream of the institutions.

When immediate pressures for resource reviews fostered a reassessment for which black staff and white administrators were ill-prepared, a myriad of issues reflecting the lack of a legitimate review process emerged. What was to be the order of a review? Who would be represented in this review process? Blacks suggested that unsupportive faculty from other units were not appropriate participants. Whites were suspicious of self-reviews or reviews by black groups from other institutions. What data would be utilized in such reviews? Even if everyone could agree on criteria, questions concerning the adequacy, accuracy, and confidentiality of data introduced further difficulties. The basic dilemma rested on the degree to which rational or political self-interest considerations would control the review process and, therefore, its outcomes.

Another question concerned the role that other racial and nonracial minority groups would play. Were they to be political allies of the blacks in the review, or would they present their own interests? Would all minorities band together to make each program review an affirmative action issue? These issues underscored once again the crucial nature of leadership for whites, blacks, and other minority groups as reassessment was approached.

The Response Strategies

While we can only speculate about the processes and strategies that would resolve reassessment issues, two dimensions help to make sense of the alternatives. (Table 15-4.) The first focuses on whether or not the institutions have developed and gained acceptance for a legitimate program review process, and the second on whether or not the institutional leadership had continued to place a high priority on minority commitments. The following alternatives suggest strategies that would affect the future commitment to blacks and other minorities.

Table 15-4

Future Institutional Response Strategies

| Institution's Black Program Priority | Review Process Established | |
	Legitimated Procedures	No Legitimated Procedures
High	Full Institutionalization	Partial Institutionalization
Low	Retrenchment	Termination

Full Institutionalization: There is high priority for black programs and review procedures are legitimated. Under this condition, there is likely to be further development of black and minority programs and full acceptance of them.

Partial Institutionalization: There is high priority for black programs but no legitimate review process. Under this strategy the high priority—whether in the perception of administrators, faculty, or black groups—would assure some further development; however, there is little guaranteed of continued support, especially if important groups (e.g., faculty bodies) did not participate in or concur in future decisions.

Retrenchment: There is low priority for black programs and a legitimate review process. In this situation, reduced effort in the minority area would most likely result from a tight resource situation. Some conflict is probably inevitable.

Termination: There is low black program priority and no legitimate review process. In this situation, severe retrenchment or termination are possible. Escalated conflicts may occur as blacks rally their support in order to prevent termination or reduction. In our estimation, most of the institutions in our study could not yet be placed into this typology. They had no legitimate process or procedures for program review, although they were just beginning to recognize that they needed them. They were uncertain what the commitment of the various governing bodies were to minority programs.

SUMMARY

This chapter has presented a five-phase model of the responses of colleges and universities to the increased enrollments of black students. The impact issues and dilemmas posed at each phase synthesize the common experiences of all 13 institutions, while the response strategies take account of differences among them. The flow of events, the complex impact issues, and strategies of response summarize the experiences of institutions that attempted to increase black student enrollments in a short span of time. The model suggests how colleges and universities may respond to other new groups of students, particularly those whose entry follows from changes in the society.

16

The Meaning of Response: Current and Future Questions

Robert T. Blackburn, Zelda F. Gamson,
and Marvin W. Peterson

This study has examined a selected set of colleges and universities at a particularly critical time in their histories, as they were indirectly experiencing a significant social upheaval in this country through their attempts to increase black enrollments. In this chapter, we review the impacts that appeared persistently from one campus to another, as well as the underlying patterns of response. We want to take a step back from our particular findings to look at the shared context of the study and the meaning of this recent history for the institutions and the participants. Second, we want to analyze the meaning of responsiveness in colleges and universities, especially with respect to a new group of students. Finally, we want to look into the future: How does the current environment for colleges and universities and for minorities shape the future of their lives together? What more general issues does the presence of black students raise for colleges and universities in the future?

THE STUDY IN RETROSPECT

The 1960s were a decade when American society tried to redress some of the wrongs it had imposed on blacks for three centuries. Moving blacks into the mainstream through access to higher education was seen as one solution to the problem of racial inequality. For the first time, white colleges and universities were presented with the legitimate opportunity to participate in a cause that only a few years earlier would have been resisted by many segments of the society. The psychological climate affecting white institutions of higher learning in the late 1960s could not have been more favorable for increasing black enrollments.

Conditions within higher education were equally favorable. Colleges and universities were expanding as if that would go on forever. With public support for higher education higher than it had ever been, the challenge to admit more minority students was accepted by many colleges and universities with optimism and confidence.

Further, for the 13 colleges and universities in our study, the decision to recruit significant numbers of blacks was in most instances a voluntary decision. A few predominantly white institutions in the United States already had appreciable black enrollments by the late 1960s, but many more did not. Some chose to make an effort to change the situation and failed. Others, like our 13 institutions, succeeded in increasing their black undergraduate enrollments dramatically in the short interval between 1968 and 1972.

This sanguine picture was to be shattered only a few years later. The favorable attitudes towards increasing black representation in higher education rested on assumptions which, although widely held in 1968, were shortly discovered to be fallacious. White students assumed that black students would want to be integrated with whites. While colleges and university leaders expected some changes would follow from admitting a new clientele, they assumed that the changes would take place smoothly and without conflict. Administrators and faculty members also assumed that most blacks, regardless of their educational background, would be able to perform academically in the existing environment; if not, small doses of remedial work were expected to correct inadequate preparation. These same whites also assumed that the new clientele would be satisfied with the programs and courses their institutions already offered. The notion of a course in black studies—to say nothing of a major, a department, even a degree in black studies—came unexpectedly for most white educators. In short, people in colleges and universities expected that the admission of black students into their white middle-class institutions would be accepted with gratitude.

OVERVIEW OF THE FINDINGS

Of course, this did not happen. Institutions of higher education, despite their reputation for "cognitive rationality," generally act like most other organizations when they move into spheres with which they are unfamiliar. Particularly with respect to large numbers of black students, colleges and universities had little experience from which to draw. They improvised and reacted but rarely planned or evaluated what they had done.

Part of the issue lies with the timing of the entry of large numbers of blacks into predominantly white institutions of higher education. Timing was a positive factor in the main. In the late 1960s money for minority programs and for financial aid was available in large amounts for the first time. The civil rights movement had affected the consciousness of large numbers of white Americans, and the assassination of Martin Luther King accelerated that consciousness.

These circumstances got blacks in the door, but it soon became apparent that the new students wanted and needed more—financial aid, special programs of one sort or another, space in student unions and dormitories, and influence in student government. To the surprise of college and university leaders, many blacks did not quietly adjust to the programs, standards, and mores of the white colleges. Instead of giving thanks, black students wanted and demanded more. They took over buildings and organized sit-ins for what they thought were their rights; in doing so, they often rejected white support and advice.

Thus, colleges and universities were caught up short in their ability to respond at the academic and programmatic levels. Furthermore, academic norms about how to behave in disputes—through calm, rational debate—were challenged by the black students. The charged atmosphere during particular conflict incidents thrust top administrators into major negotiating roles. Questions from the faculty regarding the legitimacy and status of new courses and programs introduced another unanticipated stress on the institutions, again especially on administrators.

The availability of federal and state funds for a variety of special programs softened the impact of these stresses for a while. But, as with the City University of New York, tightened budgets directly affected newly admitted minorities. External funding may be absolutely essential in getting new things started and for financing the initial stages of implementation but it is not very helpful in keeping them going once the money runs out. Indeed, external funding may end up distorting the institution in unintended ways.

Distortion of purpose and unintended impacts are factors that cause anxiety when changes are introduced with minimal planning. Precisely in the situation of increased black enrollments, which affected almost all levels within an institution, change was essentially irreversible. Changing back was virtually impossible for most of the 13 institutions, particularly those located in or near cities with any sizeable black populations. But the institutions did have the option of evaluating what they had done and planning for the future. By the time of our campus visits in 1974–75, two or three had begun some process of evaluation; a few others had instituted a planning process that examined minority programs along with other programs. Unfortunately, such reviews were beginning to take place before most of the minority programs had achieved some measure of stability and legitimacy. At "State University," the one place where it was clear that minority programs had reached maturity, the institution moved to further institutionalize the minority effort and to coordinate it with the other activities.

State University, which gave its minority programs time to develop, also reminds us of the importance of leadership, particularly from individuals in a position to effect change. Because of strong and early advocacy for increased minority enrollments from those at the top, these 13 institutions were able to allocate substantial internal resources to their minority effort. This was true even when they received large amounts of money from the outside. Leadership from the top was also important in some of the institutions in legitimizing the commitment to blacks and in gaining support from a variety of groups both inside and outside the institution. Unfortunately, such leadership was not maintained in some of the colleges and universities we studied. Whenever advocacy from the president and executive officers waned, so did support from other constituencies—particularly if the minority programs were still in the early stages of implementation and not well accepted or integrated into the regular patterns of the institution. Under pressure and often under time constraints, faculty and students found they had little, if any, voice in the decisions concerning black students. The result was that white students and faculty became indifferent, at best, to the black students in their midst. Changes in teaching practices and course content were less common than changes in administrative structures.

Nevertheless, these colleges and universities made substantial programmatic responses in a very short time in providing opportunities for black students. The form and pattern of response varied considerably from one campus to another. Indeed, one of the major findings of this study is the complexity of the term "responsiveness." It is to the varieties of response to black students on these white campuses that we now turn.

THE MEANING OF RESPONSIVENESS

While institutional commitment to black and minority groups must be assessed over a long span of time, it is possible to identify several dimensions of the meaning of institutional responsiveness on the basis of the experiences of the 13 colleges and universities in our sample between 1968 and 1975. In a complex organization such as a college or university, the meaning of responsiveness must be grounded in an assessment of how the institution deals with its new clientele at the organizational, program, and individual levels. Responsiveness should measure how a college or university is changed toward a closer "fit" between the characteristics and needs of the new student clientele and existing organizational patterns. Three areas of responsiveness, therefore, will be distinguished: institutional commitments; program responses; and attitudinal and perceptual climate.

Institutional Commitments

The visible commitments to and structural arrangements made for a college or university's new black student clientele were important public statements. These represented the institutional priorities for minorities and were reflected in terms of formally adopted policies and approved programmatic commitments. These, in turn, established procedures to insure implementation of programs, clarified controversial issues, and constrained unnecessary conflict. Such formal institutional commitments by leaders and official governing bodies were necessary to establish some trust and commitment, particularly at the beginning. The dimensions in this area are shown in Table 16-1.

Program Responses

This study identified five programatic areas which dealt most directly with the needs and concerns of black students. Merely iden-

tifying an area of minority activity and finding out who was responsible for it was not adequate to deal with legitimate concerns of new
students. A number of issues described the adequacy of, support for,
and critical relationships of those programs if they were to be effective and were seen to be important. Responsiveness meant the establishment of programs which were able to function effectively. Dimensions for assessing responsiveness at this level are included in
Table 16-1.

Attitudinal and Perceptual Dimensions of Minority Commitment

The attitudes which members of a college or university held
toward minorities, what they thought about their institution's goals
for and commitment to minority programs, and their perceptions of
racial climate and trust were important features of the way members of colleges and universities thought about the issues surrounding minority enrollments. Secondary data reduction of the key questions and indices in our survey data identified five dimensions
describing how people on each campus viewed the presence of minorities, their needs and concerns, and the varieties of institutional
responses to them. These were discussed in Chapter 12 and are
presented in Table 16-1.

TABLE 16-1.

Assessing Institutional Responsiveness

Institutional Commitments

Institutional Goals for Minority Efforts
1. Are there institutional goals or targets for minority student enrollments de-
    rived from some assessment of the available student pool?
2. Do the goals specify which minority groups are targeted? Do they provide
    some means for delineating a "special student"?
3. Are there policy commitments to provide appropriate academic and support
    programs, staff, and resources to deal with the needs of the new minority
    student population?

Official Endorsement or Legitimation
1. Does the institutional goal or policy commitment to minority students and
    programs have official approval of a comprehensive (or constituent) gover-
    nance body?
2. Of the Board of Trustees?
3. Of a state agency, if appropriate?

Program Comprehensiveness
1. Is there a commitment to providing an adequate range of programs or ser-
    vices for the minority student clientele in recruitment and admissions?

TABLE 16-1 continued

2. Financial aids?
3. Supportive services?
4. Ethnic or minority academic programs or courses?
5. Social and cultural programs, facilities, or activities?

Programming Strategy
1. Are there separate programs for different minority groups or are they ethnic or mulit-ethnic in focus?
2. Is there some anticipated strategy for structuring minority programs in relation to each other and to existing units?
3. Are minority programs separate from, integrated with, or coordinated with similar nonminority programs and activities?
4. Is it clear where minority program directors report and the degree of autonomy directors have to operate their programs?

Resource Support Strategy
1. Is there an understanding of the way resources are to be allocated to these programs and the future implications of that strategy?
2. Are resources (staff, facilities, operating budgets) allocated to minority programs on the same or different basis than similar nonminority programs?
3. What is the balance of internal/external funding currently? What is it likely to be in the future?
4. Are there plans for funding transitions to new sources when needed? Have all potential sources been explored?

Evaluation and Assessment Strategy
1. Are there clearly understood institutional process, group, and criteria for evaluating or assessing academic and non-academic units?
2. Are minority programs evaluated the same as nonminority programs?

Student Life Concerns
1. Are there mechanisms for distributing student activities funds to minority and nonminority organizations and for coordinating their activities?
2. Are there mechanisms for dealing with interracial problems?
3. Are there formal procedures for dealing with grievances?
4. Is there an attempt to collect and analyze data on minority student needs and concerns? On student racial climate?

Top Level Administrative Commitment
1. Are there blacks in higher academic or non-academic administrative posts?
2. Is there an awareness of and mechanisms for relating to external, noncampus minority groups?
3. Is the affirmative action office adequately staffed and operating?

Program Responses

For successful implementation and operation, a number of program-related issues must be considered. Within each of the five areas of organized or programmatic activity for minority students below, these questions can be asked:
1. How *extensive* is the activity (range of services)?
2. How extensive is the *commitment* (degree of staff and financial support)?
3. How is it *coordinated* with other minority programs or activities?
4. How is it *integrated* with related non-minority units?
5. What is the *status* of the program (type of unit, reporting level, and degree of autonomy)?
6. What is the *status* of the director and *staff* (nature of appointment, professional perquisites, and promotional procedures)?

TABLE 16-1 continued

Recruitment and Admissions
1. Is there a clear recruitment region and strategy?
2. Are there admissions criteria and/or procedures for assessing student academic needs or disabilities?

Financial Aids
1. Are all sources of financial aid for minority students utilized?
2. Is there a clear procedure for needs assessment and policy for distribution of various forms of aid?

Supportive Services

Minority Academic Programming
1. Is the focus on a particular racial or ethnic group or is it multi-ethnic?
2. Is the orientation academic, activist, outreach or a combination?
3. What is the level of offerings—noncredit and/or credit courses, undergraduate majors, graduate offerings, institutes, etc.?

Social and Cultural Programming
1. Is it a separate program or activity or a part of other minority efforts?
2. Does it require separate facilities and/or locations?

*Attitudinal and Perceptual Dimensions**

Role of Minorities in Colleges and Universities: a series of attitudinal questions and indices on a variety of issues—*the philosophical view* about the role colleges and universities play in the larger social issue; Table 12-6.

Breadth of Institutional Goals for Blacks: a set of perceptual measures of constituents views of their institution's goal commitments to Black and minority concerns—the *ideology* of the institution; Table 12-2.

Willingness and Commitment to Support Minority Programs: a set of attitudes expressing personal and institutional support for minority programs—the *intent* of constituents; Table 12-3.

Racial Climate and Activism: Measures of the perception of constituents on dimensions of racial and interracial activity—the perceived *actual behavior* on campus; Table 12-4.

Interracial Trust and Conflict: perceptual measures of the degree of trust and hostility among racial groups and between racial groups and whites—a *psychological* measure of the racial climate; Table 12-5.

*See Table 12-1 and Appendix E for an identification of all survey indices used in this study.

These multiple levels for assessing responsiveness—institutional, programmatic, and individual—reflect the complexity and extensiveness of impact, as well as the response patterns that we observed across the 13 colleges and universities. No institution would receive positive ratings on all of the measures, nor could we identify an ideal pattern of responsiveness at all levels. However, it is important to address all of them. We learned in our study that failure to deal with any of the particular issues listed in Table 16-1 was likely to become a source of difficulty at some point in these institutions' relationships with minorities.

PRESENT CONDITIONS AND THE FUTURE

The consequences of increased black enrollments for white colleges and universities do not end here, for recent changes affecting higher education have new implications for blacks. Higher education in the 1970s has had to compete in the wider society with other public goods, a competition that is likely to intensify in the 1980s as demographic changes and an unpredictable economy lead to declining enrollments in colleges and universities. In this atmosphere, doubts are cast on the value of a college degree, and dollar support for higher education has not kept pace with rising costs and inflation. Some of these factors have already begun to affect black enrollments. While black graduate and professional school enrollments have increased, new black undergraduate enrollments have leveled off short of the 14 percent which blacks represent in the U.S. population. High levels of black undergraduate attrition have further reduced the presence of blacks in colleges and universities in the 1970s.

The Bakke case has received wide attention and commentators, regardless of their position on the case, agree that the Supreme Court's ruling will have profound effects on the gains blacks have made in the last decade. In the meantime, efforts to increase equality of opportunity have been broadened to encompass other minority groups and women. In the struggle for attention, blacks have lost their unique claims on whites. Blacks are no longer among the top concerns of hard-pressed administrators, even in the responsive institutions examined in this study.

The list of dilutions is a long one. When set in a climate which is more pessimistic than the era which ushered in the rapid entry of blacks into white colleges and universities, the recent external and internal changes affecting higher education have a potentially negative impact on the commitment to blacks. Financial aid has sometimes been cut back. Black and other minority programs have suffered declining enrollments and staff reductions.

It is clear from our examination of the 13 colleges and universities that moral fervor has its limits for long-run commitment. It may provide the momentum for a new direction, but it is not sufficient to carry decisions to the point of institutionalization, particularly when financial exigencies intervene in the process of implementing those decisions. If we add to this conclusion the recognition that the dilemma underlying the entry of black students into predominantly white institutions during the 1960s has not yet been resolved, the optimism of the 1960s must be tempered substantially.

THE BASIC DILEMMA:
INTEGRATION, SEGREGATION, OR PLURALISM

We have seen that the stage was set for a good deal of misunderstanding and conflict between the expectations of the whites who opened up their institutions to more black students and the expectations of the blacks who came. The integrationist views of whites in that period lagged behind changes in the civil rights movement, which already had experienced the emergence of black power and black separatist groups that opposed integration on the grounds that it meant the submergence of black culture to the dominant white culture. Integration might come for the generations ahead, but this was not highly valued by blacks as a step toward increasing opportunities. Pluralism—with some segregation of the races as a transition—was the desired state.

The black students who arrived on white campuses in the late 1960s and early 1970s may not have been sophisticated about such arguments, but they responded to their condition on these campuses in ways which demonstrated the case against integrationism. While they were eager for the benefits of a college education and for their share of campus resources, they wanted them on terms which did not threaten their own psychological and cultural roots. It was difficult enough for these predominantly first-generation college students to deal with the academic demands placed on them. Culturally and socially, most of them felt on alien territory. Given the rapid increase in the black student population, black students found like-minded souls with whom they could band together. Particularly in the informal social life of the colleges and universities we studied, but also in the formal side of student life, black students became an identifiable subgroup.

We do not want to overstate the degree of cohesiveness among the black students. Even in the early period of black enrollment increase, there was diversity among blacks in social class, interests, politics, and styles of life. Not all were politically active; some became involved in black fraternities and sororities and others in nonpolitical student organizations such as choirs and athletic teams. But from the vantage of the whites who did not know them well, blacks formed a group. This is probably less true now, as later student generations take the pioneers' efforts for granted. But in the early days, blacks felt visible and often embattled.

The response of whites varied. Certainly, in no case did we see the kind of racial integration that had been expected. By the time of our study, several campuses had settled down to a pattern of mutual indifference between the races. In one case, at State University, we detected the emergence of support for pluralism in the relations between blacks and whites. But on many campuses, even State, this kind of acceptance of difference did not extend to any great extent into the student culture. A placid surface only barely masked hostilities between black and white students. Faculty and administrators were more benign in their attitudes—but they did not have to live with students to the degree that students must live with one another.

The tendency on the part of most of the campuses was to minimize conflict by developing separate student organizations and separate support services and/or academic programs. This solution, combined with the diversity of interests among blacks and the entry of other minority groups, later raised serious problems. Separate programs and organizations for every minority or interest group were duplicative and expensive. Combining them, however, was also difficult. Chicano and other minority groups with whom we spoke were reluctant to participate in a larger unit in which they felt themselves to be a minority within a minority. It was difficult to introduce an overarching "ethnic studies" approach once a black studies program had begun, if only because staffing would have to be different.

Some rational efforts to coordinate the minority effort were beginning when we visited the campuses. Bowling Green in 1973–74 placed all minority programs, both academic and non-academic, under a single Vice Provost for Minority Affairs. State University tried to integrate several minority groups into its Support Services office, which had initially begun working only with blacks. What began at other places as "special" programs were beginning to be incorporated in the regular academic structure. And still other institutions dealt with organizational integration more informally.

But the underlying dilemma remained. The pattern of having separate organizational units, left over from the confrontation period, is still dominant. Race relations, particularly among students, are characterized by voluntary segregation or by indifference thinly covering interracial conflicts and feelings of mistrust. Little attention was being paid to the interpersonal aspects of race on these campuses, and organizational arrangements and social segregation reinforced the situation.

Our data indicate that such arrangements and activities may be misguided. The respondents in our 1975 surveys at Brockport, State, Metropolitan, and Kansas City presented a fairly hopeful picture for tackling the interpersonal side of the race issue—perhaps in the direction of increasing pluralism if not integration. The groups of people on these campuses showed a strong reservoir of support for commitment to minorities on the part of higher education and their own institutions (Table 16-2). Two thirds *disagreed* that colleges and universities do not have a primary responsibility to rectify racial injustice. There was little opposition to black or minority programs, a good deal of passive support among faculty, and more active support among administrators. Students were more opposed than either faculty or administrators, although a plurality seemed to be indifferent. But when asked about their *own* support for their institutions' commitments to blacks and other minorities, few respondents admitted being opposed. Half claimed they passively supported minority programs and services, and another quarter said they were active supporters. Indeed, combining both active and passive support, more respondents described *themselves* as being supportive than they did any other group.

Views of the future were surprisingly optimistic in this group as a whole. The overwhelming majority—more than 80 percent—believed that their own institutions would either maintain or increase their support of programs and services for blacks in five areas; particularly strong was the belief that black faculty and staff recruitment would be increased.

These are, of course, *perceptions* of current and future commitments. They may not fully recognize real limitations in resources, and the future may change in unpredictable ways. Yet the belief among these respondents in their institutions' commitment, combined with their own personal commitment, provides some reason for optimism in the generally pessimistic picture we have drawn in this chapter. The beliefs we have just presented are as much a reality affecting the future of blacks and other minorities in higher education as shrinking resources and enrollment declines, for they provide the latent support for minorities in colleges and universities. Of course, the support remains primarily passive rather than active. But such support could potentially be mobilized by leaders within and outside higher education for the same moral ends that brought large numbers of blacks into colleges and universities in the first place. At the present time evidence of current attempts to begin that mobilization is difficult to find. However, where there is such potential support in the face of the constrained future, the risk of mobilizing it is small—and the potential gains for whites, as well as for blacks and other minorities, are enormous.

TABLE 16-2

Current and Future Commitment to Minorities

	Agree		Disagree	
"Despite our concern over racial injustice, colleges and universities *do not* have a primary responsibility to rectify that situation."	33%		67%	

"How would you rate the *current commitment* of each of the following to the development of black or minority programs and services?"	Opposition	Indifference	Passive Support	Active Support
Executive Officers	12%	17%	34%	36%
Academic Administrators	11%	19%	42%	28%
Faculty	10%	34%	45%	11%
White Students	21%	45%	29%	5%
Your Own Commitment	6%	18%	50%	26%

"How would you assess your institution's *future commitment to continued support* of programs and services for blacks in each of the following areas?"	Will be Increased	Will be Maintained	Will be Decreased
Student Recruitment, Admissions, and Financial Aid	32%	52%	16%
Tutoring, Counseling, and Advising Services	31%	57%	12%
Black or Ethnic Studies and Other Black-Focused Curricula	28%	56%	16%
Social and Cultural Activities	24%	61%	15%
Black Faculty and Staff Recruitment	42%	48%	10%

Overall N = 1,391

Appendix A

Research Design Abstract

STAGE I

The beginning phase of our study focuses on the internal dynamics of the responses to increased numbers of black students by four-year colleges and universities. Unlike most of the research to date, this is not a study of the response of black students to white institutions nor is it a descriptive survey of institutional enrollment characteristics, minority programs, affirmative action, or staffing patterns. Institutional responses are investigated in four areas: administrative responses, faculty responses, academic or curricular responses, and responses in the student culture. Four research questions cut across these areas: (1) What were the events and conditions leading to increased black enrollments and how were they reflected in each area? (2) What changes in program and structure have taken place in response to black students in the four areas? (3) How do changes affect existing structures, roles, and performance? (4) What has been the impact on decision making, communication, allocation of resources, and other important processes or patterns in each area?

The study was conducted in two stages. In this *first stage*, we visited a sample of institutions which have experienced a substantial increase in black enrollment between 1968 and 1972. A two or three member research team spent approximately three days on each campus, conducting open-ended interviews with clearly identified administrators, faculty, and student representatives. We also collected appropriate public documents to better understand your institution's pattern of response. The second stage of the study was designed to focus on a more limited set of institutions, utilizing additional interviews and brief questionnaires dealing with the dynamics and issues raised in the Stage I visits.

The data obtained from the study has been used: (1) as the basis for designing approaches and instrumentation for more extensive institutional or research use; (2) as feedback to the participating institutions to help them deal more successfully with this crucial area of concern; and (3) as a basis for articles in both scholarly and popular journals. Participation by an institution, of course, was voluntary at each stage of the study, although it was our hope that colleges and universities participating in the initial stage would find continued participation in Stage II beneficial to their own interests.

The purpose of the study is decidedly not evaluative. Rather, its focus is on the identification of important forces, variables, and resultant issues raised as institutions have responded to increased black enrollments under differing conditions. The analytic concepts and instruments developed should be useful to other institutions in assessment of their own experience. We focus on blacks because they were the first minority group in recent years to have expanded enrollments in white institutions in this region. We are, however, interested in the more general question of institutional response and/or adaptation to new groups of students, whoever they are.

STAGE II

This second stage, utilizing information gained in the Stage I institutional visits, had as its principal focus the development of survey instruments which identify, measure, and assess the impact on and responses of institutional members to the increased black enrollment. Survey feedback was provided to the participating institutions on the dynamics of this phenomenon. Institutions selected for Stage I were a sample of four-year colleges and universities which had low black enrollments in 1968 and had experienced a substantial increase by 1970 or 1972. Institutions selected for participation in Stage II were selected according to three criteria: (1) their comprehensive range of activities or programs related to that enrollment change, (2) their diversity of institutional types, and (3) their varied pattern of structural integration of such programs and activities.

This second stage involved the distribution of fixed-response questionnaires to the faculty of the arts and science colleges, to a sample of black and non-black undergraduate students in those colleges, and to selected administrators (nine department chairpersons were also interviewed). The questionnaire encompassed institutional variables, dynamics, and issues affected by the change in enrollment pattern identified during our Stage I institutional visits. The questionnaire was designed to tap the attitudes and perceptions of the respondent groups. It was designed to provide an overall assessment of the impact on or response of the institution, but it was *not designed as an assessment or evaluation of specific black or minority-related programs.* Neither was the questionnaire an assessment of the institution's affirmative action program. The areas covered in the questionnaire were as follows:

1. General attitudes about role of blacks and other ethnic minorities in higher education.
2. Perception of institutional goals for black or minority activities.
3. Individual goals with regard to black or minority activities.
4. Perceptions of the institution's general racial climate.
5. Internal and external supports for and constraints on the institution's black or minority efforts.
6. Identification of black and minority student needs.
7. Perceptions of the institution's general responsiveness and effectiveness in relating to black and minority students.
8. Impacts of black or minority enrollment and activities on institutional processes and functions.
9. Identification of impacts on individuals caused by the changing enrollment patterns.
10. Areas of future concern.

Both the data collection and the analysis resulting from this survey have been treated to *guarantee individual anonymity.* While tests of response reliability and validity have been conducted to refine the questionnaire, the institutional analysis profiles institutional response patterns for faculty, administrative staff, and black and white students. No racial profiles were made for the administration or faculty in order to insure individual anonymity. Additionally, institutional anonymity has been guaranteed in all reports and publications related to this study.

The participating institutions have received, in addition to the institutional case study and comparative institutional analysis conducted during Stage I, a report of the Stage II survey including the profile of responses to all questionnaire items by the respondent groups identified above. While the intent and budget of this study has not allowed us to expand the survey sample, we will have provided participating institutions with questionnaires (at duplicating cost), coding information, and profile analysis guidelines should they wish to use them in other areas of their institutions.

Appendix B

Interview Guide (Stage I)

I. INTRODUCTORY INFORMATION

A. Introductory Information for Interviewee:

We are (I am) part of a team from the University of Michigan's Institute for Social Research conducting a study on a grant from the National Institute of Mental Health. The study is concerned with the ways in which predominantly white institutions of higher education have increased their Black enrollments, how they have responded to that student clientele, and how they are changed or affected by the shift. Your institution is one of a limited number which were selected primarily on the basis of its substantial influx of Black students primarily between 1968-1972 and its publicly documented program of response.

The study itself has been reviewed with (persons or groups) at your institution. It has also been cleared with both the University of Michigan and the National Institute of Mental Health's Human Subjects Review committee. Your institution will also get a copy of our report that results from this trip. There is a second phase to the study which will look more intensely at certain institutions but participation beyond this first phase will be reviewed later.

Because of your position (elaborate) we think you can give us an important perspective on some aspects of your institution's general experience with this phenomena as well as information on some precise responses or impacts. In the report of the study your individual responses and the institution will remain anonymous. We would like to ask you about several areas (identify sections of questionnaire you intend to use).

Are there any questions?

B. Reminder to the Interviewer

1. Be on schedule, know your respondents areas of responsibility, and sections of questionnaire you intend to use.

2. Have you obtained copies of or leads to reports on minority activity in the interviewee's area of expertise?

3. Have you asked about others to talk to?

4. Have you given the interviewee a chance to suggest important things that you did not ask him about?

5. Build rapport where appropriate! We may want to come back.

327

C. A SUGGESTED PATTERN FOR QUESTIONNAIRE GUIDE USE

INTERVIEWEE	A	B	C	D1	D2	D3	D4	D5	E	F
Pre-Scheduled:										
President	X	X	0—0	X	?		X	X	X	X
V.P. Academic	X	X	0—0		X		X	X	?	X
V.P. Students	X	X	0—0			X	X	X	?	X
V.P. Business and Finance	X	X	0—0					X	?	X
Undergraduate Dean	X	X	0—0	X			X	X	?	X
Chairperson Faculty Senate (Prior One)	X	X	0—0				X	X	?	X
2-3 Department Chairpersons	X	X	0—0				X	X	?	X
Directors of Minority Program	X	X	0—0	0—0					X	
Directors of Admissions	X	X	0—0	X	?			?		
Directors of Financial Aids	X	X	0—0	X	?				X	
Director of Institutional Research	X	X								
Other:										
Affirmative Action Officer	X	X	0—0	0—0				?	X	
Head of Student Government	X	X			X				?	X
Black Student Organizations	X	X			X					X
White Faculty and Black Faculty	X	X		0—0	0—0		X			X
Other Minority Groups	X	X								X
Athletic Director	X	X	0—0	X	?					
Housing Director	X	X	0—0					X	X	
Trustees	X	X						X	X	

X = definite
0—0 = most appropriate section
? = Possible

INSTITUTION _____

INTERVIEWER _____

A-1

A. INTERVIEWEE BACKGROUND

Name

1. Name: _____

Position

2. Current Position(s): [Indicate Faculty Rank, if held]

   _____

   _____

Year of employment

3. When were you first employed by this institution? Year: _____

Prior position

4. Where were you prior to coming here and what position did you hold there?

   Previous employer: _____

   Position held: _____

   Dates: From _____ to _____.

FOR INSTRUCTIONAL FACULTY, ASK QUESTIONS 5, 6, 7, 8

FOR ADMINISTRATORS AND OTHER ACADEMIC STAFF, ASK QUESTIONS 9, 10, 11, 12, and 13

Faculty rank

5. Prior to your current rank, what other academic positions have you held here? When?

   Current rank: _____ From _____ to _____

   Prior positions: _____ From _____ to _____

   _____ From _____ to _____

Faculty committees

6. On what committees or faculty organizations are you serving now or have you served during the past two years?

   _____ From _____ to _____

   _____ From _____ to _____

   _____ From _____ to _____

Work with Other Units

7. Are there any offices or units, other than your department, with which you work regularly?

   If yes, what are they and what is the nature of your involvement with them?

A-3

Faculty responsibility
8. Please indicate which of the following you are currently responsible for?

a. Undergraduate course instruction
b. Undergraduate student counselling, advising
c. Graduate course instruction and advising
d. Academic administration
e. Research
f. Other (Identify:)

Primary responsibility
Probe: Which would you say is your primary responsibility?

FOR INSTRUCTIONAL FACULTY: GO TO QUESTION 14

Positions held
9. Prior to your current position, what other positions have you held here and for how long?

Current position: From____ to 1974
Prior positions: From____ to____
From____ to____

Supervisor
10. To whom do you report in your current position?

Other offices
11. Are there other offices with which you work closely?
If yes, what, are they and what is the nature of your work with them?

Responsibility
12. What would you define as your specific areas of responsibility in this current position?

Involvement in minority areas
13. During the years you have been at this institution have you been involved in racial or minority concerns within the institution? ____
If yes, what, in general, were your major involvements? Please indicate which were self-initiated and which were required by the formal duties of your position.

IF INTERVIEWEE CAME TO THE INSTITUTION IN 1970 OR LATER GO TO SECTION B, THEN TO SECTION D

Major Institutional Changes
14. Reflecting on your institution from about 1964 to the present, what would you identify as the two or three major forces, events, or changes that have had the greatest impact on the institution?

IF INTERVIEWEE DOES NOT MENTION INCREASE IN BLACK ENROLLMENT,

Minority related issues
Probe: Would you say that increased enrollment of Blacks and other minorities has not had a major impact on your institution?

How affected
15. How have the non-minority related forces or changes you mentioned affected the direction of your institution? Give examples if possible.

How Responded
16. How did your institution respond or react to these forces or changes? Would you say it was prepared for them? Was it easy or difficult?

A-- 4

General
Response
Overview

17. We have tried to identify the major programs and organization patterns which have emerged in your institution as a result of the increased Black enrollments. In the following areas, could you indicate which you are most familiar with and identify ones that we have missed?

[STRESS IDENTIFICATION NOT DISCUSSION]

a) Black and minority academic programs [NAME THEM]

b) Black or minority admissions and financial aids programs [NAME THEM]

c) Black or minority student support service programs (Remedial programs, counseling, housing, etc. [GIVE EXAMPLES]

d) Principal Black or minority student organizations [GIVE EXAMPLES]

e) Black or minority faculty groups, if any [GIVE EXAMPLES]

f) Special administrative offices for Black or minority Affairs [GIVE EXAMPLES]

Probe: Are there other important ones that were tried and discontinued?

[USE ABOVE TO GET FEEL FOR RESPONDENTS KNOWLEDGE OF DIFFERENT AREAS. IT MAY FOCUS YOUR USE OF APPROPRIATE PARTS OF SECTION D LATER.]

B-1

B. RECENTLY ARRIVED INTERVIEWEE'S VIEW OF INSTITUTION

[ONLY FOR INTERVIEWEES WHO ARRIVED AT INSTITUTION IN 1970 OR LATER]

Major changes

1. Since your arrival at this institution, what would you identify as the two or three major changes that have had the greatest impact on the institution?

[IF INTERVIEWEE DOES NOT MENTION ETHNIC OR MINORITY ISSUES]

Minority related changes

Probe: Would you say that changes related to racial or ethnic minorities have not had a major impact on this institution? Why?

Particular attraction

2. What was the particular attraction for you in deciding to come to this institution?

Satisfaction

Probe: Has the institution lived up to your expectations in that regard?

General perception of institution

3. At the time of your arrival, was any formal position, group or program identified with each of the following? How would you characterize your institution's stance on each?

a. Curricular or academic programming focused on minority content or issues.

b. Minority student recruitment and admissions programs, procedures, and criteria.

c. Financial aids for minorities

B-2

d. Other student services supportive programs.

e. Special offices, such as Special Projects, Minority Affairs, Affirmative Action, Ombudsman, etc.

f. Black faculty and/or administrative staffing and Black or minority faculty or staff associations.

> AFTER COMPLETING SECTION B, FOR RECENT ARRIVALS, GO TO SECTION D

C-1

C. INCREASING BLACK ENROLLMENTS AND INSTITUTIONAL CONTEXT

> Early in our visit we will develop a chronology of events and decisions. Refer to these events and decisions in this section to show you know quite a bit already. Use the interview to clarify points that are missing from the chronology.

Black undergraduate enrollments according to Civil Rights reports, seemed to increase rapidly from less than (____%) in 1968 to over (____%) in 1972 at _____ college. Do these figures agree with your recollection? As best you can recall we would like you to focus briefly on the actual dynamics of black enrollments during that period.

Catalyst or Reason — 1. What was the major catalyst or reason for the rather sudden increase in Black enrollments? Was there a particular event or issue which triggered it?

Conflict — Probe: Was there a major conflict or confrontation internal and external to the institution?

> IF NO, SKIP TO QUESTION 5

Key Parties — Probe: Who were the key parties (individuals and groups)?

Proponents Opponents — Probe: Who were the major proponents of increasing Black (or minority) enrollments? The major critics or resistors?

Original Demands — Probe: What were the original demands or issues?

Influence Techniques — Probe: How did the parties in the conflict attempt to influence the resolution of the issue? What means did they use to bring pressure to bear on the institution?

How Resolved — Probe: If there was conflict, describe how the opposing groups worked out a resolution, if any.

> IF CONFLICT, GO TO QUESTION 3

C-2

If No Conflict, Why Increased Enrollments?

2. If there was not a major issue or conflict, how did it happen that Black enrollments rose appreciably in such a short period of time?

Intentional? How and Who?

Probe: Was it intentionally planned? How and by whom?

Natural Rise?

Probe: Was it merely a natural rise in applications represented by the interest of minorities at this time?

Other Reasons?

Probe: Other?

Formal Decisions To Implement and How Made

3. Was there any formal decision or commitment to increase Black enrollments (and/or provide the means for accomplishing it)? How was that made? By whom?

IF NO, SKIP TO QUESTION 4

How Decision Transmitted

4. If there was some formal commitment or decision to increase Black enrollments, how was that transmitted to the faculty and staff in the institution? How was it received?

Monitoring and Review Mechanisms

5. Was there any clearly understood mechanism, administrator, or group designated to monitor and/or review the attempt to increase Black enrollments? Who was involved? How has it worked?

Was This Consistent With Usual Decision Making?

6. Was the way in which this decision to increase and monitor Black enrollments made consistent with the normal institutional decision making pattern for such decisions? If it was different, how? Why?

Strength of Commitment

7. How strong would you say the commitment was? Evidence? Where was the commitment the strongest? Weakest?

C-3

New Programs, Offices, Hirings

8. At the time of the decision to increase enrollments of Blacks, was any formal program developed, offices created, or persons hired or appointed to insure the increase of Black enrollments?

Probe: Recruitment?

Probe: Financial Aids?

Probe: Publicity of an extensive or unusual nature?

Probe: Creation of other special offices or staffing to accomplish it?

Probe: Other?

Initial Problems

9. During the initial stages of increased Black enrollment, in what areas did the most critical problems, issues, or concerns, arise in your judgment?

Probe: a) Board or President
b) Executive offices for academic, student or business affairs
c) The faculty
d) The student body
e) The community

Prior to this period of rapidly increasing Black enrollments (pre-196__), let me ask you two or three brief questions.

Pre-1968 Catalyst or Reasons

10. During the period prior to 196__ (above), were there any issues or events that raised concerns over racial and ethnic minority enrollments or problems on this campus itself?

IF NO, GO TO QUESTION 11

Issue

Probe: What was the issue raised?

C-4

Key Parties	Probe: By whom? Or by what groups?
Proponents and Opponents	Probe: Who were the active supporters and critics of these early issues or events?
Context	Probe: In what context? [Be brief]
Formal Mechanisms	Probe: Was the issue given active or formal consideration? By what body or institutional mechanism?

[If Relevant]

External Groups
11. During the period prior to 1968 were there any active groups external to the campus raising issues or bringing pressures on the institution regarding minority issues (Civil Rights groups, legislature, community bodies, individuals, etc.)

[IF NO, SKIP TO QUESTION 12]

Who?	Probe: Who were they?
Concerns	Probe: What were their concerns?
Influence	Probe: How did they bring pressure, if any, on the campus?
Techniques	Probe: Did they work with or through any campus-based groups or individuals? (be explicit)

[For Administrators Only:]

Pre 1968 Minority Programs
12. Prior to 1968 (pre Black enrollment increase) can you identify their any formal administrative position, program or group concerned with minorities under your jurisdiction?

Focus
Probes: Name of the unit, approximate founding date, purpose, precursor to current group?

D: 1-1

D. INSTITUTIONAL RESPONSES, PATTERNS, PROGRAMS, AND IMPACTS

Note to interviewer: Explain to interviewee that you now want to focus on some very specific areas, identify what those areas are, and ascertain his or her familiarity with the area. Section A, Question 17 should have already partially apprised you of this.

D: 1 ACADEMIC PROGRAMS FOR BLACKS AND OR MINORITIES

Context
1. Let me briefly identify some (academic, counseling, or housing, other supportive) programs with which you appear to be familiar and about which I would like to ask you for some information.
[Identify them]
1.
2.
3.

Sequence
Probe: What was the sequence (dates? of establishing these programs?

Current Program Description
2. Could you describe (each) program in terms of the following?

a) Title of director? Nature of faculty appointment? Position on major institutional committee?

informal ties
b) To whom does the director report?
Probe: Formally and frequently?
Probe: Are there other administrators with whom the director works frequently and regularly?

Staff size
c) Size of professional personnel? Staff? [Get FTE Breakdown]

Nature of appointments
Probe: Are there appointments to this unit only?

Services
d) What services are offered by this program?
Activities? Courses? Special events?
[Get brochures,if any]

D:1--2

Probe: If academic or supportive program, what is the credit/non-credit arrangement?

Organizational structure   e) Internally how is this program organized? Functional division? Administrative structure?

Funding   f) Size and services of financial support?

Physical facilities   g) What are your physical facilities?

What are your needs? Expansion forseen?

Program initiation   3. How did the program get developed?

developers   Probe: Who developed the program idea (individual or group)? When? Under what circumstances?

Threatening to whom   Probe: Did the proposal threaten any specific individuals or groups? Why?

Support   Probe: Who voiced strong support? Strong opposition? How was it resolved?

Appropriate Need   Probe: Specific issues pro and con

D:1--3

Decision process 4. How was the decision made to adopt this program?

consistency   Probe: Was the decision making consitent with the way such decisions are usually made there? If not, why?

Purpose of program   5. What was the original purpose or purposes of this program?

Need   Probe: Was it directed to a specific need? What need? Whose?

Benefits   Probe: Who benefited from it?

Current Goals   Probe: What is the focus or goals?

Goal shift   Probe: If these goals have changed, why?

Planning   Probe: What are the long-range goals? How established?

Coordination 6. [For Director Only] How and in what areas is this program coordinated with others in the institution?

Other minority services   Probe: Other Black or minority academic programs or supportive services?

non-minority groups   Probe: With non-minority administrative offices, academic programs (departments), or student services?

cooperation competition antagonism   Probe: What is level of cooperation/competition or antagonism you feel in trying to work with these other porgrams?

D:1--4

Communication   Probe: Is there any regular communication with these groups?

Decision Autonomy

7. How free is this program to define its own direction, hire staff, use its allocated funds for different purposes? Explain:

Limits   Probe: What are the limits on what your program can do? Where do these come from?

Review of decisions   Probe: Are major decision of this program regularly reviewed? Which ones? By whom?

University Perspective

8. How is the program viewed by:

a) Minority students (in terms of their interests, participation)?

b) Non-minority students?

c) Faculty?

d) Administrators or trustees?

e) Community people or others outside the institution?

Probe: Social, political climate?

D:1--5

Reports, Research Evaluations

9. Are there any reports of level of operations, evaluation studies, or research on this program? What are those? Could we get copies?

Probe: Are they done regularly? By whom?

Current Issues or Concerns

10. What are the critical problems facing this program today.

internal   Probe: Internally? Program, staffing, funding, etc.?

external   Probe: Externally, in the larger institution?

Resolution   Probe: How do you see these issues being resolved?

Check on program discussion

11. Are there any issues, events, or circumstances regarding these programs for Blacks and minorities which we haven't covered which you think are important? What are they?

D:2--1

D: 2 STUDENT SUPPORT SERVICES

The four subsections which follow are primarily aimed at the chief administrative officer in Admissions, Financial Aid, counseling, and Housing. If these areas have separate programs for minorities section D-1 may be more appropriate.

D:2A ADMISSIONS

Before beginning, ask about the existence of reports or documents which would provide data on the following general areas: 1) Freshmen class characteristics 1968, 72, 74 2) Minority student characteristics, same years 3) Retention-attrition 4) Applicant to enrollment rates for minority and non-minority 5) other institutional research on these topics.

General Overview: Admissions

1. How would you describe the admissions operation in terms of :
   A. Number of professionals and staff
   B. Recruiting area and scope of travel
   C. Operating budget

Minority Emphasis

2. To what degree is your current minority recruitment effort a clearly defined area of concern?
   Probe: Professional staff member designated as minority recruiter? Title?
   Probe: Specific goals for minority enrollment?
   Probe: Earmarked budgetary support for minority recruitment?

Initial Period 1968-72

3. [If not covered in Section C] During the initial controversy over or attempts to increase Black enrollment, what was the role of the Admissions Office?
   Probe: Involved in decision: Advisory?
   Probe: Anticipatory? Already recruiting Blacks?

D:2--2

Recruiting Methods

4. During the initial phase of increasing Black enrollments what methods were employed to recruit minorities?
   Probe: Sources--geographic areas? Type of Black students sought (freshmen, transfer), strategies
   Probe: Changes since this early period?

Competition for Blacks

5. What is the current competitive situation in regards to the recruitment of Blacks for this institution?
   Probe: Application/ Admissions/Matriculation rates?
   Probe: Is the high school pool expanding or static?

Black's Selection Criteria

6. What do you consider among the primary reasons that minorities have come to ____? (Financial Aid? Academic Programs? Location? Recruiting efforts?)

Institution Selection Criteria

7. Who sets the undergraduate admissions criteria?
   Probe: How much latitude does your office have to "interpret" that criteria?

Early Admissions Criteria

8. What were the major admission criteria prior to period of increased minority enrollment? For Whites: For Blacks?
   Probe: Relative importance?

Changes in Admissions Criteria

9. How have these changed?

D:4-1

D:4   FACULTY ORGANIZATION AND FACULTY CULTURE

This section may be used to focus on either the total faculty or the departmental faculty. The former focus should be used for V.P. Academic Affairs, Dean, and head of Faculty Senate; the latter for department chairpersons; with faculty a judgment must be made. For department focus use ( ) wording. You should make it clear that we are primarily focusing on undergraduate education.

Faculty Governance Body

1. What is the major faculty governance body(ies) on your campus? (In your department?)

Faculty Involvement

2. How, if at all, were faculty involved in the original decision or actions to increase Black enrollments in your institution? (In your department?)

Conflict

   Probe: Was it a source of major conflict within the faculty? Parties or groups? Issues?

Resolution

   Probe: How was the conflict, if any, resolved? Was this satisfactory?

Faculty Involvement In Program Responses

3. In faculty & academic affairs are Black and minority issues more likely to be dealt with by department, by faculty governance bodies, or by higher levels of administration? If it varies, on the following, explain how?

   a) Recruitment policies, admissions standards, and Financial Aids Programs.

   b) Academic programs or course offerings for minorities

   c) Support programs (counseling, remedial programs, special housing, etc.)

   d) Grading policies and practices

   e) Other areas?

B:3-2

   Probe: How do they reflect Black or minority student interests? How do they relate to the Black or minority student organizations?

Student Government

3. Does your college have an active college-wide student government for all students?

Black Student Involvement

   Probe: Are minority students active in student government? How are they represented? What is the relationship of Black student organizations and the college-wide student government?

Black-White Student Issues

4. What have been the most significant problems or controversies between Black or minority students and the majority of white students? What were the issues? How were they dealt with? By whom?

Black Student In Community

5. How are your Black students accepted in the community? Have there been issues or incidents aside from those involving individuals?

   Probe: Are there community groups or organizations that Black students are involved with? That assist Black students?

Influential Black Students

6. Can you identify or describe the type of Black students who have been most influential in campus affairs and most respected by other Blacks? Are they the same?

Other Minority Groups

7. Have other minority students come into conflict with Black students or organizations? Describe groups, context, issues,

Other Students

8. Can you identify two or three outspoken Black or white student leaders that we should speak with?

D:4-2

Faculty Supportive, Critical, or Split

Probe: In the areas of faculty involvement in responses were they supportive or critical of these changes? If split, can you identify the issues and characterize those on opposing sides?

External Conflict

Probe: Did the faculty become embroiled in controversy on any of these issues with administrators? Minority groups? Or others?

New Faculty Governance Mechanisms

4. Were special institutional (departmental) procedures or mechanisms required for faculty to deal with minority issues? If so, how did the special procedures vary from traditional modes of academic governance? Where were the faculty in these new procedures?

Faculty Selection

5. How has your faculty dealt with the issue of Black and ethnic minority recruitment and selection of new faculty? Evaluation and promotion of minority faculty?

Black Faculty Leadership

6. Have Black faculty exerted a substantial leadership role in faculty (departmental) governance? On what issues? By what means?

General Faculty Response

7. In general, how have the majority white faculty members (of your department) responded to the demands of Black students? The new programs focused on Black or minority students?

Impact On Faculty Member Role

8. How has the increase of Black enrollments and the existence of Black programs directly affected individual faculty members role or behavior at this institution? (In your department). Give examples:

Probe: In institutional decision making

Probe: In departmental decision making

D:4-3

Probe: Do white faculty make special allowances for Black or minority students in grading, written or reading assignments, examinations procedures, or in other ways? Give examples.

Probe: Have white faculty altered their teaching style or content of their courses as a result of increased Black enrollments?

Probe: Have course assignments of individual faculty been changed?

Other Faculty Concerns

9. Aside from Black and minority issues, what are the two or three most pressing issues for faculty in your institution? (In your department?) Are these of higher or lower priority than minority issues?

Other Faculty

10. Can you identify 2 or 3 outspoken Blacks or white faculty we should speak with?

[For Department Chairmen Only]

Departmental Minority Picture

11. What is your current departmental picture with regard to minority faculty? Minority undergraduate majors? Is their a departmental recruitment effort for either?

Departmental Autonomy

12. How has the increase of minority enrollments and programs influenced your department's funding, program and course offerings, your self-defined purposes?

Response or Impact

Coordination

13. What minority programs and/or groups does your department work with on a regular basis? Give examples.

Department Chairperson Role

14. As department chairperson, how does the increase of Black enrollments affect your own role? Decision-making role, functions, trust, administrative style?

D: 5-1

D:5 ADMINISTRATIVE AND ORGANIZATIONAL CHANGES

QUESTIONS 1 to 4 SHOULD BE ASKED ONLY OF PRESIDENTS, VICE PRESIDENTS, AND TRUSTEES, (PERHAPS THE ACADEMIC DEAN OR FINANCIAL OFFICER IN SMALL COLLEGES, IF NO ONE HAS THE TITLE AND THEY REPORT DIRECTLY TO THE PRESIDENT).

FOR PERSONS OTHER THAN ABOVE USE THIS ALTERNATE QUESTION AND THEN GO TO #5 USING THE PARENTHETIC FORM TO RELATE IT TO THEIR AREA.
ALTERNATE QUESTION: What if any, was your involvement in the original decision to increase Black enrollments at your institution?

Awareness

Pres. and Board in Increase
1. Were you aware of the Board's discussion at the time issues related to increasing Black enrollments were discussed?
[If no, go to Question 5]
2. In the original decision, confrontation, or discussion leading to the increased enrollment of Blacks what role did the President and trustees play? How were they involved? What were the issues?

Pres. and Board in initial response
3. In the decisions to create response mechanisms (recruitment, admissions, and financial aids programs, academic and supportive services) have the President or Trustees been actively involved?

External pressures
Probe: Was the Board subjected to pressures from outside the institution? Who?

Internal Pressures
Probe: Were internal divisions critical factors in the trustees deliberations?

Attitude changes
Probe: Have there been major shifts in the Trustee's positions and attitudes toward minority enrollments and programs since then? If so, how?

Decision making consistency
4. Were the processes by which these decisions were made a departure from normal practice for such issues at your institution? If so, why?

D:5-2

5. What was the role of the executive officers in the original decision to increase Black enrollments? Were any individuals particularly influential?

Executive Involvement or leadership

6. What new review committee or advisory groups, if any, have been created at the vice-presidential or presidential level (your administrative level) to deal with Black or minority issues? Describe function and membership briefly.

New executive structures

7. Which executive officers (administrators in your area) have been most affected by the increase in Black enrollments? Why?

Impact at Exec. Level

Probe: Since 196_ has there been a change in incumbent in any or all of the top administrative officers? Was any of these related to or affected by a minority issue or decision?

Turnover

Probe: As Black enrollments increased and Black programs developed were there new administrative offices created in your area as a result of those changes? Briefly, describe function, if any?

new offices

Probe: What has been your success in hiring Black administrators

Hiring Blacks

(Use appropriate level:)
a) Top level (President and Vice-Pres)

b) Second Echelons in your area (Persons reporting to you as executive officers) Deans, Directors, etc:

c) Lower levels (Department chair persons, assistant deans, etc).

Recruitment Practices
Probe: How have you attempted to hire Black administrators? (Goals, special recruitment efforts, etc.)

D: 5-3

Conflict in hiring
   Probe: Have you had any significant conflict over hiring or releasing a Black administrator? If so, describe it briefly.

Personal Impact
8. How has the increase of Black enrollments and the existence of Black programs directly affected you as an administrative officer in this institution?

Decision making
   Probe: In institutional decision making (participation and influence)?

Functions
   Probe: In your functions or responsibilities?

Trust or personal relationship
   Probe: In the extent to which you are trusted by white faculty, and students? By minority students? By other administrators?

Style
   Probe: In your administrative style?

Current decision making level
9. Currently at what administrative level do controversial minority issues of each of the following usually get final discussion and/or settled? (i.e. where does responsibility rest)
a) Admissions—policy and standards
b) Recruitment—policy
c) Financial Aids—Program
d) New minority academic programs
e) New minority support services
f) Minority faculty hiring
g) Minority grievances

D:5-4

BE PREPARED TO SKIP Q. 10 IF RESPONDENT IS UNABLE TO RESPOND

Budgetary Process
10. From your perspective, how has the advent of minority programs and enrollments altered the budget? The budgetary process?

Communications
11. Has the pattern of communication or your network of relationship with other administrators for you as an administrator been altered as a result of the increase in Black enrollments and programs?

Constituency relationship in Governance
12. What kind of college or university governance set-up do you have? In that context has the relationship of the typical college or university constituencies (student, faculty and administrative) in the governance process been influenced or changed as a result of the increase in Black enrollments?

Participation
   Probe: Level of Participation of the constituencies in governing bodies?

Power
   Probe: Relative power or influence of each constituency?

Trust
   Probe: Trust between or among the constituencies?

FOR VP ACADEMICS, STUDENT, OR MINORITY OFFICER WITH MINORITY PROGRAMS UNDER THEIR JURISDICTION

Responsibility for Minority Programs
13. What organizational units specifically concerned with Blacks and minorities are under your direction? Describe each.

Purpose
   Probe: its purpose?

Strengths
   Probe: Strengthens and weaknesses?

D:5-5

E-1

Control

Probe: How you relate to it?

Needed Changes

Probe: How you would like to see it changed?

Other issues

14. Aside from Black and minority issues what are the two or three most pressing issues for your level of administration?

Priority

Probe: Are these higher or lower than the minority issue?

External Constraints and Influences

E. OTHER INTERVENING CONSTRAINTS AND INFLUENCES

Probes: Use only where appropriate

1. An institution's capacity to expand and/or respond to Black students is obviously affected by many other constraints and influences. Please comment, briefly, on any of the following that have affected your institution's capacity to expand Black enrollments, develop programs, and hire Black faculty or support them.

Probe: Any state legislation or guidelines on minority enrollments or programs.

Probe: State institutional appropriations or other special financial aid programs.

Probe: Federal HEW Actions or Affirmative Action guidelines

Probe: Unusual local economic, political, or social changes

Probe: Unusual institutional financial strain or reasons aside from the ubiquitous inflationary trends?

Probe: Enrollment declines

Probe: Collective Bargaining

F-1

F. THE CURRENT SCENE: RELATIONSHIP, ISSUES, AND PORTENTS

Switching to your current institutional setting we would appreciate your brief, but candid interpretation of each of the following:

[ASK ONLY IF THEY HAVE NOT ALREADY BEEN DISCUSSED]

Black Student Characteristics

1. What are the background characteristics of your Black student enrollment? (Region, family occupation and income, educational and career interests, attitudes to institution). Is it changing or likely to change? Are there studies of the student body and minorities available?

Black Needs

2. What are major concerns and unmet needs of Blacks on your campus?

Students

Probe: For current Black students at your institution? Are these different from other ethnic groups? What do you foresee being done (or not being done)?

Faculty

Probe: What are the concerns of Black faculty?

Popularity Supportive

3. In general how would you describe the Black students attitudes to the Black studies programs and supportive services and their staff on this campus? Are there problems here?

Black White Relations

4. How would you characterize the following Black-White relationships on your campus?

Black and White Students

Probe: How well do white and Black students interact on your campus? Are there particular issues that concern you?

Black Students- White Faculty

Probe: In general how do Black students relate to white faculty? Are there particular concerns here?

White Students- Black Faculty

Probe: How do white students relate to or work with Black faculty?

F-2

Other Minorities

5. How do Black student groups and programs relate to or work with other minority groups, women's groups?

Black-White Faculty and Administrative Relations

6. What is the most important issue, if any, interfering with more effective working relationships between Black and white faculty? Between Black and white administrators?

Racial Relationship Directions

7. Finally are Black-White relationships on your campus changing for the better (or worse) in any significant way? Give examples:

[LAST FIVE MINUTES]

Final Institution

I have constrained you to some fairly focused areas. Are there other concerns that you have about your institutions' attempt to increase Black enrollments and to develop response patterns and programs or in the affect that these changes have had on your institution that we really should know about?

THANK YOU FOR YOUR TIME!

Appendix C

Survey Questionnaire (Stage II)

The respondent groups addressed for the items shown are indicated on the upper right hand corner on each page.

SURVEY QUESTIONNAIRE

WHITE COLLEGES' AND UNIVERSITIES' RESPONSE TO THE ENTRY OF BLACK STUDENTS

This questionnaire is part of the second stage of a pilot research project conducted by a multi-racial research team from the Institute for Social Research at the University of Michigan.

The purpose of this questionnaire is to obtain your views of the impacts on and responses of predominantly White colleges and universities which have had a substantial increase in Black enrollments since 1968 or 1970. The purpose of the study is to help institutions assess their response to a racial minority group on a number of dimensions which were identified in the first stage of the research.

This study is neither an evaluation of specific Black or minority related programs nor an affirmative action study. The questionnaire will be treated confidentially and both individual and institutional anonymity is guaranteed in all reports and publications of this project. Your institution will receive a profile of response patterns with comparisons of faculty, administrative, and student responses. There will be no racial breakdown of faculty and administrative respondents in order to further guarantee individual anonymity. The report provided to your institution will be available to anyone interested and should be of use to students, faculty, or administrators interested in obtaining a better understanding of their campus on this topic.

Please answer all questions by checking the most appropriate response and complete the personal information at the end. The identification number on the front of the questionnaire is for follow-up purposes only and will be removed when the questionnaire is received. The questionnaire should be returned in the enclosed envelope as directed.

Administrators, Faculty, and Students

ROLE OF RACIAL MINORITIES IN COLLEGES AND UNIVERSITIES

The role of racial minorities in American colleges and universities and the responsibility of those institutions for such groups is a critical issue for persons working in colleges and universities. The following are some statements representing various views or positions on this issue. Please indicate the extent to which you agree with each. (Check one response for each item):

	STRONGLY AGREE 1	AGREE 2	DISAGREE 3	STRONGLY DISAGREE 4	
1. Black and racial minorities should meet the same academic admissions standards as all other students	☐	☐	☐	☐	(1:15)
2. Different performance standards are probably required for some racial minority students . . .	☐	☐	☐	☐	(1:16)
3. Remedial academic programs are probably necessary to insure success of some racial minority students	☐	☐	☐	☐	(1:17)
4. Increases in Black and other racial minority enrollments and special programs for them reduce academic standards	☐	☐	☐	☐	(1:18)
5. In the long run the entrance of racial minority students and the development of related programs will strengthen our colleges and universities	☐	☐	☐	☐	(1:19)
6. Diversity of life styles and separate living patterns among Blacks and other racial groups should be encouraged in colleges and universities.	☐	☐	☐	☐	(1:20)
7. Colleges and universities have an obligation to encourage racial interaction in all areas of campus life	☐	☐	☐	☐	(1:21)
8. Pluralism can be divisive and colleges and universities should not support separate educational, cultural, and social activities by various racial groups	☐	☐	☐	☐	(1:22)
9. Black or ethnic studies programs should have a strong focus on activist and/or community service activities	☐	☐	☐	☐	(1:23)
10. Despite our concern over racial injustice, colleges and universities do not have a primary responsibility to rectify that situation . .	☐	☐	☐	☐	(1:24)

Administrators and Faculty Only

	STRONGLY AGREE 1	AGREE 2	DISAGREE 3	STRONGLY DISAGREE 4	
11. Different admissions criteria and standards may be justified for some racial minority groups	☐	☐	☐	☐	(1:25)
12. Remedial education should not be offered for academic credit	☐	☐	☐	☐	(1:26)
13. Colleges and universities can best serve racial minority students by establishing explicit goals and specifying competency levels for academic performance	☐	☐	☐	☐	(1:27)
14. Racial minority students are best served by continued stress on traditional standards of academic performance	☐	☐	☐	☐	(1:28)
15. In light of current and projected enrollment declines, colleges and universities should move toward open admissions	☐	☐	☐	☐	(1:29)
16. Affirmative action, despite its underlying concern for equality, is detrimental to the viability of our colleges and universities . .	☐	☐	☐	☐	(1:30)
17. Programs for Blacks and other racial minorities will be more effective if they are given a separate departmental identity. .	☐	☐	☐	☐	(1:31)
18. Afro-American or African studies are legitimate interdisciplinary or interdepartmental majors which focus on distinct world subgroups . . .	☐	☐	☐	☐	(1:32)
19. Colleges and universities should insure the inclusion of Blacks and other racial minorities in faculty and administrative positions not specifically responsible for those groups	☐	☐	☐	☐	(1:33)
20. Despite concern for past discrimination, hiring and promotion decisions must favor the most qualified individual in colleges and universities	☐	☐	☐	☐	(1:34)
21. Ethnic studies is more appropriate than separate majors focusing on particular racial groups (e.g., Black or Chicano Studies) . . .	☐	☐	☐	☐	(1:35)

INSTITUTIONAL GOALS FOR BLACK AND RACIAL MINORITIES

Administrators and Faculty Only

Institutions of higher education by their actions, programs, and patterns of commitments often have goals, formal or informal, which are widely shared or understood. Below are some goals related to Blacks, as a racial minority group, held by some colleges and universities. Please, indicate the extent to which each is an important goal or priority for your institution, regardless of how you personally feel. (Check one box for each item):

Scale: NO IMPORTANCE 1 — SLIGHT 2 — SOME 3 — SUBSTANTIAL 4 — GREAT IMPORTANCE 5

1. The recruitment and admission of Black students at least in proportion to their population in your recruitment area. . . . (1:36)
2. The provision of a full range of remedial, academic, social, and cultural services for Blacks . . . . (1:37)
3. The creation and continuation of an academically strong Black or ethnic studies program. . . . . (1:38)
4. The recruitment and hiring of Black faculty members at least in proportion to the representation of those groups in the student body. . . . . (1:39)
5. The recruitment and hiring of Black or minority staff for top level administrative positions who are not explicitly responsible for minority affairs . . . (1:40)
6. The commitment of institutional financial resources for the support of Black or racial minority admissions, remedial, and social or cultural programs . . . . . (1:41)
7. The commitment of institutional funds for financial aid when necessary to assure that Black students can complete their undergraduate degrees. . . . . . . (1:42)
8. Including Black content in all courses related to American life or institutions (American history, literature, music). . . (1:43)
9. The development of strong institutional ties with Black groups in the surrounding community. . . . . (1:44)
10. The creation of a high level, visible administrative office or other structure which is primarily concerned with Black or racial minority issues and activities on campus . . . . (1:45)

INSTITUTIONAL RACIAL CLIMATE

Administrators, Faculty, and Students

The following statements reflect patterns of Black and White relations that have been observed on various college and university campuses. How would you assess the extent to which each is present on or descriptive of your own campus. (Check one box for each item):

Scale: VERY LITTLE 1 — SLIGHT 2 — SOME 3 — SUBSTANTIAL 4 — VERY SUBSTANTIAL 5

1. The degree of trust between Black students and
   a) White students . . . . (1:46)
   b) The faculty. . . . . (1:47)
   c) The administration . . . . (1:48)
   d) Other racial minorities . . . . (1:49)
2. The degree of racial conflict on campus. . . . . . (1:50)
3. Concern for Black issues on campus. . . . . (1:51)
4. Activism by Black groups on behalf of their own interests and concerns . . . . (1:52)
5. The degree of Black and White interaction among faculty and staff on a social and personal basis. (1:53)
6. Positive Black and White professional relationships in the faculty and the administration. . . (1:54)
7. The presence of separate but mutually accepted racial groups and interests. . . . . (1:55)
8. The degree to which Blacks and other racial minorities are sought for representation. . . . . (1:56)
9. The existence of a great diversity rather than homogeneity among Black students in their interests social groups and organizations and activities. . . . . (1:57)
10. Open discussion of Black or racial issues and concerns on campus. . . . . (1:58)
11. Blacks who are visible and influential:
    a) in the student body. . . . . (1:59)
    b) in the faculty . . . . (1:60)
    c) in the administration . . . . (1:61)
12. Active interracial social patterns among students. (1:62)

Administrators, Faculty, and Students

INSTITUTIONAL RESPONSIVENESS

In recent years your institution has established various programs and services in response to the increase of Black enrollments in order to serve some of their needs. In the next three questions, please indicate your perceptions of your institution's responsiveness to those needs. (Check one box for each item).

1. How do you rate your institution's current willingness to establish or develop programs or services for Blacks in each of the following areas?

	VERY RESISTANT (1)	SOMEWHAT RESISTANT (2)	INDIFFERENT (3)	SOMEWHAT WILLING (4)	VERY WILLING (5)	
a) Student recruitment, admissions, financial aid	☐	☐	☐	☐	☐	(1:63)
b) Tutoring, counseling and advising services	☐	☐	☐	☐	☐	(1:64)
c) Black or ethnic studies and other Black-focused curriculum	☐	☐	☐	☐	☐	(1:65)
d) Social and cultural activities	☐	☐	☐	☐	☐	(1:66)
e) Black faculty and staff recruitment	☐	☐	☐	☐	☐	(1:67)

2. In light of your perceptions of the needs of Black students, how do you rate the adequacy of your institution's effort in providing programs and services for Blacks in each of the following areas?

	NOT AT ALL ADEQUATE (1)	LESS THAN ADEQUATE (2)	ADEQUATE (3)	MORE THAN ADEQUATE (4)	VERY ADEQUATE (5)	
a) Student recruitment, admissions and financial aid	☐	☐	☐	☐	☐	(1:68)
b) Tutoring, counseling and advising services	☐	☐	☐	☐	☐	(1:69)
c) Black or ethnic studies and other Black-focused curriculum	☐	☐	☐	☐	☐	(1:70)
d) Social and cultural activities	☐	☐	☐	☐	☐	(1:71)
e) Black faculty and staff recruitment	☐	☐	☐	☐	☐	(1:72)

Administrators, Faculty, and Students

3. In general, how would you rate the current commitment of each of the following to the development of Black and minority programs and services?

	ACTIVE OPPOSITION (1)	PASSIVE OPPOSITION (2)	INDIFFERENCE (3)	PASSIVE SUPPORT (4)	ACTIVE SUPPORT (5)	
a) Executive officers (Pres., V. Pres., Prov.)	☐	☐	☐	☐	☐	(2:15)
b) Academic administrators (Deans, Asst. Deans etc.)	☐	☐	☐	☐	☐	(2:16)
c) Department chairpersons	☐	☐	☐	☐	☐	(2:17)
d) Student affairs staff	☐	☐	☐	☐	☐	(2:18)
e) Faculty governing body	☐	☐	☐	☐	☐	(2:19)
f) Student government	☐	☐	☐	☐	☐	(2:20)
g) Black faculty and staff	☐	☐	☐	☐	☐	(2:21)
h) The faculty	☐	☐	☐	☐	☐	(2:22)
i) White students	☐	☐	☐	☐	☐	(2:23)
j) Black students	☐	☐	☐	☐	☐	(2:24)
k) Your own commitment	☐	☐	☐	☐	☐	(2:25)

Administrators and Faculty Only

INSTITUTIONAL IMPACTS AND RESPONSES

The inclusion of any new group of students in substantial numbers inevitably influences or changes some patterns of institutional functioning in addition to the presence of visible programs and services for Blacks or other racial minorities. In the following questions you are asked to briefly assess the impact of increased Black enrollments in certain broad institutional dimensions. (Check one box for each item):

	1 NONE	2 A LITTLE	3 SOME	4 SUBSTANTIAL	5 A GREAT DEAL	

1. To what degree do Blacks exert influence in your institution at the following levels?

    a) The trustees. . . . . (2:26)
    b) Executive officers. . . . . (2:27)
    c) School or college level administrators or governance structures. . . . . (2:28)
    d) Departments. . . . . (2:29)
    e) The faculty in general. . . . . (2:30)
    f) The student body. . . . . (2:31)

2. To what degree do the following Black groups have influence in your institution?

    a) Black administrators and staff. . . . . . . (2:32)
    b) Black faculty . . . . (2:33)
    c) Black students . . . . (2:34)
    d) Coalitions or combinations of the above . . (2:35)

3. Relative to their numbers, would you say Black representation and involvement in institutional governance and decision making bodies is:

    _____ (1) unusually low
    _____ (2) about average   (2:36)
    _____ (3) unusually high

Administrators and Faculty Only

4. We are interested in how your institution deals with major Black or racial minority issues in contrast to the way it deals with similar non-Black or racial issues. (For example, the introduction of Black Studies as compared to another interdisciplinary program, new admissions or financial aids policies for Blacks as compared to Whites, a student racial disturbance compared to a non-racial one). Given the areas with which you are familiar, how do you rate your institution's pattern of dealing with Black or racial minority issues as contrasted to comparable non-racial issues on the following? (Check one box for each item):

a. The level at which Black or racial issues finally get settled?
    ___ (1) much more decentralized than other issues.
    ___ (2) somewhat more decentralized than other issues.   (2:37)
    ___ (3) no difference or no discernible pattern.
    ___ (4) more centralized than other issues.
    ___ (5) much more centralized than other issues.

b. The extent to which the Black or racial issues are scrutinized?
    ___ (1) much less intensely scrutinized than other issues.
    ___ (2) somewhat less intensely scrutinized than other issues.   (2:38)
    ___ (3) no difference or no discernible pattern.
    ___ (4) somewhat more intensely scrutinized than other issues.
    ___ (5) much more intensely scrutinized than other issues.

c. The manner in which Black and racial issues are discussed or deliberated.
    ___ (1) much more conflictual and adversary in nature than others.
    ___ (2) somewhat more conflictual and adversary in nature than others.   (2:39)
    ___ (3) no difference or no discernible pattern.
    ___ (4) somewhat more conflictual and adversary in nature than others.
    ___ (5) much more conflictual and adversary in nature than others.

d. The manner in which decisions on Black or racial issues are made?
    ___ (1) more closed discussions than other issues.
    ___ (2) no difference or no discernible pattern.   (2:40)
    ___ (3) more open discussions.

e. The manner in which the implementation of decisions on Black or racial issues are directed from higher administrative levels?
    ___ (1) much less directed than for other issues.
    ___ (2) somewhat less directed than for other issues.
    ___ (3) no difference for no discernible pattern.   (2:41)
    ___ (4) somewhat more directed than for other issues.
    ___ (5) much more directed than for other issues.

Administrators, Faculty, and Students

FUTURE INSTITUTIONAL COMMITMENTS, CONCERNS, AND ISSUES

In light of your institution's current situation, how would you assess your institution's <u>future</u> commitment to <u>continued support</u> of programs and services for Blacks in each of the following areas? (Check one box for each item):

	WILL BE GREATLY INCREASED (1)	WILL BE SOMEWHAT INCREASED (2)	WILL BE MAINTAINED (3)	WILL BE SOMEWHAT REDUCED (4)	WILL BE SUBSTANTIALLY REDUCED (5)	
a. Student recruitment, admissions and financial aid	☐	☐	☐	☐	☐	(2:42)
b. Tutoring, counseling and advising services	☐	☐	☐	☐	☐	(2:43)
c. Black or ethnic studies and other Black-focused curricula	☐	☐	☐	☐	☐	(2:44)
d. Social and cultural activities	☐	☐	☐	☐	☐	(2:45)
e. Black faculty and staff recruitment. . .	☐	☐	☐	☐	☐	(2:46)

2. Identify briefly the two or three issues, either directly or indirectly related to Black or racial minority affairs, which you think will be significant problems or conflicts within the next year.

(2:47)

(2:48)

Administrators Only

IMPACT AND RESPONSES IN ADMINISTRATIVE AREAS

As your institution has increased in its enrollment of Black students and developed response programs and services, these may have affected areas of administrative activity. In the following questions we are interested in your perceptions of how these changes have affected the areas with which you are most familiar. (Check one box for each question or item):

1. To what degree have Black and minority issues, pressures, or considerations <u>altered</u> the way <u>your</u> office meets its responsibilities?

   (1) Very little
   (2) Somewhat
   (3) A great deal   (2:49)

2. As an administrator, to what extent have the following <u>influenced</u> or <u>significantly altered</u> the way <u>your office</u> meets its responsibilities?

	NOT AT ALL (1)	SLIGHT (2)	SOMEWHAT (3)	SUBSTANTIAL (4)	A GREAT DEAL (5)	
a. The increased Black student enrollment.	☐	☐	☐	☐	☐	(2:50)
b. The addition of Black faculty.	☐	☐	☐	☐	☐	(2:51)
c. The increase of Black administrators	☐	☐	☐	☐	☐	(2:52)
d. Increased enrollment of other racial minorities	☐	☐	☐	☐	☐	(2:53)
e. Affirmative Action	☐	☐	☐	☐	☐	(2:54)
f. The addition of Black staff to your immediate area. . .	☐	☐	☐	☐	☐	(2:55)
g. The creation of Black or other minority programs or activities in your area.	☐	☐	☐	☐	☐	(2:56)
h. Black or racial minority groups off campus.	☐	☐	☐	☐	☐	(2:57)

3. To what extent have Black or minority issues <u>influenced</u> the following in your administrative area? (Check one box for each item):

	SUBSTANTIALLY DECREASED (1)	SOMEWHAT DECREASED (2)	UNCHANGED (3)	SOMEWHAT INCREASED (4)	SUBSTANTIALLY INCREASED (5)	
a. Services offered	☐	☐	☐	☐	☐	(2:58)
b. Our resources	☐	☐	☐	☐	☐	(2:59)
c. Our staff	☐	☐	☐	☐	☐	(2:60)
d. Quality of our services	☐	☐	☐	☐	☐	(2:61)

Administrators Only

4. How would you say that the impact or alterations resulting from these Black or racial minority influences compares to other important non-minority issues and influences in your administrative area?

_____ (1) Minority issues much less significant than others.

_____ (2) About the same as others.

_____ (3) Minority issues much more significant than others.   (2:62)

5. To what extent have Black or minority issues been a significant factor in any of the following in your administrative area.

	LITTLE OR NO SIGNIFICANCE 1	SLIGHT 2	SOME 3	SUBSTANTIAL 4	A GREAT DEAL OF SIGNIFICANCE 5	
a. The release, transfer, or resignation of a non-minority staff member	☐	☐	☐	☐	☐	(2:63)
b. The addition of Black or minority staff	☐	☐	☐	☐	☐	(2:64)
c. The reorganization of the area	☐	☐	☐	☐	☐	(2:65)

6. Within the administrative staff meetings, discussions and decision groups in which you regularly participate, how are minority issues generally treated or viewed? (Circle appropriate number and assume 1=very; 5=very):

	1	2	3	4	5		
Seldom	1	2	3	4	5	Often	(2:66)
Antagonistically	1	2	3	4	5	Supportively	(2:67)
Indecisively	1	2	3	4	5	Decisively	(2:68)
With little minority input	1	2	3	4	5	With substantial minority input	(2:69)
Under external pressure	1	2	3	4	5	No external pressure	(2:70)
Divisively	1	2	3	4	5	Cooperatively	(2:71)

Administrators Only

7. How would you assess the relationship of your White administrative colleagues with Black administrators, faculty, or staff? (Circle appropriate number):

	1	2	3	4	5		
Disrespectful	1	2	3	4	5	Respectful	(3:15)
Guarded	1	2	3	4	5	Open	(3:16)
Formal	1	2	3	4	5	Personal	(3:17)
Antagonistic	1	2	3	4	5	Supportive	(3:18)
Conflictual	1	2	3	4	5	Unconflictual	(3:19)
Indifferent	1	2	3	4	5	Concerned	(3:20)
Insignificant	1	2	3	4	5	Crucial	(3:21)

8. How has the presence of more Black students, faculty, and staff in your institution affected your personal administrative role and responsibilities? (Check one box for each item):

	GREATLY REDUCED 1	SOMEWHAT REDUCED 2	UNCHANGED 3	SOMEWHAT INCREASED 4	GREATLY INCREASED 5	
a. Degree of tension	☐	☐	☐	☐	☐	(3:22)
b. Personal satisfaction	☐	☐	☐	☐	☐	(3:23)
c. Concern for minority issues	☐	☐	☐	☐	☐	(3:24)
d. Time demands	☐	☐	☐	☐	☐	(3:25)
e. Flexibility	☐	☐	☐	☐	☐	(3:26)
f. Job challenges	☐	☐	☐	☐	☐	(3:27)
g. Job constraints	☐	☐	☐	☐	☐	(3:28)
h. Personal effectiveness	☐	☐	☐	☐	☐	(3:29)
i. Job clarity	☐	☐	☐	☐	☐	(3:30)
j. Personal commitment to the institution	☐	☐	☐	☐	☐	(3:31)

Administrators Only

PERSONAL INFORMATION ON ADMINISTRATORS

1. Administrative level (Check one):

____ (1) Executive officer (Vice president or above)
____ (2) Dean, Director, or other officer reporting to a Vice President or the President
____ (3) Assistant and Associate Dean or Director or other title   (3:32)

2. Primary area of Responsibility (Check one):

____ (1) Academic affairs
____ (2) Business or financial affairs
____ (3) Student affairs
____ (4) Black or minority programs or affairs   (3:33)
____ (5) Other:

3. If you are not primarily responsible for minority programs or affairs, do you (Check as many as apply):

____ (1) Have a specific minority program or activity reporting to you?   (3:34)
____ (2) Coordinate regularly with a Black or minority program?   (3:35)
____ (1) Report to a Black administrator?   (3:36)
____ (1) Have a Black administrator reporting directly to you?   (3:37)

4. How many years have you been in:

Your current position _____   (3:38)

This institution _____   (3:39)

5. Prior to your current position was your primary responsibility (Check one):

____ (1) Teaching or other academic work in a college or university?
____ (2) Administration in a college or university?   (3:40)
____ (3) Work in another type of institution?

6. If you were previously in college or university administration, were you primarily responsible for (Check one):

____ (1) Academic affairs
____ (2) Business or financial affairs
____ (3) Student affairs
____ (4) Black or ethnic minority affairs   (3:41)
____ (5) Other:

7. What is your highest degree level? (Check one):

____ (1) Less than Bachelors level
____ (2) Bachelors degree
____ (3) Masters or first professional degree   (3:42)
____ (4) Doctoral degree

THANK YOU! PLEASE RETURN IN ENVELOPE PROVIDED

Faculty Only

IMPACTS AND RESPONSES IN FACULTY AND DEPARTMENTAL ACTIVITY

As the number of Black students has increased at this institution, we are interested in the techniques, evaluation practices, and teaching styles faculty employ in order to accomplish their educational goals. Indicate whether the items listed below are employed for minority students more or less frequently than for non-minority students.

IMPORTANT: We are asking for your pattern of usage and not whether you use minority status as a criterion for the selection of the technique.

Faculty Impacts And Responses.

	SELDOM OR NEVER WITH ANY STUDENTS (1)	LESS WITH BLACKS THAN WITH OTHERS (2)	SAME FOR ALL STUDENTS (3)	SOMEWHAT MORE WITH BLACKS THAN WITH OTHERS (4)	MUCH MORE WITH BLACKS THAN MY OTHER STUDENTS (5)	
1. Teaching Techniques and Styles Employed:						
a. Set up group or individual sessions to provide academic help.	☐	☐	☐	☐	☐	(2:49)
b. Extend deadlines.	☐	☐	☐	☐	☐	(2:50)
c. Relate course content to concrete examples of student's personal experience. . . .	☐	☐	☐	☐	☐	(2:51)
d. Give extra assignments.	☐	☐	☐	☐	☐	(2:52)
e. Refer students to tutorial services. . .	☐	☐	☐	☐	☐	(2:53)
f. Allow a wider range of topics and projects to fulfill course requirements.	☐	☐	☐	☐	☐	(2:54)
g. Permit students to rewrite papers or exams.	☐	☐	☐	☐	☐	(2:55)
2. Evaluation Practices Employed:						
h. Written essay exams.	☐	☐	☐	☐	☐	(2:56)
i. Oral exams	☐	☐	☐	☐	☐	(2:57)
j. Objective exams	☐	☐	☐	☐	☐	(2:58)
k. Competency/Proficiency exams.	☐	☐	☐	☐	☐	(2:59)
l. Subjective evaluation of student efforts .	☐	☐	☐	☐	☐	(2:60)
m. Evaluation of class participation. . . .	☐	☐	☐	☐	☐	(2:61)
n. Other _____						☐ (2:62)

Faculty Only

5. In general to what degree have Black and racial minority issues, pressures, or considerations altered your role as a faculty member: (3:25)
   ___ (1) very little
   ___ (2) somewhat
   ___ (3) a great deal

6. If you answered somewhat or a great deal in 5, to what degree have each of the following been influential in this change? (Check one box for each item):

	NO INFLUENCE (1)	SLIGHT (2)	SOME (3)	SUBSTANTIAL (4)	A GREAT DEAL OF INFLUENCE (5)	
a. Black students in my classes	☐	☐	☐	☐	☐	(3:26)
b. Black students in this institution	☐	☐	☐	☐	☐	(3:27)
c. Black colleagues in my department	☐	☐	☐	☐	☐	(3:28)
d. Black faculty and staff in this institution	☐	☐	☐	☐	☐	(3:29)
e. My dean or department chairman	☐	☐	☐	☐	☐	(3:30)
f. Other faculty and/or administrators:	☐	☐	☐	☐	☐	(3:31)

Departmental Impacts and Responses

7. To what extent have minority issues, pressures, or considerations made the following departmental concerns more or less difficult:

	MUCH LESS DIFFICULT (1)	LESS DIFFICULT (2)	UNCHANGED (3)	MORE DIFFICULT (4)	MUCH MORE DIFFICULT (5)	
a. Hiring and appointment decisions	☐	☐	☐	☐	☐	(3:32)
b. Relationships with the central administration	☐	☐	☐	☐	☐	(3:33)
c. Promotional and salary decisions	☐	☐	☐	☐	☐	(3:34)
d. Maintenance of academic reputation	☐	☐	☐	☐	☐	(3:35)

8. In general how much impact have Black and minority issues, pressures, or considerations had on your department? (3:36)
   ___ (1) Very little
   ___ (2) Somewhat
   ___ (3) A great deal

Faculty Only

3. We are interested in the impact that Black students have had on more general changes in patterns of faculty activity. Below are a number of items which may have been affected by increasing numbers of Black students at your institution. (Check one response for each item):

	SIGNIFICANTLY DECREASED (1)	SOMEWHAT DECREASED (2)	REMAINED THE SAME (3)	SOMEWHAT INCREASED (4)	SIGNIFICANTLY INCREASED (5)	
a. My time spent in teaching and class preparation	☐	☐	☐	☐	☐	(2:63)
b. My creative and scholarly work accomplished	☐	☐	☐	☐	☐	(2:64)
c. My time spent in counseling students	☐	☐	☐	☐	☐	(2:65)
d. My interaction with student services staff and counselors	☐	☐	☐	☐	☐	(2:66)
e. Black content in my courses	☐	☐	☐	☐	☐	(2:67)
f. My class discussions centered on racial issues	☐	☐	☐	☐	☐	(2:68)

4. Compared to other students, Black students in my classes:

	MUCH LESS THAN OTHER STUDENTS (1)	SOMEWHAT LESS THAN OTHER STUDENTS (2)	ABOUT THE SAME (3)	SOMEWHAT MORE THAN OTHERS (4)	MUCH MORE THAN OTHER STUDENTS (5)	
a. Participate in class discussions	☐	☐	☐	☐	☐	(3:15)
b. Speak to me on campus	☐	☐	☐	☐	☐	(3:16)
c. Come to my office to discuss academic problems, seek extra help	☐	☐	☐	☐	☐	(3:17)
d. Come to see me about personal problems	☐	☐	☐	☐	☐	(3:18)
e. Discuss career or graduate school plans	☐	☐	☐	☐	☐	(3:19)
f. Raise questions about their grades	☐	☐	☐	☐	☐	(3:20)
g. Request extra assignments	☐	☐	☐	☐	☐	(3:21)
h. Suggest changes in my course content	☐	☐	☐	☐	☐	(3:22)
i. Suggest changes in my teaching style	☐	☐	☐	☐	☐	(3:23)
j. Other _____	☐	☐	☐	☐	☐	(3:24)

Faculty Only

9. Departments may vary on how they approach the education of minority students. Below are a number of phrases which could be used to describe the racial and academic climate of a department. For each item please check the one item which expresses how characteristic the item is of your department. (Check one box for each item):

	DEFINITELY NOT TRUE OF MY DEPARTMENT	GENERALLY NOT TRUE	GENERALLY TRUE	DEFINITELY TRUE OF MY DEPARTMENT	
	1	2	3	4	

Racial Climate of My Department

a. The faculty make special efforts to ensure the success of Black students . . . . □ □ □ □ (3:37)

b. Faculty present curriculum in order to have an appeal and interest to Black students . . . . □ □ □ □ (3:38)

c. Faculty make the same academic demands on Blacks as Whites . . . . □ □ □ □ (3:39)

d. Different opinions on Black and minority issues has caused polarization in this department . . □ □ □ □ (3:40)

e. Faculty accept cultural differences between Whites and Blacks. . . . . □ □ □ □ (3:41)

Academic Climate of My Department

f. Faculty are more oriented toward research and graduate instruction than to undergraduate teaching. . . . . □ □ □ □ (3:42)

g. Faculty are involved in the community in a variety of departmental activities . . . . □ □ □ □ (3:43)

h. Faculty are actively concerned about the "job market" for their graduates . . . . □ □ □ □ (3:44)

i. Faculty place greater demands on departmental majors than what is the norm for the institution as a whole . . . . □ □ □ □ (3:45)

Faculty Only

PERSONAL INFORMATION ON FACULTY

1. Department of Primary Appointment: _____ (3:46)

2. Other Department Appointment: _____ (3:47)

3. Academic Rank:
   ___(1) Professor
   ___(2) Associate Professor (3:48)
   ___(3) Assistant Professor
   ___(4) Instructor

4. Sex: ___(1) Male ___(2) Female (3:49)

5. Age: _____ (3:50)

6. Tenure: ___(1) Yes ___(2) No (3:51)

7. Highest Degree Earned:
   ___(4)Doctorate
   ___(3)Masters or First Professional Degree (3:52)
   ___(2)Bachelors Degree
   ___(1)Less than Bachelors Degree

8. How many years have you been in: Your current position? _____ (3:53)
   This institution? _____ (3:54)

9. Do you currently serve on any departmental committees concerned primarily with minority issues? Please list: (3:55)
   a. _____
   b. _____

10. Do you currently serve on any other institutional committees or advisory groups primarily concerned with minority issues? Please list: (3:56)
    a. _____
    b. _____

11. Please indicate:

	Number	Approximate Total Enrollment	Approximate Black Enrollment
Number of introductory courses taught this academic year	_____	_____	_____ (3:57)
Number of advanced undergraduate courses	_____	_____	_____ (3:58)
Number of graduate courses	_____	_____	_____ (3:59)

THANK YOU. PLEASE RETURN IN THE ENVELOPE PROVIDED.

Students Only

STUDENT RACIAL CLIMATE

Institutions vary considerably in the way different races relate to each other. Usually there is a "climate" or "campus atmosphere" which can often be described along several scales. Please circle the one number for each of the following scales which best characterizes this racial climate at your campus. (Interpret the scale as 1 = very relaxed; 5 = very tense; 3 = neutral)

Relaxed	1	2	3	4	5	Tense	(1:37)
Friendly	1	2	3	4	5	Hostile	(1:38)
Cooperative	1	2	3	4	5	Competitive	(1:39)
Socially integrated	1	2	3	4	5	Socially separated	(1:40)
Communicative	1	2	3	4	5	Reserved	(1:41)
Concerned	1	2	3	4	5	Indifferent	(1:42)
Guarded	1	2	3	4	5	Open	(1:43)
Respectful	1	2	3	4	5	Disrespectful	(1:44)
Optimistic	1	2	3	4	5	Pessimistic	(1:45)

Students Only

INSTITUTIONAL ATTRACTIVENESS FOR BLACK STUDENTS

The enrollment of Black students at this institution has been increasing. In your opinion, how significant are each of the factors listed below in attracting Black students?

BLACK STUDENTS: Rate the significance of these factors for your being attracted to this institution.

OTHER STUDENTS: Rate how significant you think these are for Black students at this institution. (Check one response for each item):

	OF NO SIGNIFICANCE 1	SLIGHT 2	SOME 3	SUBSTANTIAL 4	OF VERY GREAT SIGNIFICANCE 5	
1. Black or minority recruitment and admission program	☐	☐	☐	☐	☐	(1:25)
2. Presence of Black faculty and/or active, visible Black students on campus	☐	☐	☐	☐	☐	(1:26)
3. Location in an urban area or presence of nearby Black communities	☐	☐	☐	☐	☐	(1:27)
4. Availability of Black social life and cultural activities oriented to Black people on campus	☐	☐	☐	☐	☐	(1:28)
5. Acquaintance with students who attended the institution or its reputation among Blacks	☐	☐	☐	☐	☐	(1:29)
6. Availability of financial support	☐	☐	☐	☐	☐	(1:30)
7. Desire to be near home or live at home	☐	☐	☐	☐	☐	(1:31)
8. Opportunity to participate in intramural or inter-collegiate athletics	☐	☐	☐	☐	☐	(1:32)
9. Good academic reputation of institution	☐	☐	☐	☐	☐	(1:33)
10. Availability of a good program in preferred major	☐	☐	☐	☐	☐	(1:34)
11. Desire to be away from home	☐	☐	☐	☐	☐	(1:35)
12. Existence of Black or ethnic studies program	☐	☐	☐	☐	☐	(1:36)

Students Only

BLACK STUDENTS' NEEDS OR CONCERNS

The following items have often been identified as needs and concerns of Black students on many campuses. To what extent do these represent *important* needs or concerns of Black students at your institution? (Check one response for each item.)

	NO IMPORTANCE (1)	SLIGHT IMPORTANCE (2)	SOME IMPORTANCE (3)	OF GREAT IMPORTANCE (4)	
1. Increased financial aid	☐	☐	☐	☐	(2:26)
2. More Black oriented cultural events and activities. .	☐	☐	☐	☐	(2:27)
3. Additional Black faculty and administrators.	☐	☐	☐	☐	(2:28)
4. Improved academic support services and remedial coursework.	☐	☐	☐	☐	(2:29)
5. Additional Black or racial minority oriented, extra-curricular organizations.	☐	☐	☐	☐	(2:30)
6. More minority housing options (e.g., a Black dorm, house, or other residence arrangements)	☐	☐	☐	☐	(2:31)
7. Opportunities to render service to Black communities. .	☐	☐	☐	☐	(2:32)
8. Facilities for Black or minority recreational, cultural and social meetings or activities.	☐	☐	☐	☐	(2:33)
9. Improved faculty contact and support.	☐	☐	☐	☐	(2:34)
10. More Black or other ethnic courses and programs (e.g., Black History, Black literature).	☐	☐	☐	☐	(2:35)
11. A more favorable racial climate on campus.	☐	☐	☐	☐	(2:36)
12. Additional minority oriented counseling and advising. .	☐	☐	☐	☐	(2:37)
13. A more favorable racial climate in the area surrounding the institution.	☐	☐	☐	☐	(2:38)
14. Opportunities to recruit other Black students	☐	☐	☐	☐	(2:39)
15. Additional Black clerical and non-professional staff. .	☐	☐	☐	☐	(2:40)
16. Increased racial sensitivity by all clerical personnel.	☐	☐	☐	☐	(2:41)

Students Only

IMPACTS ON STUDENT LIFE

1. In each of the following areas, to what extent are there important problems or issues in Black/White student relationships on your campus? (Check one response for each item):

Rate the *importance of problems* in each area:

	NOT A PROBLEM (1)	SLIGHT (2)	SOME (3)	SUBSTANTIAL (4)	A CRUCIAL PROBLEM (5)	
a. Representation of Blacks in student government organizations	☐	☐	☐	☐	☐	(2:49)
b. Relationship of Black and White student leaders . .	☐	☐	☐	☐	☐	(2:50)
c. Allocation of funds to Black student organizations. .	☐	☐	☐	☐	☐	(2:51)
d. Room assignments and selection by race.	☐	☐	☐	☐	☐	(2:52)
e. Tension in living arrangements	☐	☐	☐	☐	☐	(2:53)
f. Separate seating patterns in dining facilities. . . .	☐	☐	☐	☐	☐	(2:54)
g. Interracial dating and friendships	☐	☐	☐	☐	☐	(2:55)
h. White participation in Black oriented events	☐	☐	☐	☐	☐	(2:56)
i. Conflicts over areas for socializing.	☐	☐	☐	☐	☐	(2:57)
j. Concern about differential allocations in financial aid	☐	☐	☐	☐	☐	(2:58)
k. Black participation in all-campus events	☐	☐	☐	☐	☐	(2:59)
l. Concern about differential access to graduate and professional school.	☐	☐	☐	☐	☐	(2:60)
m. Concerns about job discrimination	☐	☐	☐	☐	☐	(2:61)
n. Amount of Black content in class discussions and reading assignments.	☐	☐	☐	☐	☐	(2:62)
o. Racial insensitivity and intolerance in the classroom by students of the opposite race.	☐	☐	☐	☐	☐	(2:63)

2. Think of your three best friends currently. Please, identify each friend on the following four characteristics. (Check one for each item):

Friend #1 a. ___ (1) Male or ___ (2) Female (2:64)

b. ___ (1) Black ___ (2) White ___ (3) Other (2:65)

c. ___ (1) Student here ___ (2) Not student here (2:66)

d. If student here: ___ (1) Fr. ___ (2) So. ___ (3) Jr. ___ (4) Sr. (2:67)

Friend #2 a. ___ (1) Male ___ (2) Female (2:68)

b. ___ (1) Black ___ (2) White ___ (3) Other (2:69)

c. ___ (1) Student here ___ (2) Not student here (2:70)

d. If student here: ___ (1) Fr. ___ (2) So. ___ (3) Jr. ___ (4) Sr. (2:71)

Friend #3 a. ___ (1) Male ___ (2) Female (3:15)

b. ___ (1) Black ___ (2) White ___ (3) Other (3:16)

c. ___ (1) Student here: ___ (2) Not student here (3:17)

d. If student here: ___ (1) Fr. ___ (2) So. ___ (3) Jr. ___ (4) Sr. (3:18)

3. We are interested in the ways in which your ideas have changed about race and race relations since attending college. Which of the following best describe what has happened to you?

a. My feelings are (circle one):

1	2	3	4	5	
Much more antagonistic to people of other races	Somewhat more antagonistic	Not changed	Somewhat friendlier	Friendlier toward people of other races	(3:19)

b. My attitudes about racial separatism and integration reflect (circle one):

1	2	3	4	5	
Much stronger belief in separatism	Somewhat stronger belief in separatism	No change	Somewhat stronger belief in integration	Much stronger belief in integration	(3:20)

4. Various majors in the area of Arts and Sciences at any institution differ on how demanding and competitive they are. From your own experience and from what you hear from friends, which majors have the reputation of being:

a. The toughest or most demanding?

1) _____ (3:21)

2) _____ (3:22)

3 _____ (3:23)

b. The easiest or least demanding?

1) _____ (3:24)

2) _____ (3:25)

3) _____ (3:26)

5. Departments have another kind of reputation as well. Some are helpful and supportive of students; others are thought to be indifferent and unsupportive. From your own experience and from what you hear from your friends which departments have the reputation as:

a. The most helpful and supportive?

1) _____ (3:27)

2) _____ (3:28)

3) _____ (3:29)

b. The most indifferent and unsupportive?

1) _____ (3:30)

2) _____ (3:31)

3) _____ (3:32)

Students Only

FACULTY AND CLASSROOM BEHAVIOR

In your classroom activities and academic endeavors, do faculty treat Black students differently than other students? Indicate whether faculty use the following more or less frequently with Black students. (Check one box for each item):

	SELDOM OR NEVER WITH ANY STUDENTS	LESS WITH BLACKS THAN WITH OTHER STUDENTS	SAME WITH ALL STUDENTS	SOMEWHAT MORE WITH BLACKS THAN OTHER STUDENTS	MUCH MORE WITH BLACKS THAN OTHER STUDENTS	
1. Extend deadlines	☐	☐	☐	☐	☐	(3:33)
2. Provide individual academic help	☐	☐	☐	☐	☐	(3:34)
3. Refer students to counseling or tutorial services	☐	☐	☐	☐	☐	(3:35)
4. Accept suggestions for changes in course content or teaching style	☐	☐	☐	☐	☐	(3:36)
5. Treat students indifferently	☐	☐	☐	☐	☐	(3:37)
6. Use objective exams and evaluations	☐	☐	☐	☐	☐	(3:38)
7. Use subjective evaluations	☐	☐	☐	☐	☐	(3:39)
8. Take personal interest in individuals	☐	☐	☐	☐	☐	(3:40)

Students Only

PERSONAL INFORMATION ON STUDENTS

1. Age: _____ (3:41)

2. Sex: _____ (1) Male _____ (2) Female (3:42)

3. Major field: _____ (3:43)

4. Marital Status: _____ (1) Married _____ (2) Single (3:44)

5. Racial origin or ethnic group: (3:45)
   _____ (1) Black or Afro-American
   _____ (2) White or Caucasian
   _____ (3) Spanish Origin (Chicano, Mexican American, Puerto Rican, other Hispanic group)
   _____ (4) Oriental
   _____ (5) Native American
   _____ (6) Other (describe)

6. Citizenship Status: _____ (1) U. S. _____ (2) Other (3:46)

7. Are you considered a full-time student: _____ (1) Yes _____ (2) No (3:47)

8. Are you from: _____ (1) In-state _____ (2) Out of state (3:48)

9. Check one of the following characteristics which best describe the place where you lived most of your life. (Estimate population as accurately as possible.) (3:49)
   _____ (1) Suburb of a metropolitan area
   _____ (2) In a city of about one million or more
   _____ (3) In a city (not a suburb) of 50,000-1,000,000 population
   _____ (4) In a city or town of 10,000 to 50,000
   _____ (5) In a town of less than 10,000
   _____ (6) Ranch or rural area

10. What is your class standing? (3:50)
   _____ (1) Freshman
   _____ (2) Sophomore
   _____ (3) Junior
   _____ (4) Senior
   _____ (5) Graduate

11. What is the highest degree you plan to receive? (3:51)
   _____ (1) B.A. or B.S.
   _____ (2) M.A. or M.S.
   _____ (3) Specialist
   _____ (4) Professional
   _____ (5) Ph.D or Ed. D.
   _____ (6) Other: (Specify)

Students Only

12. Approximately how many hours per week are you spending in paid employment during this year in college?

   (1) None
   (2) Less than 11 hours a week
   (3) 11-20 hours
   (4) 21-30 hours
   (5) More than 30 hours a week   (3:52)

13. Please indicate your involvement in the following Black oriented activities. Check as many as are appropriate:

   (1) Black tudent Association or Union   (3:53)
   (1) Tutorial work with Black students (as a tutor)   (3:54)
   (1) Black-consciousness or Black Studies course (e.g., Black History, Afro-American History, etc.)   (3:55)
   (1) Tutorial work helping young Black children   (3:56)
   (1) Other cultural or political organizations focusing on Black people   (3:57)
   (1) Other: (Specify)   (3:58)

14. Are you a member of a Greek social organization: ___ (1) Yes ___ (2) No   (3:59)

If yes, is it predominantly: ___ (1) White ___ (2) Black ___ (3) Both   (3:60)

15. Have you received any financial aid from your university? ___ (1) yes   (3:61)
   ___ (2) no

Specify the type(s): (E.g., NDSL, Work-Study, Grant, Scholarships, etc.)

_____

_____

_____   (3:62)

16. Where do you live while attending college?

   (1) In the dorm
   (2) Off-campus
   (3) At home with parents   (3:63)

17. From what type of high school or secondary school did you graduate?

   (1) Public high school
   (2) Private, religious high school
   (3) Other private, non-religious high school   (3:64)

18. How would you describe the neighborhood in which you lived during high school?

   (1) Completely Black neighborhood
   (2) Mostly Black neighborhood
   (3) An equally integrated neighborhood
   (4) Mostly White neighborhood
   (5) Completely White neighborhood   (3:65)

Students Only

19. To what extent was your high school integrated?

   (1) Almost entirely White
   (2) Integrated but mostly White
   (3) Integrated about equally
   (4) Integrated, but mostly Black
   (5) Almost entirely Black   (3:66)

20. How much schooling have your parents had? (Check one for each parent):

	Father	Mother
Completed grade school or less	(1) ___	
Some high school	(2) ___	
Completed high school	(3) ___	Father (3:67)
Some college	(4) ___	
Completed College	(5) ___	Mother (3:68)
Graduate or professional school	(6) ___	
Don't know, or does not apply	(7) ___	

21. Do any of the following come reasonably close to describing your father's and mother's occupation presently?

(Check one for each parent):

	Father	Mother
(1) Blue collar	___	
(2) White collar	___	Father (3:69)
(3) Professional or managerial	___	
(4) Unemployed	___	Mother (3:70)
(5) Don't know	___	

22. What is your cumulative grade point average in college _____?   (3:71)

23. How certain are you about your average?

   (1) I am quite certain
   (2) I know it approximately
   (3) I am mostly guessing   (3:72)

THANK YOU! PLEASE RETURN IN ENVELOPE PROVIDED.

Appendix D

Survey Populations, Samples, and Institutional Response Rates (Stage II)

The study and the Stage II institutional survey focused on the entry of black undergraduate students—primarily those enrolled in the arts and sciences college or related programs. This focus constrained to some degree the population of respondents which we chose to survey. The population and sampling procedure were as follows:

Administrators

Questionnaires were distributed by campus mail to all executive officers (vice presidents and above), all deans or directors reporting directly to them, all administrative officers reporting directly to the Dean of Arts and Sciences (or equivalent title), the directors and professional staff of black or minority programs, and racial minority persons in professional administrative positions identified by the institution. One phone call and one mail follow up were sent.

Faculty

Questionnaires were distributed by campus mail to all full-time faculty members at the instructor, and assistant, associate, or full professor ranks who held appointments in the Arts and Sciences College. Since nine departments were targeted for analysis in our larger study, members of those departments received phone call reminders, which accounts for their higher response rate. All faculty members received a mail follow up.

Students

Questionnaires were distributed by U.S. mails to all black students and an equal size random sample of non-black students enrolled in the undergraduate Arts and Sciences College. Phone call reminders were made to all students receiving the questionnaire.

TABLE D-1

Response Rates by Institution and Respondent Group

Institution and Respondent Group	Adjusted Sample (N)	Usable Returns(N)	Percentage Usable Returns
University of Missouri–Kansas City			
Administrators	60	36	60.0
Arts and Science Faculty	217	102	47.0
Faculty in Nine Focal Departments	135	77	57.0
Undergraduate Arts and Sciences Students*	454	99	21.8
Black Students†	225	34	15.1
White Students†	200	55	27.5
All Respondents	731	237	32.4
"Metropolitan University"			
Administrators	34	21	61.8
Arts and Science Faculty	194	100	51.5
Faculty in Nine Focal Departments	93	58	62.4
Undergraduate Arts and Sciences Students*	476	137	28.8
Black Students†	220	57	25.9
White Students†	225	68	30.2
All Respondents	704	258	36.6
"State University"			
Administrators	61	49	80.4
Arts and Science Faculty	595	229	38.5
Faculty in Nine Focal Departments	223	122	54.7
Undergraduate Arts and Sciences Students*	707	218	30.8
Black Students†	220	59	26.8
White Students†	380	128	33.7
All Respondents	1,363	496	36.4
SUNY-Brockport			
Administrators	46	35	76.1
Arts and Sciences Faculty	559	240	42.9

TABLE D-1 continued

Institution and Respondent Group	Adjusted Sample (N)	Usable Returns(N)	Percentage Usable Returns
Faculty in Nine Focal Departments	216	106	49.1
Undergraduate Arts and Sciences Students*	750	141	18.8
Black Students†	294	31	10.5
White Students†	395	90	22.8
All Respondents	1,355	416	30.7
TOTAL			
Administrators	201	141	70.1
Arts and Science Faculty	1,565	671	42.9
Faculty in Nine Focal Departments	667	363	54.4
Undergraduate Arts and Sciences Students*	2,387	595	24.9
Black Students†	959	181	18.9
White Students†	1,200	341	28.4
All Respondents	4,153	1,407	33.9

†Black and White Students do not add to total, which includes "other" minority respondents. Estimates, plus or minus 5.

TABLE D-2

Response Rate by Institution and Faculty in Nine Focal Departments

Institution and Department	Adjusted Sample (N)	Usable Returns (N)	Percentage Usable Returns
University of Missouri–Kansas City			
English	17	10	58.8
History	15	9	60.0
Biology	16	12	75.0
Chemistry	16	8	50.0
Mathematics	20	6	30.0
Economics	8	5	62.5
Political Science	9	6	66.7
Psychology	21	14	66.7
Sociology	13	7	53.8
All Focal Departments	135	77	57.0
"Metropolitan University"			
English	15	11	73.3
History	13	5	38.5
Biology	9	5	55.6
Chemistry	10	7	70.0
Mathematics	9	6	66.7
Economics	7	3	42.9
Political Science	6	4	66.7
Psychology	16	12	75.0
Sociology	8	5	62.5
All Focal Departments	93	58	62.4
"State University"			
English	48	24	50.0
History	21	12	57.1
Biology*	18	10	55.6
Chemistry	21	11	52.4

TABLE D-2 continued

Institution and Department	Adjusted Sample (N)	Usable Returns (N)	Percentage Usable Returns
Mathematics	31	15	48.4
Economics	19	6	31.6
Political Science	19	15	78.9
Psychology	27	16	59.3
Sociology	19	13	68.4
All Focal Departments	223	122	54.7
SUNY-Brockport			
English	35	16	45.7
History	28	16	57.1
Biology	27	17	63.0
Chemistry	12	7	58.3
Mathematics	20	8	40.0
Economics	25	10	40.0
Political Science	25	10	40.0
Psychology	26	15	57.7
Sociology	18	7	38.9
All Focal Departments	216	106	49.1
TOTAL			
English	115	61	53.0
History	77	42	54.5
Biology	70	44	62.9
Chemistry	59	33	55.9
Mathematics	80	35	43.8
Economics	59	24	40.7
Political Science	59	35	59.3
Psychology	90	57	63.3
Sociology	58	32	55.2
All Focal Departments	667	363	54.4

*Institution has departments of Zoology (included here as a focal department) and Botany (not included as a focal department).

Appendix E

Factor Analysis of Indices for the Three Respondent Groups

Data reduction was accomplished by utilizing factor analysis and employing a pairwise varimax solution with normalized loadings. Within each major section of the questionnaire, a factor analysis was performed for each of the respondent groups and for certain combinations. The following table identifies the name of each factor-derived index by section of the questionnaire and the respondent group employed in the factor analysis. Individual items included in each factor index are also shown with a key to the questionnaire and the loading of the item on the factor. Items loadings were cross-checked against the correlation matrix of the items. A minimum factor loading of .40 was required for inclusion of an item in a factor; however, some items were excluded on conceptual grounds. Appropriate respondent groups were selected on the basis of several criteria. For example, common attitude indices were selected for faculty and administrators for comparative purposes even though the two groups occasionally showed somewhat different results on separate factor analyses. In the case of black student needs/concerns, black students alone rather than all students were selected as the appropriate respondent group.

TABLE E-1

Factor Analysis of Indices for the Three Respondent Groups

Index* (High = Direction; Scale)	Questionnaire Items Comprising Index†	Respondent Group‡	Factor Loading
Role of Racial Minorities in Colleges			
and Universities			
Universal-Particular Standards	1	AF	.66
(H = Universal; 0–9)	2		−.61
	11		−.58
Long-Term Minority Impact	4	F	.76
(H = Positive; 0–9)	5		−.46
	16		.44
Institutional Separation-Integration	6	F	−.56
(H = Integration; 0–9)	8		.61
	17		−.41
Institutional Goals for Blacks and			
Racial Minorities			
Institutional Black Priority	1	AF	.71
(H = Important; 0–32)	2		.75
	3		.58
	4		.50
	5		.48
	6		.78
	7		.69
	10		.46
Non-Academic Support	1	AF	.71
(H = Important; 0–16)	2		.75
	6		.78
	7		.69
Affirmative Action	4	AF	.58
(H = Important; 0–8)	5		.48
Integrating Concern for Blacks	5	AF	.58
(H = Important; 0–12)	8		.74
Institutional	9		.68
Racial Climate			
Black-White Trust	1a	ALL	.59
(H = Trust; 0–12)	1b		.81
	1c		.68
Openness and Inclusiveness	3	ALL	.44
(H = Open; 0–12)	8		.64
	10		.54
Administrative, Faculty, Staff	5	ALL	.57
Interaction	6		.69
(H = Positive; 0–8)			
Black Visibility and Influence	11a	ALL	.53
(H = Visible; 0–12)	11b		.78
	11c		.83
Institutional Responsiveness:			
Willingness	1a	ALL	.67
(H = Willing; 0–20)	1b		.52
	1c		.70
	1d		.65
	1e		.72

TABLE E-1 continued

Index* (High = Direction; Scale)	Questionnaire Items Comprising Index†	Respondent Group‡	Factor Loading
Adequacy	2a	ALL	.60
(H = Adequate; 0–20)	2b		.52
	2c		.79
	2d		.77
	2e		.67
White Commitment to Blacks	3a	ALL	.72
(H = Active Support; 0–32)	3b		.80
	3c		.86
	3d		.68
	3e		.84
	3f		.66
	3h		.70
	3i		.56
Administrative Commitment	3a	ALL	.72
(H = Active Support; 0–16)	3b		.80
	3c		.86
	3d		.68
Faculty Commitment	3e	ALL	.84
(H = Active Support; 0–12)	3g		.42
	3h		.70
Student Commitment	3f	ALL	.66
(H = Active Support; 0–8)	3i		.56
Black Commitment	3g	ALL	.40
(H = Active Support; 0–8)	3j		.80
Institutional Impacts and Responses			
Black Influence Exertion	1a	AF	.51
(H = A Great Deal; 0–24)	1b		.70
	1c		.82
	1d		.78
	1e		.79
	1f		.52
Total Black Influence	2a	AF	.67
(H = A Great Deal; 0–16)	2b		.82
	2c		.72
	2d		.72
Authoritarian Treatment	4a	AF	.76
(H = Authoritarian; 0–12)	4b		.69
	4e		.71
Future Institutional Commitments			
Future Commitment	1a	ALL	−.76
(H = Reduced; 0–20)	1b		−.74
	1c		−.63
	1d		−.74
	1e		−.70
Impacts and Responses in Administrative Areas			
Black and Minority Enrollment Impact	2a	A	.74
(H = A Great Deal; 0–8)	2d		.89

TABLE E-1 continued

Index* (High = Direction; Scale)	Questionnaire Items Comprising Index†	Respondent Group‡	Factor Loading
Black Staff and Program Impact	2b	A	.67
(H = A Great Deal; 0–24)	2c		.77
	2e		.67
	2f		.69
	2g		.57
	2h		.53
Intensity of Black Issues	6a	A	.79
(H = Intense; 0–8)	6d		.65
Antagonistic-Supportive Treatment	6b	A	.75
(H = Supportive; 0–12)	6c		.64
	6f		.78
Positive-Negative Relationships	7a	A	.76
(H = Positive; 0–28)	7b		.79
	7c		.70
	7d		.85
	7e		.75
	7f		.81
	7g		.64
Situational Role Constraints	8d	A	.51
(H = Increased; 0–8)	8g		.63
Personal Openness	8b	A	.74
(H = Increased; 0–24)	8c		.63
	8e		.58
	8f		.65
	8h		.70
	8j		.66
Impacts and Responses in Faculty *and Departmental Activity*			
Help and Accommodation	1a	F	.52
(H = Helpful; 0–20)	1b		.64
	1e		.57
	1f		.65
	1g		.61
Subjective Evaluation	2l	F	.67
(H = Subjective; 0–8)	2m		.72
Objective Evaluation	2j	F	.62
(H = Objective; 0–8)	2k		.77
Time Demand	3a	F	.62
(H = Increased; 0–16)	3b		−.51
	3c		.76
	3d		.55
Black Course Content	3e	F	.77
(H = Increased; 0–8)	3f		.81
Personal Interaction	4a	F	.48
(H = More; 0–16)	4b		.64
	4d		.57
	4e		.62

TABLE E-1 continued

Index* (High = Direction; Scale)	Questionnaire Items Comprising Index†	Respondent Group‡	Factor Loading
Style and content	4h	F	.84
(H = More; 0–8)	4i		.85
Black Student Influence	6a	F	.72
(H = A Great Deal; 0–8)	6b		.64
Black Faculty and Staff Influence	6c	F	.47
(H = A Great Deal; 0–8)	6d		.40
Faculty and Administrative Influence	6e	F	.68
(H = A Great Deal; 0–8)	6f		.84
Departmental Black Concern	9a	F	.68
(H = Concern; 0–6)	9b		.71
Departmental External Orientation	9g	F	.42
(H = External; 0–6)	9h		.69
Institutional Attractiveness for Blacks			
Black Visibility	1	S	.54
(H = Significant; 0–20)	2		.77
	4		.81
	5		.60
	12		.76
Location	3	S	.65
(H = Significant; 0–8)	7		.59
Academic Reputation	9	S	.79
(H = Significant; 0–8)	10		.83
Student Racial Climate			
Tension-Hostility	1	S	.72
(H = Tense, Hostile; 0–24)	2		.78
	3		.67
	4		.63
	8		.74
	9		.77
Indifference	5	S	.73
(H = Indifferent; 0–8)	6		.63
	7		−.34
Black Students Needs or Concerns			
Institutional Support	1	Black	.75
(H = Important; 0–9)	3	Students	.49
	9		.44
Black Extracurricular	2	Black	.77
(H = Important; 0–6)	5	Students	.67
Minority Support Services	4	All	.49
(H = Important; 0–12)	6	Students	.75
	12		.54
	15		.42
Black Identity Expression	7	Black	.50
(H = Important; 0–12)	8	Students	.50
	10		.62
	14		.65

TABLE E-1 continued

Index* (High = Direction; Scale)	Questionnaire Items Comprising Index†	Respondent Group‡	Factor Loading
Supportive Racial Climate	11	Black	.72
(H = Important; 0–9)	13	Students	.66
	16		.47
Impacts on Student Life			
Student Government	1a	S	.78
(H = Problem Area; 0–12)	1b		.73
	1c		.67
Dormitory Life	1d	S	.70
(H = Problem Area; 0–8)	1e		.78
Student Separation-Integration	1f	S	.45
(H = Problem Area; 0–20)	1g		.53
	1h		.55
	1i		.58
	1k		.48
Career Access	1l	S	.80
(H = Problem area; 0–8)	1m		.73
Classroom Comfort	1n	S	.46
(H = Problem area; 0–8)	1o		.36
Faculty and Classroom Behavior			
Personal Concern	1	S	.46
(H = Concerned; 0–16)	2		.68
	4		.54
	8		.70
Indifference	5	S	.75
(H = Indifferent; 0–8)	7		.42

*See Table 12-1 for description of each index used in this book.

†Numbers refer to question number in section of questionnaire for respondent group (App. C).

‡Respondent groups included in factor analysis on which index was constructed: A = Administrator; F = Faculty; S = Student; AF = Administrator and Faculty Combined; ALL = all respondents (A, F, and S).

§Adjustments for negative factor loadings were made in creating additive indices.

Appendix F

Factor Analysis of Indices and Other Interesting Items for Faculty and Administrators Combined

Index	Factors* 1	2	3	4	5
Role of Racial Minorities in Colleges and Universities					
Universal–Particular Standards (H = Universal)					−.50
Long-Term Minority Impact (H = Positive)					.55
Institutional Pluralism– Integration (H = Integration)					−.47
Institutional Goals for Blacks and Racial Minorities					
Institutional Black Priority (H = Important)	−.94				
Non-Academic Support (H = Important)	−.83				
Affirmative Action (H = Important)	−.85				
Integrating Concern for Blacks (H = Important)	−.73				
Institutional Racial Climate					
Black/White Trust (H = Trust)				.77	
Openness and Inclusiveness (H = Open)			.65		
Administration, Faculty, Staff Interaction (H = Positive)			.57		
Black Visibility and Influence (H = Visible)			.75		
Institutional Responsiveness					
Willingness (H = Willing)		.48	.40		

Index	1	2	Factors* 3	4	5
Adequacy (H = Adequate)			.47		−.42
White Commitment to Blacks (H = Active Support)		.87			
Administrative Commitment (H = Active Support)		.79			
Faculty Commitment (H = Active Support)		.86			
Student Commitment (H = Active Support)		.75			
Black Commitment (H = Active Support)		.73			
Institutional Impacts					
Black Influence Exertion (H = Great Deal)			.70		
Total Black Influence (H = Great Deal)			.78		
Authoritarian Treatment (H = Authoritarian)					
Future Institutional Commitments					
Future Commitment (H = Reduced)					
Other Interesting Items					
Black Trust of Other Minorities				.52	
Campus Racial Conflict				−.49	
Black Activism			.49		
Pluralism or Separatism			.42		
Black Student Diversity					
Student Interracial Patterns			.45		
Black Representation			.48		

*Description of factors:
 Factor #1 Breadth of Goals for Blacks (Institutional Ideology)
 Factor #2 Willingness and Commitment (Intent)
 Factor #3 Racial Climate and Activity (Perceived Behavior)
 Factor #4 Interracial Trust/Conflict (Psychological Feeling)
 Factor #5 Pluralism–Integration (Belief System)
Criteria for inclusion on a factor after varimax rotated solution:
 (1) heaviest loading of item on factor and
 (2) loading .40 or over.

Appendix G

Mean Scores on Indices for Faculty and Administrators

Index	Administrators	Faculty	F Score	p (<)
Role of Racial Minorities in				
Colleges and Universities				
Particular-Universal Standards				
(H = Universal; 0–9)	4.25	4.72	6.03	.01
Long-Term Minority Impact				
(H = Positive; 0–9)	6.51	5.93	14.48	.02
Institutional Pluralism–				
Integration (H = Integration; 0–9)	4.95	5.21	2.87	.09
Institutional Goals for Blacks				
and Racial Minorities				
Institutional Black Priority				
(H = Important; 0–32)	20.19	18.07	16.01	.00
Non-Academic Support				
(H = Important; 0–16)	10.65	9.66	12.62	.00
Affirmative Action				
(H = Important; 0–8)	4.98	4.28	15.74	.00
Integrating Concern for				
Blacks (H = Important; 0–12)	6.70	5.55	24.97	.00
Institutional Racial Climate				
Black/White Trust (H = Trust; 0–12)	5.92	5.95	.02	.88
Openness and Inclusiveness				
(H = Open; 0–12)	6.34	5.97	3.08	.08
Administrative, Faculty, Staff				
Interaction (H = Positive; 0–8)	4.16	4.06	.33	.56
Black Visibility and				
Influence (H = Visible; 0–12)	5.21	4.92	1.63	.20
Institutional Responsiveness				
Willingness (H = Willing; 0–20)	15.99	15.61	1.23	.27
Adequacy (H = Adequate; 0–20)	9.66	10.50	4.72	.03
White Commitment to Blacks				
(H = Active Support; 0–32)	23.40	22.79	1.40	.24

Index	Administrators	Faculty	F Score	p (<)
Administrative Commitment				
(H = Active Support; 0–16)	12.70	12.06	4.86	.03
Faculty Commitment				
(H = Active Support; 0–12)	9.05	8.90	.57	.45
Student Commitment				
(H = Active Support; 0–8)	5.33	5.21	.63	.43
Black Commitment				
(H = Active Support; 0–8)	7.04	6.58	11.25	.00
Institutional Impacts				
Black Influence Exertion				
(H = Great Deal; 0–24)	10.15	9.56	2.49	.12
Total Black Influence				
(H = Great Deal; 0–16)	7.83	7.21	6.11	.01
Authoritarian Treatment				
(H = Authoritarian; 0–12)	8.24	7.31	27.12	.00
Future Institutional				
Commitments				
Future Commitment				
(H = Reduced; 0–20)	8.89	9.07	.37	.54
Impacts and Responses in				
Administrative Areas				
Black and Minority Enrollment				
Impact (H = Great Deal; 0–8)	2.54			
Black Staff and Program				
Impact (H = Great Deal; 0–24)	6.65			
Intensity of Black Issues				
(H = Intense; 0–8)	3.96			
Antagonistic–Supportive				
Treatment (H = Supportive; 0–12)	7.82			
Positive–Negative Relationships				
(H = Positive; 0–28)	19.39			
Situational Role Constraints				
(H = Constrained; 0–8)	4.82			
Personal Openness (H = Open; 0–24)	15.48			
Impacts and Responses in Faculty				
and Departmental Activity				
Help and Accomodation				
(H = Helpful; 0–20)		11.40		
Subjective Evaluation				
(H = Increased; 0–8)		4.18		
Objective Evaluation				
(H = Increased; 0–8)		4.03		
Time Demand				
(H = Decreased; 0–12)		14.81		
Black Course Impact				
(H = Increased; 0–8)		4.53		
Personal Interaction				
(H = More; 0–16)		7.09		
Style and Content				
(H = More; 0–8)		3.69		

Index	Administrators	Faculty	F Score	p (<)
Black Student Influence (H = Increased; 0–8)		3.92		
Black Faculty and Staff (H = Increased; 0–8)		3.44		
Faculty and Administrative Influence (H = Increased; 0–8)		3.35		
Departmental Black Concern (H = Concern; 0–6)		2.72		
Departmental External Orientation (H = External; 0–6)		3.72		

Administrators, N = 141
Faculty, N = 671
Total, N = 812

BIBLIOGRAPHY

Academy for Educational Development. *Black Studies: How It Works at Ten Universities.* New York: Academy for Educational Development, 1971.

Allen, Robert L. "Politics of the Attack on Black Studies." *The Black Scholar—Journal of Black Studies and Research* 6 (September 1974): 2–7.

Andrews, Frank M.; Morgan, James N.; and Sonquist, John A. *Multiple Classification Analysis.* Ann Arbor: Institute for Social Research, The University of Michigan, 1967.

Andrulis, Dennis P.; Iscoe, Ira; Sikes, Melvin P.; and Friedman, Thomas. "Black Professionals in Predominantly White Institutions of Higher Education—An Examination of Some Demographic and Mobility Characteristics." *Journal of Negro Education* 44 (Winter 1975): 6–11.

Antonovsky, Aaron. "Aspirations, Class, and Racial-Ethnic Membership." *Journal of Negro Education* 36 (1967): 385–393.

Arce, Carlos H. "Historical, Institutional, and Contextual Determinants of Black Enrollment in Predominantly White Colleges and Universities, 1946 to 1974." Ph.D. dissertation, The University of Michigan, 1976.

Astin, Alexander W. "Racial Considerations in Admissions." *The Campus and the Racial Crisis.* Background paper for participants in the 52nd annual meeting of the American Council on Education. Washington, D.C.: American Council on Education, 1969.

———; Astin, Helen S.; Boyle, Alan E.; and Bisconti, Ann S. *The Power of Protest: A National Study of Student and Faculty Disruptions with Implications for the Future.* San Francisco: Jossey-Bass, 1975.

Atkinson, Carolyn O.; Etzioni, Amitai; and Inker, Irene. *Post-Secondary Education and the Disadvantaged Student: A Policy Study.* New York: Center for Policy Research, 1969.

Bayer, Alan E., and Boruch, Robert F. "Black and White Freshmen Entering Four-Year Colleges." *Educational Record* 50 (Fall 1969): 371–386. (a)

———, and Boruch, Robert F. "The Black Student in American Colleges." *ACE Research Reports* 4 (1969). (b)

Blackburn, Robert T. *Tenure: Aspects of Job Security on the Changing Cam-*

377

pus. Research Monograph No. 19. Atlanta, Ga.: Southern Regional Education Board, 1972.

————; Armstrong, Ellen; Conrad, Clifton; Dinham, James; and McKane, Thomas. *Changing Practices in Undergraduate Education.* Berkeley: Carnegie Council on Policy Studies in Higher Education, 1976.

Blassingame, John W. *New Perspectives on Black Studies.* Urbana: University of Illinois Press, 1973.

Blauner, Robert. *Racial Oppression in America.* New York: Harper and Row, 1972.

Bowles, Frank, and DeCosta, Frank A. *Between Two Worlds.* New York: McGraw-Hill, 1971.

Boyd, William M. *Desegregating America's Colleges: A Nationwide Survey of Black Students, 1972–73.* New York: Praeger, 1974.

Bradshaw, Ted K. "The Impact of Peers on Student Orientation to College: A Contextual Analysis." In *Teachers and Students,* edited by Martin Trow. New York: McGraw-Hill, 1975.

Brick, Michael, and McGrath, Earl J. *Innovation in Liberal Arts Colleges.* New York: Teachers College Press, 1969.

Brooks, Glenwood C., and Sedlacek, William E. "The Black Student on the White Campus: A Summary of Relevant Research." *American College Personnel Association Newsletter,* June 1973.

Brubacher, John S., and Rudy, Willis. *Higher Education in Transition.* New York: Harper and Row, 1968.

Campbell, Angus. *White Attitudes Toward Black People.* Ann Arbor: Institute for Social Research, The University of Michigan, 1971.

————, and Schuman, Howard. *Racial Attitudes in 15 American Cities.* Ann Arbor: Institute for Social Research, The University of Michigan, 1968.

Caplan, Nathan S., and Paige, Jeffrey M. "A Study of Ghetto Rioters." *Scientific American* 219 (1968): 15–21.

Carmichael, Stokely, and Hamilton, Charles V. *Black Power.* New York: Random House, 1967.

Cartey, Wilfred, and Morrison, Anne. "Compensatory Education Programs in Higher Education: A Nationwide Survey." *Research in Education,* 1970.

Catlin, Jamie B. "The Impact of Interracial Living on White College Students' Racial Attitudes, Values, and Intergroup Relations." Ph.D. dissertation, The University of Michigan, 1977.

————; Seeley, Joan A.; and Talburtt, Margaret A. *Affirmative Action: Its Legal Mandate and Organizational Implications.* Ann Arbor: Center for the Study of Higher Education, The University of Michigan, 1974.

Centra, John A. "Black Students at Predominantly White Colleges: A Research Description." *Sociology of Education* 43 (Summer 1970): 325–339.

Clark, Kenneth B., and Plotkin, Lawrence. *The Negro Student at Integrated Colleges.* New York: National Scholarship Services and Fund for Negro Students, 1963.

Clift, Virgil A. "Higher Education of Minority Groups in the United States." *Journal of Negro Education* 38 (Summer 1969): 291–302.

Coleman, James S.; Campbell, Ernest; Hobson, Carol J.; McPartland, James; Mood, Alexander M.; Weinfeld, Frederic; and York, Robert L. *Equality of Educational Opportunity.* Washington, D.C.: U.S. Government Printing Office, 1966.

Cox, Otha, Jr. "A Comparative Analysis of Self-Perceived Roles of Black and Non-Black Administrators in Predominantly White Institutions of Higher Education." Ph.D. dissertation, Michigan State University, 1971.

Cross, K. Patricia. "The Instructional Revolution." Unpublished paper presented at a meeting of the American Association of Higher Education, 8 March 1976, Chicago, Illinois.

Crossland, Fred E. *Minority Access to College—Ford Foundation Report.* New York: Schocken Books, 1971.

Dressel, Paul L., and DeLisle, Frances H. *Undergraduate Curriculum Trends.* Washington, D.C.: American Council on Education, 1969.

Duncan, Otis D.; Schuman, Howard; and Duncan, Beverly. *Social Change in a Metropolitan Community.* New York: Russell Sage Foundation, 1973.

Dutton, Jeffrey E. *Courses and Enrollment in Ethnic/Racial Studies.* Washington, D.C.: American Council on Education, 1973.

Egerton, John. *State Universities and Black Americans: An Inquiry into Desegregation and Equity for Negroes in 100 Public Universities.* Atlanta, Ga.: Southern Education Foundation, 1969.

Ellison, Mary. *The Black Experience: American Blacks Since 1965.* London: Batsford, 1974.

Etzioni, Amitai. "Faculty Response to Racial Tensions." In *The Campus and the Racial Crisis,* edited by David C. Nichols and Olive Mills. Washington, D.C.: American Council on Education, 1970.

Fair, Martha H. "Special Programs for Disadvantaged Students in Higher Education." Ph.D. dissertation, Northern Illinois University, 1973.

Feldman, Saul D. *Escape from the Doll's House.* New York: McGraw-Hill, 1974.

Fenstemacher, William P. "A Study of the Relationship of Instrumental and Intellectual Orientations to the Educational Experiences of Black Students at The University of Michigan." Final Report, Project No. 9-E-072, U.S. Department of Health, Education, and Welfare, Office of Education, April 1971.

Fischer, George. *Urban Higher Education in the United States.* New York: City University of New York, 1974.

Ford, Nick Aaron. *Black Studies: Threat or Challenge.* Port Washington, New York: Kennikat Press, 1973.

Forgianni, Dominic Albert. "Impact of Black Student Activism on Institutional Response to Blacks in Higher Education." Ph.D. dissertation, Indiana University, 1973.

Garcia, Richard L. "Affirmative Action Hiring: Some Perceptions." *Journal of Higher Education* 45 (April 1974): 268–272.

Goldstein, Rhoda L. *The Status of Black Studies Programs at American Colleges and Universities.* Washington, D.C.: U.S. Department of Health, Education, and Welfare, 1972.

Gordon, Edmund W., and Wilerson, Doxy A. *Compensatory Education for the Disadvantaged.* New York: College Entrance Examination Board, 1966.

Greeley, Andrew M., and Sheatsley, Paul B. "Attitudes Toward Racial Integration." *Scientific American* 225 (1971): 13–19.

Gurin, Patricia, and Epps, Edgar G. *Black Consciousness, Identity, and Achievement.* New York: Wiley, 1975.

Harrison, E. C. "Achievement Motivation Characteristics of Negro College

Freshmen." *Personnel and Guidance Journal* 38 (October 1959): 146–149.

Hayashi, Patrick S. "The Institutional Accommodation of the Department of Ethnic Studies at The University of California–Berkeley, from 1958 to 1972." Master's thesis, University of California–Berkeley, 1972.

Henry, David. *Challenges Past, Challenges Present: An Analysis of American Higher Education Since 1930.* San Francisco: Jossey-Bass, 1975.

Hodgkinson, Harold L. *Institutions in Transition: A Study of Change in Higher Education.* Berkeley: Carnegie Commission on Higher Education, 1971.

Hunt, David E., and Hardt, Robert H. "The Effect of Upward Bound Programs on Attitudes, Motivation, and Academic Achievement of Negro Students." *Journal of Social Issues* 25 (1969): 117–129.

Institute for Social Research, The University of Michigan. "Cross-Racial Contact Increases in the Seventies: Attitude Gap Narrows for Blacks and White." *ISR Newsletter,* Autumn 1975.

Jacoby, Susan. "The Megapopulist Multiversity: Michigan State Redefines the Land Grant Philosophy." *Saturday Review,* November 1972, pp. 63–67.

Jencks, Christopher, and Riesman, David. *The Academic Revolution.* New York: Doubleday, 1968.

Kandel, Denise B. "Race, Maternal Authority, and Adolescent Aspiration." *American Journal of Sociology* 76 (May 1971): 990–1020.

Kendrick, S. A. "The Coming Segregation of our Selective Colleges." *College Board Review* 66 (1967–68): 6–13.

Kirkmon, Talmadge D. "Utilizing Administrative Concepts as Conditional Constraints to Determine Comparative Leadership Behavior in Black and Brown Administrators in Community Colleges." Ph.D. dissertation, Claremont Graduate School, 1972.

Knoell, Dorothy M. *People Who Need College: A Report on Students We Have Yet to Serve.* Washington, D.C.: American Association of Junior Colleges, 1971.

Ladd, Everett, C., Jr., and Lipset, Seymour M. "Professors' Religious and Ethnic Backgrounds." *The Chronicle of Higher Education,* 22 September 1975, p. 2.

Lester, Richard A. *Anti-Bias Regulation of Universities: Faculty Problems and their Solutions.* New York: McGraw-Hill, 1974.

Lindahl, Charles W. "Attrition of College Administrators: Causes and Some Cures of the Situation Leading to Short Tenure." *Intellect* 101 (February 1973): 289–293.

Lipset, Seymour M., and Ladd, Everett C., Jr. "The Politics of American Sociologists." *American Journal of Sociology* 78 (July 1972): 67–104.

Lyons, James E. "The Response of Higher Education to the Black Presence." *Journal of College Student Personnel* 13 (September 1972): 388–94.

———. "The Adjustment of Black Students to Predominantly White Colleges." *Journal of Negro Education* 42 (Fall 1973): 462–466.

Martin, Warren B. *Conformity: Standards and Change in Higher Education.* San Francisco: Jossey-Bass, 1969.

Mays, Benjamin E. "Black Colleges: Past, Present, and Future." *The Black Scholar—Journal of Black Studies and Research* 6 (September 1974): 32–37.

McKee, James W. "Patterns of Institutional Response to Blacks in Higher Education." Ph.D. dissertation, Indiana University, 1971.
Melnick, Murray. "Higher Education for the Disadvantaged: Summary." Hofstra University, Center for the Study of Higher Education, Abstracts and Reviews of Research in Higher Education 12 (April 1971).
Midwest Committee for Higher Education Surveys, 1970. Admission of Minority Students in Midwestern Colleges. Report M-1. Evanston, Ill.: College Entrance Examination Board, 1970.
Milton, Ohmer. Special Opportunity Students: Weighed in the Balance. Knoxville, Tenn.: Learning Research Center, University of Tennessee, 1970.
Mingle, James R. "Faculty and Departmental Response to Increased Black Student Enrollments: Individual and Contextual Predictors." Ph.D. dissertation, The University of Michigan, 1976.
Moore, William, Jr., and Wagstaff, Lonnie H. Black Educators in White Colleges. San Francisco: Jossey-Bass, 1974.
Nash, George; Waldorf, Dan; and Price, Robert E. The University and the City: Eight Cases of Involvement. Report prepared for the Carnegie Commission. New York: McGraw-Hill, 1973.
Nichols, David C., and Mills, Olive, eds. The Campus and the Racial Crisis. Washington, D.C.: American Council on Education, 1970.
Pace, C. Robert. The Demise of Diversity? A Comparative Profile of Eight Types of Institutions. Berkeley, Ca.: Carnegie Commission on Higher Education, 1974.
Paussaint, Alvin. "The Black Administrator in the White University." The Black Scholar—Journal of Black Studies and Research 6 (September 1974): 8–14.
Pfeifer, C. Michael, and Schneider, Benjamin. "University Climate Perceptions by Black and White Students." Journal of Applied Psychology 59 (October 1974): 660–662.
Rafky, David M. "Attitudes of Black Studies Faculty toward Black Students: A National Survey." Journal of College Student Personnel 14 (January 1973): 25–30.
Record, Wilson. "Some Implications of the Black Studies Movement for Higher Education in the 1960s." Journal of Higher Education 44 (March 1973): 191–216.
———. "Response of Sociologists to Black Studies." Journal of Higher Education 45 (May 1974): 364–391. (a)
———. "White Sociologists and Black Students in Predominantly White Universities." Sociological Quarterly 15 (Spring 1974): 164–182. (b)
Riesman, David, and Stadtman, Vern A. Academic Transformation. New York: McGraw-Hill, 1973.
Rist, Ray C. "Black Staff, Black Studies at White Universities: Study in Contradictions." Journal of Higher Education 41 (November 1970): 618–629.
Robinson, Armstead; Foster, Craig C.; and Ogilvie, Donald H. Black Studies in the University. New York: Bantam Books, 1969.
Rosovsky, Henry. "Black Studies at Harvard: Personal Reflections Concerning Recent Events." American Scholar 38 (Autumn 1969): 562–572.
Rossman, Jack E.; Astin, Helen S.; Astin, Alexander W.; and El Khawais, Elaine S. Open Admissions at SUNY: An Analysis of the First Year. Englewood Cliffs, N.J.: Prentice Hall, 1975.

Schuman, Howard, and Laumann, Edward O. "Do Most Professors Support the War?" *Trans-action* 5 (November 1967): 32–35.

———, and Hatchett, Shirley. *Black Racial Attitudes: Trends and Complexities.* Ann Arbor: Institute for Social Research, The University of Michigan, 1974.

Sedlacek, William E.; Brooks, Glenwood C.; and Mindus, L. A. "Black and Other Minority Admissions to Large Universities: Three Year National Trends." *Journal of College Student Personnel* 14 (January 1973): 16–24.

———; Merritt, Mary Stander; and Brooks, Glenwood C. "A National Comparison of Universities, Successful and Unsuccessful in Enrolling Blacks over a Five-Year Period." *Journal of College Student Personnel* 16 (January 1975): 56–63.

Sheatsley, Paul B. "White Attitudes Toward the Negro." *Daedalus* 95 (1960): 217–238.

Sherman, Barbara. "Dimensions of Faculty Effectiveness as Perceived by College Students." Ph.D. dissertation, The University of Michigan, 1973.

Shoenfeld, Janet D. "Student-Initiated Changes in the Academic Curriculum." Occasional Paper 72-1, ERIC Clearinghouse on Higher Education. Washington, D.C., July 1972 (ED 065105).

Steinberg, Stephen. *The Academic Melting Pot.* New York: McGraw-Hill, 1974.

Swartz, Mildred. *Trends in White Attitudes Toward Negroes.* Chicago: National Opinion Research Center, 1967.

U.S. Department of Health, Education, and Welfare, Office for Civil Rights. *Undergraduate Enrollment by Ethnic Group in Federally Funded Institutions of Higher Education, 1968.* Washington, D.C.: U.S. Government Printing Office, 1969.

———. *Racial and Ethnic Enrollment Data from Institutions of Higher Education, Fall 1970.* Washington, D.C.: U.S. Government Printing Office, 1973.

———. *Racial and Ethnic Enrollment Data from Institutions of Higher Education, Fall 1972.* Washington, D.C.: U.S. Government Printing Office, 1975.

Veroff, Joseph, and Peele, Stanton. "Initial Effects of Desegregation on the Achievement Motivation of Negro School Children." *Journal of Social Issues* 25 (1969): 71–91.

Veysey, Lawrence R. *The Emergence of the American University.* Chicago: University of Chicago Press, 1965.

Watley, Donivan. "Black and Non-Black Youth: Finances and College Attendance." *National Merit Scholarship Corporation Research Reports* 7 (1971).

Willie, Charles V., and Sakuma, Arline. *Black Students at White Colleges.* New York: Praeger, 1972.

Willingham, Warren H. *Admission of Minority Students in Midwestern Colleges.* Higher Education Survey Report M-1. New York: College Entrance Examination Board, May 1970.

Yetman, Norman R., and Steele, C. Hoy. *Majority and Minority: The Dynamics of Racial and Ethnic Relations.* Boston: Allyn and Bacon, 1972.

RELATED PUBLICATIONS

Dissertations

In addition to the works by Arce and by Mingle, already cited, the following dissertations are either direct products of the present study or in part utilize its data and/or methodology.

Copeland, Largé L. "An Exploration of the Causes of Black Attrition at Predominantly White Institutions of Higher Education." Ph.D. dissertation, The University of Michigan, 1976.

Davenport, Roselle W. "Institutionalizing Black/Ethnic/and Other Interdisciplinary Studies in College Curricula." Ph.D. dissertation, The University of Michigan (in progress).

Delgado, Paul A. "Institutional Response to Minorities in Graduate Schools of Social Work." Ph.D. dissertation, The University of Michigan, 1978.

Farmer, Vernon L. "A Response of a Predominantly White University to Black Students' Entry (Particularly Black Students' Demands)." Ph.D. dissertation, The University of Michigan (in progress).

Shoemaker, Daniel P. "The Relationship between Background, Context, Student and Institutional Racial Climate, and Change in Attitude toward Race." Ph.D. dissertation, The University of Michigan (in progress).

Wright, Baxter B. "An Examination of the Response of a Midwestern School of Social Work to Minority Students as Reported by Students." Ph.D. dissertation, The University of Michigan (in progress).

Papers and Articles

Blackburn, Robert T., and Peterson, Marvin W. "Administrator and Faculty Responses to Increased Black Enrollment in White Universities." American Education Research paper, in *Resources in Education* 11 (October 1976): 94.

Gamson, Zelda, F. "Colleges, Clients, and Controversy: Synopsis of a Study of Black Students on White Campuses." Paper presented at a conference on "The Responsibility of the University in Providing Opportunities to Minorities," October 1977, Syracuse, New York.

Gamson, Zelda F.; Blackburn, Robert T.; and Peterson, Marvin W. "Issues and Impacts: Black Student on White Campuses." Paper presented at a meeting of the Association for the Study of Higher Education, March 1978.

Mingle, James R. "Faculty and Departmental Response Patterns: Individual and Contextual Predictors." *Journal of Higher Education* (in press).

Index

Abernathy, Ralph, 119
Academic support for minorities. *See* Black students
Activism, 11, 18–19, 29, 75, 94–95, 118, 119, 195–98, 207, 289. *See also* Civil rights
Administrators in higher education: black, 215–18, 255; and black students, 38–39, 47, 118, 156, 158–60, 209–19, 228, 242–43, 247, 249, 251–52, 255, 284, 287, 297, 307; trustees, 210–11, 222
Admissions: criteria for, 168–70; open, 37, 40, 169. *See also* Recruitment
Affirmative action, 156, 231–32, 268, 273, 297. *See also* Admissions; Black students
Afro-American studies. *See* Black studies

Black enrollments in higher education, 26–31, 68–71, 105–09, 111–25, 131–40, 148, 156, 160, 195–96, 220–21, 249, 287, 310, 312, 317
Black Muslims, 18
Black Panthers, 19, 157
Black students: academic support for, 34, 36, 46, 137, 174, 177–80, 264–65; attitude towards universities, 6–7, 36, 39–40, 207, 318; background of, 163–64; and faculty, 221–22; organizations of,

34–35, 148, 156, 158–59, 197, 199–204, 302; relations with white students, 198, 204–06, 301. *See also* Black enrollments in higher education; *names of specific schools*; Recruitment
Black studies, 31–37, 46–47, 149, 164, 181, 183, 185–87, 263–64, 301, 304, 307, 317, 319; development of, 187–190. *See also names of specific schools*
Blauner, Robert, 36
Bowling Green State University, 70, 72–74, 121–22, 124, 143–44, 157, 197, 210, 298; academic support for minorities, 174, 180; black staff at, 73–74, 210; black student enrollment in, 70, 111, 131, 137–38; and financial aid for minorities, 170–71, 173, 174; and recruitment of minorities, 166–68 *passim*; student organizations at, 73
Bradley University, 94–96, 112, 119, 123, 124, 143–44, 157, 197, 219, 221, 298; academic support for minorities, 174; black staff at, 94, 96; black student enrollment in, 94–95, 118, 131, 140–42, 148; and black studies, 95, 183, 185–89 *passim*; and financial aid for minorities, 170–71; and recruitment of minorities, 300; student organizations at, 96
Brown, Rap, 18, 19, 119

385